Korean Communication, Media, and Culture

Korean Communication, Media, and Culture

An Annotated Bibliography

Edited by
Kyu Ho Youm and Nojin Kwak

Foreword by
Charles R. Berger

LEXINGTON BOOKS
Lanham • Boulder • New York • London

Published by Lexington Books
An imprint of The Rowman & Littlefield Publishing Group, Inc.
4501 Forbes Boulevard, Suite 200, Lanham, Maryland 20706
www.rowman.com

6 Tinworth Street, London SE11 5AL, United Kingdom

This work was supported by the Core University Program for Korean Studies through
the Ministry of Education of the Republic of Korea and Korean Studies Promotion
Service of the Academy of Korean Studies (AKS-2016-OLU-2240001).

British Library Cataloguing in Publication Information Available

Library of Congress Cataloging-in-Publication Data Available

ISBN 978-1-4985-8332-9 (cloth : alk. paper)
ISBN 978-1-4985-8334-3 (pbk. : alk. paper)
ISBN 978-1-4985-8333-6 (electronic)

To the Founders of the Korean American
Communication Association (KACA)

To all KACA members—past, present, and future

and

To the many others interested in Korean
communication, media, and culture.

Contents

Foreword

In an era when such terms as globalization, interconnectivity, information society, and similar emotionally evocative terms have devolved into clichés that continue to be trumpeted far and wide by politicians, marketers, purported visionaries, and some academic hucksters, it is ironic that some of the contributions of highly productive communication researchers outside of the Western Hemisphere remain opaque to those residing within it. Almost two decades ago, the International Monetary Fund (IMF) identified trade, capital movement, movement of people, and spread of knowledge (and technology) as four key aspects of globalization. The IMF warned that of these four aspects, knowledge flows among countries was the one that probably would be most ignored in discussions of globalization.[1]

In the face of the substantial hyperbole surrounding the use of the "globalization" and related terms and their alleged "transformational" and "game-changing" impact, the present bibliographic project provides a vivid illustration of the somewhat more uneven reality that these now-hackneyed locutions depict, especially within the domain of knowledge diffusion. Some of the authors involved in this project express disappointment with the degree to which the considerable research corpus generated by Korean communication scholars has been inaccessible to communication researchers residing outside of Korea's borders. For example, apparently, few books are available that focus on political communication in Korea, and there are almost no books on Korean communication law that have been translated from Korean to English. By contrast, there are many volumes on the Korean news industry that have appeared in English over a number of decades.

---

1. International Monetary Fund Staff, *Globalization: Threat or Opportunity* (Washington, DC: International Monetary Fund, 2000), https://www.imf.org/np/exr/041200to.htm#1.

As the direct result of the exponential growth of the Korean economy commencing in the early 1980s, such research areas as advertising and public relations have shown strong concomitant growth in English publications. Similarly, Korean cinema studies publications focused on Korean films made before 1980 are relatively rare, while that rate has increased since 1980; however, very little of this scholarship has focused on North Korean films. Nevertheless, cinema studies publications have exerted considerable influence in more general research areas such as Korean cultural studies. Although Korean popular culture (graphic arts, popular music, and films), as embodied in the *Hallyu* (Korean Wave) phenomenon, has shown immense growth in public interest, first in East Asia beginning in 1997 and then world-wide diffusion beginning in 2010, the vast majority of scholarship in this area has been published in Korean by Korean scholars; however, there are signs that the numbers of English-language publications have been increasing since 2010.

In stark contrast, as reported in the Intercultural Communication compilation, the amount of collaborative publication in English involving Korean and American researchers has shown a very high rate of growth since the late 1970s. However, this trend has led to considerable consternation about potential, but unintended biases in such comparative research and the application of naïve notions regarding the homogeneity of Korean and American cultures (sometimes there is more variance within than between cultures). Moreover, theorizing about rapidly changing phenomena presents potentially daunting challenges.

Although relatively new areas of inquiry, there are some encouraging signs that within Communication Technology and Health Communication domains, the substantial amounts of research conducted in Korea will appear in future English-language publications. However, as is often the case with newer areas of inquiry, substantive theory that guides research may be underdeveloped (see Communication Technology), and early research studies may provide more breadth than depth (see Health Communication). Moreover, in the case of Advertising research, specific research sub-areas may be highly active with substantial publication in English (for example, the effects of advertising), while other areas within the domain of inquiry may be relatively inactive (for example, advertising law).

The attenuated diffusion of some of the Korean research corpora can be partially explained by translation problems and other structural impediments (public policies) to information flows across international boundaries and linguistic communities. In any case, the bibliographic compilations presented in this volume vividly illustrate the steep price to be paid for ignoring this burgeoning Korean research corpus.

Even a cursory glance at the research areas presented in this volume immediately reveals the extremely broad panorama of research areas represented within the Korean communication research community. A highly diverse set of topics, ranging from Communication Law, Political Communication and Journalism through Public Relations and Advertising to Intercultural Communication, *Hallyu* Studies (Korean Wave popular culture) and Korean Cinema research, along with such topics as Communication and Technology and Health Communication, not only represent traditional areas of communication research but some of them far exceed the gamut of these traditional research areas. Several unique aspects of Korean popular culture, for example K-Pop (popular music) and Korean dramas, are not only unique to Korea, but they have garnered considerable acceptance in several other countries and have done so using digital platforms. This condition not only attests to the intellectual vitality of Korean communication research enterprise as a whole but its distinct penchant to expand traditional research boundaries.

In their introductions, the authors demonstrate their extensive knowledge of the history and scope of their respective areas. Each of the authors conducted extensive literature searches and went to great lengths to identify relevant research to be included in their bibliographies. Consequently, readers who are less familiar with Korean communication research will find these compilations to be a most valuable orientation to Korean communication scholarship writ large. Readers who are more familiar with the outlines of Korean communication research will find that each area's bibliography provides them with both a clear and cogent orientation to research available within each research domain.

Finally, there are numerous unique areas of study lurking in this volume's compilations, attesting to the work's heuristic provocativeness. For example, the fact that Korean serial dramas have penetrated television markets in Japan, China, and even North Korea, where there are severe penalties for watching such media fare, suggest the inherent dangers in simplistic characterizations featuring the purported similarities of East Asian cultures. Tellingly, Korean dramas have also gained wide popularity in Southeast Asian countries ranging from Bangladesh to Singapore and the Philippines, and Korean dramas have sparked considerable audience involvement outside of Asia. A similar dynamic can be observed with Korean popular music (K-Pop). Understanding why such effects are occurring and why Korean popular culture in particular is at the forefront of this extensive movement is, in the final analysis, the very rasion d'être of communication research.

Charles R. Berger
Professor Emeritus
Department of Communication
University of California, Davis

Preface

The reality facing those who are interested in the fast-growing area of English-language Korean communication research is that relatively few reference works are available. As Professor Han-Kyo Kim at the University of Cincinnati cogently observed in *Studies on Korea: A Scholar's Guide*, "[i]t is an obvious handicap but also a challenge for those who toil in this field of inquiry [i.e., Korean studies]."[1] Even more of a challenge is the difficulty in finding the sources that do exist.

Hopefully, this bibliography will allow communication researchers to successfully take up the challenge. The primary objective of our work is to provide annotated information on English-language publications for domestic and international college-level readers.

GENESIS OF THE PROJECT

The genesis of this annotated bibliography project dates back to 2015. During the "Digital Korea: History, Use, and Effects of New Communication Technologies" conference hosted by the University of Michigan Nam Center for Korean Studies at the University of Michigan in November of that year, it was proposed at a roundtable Korean American Communication Association (KACA) forum that KACA consider publishing books as part of its fortieth anniversary celebration in 2018. One of the books would be a handbook on Korean communication; the other an annotated bibliography of Korean communication publications in English.

---

1. Han-Kyo Kim, *Studies on Korea: A Scholar's Guide* (Honolulu: University of Hawaii Press, 1980), 4.

When conference participants wondered who would lead the ambitious two-book project, Professor Kyu Ho Youm (University of Oregon) said, "If Dr. [Dal Yong] Jin takes care of the handbook, I'll be happy to edit the bib volume." With the unqualified support of KACA President Seungahn Nah and his KACA officers and Professor Nojin Kwak, director of the Nam Center, Jin and Youm, along with Kwak as a co-editor for both projects, pledged to take on the leadership of these challenging but exciting book projects for the KACA.

BACKGROUND: NEED FOR THE BIBLIOGRAPHY

A historical look at Korean journalism and communication publications illustrates the need for an English-language bibliography. Despite an increasing number of English-language publications on Korean communication studies, researchers have been stymied by an inability to locate such publications easily.

South Korea's journalism education is considered to be among the "most developed" systems in Asia. In fact, the 1993 report of the Freedom Forum Media Studies Center at Columbia University noted that "in terms of the number of schools offering journalism degrees and journalism training institutes, [Korea] is perhaps second only to the United States."[2]

However, English-language Korean journalism and communication research had been limited until the late 1990s. Therefore, it is hardly surprising that not one single chapter in *Studies on Korea: A Scholar's Guide*[3]— the sixteen-chapter, 438-page annotated bibliography of Korean studies in English and other non-Korean languages published in 1980—was devoted to communication, media, or culture in Korea. Professor Han-Kyo Kim, the editor of that majestic Korean studies guide, which has inspired our bibliography project, noted thus:

> Much needs to be done in collecting and making available basic research source materials in Korean studies and in synthesizing the fruits of past scholarship. There is also a continuing need to refine research methodology and to promote more rigorous standards of scholarship that are free of preconceived biases or a priori value judgments.[4]

---

2. Jon Vanden Heuvel and Everette E. Dennis, "South Korea," in *The Unfolding Lotus: East Asia's Changing Media* (New York: Freedom Forum Media Studies Center, Columbia University, 1993), 21.

3. Kim, *Studies on Korea: A Scholar's Guide.*

4. Kim, *Studies on Korea: A Scholar's Guide*, xix.

Korea-related publications in English have risen to the challenge since then, and numerous materials now exist for Korean and non-Korean communication scholars. Nonetheless, there is still a paucity of information about certain communication-related topics, and few of the available materials are widely known to those who are looking for such scholarly publications and reference sources.[5]

For example, in the early 2010s, Professor Sherri Ter Molen at DePaul University wanted to write a paper on Korean pop culture. When she proposed the Korean Wave (*Hallyu* in Korean) as a topic for her course paper, her professor questioned whether there would be enough published material for her required review of literature. "Indeed, the corpus of English-language *Hallyu* literature was quite small at the time," Ter Molen said, "but Dr. [Dal Yong] Jin's works were salient among what was available. My professor gave me the green light to move forward with my paper."[6]

SCOPE OF THE BIBLIOGRAPHY

In order to address the needs of those interested in Korean communication research, the scope of this bibliography is as broad and comprehensive as possible. Coverage is comprehensive enough to make the bibliography an essential guide for not only academic but also nonacademic researchers.

---

5. In his email to President Seungahn Nah of the Korean American Communication Association (KACA), Kyu Ho Youm, co-editor of this annotated bibliography book, said the value of the KACA's fortieth-anniversary book projects "should be not only substantive but also enduring to JMC [journalism and mass communication] and non-JMC scholars interested in Korean studies as a whole. It should be symbolic to the scholarly community outside JMC: Korean JMC scholarship is far more extensive and in depth than often assumed." Kyu Ho Youm, email message to Seungahn Nah, August 15, 2016. See also the mission statement of the "Korean Communication Research and Practice: Looking Back, Looking Forward" conference in Hawaii on July 27–28, 2017: "During the past decades, Korean communication scholars have established a solid reputation in communication research internationally. Along with an increasing fascination among many scholars about the changing social, cultural, political and media landscape in contemporary Korea, there has been a substantial body of communication research published in English that concern various aspects of Korea." "Korean Communication Hawaii Conference: Conference Mission," July 9, 2017, https://perma. cc/27LZ-J5MN. The conference, which the University of Hawaii-Manoa Center for Korean Studies and the University of Michigan Nam Center for Korean Studies, among others, hosted, offered a timely occasion for the principal chapter authors of Communication, Digital Media, and Popular Culture (2018) then in the works to "critically evaluate the existing scholarship on Korean communication in key topic areas," "dialogue about the gaps in the current research literature," and "exchange ideas and perspectives about the future directions of communication research about Korea." "Korean Communication Hawaii Conference: Conference Mission."

6. Sherri L. Ter Molen, email message to Kyu Ho Youm, March 31, 2018. Ter Molen wrote her paper using Professor Jin's *Hallyu* research publications, presented it at a Korean studies conference, and published it as a book chapter in 2014. "If it had not been for Dr. Jin's early English-language contributions to the field," said Ter Molen, "my professor might not have approved my project, and in that case, I would have missed out on these premier opportunities." Ter Molen, email message.

Scope of English-Language Works

In an email to Seungahn Nah, then KACA president, and others, Kyu Ho Youm, a co-editor of this book, stated in August 2016:

> The bib should be as comprehensive as possible. . . . The bib should cover all the *major* English-language books, journal articles, theses/dissertations, [and] conference papers (AEJMC, ICA, NCA, etc.) on Korean JMC [journalism and mass communication] if and only if they are accessible in hard or soft copies, although link rots will be a fact of life in the digital world.[7]

However, the editors' initially ambitious plan had to be adjusted to some extent. Thus, the annotations are limited to English-language books, articles, theses, and dissertations; refereed conference research papers were excluded.

Nonetheless, some chapters are not necessarily confined to the usual types of scholarly publications. For example, the "Communication Law" chapter includes several master of laws (LLM), doctor of juristic science (JSD), and doctor of juridical science (SJD) projects. It was a formidable challenge to access the LLM theses and JSD/SJD dissertations, which often were not listed on ProQuest.

The chronological boundaries for our annotations were deliberately open-ended. Our goal was to present a comprehensive bibliography, so we included very early publications and even forthcoming publications in nearly all the chapter bibliographies. As noted, our bibliography is inspired by *Studies on Korea: A Scholar's Guide*; as such, we wanted to do as much as we could "in collecting and making available basic research source materials in Korean [communication] studies and in synthesizing the fruits of past scholarship."[8] Therefore, our annotations include two 1950s publications in the "Journalism and Broadcasting" chapter, and more than a dozen articles and books are from the 1960s and 1970s. At the same time, however, our chapter authors were adjured to include impending publications insofar as they were verifiable, and they almost invariably rose to the editors' challenge. Hence, a number of forthcoming journal articles, book chapters, and other sources are annotated.

Scope of Communication Topics

This bibliography book, as noted earlier, is a companion volume to a KACA communication handbook, *Communication, Digital Media, and Popular*

---

7. Kyu Ho Youm, email message to Seungahn Nah, Nojin Kwak, and Dal Yong Jin, August 14, 2016 (emphasis in original).

8. Kim, *Studies on Korea: A Scholar's Guide*, xix.

Culture in Korea: Contemporary Research and Future Prospects, published for the KACA's fortieth anniversary in 2018.[9] This annotated bibliography follows the general structure of the eighteen-chapter KACA communication handbook by Professors Dal Yong Jin (Simon Fraser University) and Nojin Kwak (University of Michigan), but the bibliographical subjects for annotation are more limited due to practical reasons.

Excluded from the bibliography are the topics for eight chapters in *Communication, Digital Media, and Popular Culture in Korea*: communication theory; political economy; digital media; game studies; urban communication and community; visual communication; sports communication; and lesbian, gay, bisexual, and transgender (LGBT) studies. The primary reason for excluding these topics was that English publications were so scanty that separate chapters were not warranted for this annotated project. In addition, we could not recruit a well-qualified contributor of Professor Jin's caliber for a chapter on game studies; Jin, the game studies author for the communication handbook, opted to cover *Hallyu* for our bibliography project. Likewise, we could not find a suitable replacement for Professor Jeong-Nam Kim (University of Oklahoma), who wrote the communication theory chapter for the KACA communication handbook.

PARTICIPATION OF NON-KOREAN SCHOLARS

Most of the contributors are the leading authorities on Korean communication, media, and culture, and they have published extensively about their topics over the years.

What distinguishes the authorial lineup of this bibliography from that of the Korean communication handbook, though, is the participation of non-Korean communication scholars. By involving non-Korean scholars in our bibliography project, we have hoped to dispel the perception that Korean communication research is populated only by native Korean scholars.

Admittedly, it was a daunting task to identify and invite non-Korean communication scholars to our project because few non-Korean scholars, especially those established in their research fields, have published about Korea-related communication. However, we assembled a group of seven non-Korean co-authors. John Carpenter, a PhD candidate at the University of Iowa, who co-authored the "Journalism and Broadcasting" chapter, noted that he "appreciate[s] KACA's decision to reach out to non-Korean academics to participate in the project." Carpenter observed that "Korea-related

---

9. Dal Yong Jin and Nojin Kwak, eds., *Communication, Digital Media, and Popular Culture in Korea: Contemporary Research and Future Prospects* (Lanham, MD: Lexington Books, 2018).

communication topics are of interest and importance to a broader, global academic community, so I hope that any future revisions of the book also reflect this reality."[10]

---

10. John Carpenter, email message to Kyu Ho Youm, March 30, 2018.

Acknowledgments

Kyu Ho Youm and Nojin Kwak would like to thank those who, in addition to the individual authors, have provided their unstinting support and helped give life to this book.

First, we are especially grateful to Professor Emeritus Charles Berger (University of California-Davis), former president of the International Communication Association (ICA), for his foreword. When asked to share his thoughts on the project in August 2017, Professor Berger accepted the invitation from Youm and Kwak with alacrity, noting "I could write a cogent foreword." His, indeed cogent, foreword adds gravitas to this volume. Professor Berger is one of the most influential communication scholars in the United States and holds a genuine interest in South Korea and its people. Berger, whose Korean name is Pang Chol Su, served as a Korean linguist in the U.S. Army in Korea from 1963 to 1964—an experience he described recently as life-changing "in enduring and positive ways."

Second, we owe a great deal to sixteen American and international reviewers for their careful examination of the ten chapters of annotated bibliographies that make up this volume: William P. "Chip" Eveland (Ohio State University); Thomas Hove (Hanyang University); Jisu Huh (University of Minnesota); Taejin Jung (State University of New York—Oswego); Minjeong Kim (Hankuk University of Foreign Studies); Yang Soo Kim (Middle Tennessee State University); Gary L. Kreps (George Mason University); Ki-Sung Kwak (University of Sydney); Eun-Ju Lee (Seoul National University); Seung-Sun Lee (Chungnam National University); Rich Ling (Nanyang Technological University); Kyung Sin Park (Korea University); S. Shyam Sundar (Pennsylvania State University); Maureen Taylor (University of Tennessee-Knoxville); Esther Thorson (Michigan State University); and Wayne Wanta (University of Florida).

Third, we are most appreciative of timely assistance from a number of librarians with both our own and our co-authors' research: Deanna Barmakian (Harvard Law School Library); Elizabeth M. Evans (New York University School of Law Library); Carolina Hernandez (University of Oregon Library); Jordan Jefferson (Yale Law School Lillian Goldman Law Library); Jootaek Lee (Northeastern University Law Library); Karin Loevy (New York University Law School JSD Program); Kelly Reynolds (University of Oregon Law Library); Heija Ryoo (University of Washington East Asia Library); Margaret A. Schilt (University of Chicago Law School D'Angelo Law Library); Merle Slyhoff (University of Pennsylvania Law Library); Yunah Sung (University of Michigan Library); and George Wilson (Stanford University Law Library).

Fourth, we are indebted to Jessica Garcia (University of Texas-San Antonio) for helping Seok Kang (University of Texas-San Antonio) collect bibliographical sources; Sae-Eun Kim (Kangwon National University) for providing a copy of *Understanding of Journalism in Korea* (2015); Dan Lane (University of Michigan) for creating the KACA Bib Project's Google Drive folder; Beth Luey, author of *Handbook for Academic Authors* (5th ed., 2010), for previewing our book proposal and offering her directional advice on our project; and Kie-Hyuk Shin (Koshin University) for facilitating access to his co-authored article of 2011 on American influence on Korean advertising.

And finally, Youm wishes to express his appreciation to Michelle Dreiling, Matt Eichner, and Ricardo Valencia at the University of Oregon School of Journalism and Communication for their able research assistance throughout this book project. Most importantly, he thanks the Jonathan Marshall First Amendment Endowment at the University of Oregon School of Journalism and Communication for funding the professional assistance he sought for his project.

Kwak would like to thank Adrienne Janney in the Department of Communication Studies and Do-Hee Morsman at the Nam Center for Korean Studies, both at the University of Michigan, for their administrative assistance with various phases of this book project, which had its genesis at the "Digital Korea: History, Use, and Effects of New Communication Technologies" conference of 2015—part of the annual "Perspectives on Contemporary Korea" conference series held in Ann Arbor, Michigan. Many thanks also go to the Academy of Korean Studies and the University of Michigan Nam Center for Korean Studies for providing financial and other support for the project.

Introduction

Kyu Ho Youm and Nojin Kwak

South Korea in the twenty-first century is no longer the so-called impossible country.[1] As the world's most networked country,[2] Korea is showcasing the global influence of its soft power. Furthermore, the Asian country has emerged economically as one of the "four Asian tigers" and is enjoying its newly enviable status as a vibrant democracy.

This newfound success has led to the growing international popularity of not only Korea in general but also Korean communication in particular since the late 1980s in the wake of the Seoul Olympics. In fact, Korean communication, media, and culture are attracting more attention than ever globally as topics for teaching and research. For example, an increasing number of colleges and universities in the United States and abroad are offering Korean cinema and related subjects.[3]

This book, an annotated bibliography, focuses on English-language publications about Korean communication. It is primarily intended to help non–Korean speaking researchers find information about Korean communication. In addition, from an institutional perspective, Korean American Communication Association (KACA) members wanted "to review and . . .

---

1. Daniel Tudor, *Korea: The Impossible Country* (Tokyo: Tuttle Publishing, 2012).
2. Jacqueline Kelleher, "Most Connected Countries in the World: South Korea on Top, Hong Kong Resting at 9th Place, and Singapore Ranks 19th," *OpenGov*, October 27, 2017, accessed April 1, 2018, https://perma.cc/7ND2-3QWM.
3. Professor Sang Joon Lee at Nanyang Technological University (NTU) in Singapore, co-editor of Hallyu *2.0: Korean Wave in the Age of Social Media*, has noted that more than twenty academics teach Korean cinema once a year in the United States, United Kingdom, Canada, Australia, Japan, Hong Kong, and the United Arab Emirates, in addition to "at least" fifteen to twenty others teaching *Hallyu* or Korean popular culture—or both—in North America and Europe. Lee is teaching and researching Asian cinema at NTU, and he is scheduled to offer a course on Korean cinema during the fall of 2018 at the NTU Wee Kim Wee School of Communication and Information. Sang Joon Lee, email messages to Kyu Ho Youm, April 2–3, 2018.

1

document the growth of KACA as a significant academic association"[4] through our bibliography project as its companion handbook, *Communication, Digital Media, and Popular Culture in Korea: Contemporary Research and Future Prospects*, did.

ENGLISH-LANGUAGE PUBLICATIONS: GROWTH OVER THE YEARS

English-language publications about Korean communication, while still not prolific in comparison to other areas of Korean research, have been steadily increasing over the years, in particular since the 2000s.

The Korean Society for Journalism and Communication Studies (KSJCS) deserves credit for its important role in globalizing Korean journalism and communication research. In 1994, the KSJCS, hosting the International Association for Mass Communication Research (IAMCR) conference in Seoul, the first of its kind in Asia, published *Elite Media amidst Mass Culture: A Critical Look at Mass Communication in Korea*. IAMCR President Cees J. Hamelink wrote in his foreword that "[i]t is . . . important to have a publication like the present one which provides the communication research community at large with the opportunity to be informed about Korea's mass communication."[5]

Broadcasting in Korea,[6] a more sharply focused book than *Elite Media amidst Mass Culture*, was also published in Korea in 1994. Two years later, *Press Law in South Korea*[7] followed in the United States.

Few dispute the marked change in the scholarly topography for Korean communication research in English in the 2000s and onward. In exploring a possible English-language communication research journal with a Korean academic organization in Seoul, the KACA stated in the mid-2010s: "The contribution of communication research by *Korean* and East Asian scholars in the communication field has been notable over the past three decades. The number of *Korean* and East Asian communication research [publications in English] has also increased dramatically."[8]

---

4. Dal Yong Jin and Nojin Kwak, "Introduction," in *Communication, Digital Media, and Popular Culture in Korea: Contemporary Research and Future Prospects*, ed. Dal Yong Jin and Nojin Kwak (Lanham, MD: Lexington Books, 2018), xviii.

5. Cees J. Hamelink, "Foreword," in *Elite Media amidst Mass Culture: A Critical Look at Mass Communication in Korea*, ed. Chie-woon and Jae-won Lee (Seoul: NANAM Publishing House, 1994), v.

6. Kim Kyu, Won-Yong Kim, and Jong-Geun Kang, *Broadcasting in Korea* (Seoul: NANAM Publishing House, 1994).

7. Kyu Ho Youm, *Press Law in South Korea* (Ames: Iowa State University, 1996).

8. [Korean American Communication Association], "Taylor & Francis Journals New Journal Proposal Guideline" (n.d.) (emphasis added).

Especially since 2000, Korean and non-Korean scholarship in communication and related areas has generated a substantial number of books, journal articles, theses, and dissertations in English. More than 80 percent of the English publications relating to Korean communication have been published since the early 2000s.

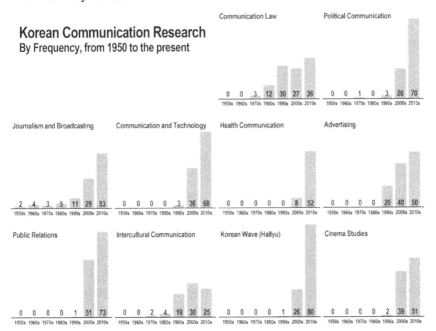

Korean Communication Research
By Frequency, from 1950 to the present

Communication scholars in Korea have endeavored to introduce their research to the global community. In 2001, the KSJCS issued a special English edition of its flagship research publication, *Korean Journal of Journalism & Communication Studies*, in preparation for the International Communication Association convention in Korea in 2002. And in 2015, the Korean Association for Broadcasting & Telecommunication Studies published an edited English volume titled *Understanding Journalism in Korea*. Unfortunately, neither of the publications is easily accessible either online or off-line.

More recently, Professor Dal Yong Jin, a prolific Korean-born communication scholar at Simon Fraser University in Canada, has authored *New Korean Wave*,[9] *Korea's Online Gaming Empire*,[10] *Smartland Korea*,[11] and *Hands On/*

---

9. Dal Yong Jin, *New Korean Wave: Transnational Cultural Power in the Age of Social Media* (Urbana: University of Illinois Press, 2016).

10. Dal Yong Jin, *Korea's Online Gaming Empire* (Boston: MIT Press, 2010).

11. Dal Yong Jin, *Smartland Korea: Mobile Communication, Culture, and Society* (Ann Arbor: University of Michigan Press, 2017).

Hands Off.[12] Equally notable is Professor Jiyeon Kang's 2016 book, *Igniting the Internet: Youth and Activism in Post Authoritarian South Korea*.[13]

While single-authored or multi-authored books in English about Korean communication are still few and far between in comparison with those about Korean history, politics, and literature, a number of book chapters (for example, in *The Unfolding Lotus*,[14] *Institutional Reform and Democratic Consolidation in Korea*,[15] and *Media, Advertising & Entertainment Law throughout the World*[16]) and journal articles (for example, in *Journalism & Mass Communication Quarterly*, *Journal of Advertising*, and *Public Relations Quarterly*) have been published.

Furthermore, many theses and dissertations in English have delved into Korean communication as a topic; however, they have rarely been turned into books and journal articles, so they have remained underused or unused resources. Consequently, few of them have attracted attention, except from those unusually dogged researchers who are willing to engage in a scavenger hunt.

ORGANIZATION OF THE BOOK

The book includes ten bibliographical chapters, each one researched by two or more authors. Chapters include varying numbers of annotations; there are some topics for which a greater breadth of English publications is available, due at least in part to the newness of a topic. For example, journalism and broadcasting has been a longstanding research subject, with sources dating back to the 1950s; in contrast, there were few pre-2000 English-language publications on topics such as *Hallyu*[17] and health communication[18] because they are newer areas of research.

In addition to the actual annotations, each chapter includes introductory commentary by the authors. All of the authors were expected to contextualize their chapters in connection with how their topics have been addressed in

---

12. Dal Yong Jin, *Hands On/Hands Off: The Korean State and the Market Liberalization of the Communication Industry* (Cresskill, NJ: Hampton Press, 2011).

13. Jiyeon Kang, *Igniting the Internet: Youth and Activism in Post Authoritarian South Korea* (Honolulu: University of Hawaii Press, 2016).

14. Jon Vanden Heuvel and Everette E. Dennis, "South Korea," in *The Unfolding Lotus: East Asia's Changing Media* (New York: Freedom Forum Media Studies Center, Columbia University, 1993).

15. Seung-Mock Yang, "Political Democratization and the News Media," in *Institutional Reform and Democratic Consolidation in Korea*, ed. Larry Diamond and Doh Chull Shin, (Stanford, CA: Hoover Institution Press, 2000), 149–70.

16. Kyu Ho Youm et al., "Korea," in *Media, Advertising & Entertainment Law throughout the World*, ed. Julie A. McConihay (St. Paul: Thomson/West, forthcoming).

17. Only one publication on *Hallyu* was available prior to 2000.

18. There was not a single annotated research paper on health communication prior to 2000.

English. More often than not, they historicized their findings. The authors not only described their topics concisely but also offered a prescriptive analysis of the direction that English-language published research on Korean communication should take.

Communication Law

The volume turns first to "Communication Law." In their study of Korean communication law, Professor Kyu Ho Youm (University of Oregon), Professor Yoonmo Sang (Howard University), and Dr. Ahran Park (Korea Press Foundation) discuss freedom of speech and the press as a communication law issue. They pay attention to communication law research inside and outside Korea and to Korean law from a comparative and methodological perspective.

Youm, Sang, and Park assess the relative dearth of English-language research on Korean law, claiming that there is a growing need for English publications on communication law in Korea. In explaining why the communication law bibliography is valuable to studying Korean law, they expressed the belief that it "will facilitate further inquiry into Korean law publications in English as a worthwhile subject."

The bibliography of 108 annotations is divided into approximately a dozen sections, including "Broadcasting," "Copyright," "Defamation," "Internet," "National Security," "North Korea," and "U.S. Military Government."

Political Communication

Political communication in Korea was rarely a topic for research before the late 1980s, when Korean politics began to move toward an open, democratic process. Since 2000, however, political communication has been a topic for a dramatic number of scholarly publications in English.

In their "Political Communication" chapter, Professors Seok Kang (University of Texas at San Antonio), Seungahn Nah (University of Oregon), and Matthew Shapiro (Illinois Institute of Technology) suggest that English scholarship in Korean political communication turn to theoretical research on political culture unique to Korea. They also mention a need for lab-based experiments and longitudinal panel surveys as research methods. Further, Kang, Nah, and Shapiro contend that political communication scholars should "provide policy implications and practical applications" for Koreans' political system.

Kang, Nah, and Shapiro note that researchers have examined elections and campaigns, social movements, politicians, political engagements, and information and communication technologies (ICTs) in Korea. Their 100 annotations focus on "Political Engagement," "National and Cultural Comparisons," "Politicians and Bureaucrats," "Media and Public Opinion," and "Presidential Campaigns and General Elections."

Journalism and Broadcasting

Although other chapters have a similarly large number of annotations, what sets the chapter on "Journalism and Broadcasting" apart is that English research publications in this area have been far more extensive than those in other areas *throughout the years*.

Professor Hun Shik Kim (University of Colorado) and John Carpenter (University of Iowa), a PhD candidate, present an informative overview of Korean journalism and broadcasting research that covers the trends and topics of English publications from the 1950s (two *Journalism Quarterly* articles) to the 2010s. Despite the quantity of available resources, the authors note areas of improvement. They point out that

> [g]iven that event-driven journalism research has been a driving force behind developing and confirming new theoretical foundations and perspectives, Korean and non-Korean journalism scholars have yet to catch up with some of the most recent events and issues in Korea by conducting timely research and have their findings published in English-language academic journals.[19]

Their extensive twelve-section, 107-entry bibliography relates to press freedom, press ethics, news audience, international and North Korean news, journalism history, media economics, online and citizen journalism, social media, and political controversies. Specific sections include "Disruptive Realignment of Traditional News Media," "International Journalism," "Journalistic Work Environments," and "Political Outrage and Protests."

Communication and Technology

Among the most popular subjects for Korean communication research in English is "Communication and Technology." According to Professors Namkee Park (Yonsei University), Seungyoon Lee (Purdue University), and Jae Eun Chung (Howard University), the study of communication and technology in Korea is relatively new. They attribute the recent voluminous research on communication and technology in major scholarly journals to the

---

19. Hun Shik Kim and John C. Carpenter, "Journalism and Broadcasting," in *Korean Communication, Media, and Culture*, 71–103.

significant increase in the number of U.S.-educated Korean communication scholars since the mid-1990s and their active publications.

While emphasizing the contributions of communication and technology works to the growing research on Korean communication, Park, Lee, and Chung assert that "there is room for further growth" in Korean communication and technology research in English. They recommend, in part, qualitative methods and mixed-methods research approaches, development of theories, and reassessment of "easy" Korea and United States comparisons.

The "Communication and Technology" chapter of 107 bibliographic entries comprises nearly ten research sections, including "Computer-Mediated Communication," "Human-Computer Interaction," "Technology Use and Political Participation," "Game Studies," and "Communication Technology Policy and Economics."

Health Communication

Professor Hye-ryeon Lee (University of Hawaii at Manoa) and her co-authors Professors Hye-Jin Paek (Hanyang University), Minsun Shim (Inha University), and Peter J. Schulz (University of Lugano) of the "Health Communication" chapter state that "a considerable body of health communication research has been published in English on Koreans in Korea or Korean immigrants abroad." Nonetheless, this bibliography chapter of sixty annotations has far fewer entries than any other chapter in this book.

The "Health Communication" authors explain why their chapter has a relatively low number of entries:

> Given the explosive growth of health-related research, it is not possible to succinctly survey research on health communication broadly defined, and the included studies represent publications that fit the narrow definition of health communication research as accepted by [the] *communication* discipline.[20]

All of the annotated publications date from 2001 to January 2017, and they were located through six electronic databases, including Communication and Mass Media Complete (CMMC), originally for the health communication chapter of *Communication, Digital Media, and Popular Culture in Korea*,[21] the companion volume of this book. The "Health Communication"

20. Hye-ryeon Lee, Hye-Jin Paek, Minsun Shim, and Peter J. Schulz, "Health Communication," in *Korean Communication, Media, and Culture* (emphasis added), 137–160.

21. Hye-ryeon Lee, Hye-Jin Paek, and Minsun Shim, "A Survey of Health Communication Scholarship on Korea: Breadth, Depth, and Trends of Published Research," in *Communication, Digital Media, and Popular Culture in Korea*, 175–214.

bibliography revolves around "messages, audience characteristics and processes, new media, and culture."

To some communication scholars, whether Korean or non-Korean, the "Health Communication" bibliography may seem surprisingly limited. However, discerning scholars will recognize that the entries in the chapter representing health communication publications in English are, in fact, a significant offering for such a new topic.

Advertising

The "Advertising" chapter begins with a quick historical overview of advertising in Korea, which started in the late nineteenth century. The authors Professors Chang-Dae Ham (University of Illinois at Urbana-Champaign), Yongick Jeong (Louisiana State University), and Jacqueline Hitchon (University of Illinois at Urbana-Champaign) explain why advertising scholarship in English has expanded considerably in recent years. According to Ham, Jeong, and Hitchon, economic growth in Korea since the 1970s has led the Korean advertising industry to globalize; thus, an increasing number of communication scholars in Korea and abroad have focused on Korean advertising for research.

The chapter is a systematic analysis of Korean advertising research in major English books, journals, and dissertations. It first approaches advertising as an academic discipline and then takes a critical look at what topics have been the notable subjects of research in English for Korean and non-Korean scholars.

Advertising is one of the most extensively annotated topics in our book. The chapter's 110-entry bibliography has six sections ("American Influence on Advertising," "Cultural Influence on Advertising Content and Reponses," "Industry Issues and Practitioner Perspectives," "Advertising Effect in Specific Contexts," "Research on Particular Audience Segments," and "Digital Interactive Advertising") and twelve subsections. In particular, the "American Influence on Korean Advertising" annotation is noteworthy.

Public Relations

Public relations (PR) research in English began in the late 1990s and has expanded considerably since then. The first annotated English publication on Korean PR was in 1998 by Professor Yungwook Kim in Korea, who taught in the United States before moving to Seoul in 2000. In their "Public Relations" chapter, Professors Jae-Hwa Shin (University of Southern Mississippi), Eyun-Jung Ki (University of Alabama), and Arunima Krishna (Boston University) wrote thus:

For the past 20 years, public relations scholars have been prolific in publishing their Korea-related research in English. An increasing number of Korean academics have hit their stride in the global PR scholarship. This is evident from the fact that almost all of the English publications annotated for our chapter have been published since 2000, and about 60 percent of them have appeared since 2010.[22]

The "Public Relations" chapter is more voluminously annotated than any other Korean communication research topic, with a total of 125 entries. This chapter is divided into nine sections, which include "Media Relations, Source-Reporter Relationship, and Agenda Building," "Public Relations Theory Building," "Publics and Activism," "Ethics and Corporate Social Responsibility," and "International Public Relations, National Image, and Public Diplomacy."

Intercultural Communication

Since the 1990s, according to "Intercultural Communication" chapter authors Professors Min-Sun Kim (University of Hawaii at Manoa) and Akira Miyahara (Seinan Gakuin University), intercultural communication publications on Koreans have expanded "tremendously," especially in the 2000s and 2010s. Study of intercultural communication, however, dates back to the 1970s, when it was first studied by American and Korean communication scholars focusing on U.S. and Korean communication behavior. The co-authors acknowledge the immeasurable contribution by the leading Korean-American intercultural communication scholar Young Yun Kim (University of Oklahoma), who wrote her Northwestern dissertation in the 1970s on Korean immigrants' acculturation.

Kim and Miyahara identify two basic approaches to communication and culture as a whole. They find that Koreans and Americans are compared in "typical" English intercultural communication studies of Koreans. And cross-cultural adaption, cultural bias, and multiculturalism and hybrid identity are given due notice as the significant areas of existing and new research for communication scholars in English.

The "Intercultural Communication" chapter has more *book* annotations than any other chapters except "Korean Wave (*Hallyu*)." The total number of annotations in this chapter is eighty.

---

22. Jae-Hwa Shin, Eyun-Jung Ki, and Arunima Krishna, "Public Relations," in *Korean Communication, Media, and Culture*, 193–225.

Korean Wave (*Hallyu*)

The "Korean Wave (*Hallyu*)" chapter stands out from other chapters not only because of its newness as a research area but also because of its Korea-central topicality.

Professor Dal Yong Jin (Simon Fraser University) and his co-author, Professor Ju Oak Kim (Texas A&M International University), background their readers on *Hallyu*. Their contextual discussion of *Hallyu* is refreshingly informative. Jin deserves the credit for creating *Hallyu* as an important topic for communication research for the past ten years. His most recent book, *New Korean Wave*, was published in 2016.

Nearly three-quarters of the English *Hallyu* publications appeared in the 2010s. *Hallyu* books in English, whether published by Korean or non-Korean scholars, are noteworthy for their breadth and depth. About twenty books are annotated in the chapter's bibliography.

In total, the chapter includes 107 annotations, which are arranged by topic. The key sections include "Policy and Diplomacy," "Audience and Fandom," "Digital *Hallyu* Studies," and "Social Media."

Cinema Studies

Professor Dong Hoon Kim (University of Oregon) and his three co-authors, Professors Hye Seung Chung (Colorado State University) Ji-yoon An (Eberhard Karls Universität Tübingen), and Trace Cabot, a PhD student (University of Southern California), selected the publications for annotation in the "Cinema Studies" chapter after considering each publication's contribution to the field. The bibliography covers books, book chapters, journal articles, and dissertations on Korean cinema. They prioritized monographs, i.e., single-authored books.

Kim and the other co-authors historicize their chapter, noting that the academic interest in Korean cinema did not emerge globally until the 1990s, when Korean films were recognized at prestigious international film festivals. Among the new developments in Korean cinema studies are analyses of different periods of film history, transnational film practices, and film cultures. North Korean cinema is also included in the chapter; six annotated publications, including two books, relate to North Korean cinema.

The chapter's bibliography, which contains 92 annotations, is categorized into several major sections, such as "South Korean Cinema," whose subcategories encompass film history, film industry, authorship, film genre, film analysis, identity politics, and screen personae.

Chapter 1

Communication Law

Kyu Ho Youm, Yoonmo Sang, and Ahran Park

Communication law has been a significant topic of interest to journalism and communication scholars in South Korea throughout the years. Korean communication scholars and professionals have paid keen attention to issues of freedom of speech and the press as crucial components of their communication law environment. Until the late 1980s, freedom of expression was a never-ending challenge in Korea under the country's authoritarian politics.

In the wake of epoch-making political reforms in 1987, Korea moved from a rule-by-law to a rule-of-law system. The passage of freedom-friendly media statutes replaced the restrictive Basic Press Act and allowed the Korean press expanded freedoms. Korea is now considered a major media law country, and Korean communication law has been more favorably received on a global level in recent years.

The history of publications about Korean communication law has followed about one step behind that of Korean communication law itself. Recent years have brought more attention to communication law in Korean-language publications, although the library is not full, so to speak. Of particular note, though, is the scarcity of English-language publications about Korean communication law.

In a global society in which Korea offers a well-developed and well-respected body of communication law, this lack is significant. Highlighting the available English-language publications is important in order to make information about Korean communication law more accessible to the rest of the world.

COMMUNICATION LAW IN KOREA: THE
PUBLISHING WORLD TAKES NOTICE

It was not until the 1980s that Korean scholars and jurists began publishing about communication law in earnest. Korean media law scholar Wonsoon Paeng attributed the "renewed interest" in mass communication law to the ongoing press freedom debates before and after the restrictive Basic Press Act was enacted in 1980.[1]

From the 1990s onward, after Korea had transformed itself into a vibrant functioning democracy following its 1987 "People's Revolution," Korean society experienced dramatic changes socio-politically, culturally, and economically. These changes have brought about a variety of new media law issues as more Koreans asserted their rights against the media, online and offline—and these media law issues have correspondingly spawned a number of publications.

Former Judge Yongsang Park, who has exerted a foundational impact on Korean media law for nearly forty years, stated that the Korean media's abuse of citizens' reputational and privacy rights has led to "a rapid increase" in the public demands for legal resolutions.[2] Among his magisterial books in Korean on speech and press law are *Freedom of Expression*,[3] *Defamation Law*,[4] and *Freedom of the Press*.[5]

These days, communication law research in Korea has become more specialized. For instance, attorney Sangwoon Ahn published a book on Korean freedom of information law in 2015.[6] More recently, constitutional law scholar Jaewan Moon devoted a new book to the "right to be forgotten" in Korea.[7]

A Comparative Approach in Publishing

As Columbia University President Lee C. Bollinger, a noted First Amendment scholar, cogently observed, we are living in the global marketplace of ideas.[8] Hence, communication law is less nation-specific than international.

---

1. Wonsoon Paeng, *Mass Communication Beopje Iron* [Mass Communication Law Theory] (Seoul: Bopmunsa, 1984), 51.

2. Yongsang Park, *Eonrongwa Gaein Beopik* [The Press and Individual Interests] (Seoul: ChosunIlbosa, 1997), 9.

3. Yongsang Park, *Pyohyeonui Jayu* [Freedom of Expression] (Seoul: Hyeonamsa, 2002).

4. Yongsang Park, *Myeongye Hwesonbup* [Defamation Law] (Seoul: Hyonamsa, 2008).

5. Yongsang Park, *Unronui Jayu* [Freedom of the Press] (Seoul: Pakyoungsa, 2013).

6. Sangwoon Ahn, *Jeongbo Gonggaebup* [Freedom of Information Act] (Seoul: Jaeumkwa Moeum, 2015).

7. Jaewan Moon, *Ithyeojil Gwonri* [The Right to Be Forgotten] (Seoul: Jipoondang, 2016).

8. Lee C. Bollinger, *Uninhibited, Robust, and Wide-Open: A Free Press for a New Century* (Oxford: Oxford University Press, 2010).

"Globalization of journalism has accelerated in recent decades thanks to borderless cyber technologies and expanding cross-border media operations," media law researchers Ahran Park and Kyu Ho Youm have noted. "As a result, media law is no longer limited to domestic issues. International and comparative law is increasingly relevant as news media and journalists are subject to a wider range of legal and extra-legal restrictions."[9]

Significantly, media law was comparatively approached in Korea nearly 50 years ago. In his Korean book, *The Press and Human Rights: A Comparative Study of Korean and U.S. Media Law and Cases*, journalism professor Yong Chang examined freedom of the press in Korea and the United States.[10] This 1969 book, albeit narrowly focused, stood out for its in-depth and comprehensive analysis of Korean and American media law.

There is a need for more comparative studies, though; and even within comparative media studies, there should be more diversity in the coverage. Korean media laws tend to be compared only with those of the United States and a few other countries; comparative studies of Korean media laws with media laws of other nations would be a beneficial addition for communication scholars.

Methodology in Publishing

Few methodological differences are noticeable in the published Korean law studies. Most studies have turned to traditional legal research. In the rapidly changing media law environment, though, an empirical approach is worth being considered more often. Columbia Law School professor Benjamin L. Liebman's study, "Innovation Through Intimidation: An Empirical Account of Defamation Litigation in China,"[11] is a good illustration of the benefits of an empirical approach. The integration of conventional legal research methods with empirical methods helps to ensure that researchers develop a more nuanced and holistic understanding of legal issues.

---

9. Ahran Park and Kyu Ho Youm, "International and Comparative Journalism Law," *in* 2 *Encyclopedia of Journalism*, ed. Christopher H. Sterling (Los Angeles: Sage, 2009), 758. doi:10.4135/9781412972048.n198.

10. Yong Chang, *Eonrongwa Ingwon: Hanmi Bigyobupgwa Panryeui Bigyoyeongu* [The Press and Human Rights: A Comparative Study of Korean and U.S. Media Law and Cases] (Seoul: Sonmyeong Munhwasa, 1966).

11. Benjamin L. Liebman, "Innovation Through Intimidation: An Empirical Account of Defamation Litigation in China," *Harvard International Law Journal* 47 (2016): 33–177.

COMMUNICATION LAW IN KOREA: ENGLISH-LANGUAGE PUBLICATIONS IN SHORT SUPPLY

Although there is a relative surfeit of Korean-language books and other publications about Korean communication law, Korean and non-Korean journalism and communication scholars suffer from a dearth of English-language publications on the topic. Thus, it is difficult, if not impossible, for Korean law to be placed in a comprehensive context.

Insufficient English-Language Publications about Korean Media Law

The language barrier is an inhibiting factor for those who wish to publish in international journals. This linguistic challenge for Korean scholars is exacerbated by the actual or perceived lack of initiative on the part of Korean or non-Korean academic organizations in facilitating publications of their members' written works.

In the mid-1980s, the U.S. Association for Education in Journalism and Mass Communication (AEJMC) Law Division issued a curt rejection of a Korean law paper due to its members' alleged lack of interest. Although interest in and respect for Korean communication law, not only in Korea but also on a global level, has increased greatly since then, it is notable that a couple of U.S.-educated Korean journalism scholars have written their master's or doctoral theses on Korean media law, but their Korean law research for such degree projects has not been turned into English journal articles or books.

English-Language Publications: Two Steps Forward, One Step Back

This is not to say that no English-language publications about Korean media law exist. Several scholars have, in fact, published about Korean communication law in English. Nonetheless, despite a clear path forward in this regard, it has not been an entirely unimpeded journey.

In 1971, the first Korea-related communication law article appeared in *Journalism Quarterly*, the flagship journal of the AEJMC. It was a brief comparison of Japanese and Korean libel law.[12] Although the article's one-page Korea section discussed the Criminal Code of Korea, neither the Civil Code nor libel court cases in Korea were mentioned.

---

12. Hamid Mowlana and Chul-Soo Chin, "Libel Laws of Modern Japan and South Korea Are Compared," *Journalism Quarterly* 48, no. 2 (Summer 1971): 326–30.

In the 1990s and 2000s, a number of English-language works about Korean communication law were published. For example, a 1991 article in *Columbia Human Rights Law Review*[13] and a book chapter in *Elite Media Amidst Mass Culture*[14] detail the overall positive media law development in post-1987 Korea. And in 1996, the now-outdated *Press Law in South Korea*[15] analyzed Korean media law, primarily from a statutory and judicial perspective.

And to their credit, in the 2000s, the Korean Society for Journalism and Communication Studies (KSJCS) and the Korean Association for Broadcasting and Telecommunication Studies (KABTS) published a special English edition of the *Korean Journal of Journalism & Communication Studies*[16] and an English book titled *Understanding Journalism in Korea*,[17] respectively. However, although KSJCS and KABTS each have a media law division, the media law members of these premier Korean scholarly organizations rarely engage with foreign scholars. Furthermore, another important Korean group, the Korean Society for Media Law, Ethics, and Policy Research, a 16-year-old organization of media law academics and practitioners in Seoul, has published only a limited journal articles in English.

In the 2000s, too, Korean and American scholars were invited to write about Korean freedom of expression for *International Libel and Privacy Handbook*[18] and *Media, Advertising & Entertainment Law Throughout the World*,[19] as well as other books. On the other hand, Korea is still conspicuously missing from *International Advertising Law*,[20] *International Copyright Law*,[21] and *International Handbook of Social Media Laws*.[22]

Of the English-language publications about Korean media law, a majority have explored statutory and case laws and policy implications. However, there are other emerging topics that deserve increasing attention, including

---

13. Kyu Ho Youm, "Current Development: South Korea: Press Laws in Transition," *Columbia Human Rights Law Review* 22 (1991): 401–35.

14. Kyu Ho Youm, "Freedom of the Press: A Legal and Ethical Perspective." In *Elite Media Amidst Mass Culture: A Critical Look at Mass Communication in Korea*, ed. Chie-woon Kim and Jae-won Lee, 65–108. Seoul: NANAM Publishing House, 1994.

15. Kyu Ho Youm, *Press Law in South Korea* (Ames: Iowa State University Press, 1996).

16. *Korean Journal of Journalism & Communication Studies*, special English edition (2001).

17. Hyung-Cheol Kang et al., Understanding Journalism in Korea (Seoul: Communication Books, 2015).

18. Kyu Ho Youm, Minjeong Kim and Ahran Park, "Korea," In *International Libel and Privacy Handbook: A Global Reference for Journalists, Publishers, Webmasters, and Lawyers*, ed. Charles J. Glasser, Jr., KOR1-KOR24 (New York: LexisNexis, 2016).

19. Kyu Ho Youm et al., "Korea," In *Media, Advertising, & Entertainment Law Throughout the World*, ed. Andrew B. Ulmer, 1135–1207 (Eagan, Minn.: Thomson Reuters, 2017).

20. Paul Jordan, ed., *International Advertising Law: A Practical Global Guide* (London: Globe Business Publishing Ltd., 2014).

21. Ben Allgrove, ed., *International Copyright Law* (London: Globe Business Publishing Ltd., 2013).

22. Paul Lambert, ed., *International Handbook of Social Media Laws* (West Sussex, UK: Bloomsbury Professional Ltd., 2014).

privacy, the right of publicity, judicial communication, and intellectual property law.

Korea, arguably the world's most wired nation, is a fascinating free speech laboratory. Its high-tech communication innovations and developments have given rise to numerous regulatory issues, including the "real name verification" system, the regulation of online video games, the criminalization of cyber defamation and cyber insult, and the press arbitration of the Internet media. Although several scholars in the United States and Korea have published works about these Korean media law topics in English, these topics are still underrepresented in the relevant body of literature.

Finally, it is worth noting that the majority of Korean communication law publications in English are authored by only a few scholars in the United States. Thus, there is a compelling need for more researchers to direct their efforts toward publishing their Korean law research in English in order to increase the diversity of such publications. This is particularly true, given that communication scholars generally publish about Korean law as a real-life case of "reverse perspective" on foreign law in order to create understandable texts for those whose Korean proficiency is rather limited.

Supply and Demand . . . and More Demand

Considering the growing influence of Korea in the global media environment, English books and monographs on Korean law, in the vein of *Hong Kong Media Law: A Guide for Journalists and Media Professionals*,[23] are in demand. Sang Hyun Song, former dean of the Seoul National University College of Law and former president of the International Criminal Court, wrote in 2000:

> Each time I am asked to teach a course on Korean law at U.S. law schools, I am confronted with the daunting problem of providing my American students with materials in English regarding Korean law. There has always been a relative paucity of English-language scholarship on Korean law in comparison to Japanese or Chinese law.[24]

Song's comment highlights the overriding need for publications on Korean media law in English.

---

23. Doreen Weisenhaus, *Hong Kong Media Law: A Guide for Journalist and Media Professionals*, 2nd ed. (Hong Kong: Hong Kong University Press, 2014).

24. Sang Hyun Song, "Foreword," in *Recent Transformations in Korean Law and Society*, ed. Dae-Kyu Yoon (Seoul: Seoul National University Press, 2000), v.

Korean Communication Law: English-Language Resources

This chapter aims to take stock of the books, book chapters, journal articles, theses and dissertations, and other publications in English on Korean communication law. The selection of the publications for annotation has been informed by an underlying question: Does the published study examine Korean speech and press law as its central focus?

As a modest but important step forward in Korean communication law studies in the global twenty-first century, the annotated bibliography should be a valuable resource for those interested in freedom of speech and the press as a legal issue in Korea—and hopefully will facilitate further inquiry into Korean law publications in English as a worthwhile subject.

ANNOTATED BIBLIOGRAPHY

General

Chang, Won Ho. "Freedom of the Press in Korea: A Study of Its Historical Development." Master's thesis, University of Southern California, 1970. ProQuest (1643254076).

Chang's MA thesis looks at freedom of the Korean press from 1896, when Korea started its modernization, to 1964, when President Park Chung-hee repealed the Press Ethics Committee Law. According to Chang, although freedom of speech and the press was not yet completely assured, the history of Koreans' struggle for a free press should not be understated as an important precursor to the current environment of press freedoms in Korea.

Human Rights in Korea. Washington, DC: Asia Watch Committee, 1985. doi: 10.1163/2210–7975_HRD-2261–0001.

This comprehensive Asia Watch report on human rights in Korea is one of a kind, since it deals with human rights in both North and South Korea. Not surprisingly, however, nearly 340 pages of the 364-page report are devoted to South Korea. The "Freedom of Expression" chapter details the Chun Doo Hwan government's repression of freedom of speech and the press from 1980 to mid-1985, when the Asia Watch delegation visited Seoul to investigate the human rights situation in South Korea.

Kim, Chunhyo. Samsung, *Media Empire and Family: A Power Web.* London: Routledge, 2016.

In the context of family-owned media giants in Korea, Kim examines the impact of neoliberal laws and policies on advertising, newspaper, cable television, and film; media owners' use of informal relations in expanding their businesses; and the key beneficiaries of the growing media conglomerates. Kim's study focuses on Samsung, CJ, and JoongAng Ilbo as Korea's *chaebol* groups. Market censorship of the Korean media and corporate censorship by the Lee family, who owns the Samsung group, are discussed.

Mal. "'Guiding' the Press." *Index on Censorship* 16, no. 5 (1987): 28–36. doi: 10.11 77/030642208701600511.

This article illustrates how the ruling authorities in Korea controlled and regulated the news media in the 1980s. It includes the English translations of the specific instructions from the Korean government to its press on how to handle news reporting. The primary source material in the article showcases how Korean journalists and editors were controlled and oppressed by the Chun Doo Hwan administration.

Park, Sora K. "The Effect of Deregulation on the Newspaper Industry Growth: A Case Study of the Korean Market." *Korean Journal of Journalism & Communication Studies* Special English Edition (2001): 241–255.

Park examines the effects of governmental regulation and deregulation on the Korean newspaper industry. Using data of the Real GDP, the newsprint consumption, and the advertising revenues, her study shows how the Korean newspaper industry performed between 1970 and 1999. It also demonstrates that newspapers in Korea held up well against other media.

Tan, Lek Hor. "South Korea: Cabbage Pickle and Press Pay-Offs." *Index on Censorship* 19, no.10 (1990): 10–13. doi: 10.1080/03064229008534973.

An informative snapshot of South Korea's journalism in the late 1980s and the spring of 1990. Despite the press proliferation and expanded press freedom in Korea, partly due to political changes and the repeal of the Basic Press Act, the nature and quality of journalism and news content remains fatuous. The author argues that many things remain to be done in order to accomplish press freedom and promote freedom of expression in Korea.

Yoon, Young-Chul. "Democratization and Media Control in South Korea." *Korean Journal of Journalism & Communication* Special English Edition (2001): 531–555.

Yoon's study of the impact of Korea's democratization process on political journalism focuses on the government mechanisms of press control. It addresses how each news media reacted to the shifting political environment in Korea after 1987 and with what results. Yoon maintains that the media control mechanism evolved from the "state incorporation" to the "press-party parallelism" in the Kim Dae-Jung regime (1998–2003).

Youm, Kyu Ho. "Freedom of the Press in South Korea, 1945–1983: A Sociopolitical and Legal Perspective." PhD diss., Southern Illinois University at Carbondale, 1985. ProQuest (303389561).

Youm's dissertation, which was published as a book, titled *Press Law in South Korea*, in 1996, explores: (1) How has freedom of the press fared in Korea as a libertarian concept? (2) How have the executive and legislative branches of the Korean government dealt with press freedom? (3) How has the Korean judiciary interpreted press freedom? (4) In what way did the Korean press and, in some instances, the Korean public, respond to the government's restriction on their freedom?

————. "Press Freedom under Constraints: The Case of South Korea." *Asian Survey* 26, no. 8 (1986): 868–882. doi: 10.2307/2644137.

While the Korean constitutional guarantee of press freedom is not different from the press freedom guaranteed in the U.S. Constitution, Youm finds that the press in Korea in the 1980s was anything but free in practice. He examines the constrained press in Korea, mapping out the social, political, and legal ways that the government limits press freedom.

————. "Press Freedom in 'Democratic' South Korea: Moving from Authoritarian to Libertarian?" *International Communication Gazette* 43, no. 1 (1989): 53–71. doi: 10.1177/001654928904300104.

This article discusses press freedom in Korea under President Roh Tae Woo, who took over in 1988 from Chun Doo Hwan (1980–1987). It considers Roh's political philosophy with regard to freedom of the press: Roh's liberalization of the legal and political structures of Korea toward a freer press is noted. In conclusion, Youm considers further steps necessary to achieve a robust, free news media in Korea.

————. "South Korea's Experiment with a Free Press." *International Communication Gazette* 53, nos. 1–2 (1994): 111–126. doi: 10.1177/001654929405300108.

Youm takes a critical look at the "sweeping democratic reforms" of post-1987 and the expanded freedom of the press in Korea. He cautions that the press is in danger of losing its freedom within its own institutions, pointing to the lack of professional ethics on the part of the Korean press.

Youm, Kyu Ho, and Michael B. Salwen. "A Free Press in South Korea: Temporary Phenomenon or Permanent Fixture?" *Asian Survey* 30, no. 3 (1990): 312–325. doi: 10.2307/2644568.

Youm and Salwen examine freedom of the press in the first two years of President Roh Tae Woo's rule. They answer three questions: (1) What reforms has Roh enacted? (2) How have these reforms impacted the Korean press? (3) What changes in the press structure and institutions contribute to a robust "Fourth Estate" in the new Korean democracy?

Youm, Kyu Ho, Yoonmo Sang, and Ahran Park. "Communication Law in Korea: A Topic for Global Research." In *Communication, Digital Media, and Popular Culture in Korea: Contemporary Research and Future Prospects,* edited by Dal Yong Jin and Nojin Kwak, 59–79. Lanham, MD: Lexington Books, 2018.

Will or can communication scholars further globalize Korean communication law by publishing in English? In exploring this question, the authors of the book chapter take inventory of Korean law research in English. They contextualize Korean law research while noting the research gaps and suggesting future research agendas. Korean-language publications—greater in number and richer in diversity—are noted to place their discussion in perspective.

Advertising

An, Soontae. "The Republic of Korea." In *The Global Advertising Regulation Handbook*, edited by Mary Alice Shaver and Soontae An, 194–205. Armonk, NY: M.E. Sharpe, 2014. doi: 10.4324/9781315699684.

An examines the structure and operation of advertising regulation, showing the interfaces between self-regulation and public controls as well as the effectiveness of private and public controls. Regrettably, however, her book chapter lacks a look at the judicial interpretations of Korean advertising law.

Kim, Jaehong. "Government Regulation of the Korean Broadcast Advertising Industry." *Journal of Regulation Studies* 14 (1995): 59–82.

Kim ascertains that the Korean government has imposed severe restrictions upon the broadcast advertising market, which brings more harm than good. He also criticizes the "public interest" argument and casts doubt on the role of the Korea Broadcast Advertising Corporation (KOBACO) as a powerful regulator in Korea. This study concludes that the Korean broadcast advertising market needs to be deregulated.

Shin, Kie-Hyuk, and In-Sup Shin. "Advertising Laws and Regulations." In *Advertising in Korea*, 119–123. 5th ed. Seoul: Communication Books, 2013.

"Advertising Laws and Regulations" is a brief chapter of Shin and Shin's book on advertising in Korea, one of the world's 15 largest advertising markets. It provides a succinct history of Korean advertising law. In noting the legal process of advertising law in Korea, Shin and Shin mention the Korea Advertising Review Board (KARB) as a self-regulatory advertising institution. Their chapter includes an informative table of advertising-related laws and a discussion of the KARB's pre-clearance of electronic advertisements.

Broadcasting

Kim, Jae-Young. "Motives for Broadcast Deregulation in South Korea: From Government Control to Market Competition or Government Intervention?" *Korean Journal of Journalism & Communication Studies*, Special English Edition (2001): 155–171.

What underlay the broadcast deregulation in Korea? In addressing this research question, Kim provides a historical overview of broadcasting policies in Korea. His article pays critical attention to the government's deregulatory efforts and to various political, economic, international, and technological factors behind the global trend toward global broadcasting deregulation.

Kim, Kyu. "Regulations of Broadcasting." In *Broadcasting in Korea*, edited by Kyu Kim, Won-Yong Kim, and Jong-Geun Kang, 73–95. Seoul: NANAM Publishing House, 1994.

This book chapter is a brief overview of the Broadcasting Act of 1990. Also discussed in the chapter are the Cable Television Broadcasting Act, the Copyright Act, and the Telecommunications Business Act. The English texts of the Broadcasting Act and the Copyright Act are included in the appendixes.

Korea Communications Commission. *Annual Report*. Gwacheon, South Korea: Korea Communications Commission, 2008–present.

The Korea Communications Commission's (KCC) *Annual Report* offers information about the broadcasting and communications policy of the Korean government. The 2014 *Annual Report* contains the KCC's revised enforcement decree of the Broadcasting Act relating to broadcasting advertisement.

Kwak, Ki-Sung. "The Role of the State in the Regulation of Television Broadcasting in South Korea." *Media International Australia* 92, no. 1 (1999): 65–79. doi: 10.1 177/1329878X9909200109.

Kwak offers an overview of the regulatory history of television broadcasting. He highlights the inconsistent policies and regulatory practices of the state bureaucracy, attributing this problematic situation to the government as the sole player in establishing, framing, and devising broadcasting regulations.

Copyright

Choe, Kyong-Soo. "Protection of Broadcast Signals in Korea from the Perspective of Copyright Law." *Asian Business Lawyer* 11 (2013): 107–124.

The Copyright Act of Korea was amended in 2011 in accordance with the Korea-U.S. Free Trade Agreement. This article examines the newly revised Copyright Act in connection with two provisions governing the protection of broadcast signals. Choe argues that the broadcast signals provisions still need further analysis.

Choi, Chung Hwan. "Protection of Artists' Rights under the Korean Copyright Law." *Pacific Rim Law & Policy Journal* 12, no. 1 (2003): 179–197. doi: hdl.handle.net/1773.1/722.

Choi, a leading Korean entertainment lawyer, points out that artists' performances, with the advancement of technology, have become as valuable as the original works of authorship and thus need legal protection by "neighboring rights." He examines various artists' rights such as the right of reproduction, right to royalties from the reproduction, performance broadcasting right, and performer's "moral right."

Choi, Yunjeong. "Development of Copyright Protection in Korea: Its History, Inherent Limits, and Suggested Solutions." *Brooklyn Journal of International Law* 28, no. 2 (2003): 643–673.

Choi examines the cultural, legal, and historical factors of copyright protection in Korea, as well as international copyright influences. While noting the limitations on copyright protection in Korea, Choi offers potential solutions to copyright issues.

Lee, Ilhyung. "Culturally-Based Copyright Systems?: The U.S. and Korea in Conflict." *Washington University Law Quarterly* 79, no. 4 (2001): 1103–1159.

Lee elaborates on the cultural dimension of American and Korean copyright systems. He contends that Confucian attitudes have played an important role in Korean culture and its approach to copyright. Economic interest, notes Lee, has contributed to the transnational dispute in Korea over intellectual property rights in general and piracy in particular.

Ministry of Culture, Sports and Tourism [MCST], Republic of Korea. *2013 Annual Report on Copyright in Korea* (No. 11–1371000–000201–10). Sejong-si, South Korea: MCST, 2013. http://www.copyright.or.kr/eng/doc/activities/2013AR.pdf.

This white paper on copyright illuminates recent developments in Korean copyright law. It features key points of the 2013 revisions of the copyright law relating to the copyright duration and the collective management of copyrights in the music industry, among others.

Moon, Sun-Young, and Daeup Kim. "The 'Three Strikes' Policy in Korean Copyright Act 2009: Safe or Out?" *Washington Journal of Law, Technology & Arts* 6, no. 3 (2011): 171–183.

The controversial "three strikes" policy in Korean copyright law has raised constitutional concerns, which include free speech violations, separation of powers, and due process of law. This law journal article suggests possible policy revisions.

Yook, So-young. "The History and Current Status on Fair Use of Copyrighted Work in Korea." *Inha Law Review* 15, no. 3 (2012): 1–29.

This article reviews the past and present of "fair use" in Korean law. It focuses on how the fair use provision of the Copyright Act was introduced into Korea. Yook briefly notes the history of the fair use doctrine in the United States. She points out that the Copyright Act, which was influenced by the Free Trade Agreements between Korea and the United States and between Korea and EU, has been revised to better protect the copyright holders than the users of copyrighted works.

Youm, Kyu Ho. "Copyright Law in the Republic of Korea." *UCLA Pacific Basin Law Journal* 17, nos. 2–3 (1999): 276–300.

Youm places the Copyright Act in historical, textual, and doctrinal contexts, giving attention to relevant statutes and court rulings. U.S. copyright law serves as a frame of reference, but not necessarily as a comparison.

Data Privacy

Greenleaf, Graham, and Whon-il Park. "South Korea's Innovations in Data Privacy Principles: Asian Comparisons." *Computer Law & Security Review* 30, no. 5 (2014): 492–505. doi: 10.1016/j.clsr.2014.07.011.

This article examines the legislative history of the Personal Information Protection Act (PIPA). Referring to South Korea as "Asia's leader in data privacy innovation," Greenleaf and Park expound significant innovations in PIPA's principles, such as mandatory privacy officers, a compulsory privacy policy, and data minimization.

Phillips, Joe, and Se-In Park. "Litigating Personal Data Disclosure against Information and Telecommunication Service Providers: A Korea-US Comparison." *Journal of Korean Law* 15 (2015): 191–235.

Why have millions of Korean and U.S. consumers sought remedies for the unauthorized disclosure of personal information by Internet-based information and telecommunications service providers? In addressing this question, Phillips and Park compares Korean and U.S. law by focusing on the definition of "personal information," possible causes of actions, and the available remedies.

Defamation

Ham, Seok-cheon. "Court Ruling and Changes in Media Environment." *Korean Journalism Review* 5, no. 2 (2011): 31–44.

This article reviews major free-speech court decisions from the 1980s to the 2000s. Ham takes note of significant changes in media law on reputation and other personal rights. Several Supreme Court of Korea decisions in the 2000s involving critical news reporting on public officials are discussed. Ham concludes that Korean courts moved in a media-friendly direction, which led to more "breathing space" for the Korean press.

Kim, Jae Hyung. "Protection of Personality Rights under Korean Civil Law." *Columbia Journal of Asian Law* 30, no. 2 (2017): 131–159.

This article is an English translation of Korean Supreme Court Justice Jae Hyung Kim's manuscript originally published in 1999. Kim provides a general overview of the legal status and protection of personality rights under Korean civil law. After showing how personality rights can come into conflict with other fundamental rights, Kim concludes his article by calling for an amendment to the Civil Code.

Lee, Jae-Jin. "Libel Law and the Press: The Struggle of the Korean Press to Establish 'Public Person' Privilege against Libel Litigation." *International Communication Gazette* 61, no. 5 (1999): 433–446. doi: 10.1177/0016549299061005005.

In examining the "public figure" defense for the Korean press against libel claims, Lee finds that the Korean courts have not yet accepted the American "actual malice" principle. He contends that the Korean press should keep developing the concept of public figures so that courts may recognize it as a safeguard against libel lawsuits.

———. "The Implication of the Supreme Court Ruling on the Libel Case." *Korean Journalism Review* 3, no. 3 (2009): 168–171.

This is a case commentary on the Supreme Court of Korea's 2009 ruling, in which the court held that web portals should be subject to the same duty of care as news organizations. Lee considers the court decision significant because it clearly acknowledged the Internet portal's duty of care. However, he points out that the Supreme Court has failed to provide a clear guideline on the duty of care for Internet service providers in Korea.

Lee, Seung-sun. "Characteristics of Libel Suits in South Korea: With Respect to Editorial Rights and Journalists' Liabilities." *Korean Journal of Journalism & Communication* Special English Edition (2001): 653–664.

The number of libel actions against Korean news media increased rapidly in the 1990s. According to Lee's study, the success rate for individuals in suing the news media reflects the judicial tendency to prioritize personal rights over freedom of the press. Lee worries that libel lawsuits will likely force media owners to interfere with editorial decision-making to preempt libel damages.

Leitner, John M. "To Post or Not to Post: Korean Criminal Sanctions for Online Expression." *Temple International & Comparative Law Journal* 25 (2011): 43–77.

Korean courts use criminal law to punish online defamation and contempt. Leitner discusses the "Real Name Verification System," the nationwide system for verifying the identities of Internet users in Korea. Also examined are cyberdefamation and cybercontempt. Leitner proposes that the National Assembly Korea consider repealing the Cyber Contempt Law and Cyber Defamation Law, as well as decriminalizing defamation and contempt.

———. "Anonymity, Privacy, and Expressive Equality: Name Verification and Korean Constitutional Rights in Cyberspace." *Journal of Korean Law* 14 (2015): 167–212.

This article contextualizes the creation and implementation of the real name verification system in Korea. Leitner argues that the value of freedom of expression in general, and anonymous online expression in particular, is properly understood through its relationship to the right of equality and the right of privacy. He suggests that Korean experience with the real name verification system provides other democracies a valuable study of how carefully a society must evaluate the costs of attempting to remake Internet culture by force.

Mowlana, Hamid, and Chul-Soo Chin. "Libel Laws of Modern Japan and South Korea Are Compared." *Journalism Quarterly* 48, no. 2 (Summer 1971): 326–330, 348. doi: 10.1177/107769907104800217.

This comparative study is probably the earliest English-language published study of Korean libel law. The authors detail the Criminal Code of Korea, as well as statistics on defamation convictions in Korea. The Korean Press Ethics Commission's role in handling libel complaints against the Korean news media is compared with its counterpart in Japan. Few Korean libel cases are discussed, however.

Park, Ahran. "Balancing Online Freedom of Speech with Reputation in South Korea." *Media & Arts Law Review* 20, no. 4 (2015): 453–460.

Park states that Korea provides a noteworthy example of Internet service provider (ISP) jurisprudence from a global perspective. Internet laws and court decisions have burdened Korean ISPs with heavy liability for defamation by online users, which might chill freedom of cyberspeech in Korea.

Park, Ahran, and Kyu Ho Youm. "International Defamation and Privacy: Korea." In *Carter-Ruck on Defamation and Privacy*, 6th ed., edited by Alastair Mullis and Cameron Doley, 1343–1349. London: LexisNexis, 2010.

After an examination of the Civil and Criminal Codes on defamation (libel and slander) and privacy as a tort, this concise chapter of Korean defamation and privacy law looks at relevant court decisions. One of the significant libel cases of the Supreme Court of Korea relates to the judicial recognition of the "reasonable belief" standard, although the Supreme Court rejected the U.S. "actual malice" doctrine.

Park, Kyung Sin. "'Stay Still': Sewol, a Tale of Fatal Censorship, Fatal Paternalism." In *Challenges of Modernization and Governance in South Korea: The Sinking of the Sewol and Its Causes*, edited by Jae-Jung Suh and MiKyoung Kim, 121–142. New York: Palgrave Macmillan, 2017. doi: 10.1007/978–981–10–4023–8_6.

Park's book chapter on the Sewol ferry tragedy in Korea pays attention to the media's failure to report facts and censorship of the published criticisms of the Sewol ferry rescue efforts. It also reviews criminal charges for defamation as well as "truth defamation" laws. Park examines various causes of major disasters in Korea and seeks to determine a possible relationship between paternalism in Korean society and Koreans' failure to respond to disaster situations.

Park, Kyung Sin, and You Jong-Sung. "Criminal Prosecutions for Defamation and Insult in South Korea with a Leflarian Study in Election Contexts." *University of Pennsylvania Asian Law Review* 12, no. 3 (2017): 463–495.

An international law perspective guides this in-depth study of Korean criminal defamation and insult law on political campaigns. Taiwan and Japan are comparatively noted about candidate defamation and insult. In addition to introducing relevant Korean law and practices, the study includes an empirical analysis of more than 1,500 candidate defamation and insult cases in Korea from 1995 to 2015 to examine whether criminal defamation law is politically abused.

Sang, Yoonmo, and Jonathan Anderson. "Bloggers' Libel Liability: A Comparative Analysis of South Korea and the United States." *Journal of Media Law & Ethics* 3, nos. 3/4 (2012): 63–85.

This study seeks to trace, from a comparative perspective, the journalistic standards of bloggers' libel liability. Litigation over bloggers' defamation and invasion of privacy in the United States and Korea is increasingly popular as the influence of bloggers grows. The authors review court cases and statutes on bloggers' liability in the two countries.

Son, Taegyu. "The Law of Political Libel and Freedom of the Press in the Republic of Korea and the United States." PhD diss., University of North Carolina at Chapel Hill, 2002. ProQuest (305565427).

Son's doctoral dissertation analyzes political libel lawsuits against the press in Korea between 1996 and 2002. It provides a comparative analysis of political libel law in Korea and the United States as a foundation for further discussion of a desirable future direction for Korea's political libel law.

Sung, Sunje. "Resolution of Clash between Freedom of Speech and Defamation in the U.S. and Korea." SJD diss., University of Wisconsin-Madison, 2000. ProQuest (not available).

How is free speech balanced with reputational interest in Korea and the United States? In examining Korean and American constitutional law on freedom of speech versus defamation law, this SJD dissertation applies a legal and sociocultural approach. Its author proposes that freedom of speech be expanded and truth be given more leeway as a libel defense for speech on matters of public concern in Korea. He argues that Korean courts should consider the U.S. "actual malice" standard.

Youm, Kyu Ho. "The Libel Law of the Republic of Korea." *International Communication Gazette* 35, no. 3 (1985): 183–196. doi: 10.1177/001654928503 500304.

Although freedom of the press and speech are guaranteed as constitutional rights, Korean libel law has been employed by the government to restrict freedom of the press. Youm examines libel law and its impact on the Korean press, discussing a number of libel cases in their sociopolitical and historical contexts.

———. "Libel Laws and Freedom of the Press: South Korea and Japan Reexamined." *Boston University International Law Journal* 8 (1990): 53–83.

Youm finds Japan to be a "functioning" democracy with a strong separation of powers, while Korea lacks the institutions to protect its press. In Korea, the public importance of information is not given consideration when balanced with reputation. In Japan, Youm finds, there is a stronger balance between the right to protect one's reputation and the public need for free information.

———. "Libel Law and the Press in South Korea: An Update." *Maryland Series in Contemporary Asian Studies 1992*, no. 3 (1992): 1–23.

Noting an increase in libel lawsuits in Korea, Youm examines Korean libel law and the press since 1981. He looks at the statutory and constitutional status of reputation and court cases and their impact on the press. Youm finds that the increasing number of libel claims have led the Korean press to change, with journalists approaching potentially defamatory stories with greater caution.

———. "Libel Law and the Press: U.S. and South Korea Compared." *UCLA Pacific Basin Law Journal* 13, no. 2 (1994): 231–264.

This article compares American and Korean press law on reputation, as well as court interpretations and their impact on the press. Libel law is found to have become less severe over time in both countries. In the United States, it is no longer a major concern. In Korea, however, the courts are still endeavoring to formulate legal standards to balance press freedom and protection of reputation.

———. "Balancing Reputation with Press Freedom in South Korea." *Communications Lawyer* 14, no. 4 (Winter 1997): 3–4.

Noting Korea's democratization of the preceding decade, Youm describes a much freer press than had ever existed in Korea's authoritarian past. However, he describes three major threats to press freedom: the rise in libel claims against journalists and publications in the Korean courts; the common practice of journalists accepting cash, or "chonji," from sources; and the "kijaden" press club system, which is not in line with the concept of a free and open press.

————. "Defamation Law and the Internet in South Korea." *Media & Arts Law Review* 9, no. 2 (2004): 141–153.

Youm looks into the concept of reputation in Korea and its complicated relationship to press freedom. He touches on the differences between Korean and American legal traditions, noting that the Constitution of Korea does not prefer press freedom over reputation. Youm notes the recent press-friendly court rulings, which signify a move toward a distinction between public and private figures in libel law.

Youm, Kyu Ho, Minjeong Kim, and Ahran Park. "Korea." In *International Libel and Privacy Handbook: A Global Reference for Journalists, Publishers, Webmasters, and Lawyers*, edited by Charles J. Glasser, Jr., KOR-1 to KOR-24. New York: LexisNexis, 2016.

Three media law scholars examine the most frequently asked questions about libel and privacy in Korean law. Among the twenty-plus questions addressed are: "What is the fault standard(s) applied to libel?" "Is a right of privacy recognized (either civilly or criminally)?" and "Has your jurisdiction applied established media law to Internet publishers?" The book chapter's introduction of the Korean legal system is informative and up to date.

Ethics

Youm, Kyu Ho. "Chonji Journalism in Korea: An Issue for Press Ethics." *Media Asia* 20, no. 2 (1993): 100–101. doi: 10.1080/01296612.1993.11726412

Youm points out new threats to press freedom, including rising libel claims against journalists and, more significantly, an increase in the practice of "envelope journalism," which is the acceptance of cash gifts, or "chonji" from news sources. The article is peppered with many examples of the practice.

Internet

Ahn, Jungmihn. "The Proliferation of Internet Regulation in Korea." *Journal of Law & Economic Regulation* 5, no. 2 (2012): 7–19.

This brief overview of the current status of broadband in Korea discusses what has contributed to broadband development in the Asian country. After critically reviewing the Korean government's recent efforts to control the Internet, Ahn concludes that the Korean government's role should be minimized when resolving social problems associated with the proliferation of broadband Internet.

Fish, Eric S. "Is Internet Censorship Compatible with Democracy?: Legal Restrictions of Online Speech in South Korea." *Asia-Pacific Journal on Human Rights and the Law* 10, no. 2 (2009): 43–96. doi: 10.1163/138819010x12647506166519.

This article explores the tension between Korea's democratic politics and its online censorship of political speech. It shows how the incomplete liberalization of Korea has given the government cover to implement a shockingly restrictive Internet censorship bureaucracy.

Jung, Gy Yun. "Internet Total Information Provider's Liability to Libel and Defamation: Supreme Court of Korea, 2008Da53812." *Asian Business Lawyer* 6 (2010): 63–69.

This is a short commentary about a significant case of the Korean Supreme Court on the Internet service provider's liability for defamation by a third party. Highlighting the Supreme Court ruling as the first opportunity to set forth the clear standards for ISP liability, Jung contends that the case has alerted ISPs to their duty to supervise and delete harmful online contents.

Kim, You-Seung. "Freedom and Regulation on the Information Superhighway: A Study of the Internet Content Rating System in South Korea." PhD diss., University of London, 2005. ProQuest (1427427328).

Using case studies and a survey, Kim pays special attention to Korea's mandatory Internet content rating system and examines the rating system's impact on freedom of expression in Korea. His dissertation overviews government regulations of Internet content in the European Union, United States, England, Australia, and China. Also analyzed are Internet self/co-regulation and content filtering technologies.

Park, Kyung Sin. "Administrative Internet Censorship by Korea Communication Standards Commission." *Soongsil Law Review* 33 (2015): 91–115.

The Korean Communication Standards Commission (KCSC) is one of the few government agencies around the world that are empowered to block or delete online contents. Park first evaluates the KCSC structure and decisions as an administrative body and then examines the judicial oversight of the KCSC. He proposes that a discussion of an international consensus on the concept of censorship extend to post-publication administrative censorship.

West, James M. "Legal Regulation of Internet Communications in South Korea." *German Yearbook of International Law* 41 (1998): 101–27.

West focuses on Internet regulation in Korea for his analysis of freedom of expression law. He addresses how Korean courts and government agencies apply the traditional free speech rules and regulations to cyberspeech.

Youm, Kyu Ho. "The Internet and Democracy in South Korea." In *Rhetoric and Reality: The Internet Challenge for Democracy in Asia*, edited by Indrajit Banerjee, 141–178. Singapore: Eastern Universities Press, 2003.

Youm's book chapter is about Internet and digital communications as a democratizing force in Korea. Noting Korea's recent move to build up its technological infrastructure, Youm places the Internet and new media in the context of the country's history and existing framework of media laws. The chapter includes an assessment of the legal implications of the Internet for Korea's participatory democracy and freedom of expression.

Youm, Kyu Ho, and Ahran Park. "Fake News from a Legal Perspective: The United States and South Korea Compared." *Southwestern Journal of International Law* 24, no.1 (2018) (forthcoming).

Korea and the United States are comparatively examined on their "fake news" law. Youm and Park first offer the differing Korean and U.S. definitions of fake news before placing it in a legal framework. Their forthcoming law journal article concentrates on the context of the (evolving) free speech law of Korea and the United States by looking into how the two countries approach fake news as a matter of statutory and decisional law.

Japanese Colonial Rule

Youm, Kyu Ho. "Japanese Press Policy in Colonial Korea." *Journal of Asian History* 26, no. 2 (1992): 140–159.

Freedom of the press during the Japanese rule of Korea is analyzed by centering on the status of the Korean press in 1910–1945, the press laws and regulations of the Japanese colonial government in Korea, and the impact of those laws and regulations upon the Korean press. The Newspaper Law of 1907 is given extensive attention in Youm's article, the first of its kind in English.

Judicial Review

Youm, Kyu Ho. "Judicial Interpretation of Press Freedom in South Korea." *Boston College Third World Law Journal* 7, no. 2 (1987): 133–159.

This article discusses the legal framework of the Korean press from 1981 to 1987. Although the Constitution of Korea provides for a system of checks and balances and a separation of power, Youm argues that its press freedom guarantee is weakened by the authoritarian history and practices of the Korean government. A number of court cases on press freedom are examined.

———. "Press Freedom and Judicial Review in South Korea." *Stanford Journal of International Law* 30 (1994): 1–40.

How has the Constitutional Court of Korea interpreted press freedom as a constitutional right since 1988? Youm's lengthy law journal article is structured in three
parts: the statutory and constitutional framework of press freedom, constitutional
court decisions, and the impact of the constitutional court decisions on press
freedom.

————. "The Constitutional Court and Freedom of Expression." *Journal of Korean
Law* 1 (2001): 37–70.

Youm explores how the Constitutional Court of Korea has balanced freedom of
expression with various conflicting interests. He analyzes the relevant constitutional text and the major legal decisions since 1988.

Mass Communication Law

Freedom of Expression in the Republic of Korea. Washington, DC: Asia Watch,
International Human Rights Law Group; New York: American Center of
International PEN, 1988. doi: 10.1163/2210–7975_HRD-2261–0010.

This documented report is drawn from information on freedom of expression in
Korea gathered by a U.S. human rights delegation. It provides succinct, up-to-date
analyses of the Korean Constitution on freedom of expression and various direct
and indirect press statutes. The report's "Policies and Practices" section focuses on
the Korean government's actions on freedom of speech and the press since June 29,
1987, when a series of democratic reforms were announced in Korea.

Haggard, Stephan, and Jong-Sung You. "Freedom of Expression in South Korea."
Journal of Contemporary Asia 45, no. 1 (2015): 167–179. doi: 10.2139/
ssrn.2505565.

What has made civil liberties in South Korea deteriorate? Haggard and You assert
that the answer can be found in abuse of criminal defamation law, election campaign law, national security limitations on free speech, Internet restrictions, and
partisan use of state power against the media. The authors contend that the main
impetus behind fewer civil liberties in Korea appears political: The administrations
on the right and left have both limited freedom of expression in order to constrain
political opposition.

Korea Press Foundation. *The Korea Press.* Seoul: Korea Press Foundation,
1984–present.

The yearbook of the Korea Press Foundation is an annual overview of the Korean
media. It is valuable to those interested in up-to-date information about the media
industry, but it is especially relevant to communications law scholars as a source for
major Korean media court decisions and media statutes. *The Korea Press* of 2017
covers the Constitutional Court ruling on the Enforcement Decree of the Promotion
of Newspapers Act.

Lee, Seung-Sun. "Media Law and Regulations: Legal Issues of Freedom of Expression." In *Journalism Culture and Practice in Korea*, edited by Hyung-Cheol Kang, Pil-Mo Jung, Seung-Sun Lee, Jung-Kun Pae, Seog-Tae Shim, June Woong Rhee, Myung-Koo Kang, et al., 50–84. Seoul: Communication Books, 2015.

Lee's book chapter is a critical examination of Korean media laws and regulations, including the National Security Law, the Protection of Communications Secrets Act, the Public Official Election Act, and the Telecommunications Business Act. It reviews many court cases on freedom of expression. Lee argues that journalists, the civil society, and academia need to make joint efforts to expand freedom of expression.

Paeng, Won-Soon. "Main Characteristics of Korea's Press Law." *Korean Journal of Journalism & Communication Studies* 20 (1985): 35–50.

The Basic Press Act of 1980 is examined by a leading scholar on Korean media law. After reviewing the press statute's provisions, Paeng asserts that the Basic Press Act includes many press-restrictive clauses, concluding that the press law can be easily abused to control the press.

Park, Ahran. "Korean Media Law Update: Key Statutes Revised." *Media & Arts Law Review* 15, no. 1 (2010): 111–123.

Park's "update" centers on the constitutional and statutory framework of Korean media law. The 2009 revisions of the Newspaper Act, the Broadcasting Act, and the Internet Protocol Television Act are discussed. In addition, the author surveys defamation and privacy law, online defamation and ISP liability, the press arbitration system, and access to information.

Youm, Kyu Ho. "Press Law in the Republic of Korea." *New York Law School Law Review* 6, no. 3 (Spring 1986): 667–702.

The press law in Korea, both direct and indirect, prior to Korea's democratic reforms in 1987 is the topic of Youm's law review article. Through an examination of the constitution and statutes, Youm addresses the broader question of why Korea epitomizes the great gap in press freedom between law on the books and law in reality.

————. "Current Development: South Korea: Press Laws in Transition." *Columbia Human Rights Law Review* 22 (1991): 401–435.

Youm's in-depth analysis of the press law in Korea in the wake of President Roh Tae Woo's liberal reforms revolves around constitutional and statutory law. Youm compares the print and broadcasting statutes of 1987 with the abolished Basic Press Act of 1980.

―――. "Freedom of Expression and the Supreme Court: The Case of the Republic of Korea." *Free Speech Yearbook* 31, no. 1 (1993): 151–173. doi: 10.1080/08997 225.1993.10556159.

Youm gives a detailed overview of the Supreme Court of Korea's structure and processes and then explores the concept of freedom of expression under the constitution and statutes of Korea. Major Supreme Court cases are analyzed.

―――. "Freedom of the Press: A Legal and Ethical Perspective." In *Elite Media Amidst Mass Culture: A Critical Look at Mass Communication in Korea*, edited by Chie-woon Kim and Jae-won Lee, 65–108. Seoul: NANAM Publishing House, 1994.

Youm's book chapter looks at the emergence of the press in Korea as a "watchdog" on the government since 1987. Besides comparing the post-1987 press laws with the (now-abolished) Basic Press Act of 1980, Youm addresses further improvements that are needed to make the Korean press laws more compatible with the democratic politics of Korea. Other topics include press responsibility and ethics as a new issue in Korea.

―――. *Press Law in South Korea.* Ames: Iowa State University Press, 1996.

Youm's book, the first and only one of its kind, focuses on the constitutional, statutory, and decisional law affecting the Korean press. Among the key topics examined are print and broadcasting law, libel, privacy, national security, access to information, copyright, and obscenity. The book's appendixes include the English translations of the Constitution of Korea, the Periodicals Act, the Broadcast Act, the Cable Television Broadcast Act, the Copyright Act, and the Press Ethics Code.

―――. "Mass Communications Law in Transition: Defining Freedom and Control of the Media." In *Recent Transformations in Korean Law and Society*, edited by Dae-Kyu Yoon, 103–134. Seoul: Seoul National University, 2000.

Youm presents the post-1987 evolution of the press law in Korea in detail. The statutory framework that governs the Korean media has led to a freer press, but he finds many remnants of the country's authoritarian past in the text of some press statutes. Youm considers the judicial interpretations of those statutes.

―――. "Freedom of Expression and the Law: Rights and Responsibilities in South Korea." *Stanford Journal of International Law* 38 (2002): 123–151.

Youm's article is a sequence to his 1994 article in the *Stanford Journal of International Law* on freedom of the press in Korea. Youm looks at the "right to know" statute and other laws that have allowed for increased government openness. Also, he devotes a section to examining expressive rights versus "societal interests" such as privacy and reputation.

Youm, Kyu Ho, Hoo-Dong Lee, Won Hee Cho, Sanghoon Shin, Jiyeon Park, Gilhan Ahn, Hyungji Kim, Sunhong Min, and Sunggene Park. "Korea." In *Media, Advertising, & Entertainment Law Throughout the World*, edited by Andrew B. Ulmer, 1136–1207. Eagan, Minn.: Thomson Reuters, 2017.

The Korea chapter, annually updated, is a practical resource for lawyers that is divided into the many subcategories of pertinent law in South Korea. The general topics discussed include media law, advertising law, entertainment law, and art law. Each topic is addressed in depth, including its constitutional basis, history, and the statutory frameworks that regulate it.

National Security

Human Rights in Korea: Facts and Fiction. Seoul: Korean Overseas Information Service, 1990.

This booklet illustrates a rare case in which the Korean government makes global efforts to promote its rule-of-law commitment. The Roh Tae Woo administration rebuts the critics of its human right record with "facts." The history and enforcement of the controversial National Security Law (NSL) is given extensive attention. The NSL chapter discusses how Roh applied the law against several journalists, book publishers, artists, and authors.

Kim, Woo-hyung. "Freedom of Political Speech vs. National Security in Korea: A Historical Survey." *International Lawyer* 5, no. 3 (1971): 488–510.

Kim looks at freedom of political speech versus national security. His historical discussion of the speech regulations of the Yi Dynasty, Japanese colonial rule, and the U.S. military government lays out an informative foundation. Kim argues that the constitutional issues over the inherent conflict between political speech and national security would be resolved only by a proper understanding of the judicial role.

Retreat from Reform: Labor Rights & Freedom of Expression in South Korea. Washington, DC: Asia Watch Committee, 1990. doi: 10.1163/2210–7975_ HRD-2261–0034.

What's the freedom of expression record of Roh Tae Woo's first two years as president of Korea? The Asia Watch Committee's report assesses the gap between Roh's promise of freedom versus his action. Freedom of expression for the labor movement is addressed as the key focus of the report of 1990. Moreover, the National Security Act as a free speech and free press issue is duly noted.

A Stern, Steady Crackdown: Legal Process and Human Rights in South Korea. Washington, DC: Asia Watch Committee, 1987. doi: 10.1163/2210–7975_ HRD-2261–0006.

The Asia Watch Committee's report investigates the criminal justice system of Korea as an illustration of the government's political abuse of the system. To those interested in freedom of expression as a communication law issue, its section on the prosecutions of political cases is of particular interest. The National Security Law and the Criminal Code on anti-State defamation are among the Korean laws informatively analyzed.

Yang, Kun. "The Recent Decisions of the Korean Constitutional Court on Freedom of Expression." *Hanyang Journal of Law* 14 (1997): 183–191.

Yang examines two 1996 cases of the Constitutional Court of Korea on freedom of expression. The first case concerned how the National Security Act on the "subsequent punishment of speech." The second case dealt with the censorship of motion pictures as a prior restraint on expression. Yang argues that the "clear and present danger" doctrine was abused in Korea against free speech.

Youm, Kyu Ho. "Press Freedom vs. National Security in South Korea." *Communications Lawyer* 9 (Spring 1991): 16–19.

Youm examines the constitutional provisions, statutes, and judicial interpretations relating to press freedom versus national security. He concludes that the "letter and spirit" of the Constitution of Korea is not followed by the laws that have been drafted and enforced in the name of national security.

North Korea

Youm, Kyu Ho. "Press Laws in North Korea." *Asian Journal of Communication* 2, no. 1 (1991): 70–86. doi: 10.1080/01292989109359541.

Youm's article on the press law in North Korea is the first and only study of its kind. According to Youm, North Korean press law is modeled after Soviet Communism. Hence, the North Korean press is working alongside the government.

Privacy

Lee, Jae-Jin. "Disclosure of a Celebrities' [*sic*] Privacy: Limitations and Legal Issues." *Korea Journalism Review* 4, no. 1 (2010): 102–113.

In defining a celebrity and determining whether celebrities have suffered from the privacy torts, Lee examines major court cases concerning celebrities' rights of publicity and privacy. He identifies several factors for Korean courts to consider in deciding when a private citizen becomes a public figure (or celebrity) and to what extent that citizen's privacy and publicity rights may be compromised.

Lee, Seung-Sun. "Telecommunication Secrecy of Public Figures versus the Media's Freedom of News Reporting on Public Affairs: Regarding the Seoul High Court's Ruling on 'X-file Scandal.'" *Korea Journalism Review* 2, no. 3 (2008): 66–93.

This is a case analysis of a Korean appellate court ruling on a news report of a wiretapped conversation among leading public figures that referenced the manipulation of a presidential campaign. In the so-called "X-file scandal" case, the Seoul High Court found that the Korean journalist involved engaged in illegal reporting, although his access to the wiretapped phone record was legal. Lee argues that the reporter's action was justifiable.

Yoo, Eui Sun. "Comparative Studies of Privacy Issues in Old Media and New Media Environment: Focusing on Illegality, Exemptions, and Remedies." *Asian Communication Research* 3, no. 1 (2006): 129–149.

Yoo finds that basic old-media privacy principles are applicable to the new-media environment. After reviewing privacy invasion by government agencies and corporations, he brings attention to a need for more legislative efforts that allow people informational privacy.

Publicity

Nam, Hyung Doo. "The Right of Publicity in the Global Market: Is James Dean a Living Dead Even in Korea?" PhD diss., University of Washington, 2005. ProQuest (305417302).

Nam's PhD dissertation explores how the right of publicity enables a person to control the commercial use of his or her name, likeness, and/or identity within the context of global entertainment distribution. Focusing on the descendibility and universality of the right, Nam discusses how to create an international regime for the right of publicity. Recent developments in publicity rights in Korea are noted.

Nam, Hyung Doo. "The Emergence of Hollywood Ghosts on Korean TVs: The Right of Publicity from the Global Market Perspective." *Pacific Rim Law & Policy Journal* 19, no. 3 (2010): 487–518.

Nam considers the right of publicity in the United States and Korea. He argues that (1) the right of publicity needs to be understood within the context of the entertainment market and (2) a global market perspective should be adopted in discussing the right of publicity. His conclusion: An international legal regime for the right of publicity needs to be established from a global market perspective.

Right of Correction

Lee, Jae-Jin. "Right of Correction." In *The International Encyclopedia of Communication*. Edited by Wolfgang Donsbach. 10 vols. Malden, MA: Blackwell Publishing, 2008.

Lee defines the right of correction and discusses how it trumps libel litigation. He distinguishes the right of correction from the right of reply, observing that Korea and other countries recognize the right of correction as a legal right. Lee's piece takes note of a 2005 Korean law that forces media companies to correct incorrect stories when there is a need to redress reputational injury.

Right of Reply

Kim, Yung-Wook, and Lim Yu-Jin. "A Study on Press Arbitration System in South Korea: Focusing on Its Functions of Conflict Resolution and Reinforcing the Role of Mediation." *Korea Journalism Review* 4, no. 2 (2010): 71–97.

The press arbitration system in Korea as a mechanism of "mediation" for conflicts between the media and individuals or organizations is the topic of this article. Kim and Lim analyze the operation of and user satisfaction with the system as an alternative dispute resolution method.

Lee, Jae-Jin. "Press Freedom, the Press Arbitration System, and Sociopolitical Changes in South Korea, 1981–1996." PhD diss., Southern Illinois University at Carbondale, 1998. ProQuest (304453185).

Lee's doctoral dissertation explores the Korean press arbitration system from 1981 to 1996. It examines libel suits and press arbitration cases in which a right of reply was sought as a remedy. In addition, it presents a comparative analysis of Germany, France, Japan, and the United States.

———. "Press Freedom and the Right of Reply under the Contemporary Korean Libel Laws: A Comparative Analysis." *UCLA Pacific Basin Law Journal* 16, no. 2 (1998): 155–197.

Lee analyzes how press freedom and reputation in Korea are reconciled through the Press Arbitration Commission. Comparing the right of reply in Germany, France, Japan, and the United States, he concludes that the right of reply in Korean law has become an effective means to resolve libel disputes.

———. "Right of Reply." In *The International Encyclopedia of Communication.* Edited by Wolfgang Donsbach. 10 vols. Malden, MA: Blackwell Publishing, 2008.

A definition of the right of reply and a discussion of its theoretical rationale are the focus of this encyclopedia entry. Among the right of reply issues examined are its compatibility with press freedom, its applicability to the Internet media, its applicability to opinions, and its extension to government entities. This source also delves into the Press Arbitration Commission of Korea as a unique enforcement mechanism for the statutory right of reply, which has been recognized in South Korea since the early 1980s.

Lee, Jae-Jin, and Sung-Hoon Lee. "The Right of Reply System for the Last Two Decades in South Korea." *Korean Journal of Journalism & Communication* Special English Edition (2001): 395–411.

Lee and Lee examine how the right of reply system has developed since its establishment in 1981. Their study finds out that the right of reply system has effectively served the public interest of facilitating an individual's recovery from reputational injury. Analyzing court cases, the authors emphasize that the balance of interests between the press and the public should be maintained.

Lee, Jae-Jin, and Yoonmo Sang. "How to Strike a Balance between Competing Interests on the Internet: A Comparative Study of the Right of Reply between the United States and South Korea." *Journal of Media Law, Ethics and Policy* 12, no. 1 (2013): 185–215.

This comparative study of the right of reply in the United States and South Korea centers on the applicability of this right in the context of the Internet media. Several relevant legal issues are identified in the two countries. The study posits that the right of reply could help resolve the tension between freedom of expression and individuals' reputation on the Internet.

Press Arbitration Commission. *Casebook on Press Conciliation and Arbitration.* Seoul: Press Arbitration Commission, 2011.

The Press Arbitration Commission (PAC) and its structure and operation are detailed in this PAC publication. Equally important is its summarized compilation of the PAC conciliation and arbitration cases from 1981 to 2009. It is a primary source on the Korean press conciliation and arbitration system in action. A total of 100 case summaries that include the PAC orders and reasonings are included in the casebook.

Youm, Kyu Ho. "Right of Reply under Korean Press Law: A Statutory and Judicial Perspective." *American Journal of Comparative Law* 41, no. 1 (1993): 49–71. doi: 10.2307/840506.

This source features a comparison of the statutory framework of the right of reply in Korean law with the press law of Germany, the model and inspiration for the Korean approach to the right of reply. Youm charts the path of the right of reply's development in Korea as it has been interpreted by Korean courts.

———. "The Right of Reply and Freedom of the Press: An International and Comparative Perspective." *George Washington Law Review* 76 (2007): 1017–1064.

Youm's law journal article presents a comparative examination of access to the news media in Korea as part of the right of reply. It covers the United States, Germany, France, Hungary, and Denmark. Youm pays extensive attention to the United States, whose strong freedom of speech laws circumvent the right of reply.

Right to Information

Kang, Kyung-Keun. "Freedom of Information Law, the Experience in Korea." *Soongsil Law Review* 13 (2003): 57–86.

This article provides general background information relating to freedom of information law in Korea. Kang explains the meaning and necessity of freedom of information law and summarizes how the freedom of information system has worked to improve the transparency of administration.

Park, Ahran, and Kyu Ho Youm. "Judicial Communication in South Korea: Moving toward a More Open System?" In *Justices and Journalists: The Global Perspective*, edited by Richard Davis and David Taras, 184–208. Cambridge: Cambridge University Press, 2017. doi: 10.1017/9781316672228.010.

This in-depth analysis of how Korean courts interact with the public through the news media focuses on the way in which communication between the courts and the news media has changed over the past thirty years. In particular, the analysis focuses on the Supreme Court and the Constitutional Court in the context of broadcasting of court proceedings, digital communications of the courts, and access to court records.

Won, Hoshin. "Measures to Realize Sustainable and Efficient Justice from the Perspective of Information and Communications Technology Focusing on the Korean Court." *Journal of Korean Law* 16 (2016): 67–91.

This study addresses the judicial informatization of Korea, including electronic litigation systems, access to court records and legal information, and the use of artificial intelligence. After discussing several proposed measures to realize the "sustainable and efficient justice," Won suggests ideas for future improvements in Korea's judicial information systems.

Youm, Kyu Ho. "Access to Information and Freedom of Expression: The Case of South Korea Since 1996." SSRN Paper 2067875, 2010. doi: doi:10.2139/ssrn.2067875.

Youm examines the right to information (RTI) law in Korea. Beginning with a 1989 constitutional court decision, he notes, freedom of information has been enshrined in Korean law. His inquiry follows three main paths: the conceptual and theoretical RTI framework, the constitutional and statutory status of freedom of information in Korea, and the judicial interpretations of RTI in Korea.

Youm, Kyu Ho, Inho Lee, and Ahran Park. "Access to Government Information in South Korea: The Rise of Transparency as an Open Society Principle." *Journal of International Media & Entertainment Law* 7, no. 2 (2017–2018): 179–202.

How and why has freedom of information (FOI) defined Korea as a functioning participatory democracy? The Korean FOI article's central focus is on the conceptual and theoretical framework of the right to information in Korea, informational access as a constitutional and statutory right in Korea, and the judicial interpretations of FOI.

Unified Korea

Youm, Kyu Ho. "Freedom of the Press in a United Korea: A Constitutional and Statutory Framework." *Korea Observer* 25, no. 2 (1994): 229–259. doi: 10.1080/0 8821127.1991.10731337.

Youm discusses freedom of the press in North and South Korea, with an eye toward a unified Korea in the future. He discusses the recognition of a free press as a human right under international law, compares press freedom in North and South Korea, and speculates as to the type of constitutional and statutory framework that could exist for press freedom in a unified Korea.

U.S. Military Government

Youm, Kyu Ho. "Press Policy of the U.S. Military Government in Korea: A Case of Failed 'Libertarian' Press Theory?" *American Journalism* 8, nos. 2–3 (1991): 160–177. doi: 10.1080/08821127.1991.10731337.

Youm's article traces the U.S. military government's libertarian press policies and their enduring impact on the Korean media. Youm details the development of a strong Korean press and the theory of a free press in Korean culture and law.

Chapter 2

Political Communication

Seok Kang, Seungahn Nah, and
Matthew A. Shapiro

South Korea's historical framework of political communication should be identified within the context of the nearly 40 years of oppression that initially shaped its political landscape. After the end of the Korean War in 1953, President Syngman Rhee (1948–1960) enforced the U.S. military government's Ordinance Number 88 against leftist newspapers. Following the Chang Myon government (1960–1961), the general-turned-president Park Chung-hee (1961–1979) was not significantly different from Rhee in restricting the Korean press. Yet President Chun Doo Hwan (1980–1987), who succeeded Park after his assassination in late 1979, resorted to even more oppressive media controls than his predecessors, forcing the mergers of news agencies and television news networks extra-legally in 1980.

The politically repressive environment and authoritarian rule in Korea up to 1987 provided minimal substance for research on political communication in Korea until the liberalization of Korean politics in the late 1980s.[1] Political communication research on Korea was a lesser known area internationally due to scant publications in English. Since 2000, however, the number of English-language journal articles, dissertations, and international conference presentations about Korean political communication has dramatically increased. Korean scholars abroad started publishing research on political communication in major communication journals. With the publications written in English, political communication research on Korea has thus been widely introduced to international readers, scholars, and experts. Among the political communication topics published in English have been elections

---

1. June Woong Rhee and Eun-mee Kim, "Democratization and the Changing Media Environment in South Korea," in *The SAGE Handbook of Political Communication*, ed. Holli A. Semetko and Margaret Scammell (London: SAGE Publications, 2012), 415–426.

and campaigns, social movements, politicians, and political engagement embedded in information communication technologies (ICTs).

Our chapter highlights the corpus of political communication research on Korea in English. And we aim to discover how these scholarly works impact the global audience. Our selection for our bibliographical annotations is based on the conceptual definition by Stanford University's Political Communication Program: "[H]ow communication and media affect political attitudes and behaviors, as well as which communication reveals about the workings of political institutions and political systems."[2] In line with this conceptual framework, our overview of political communication research focuses on the Korean government and its political actors, the media, and the public. The topics of nearly all the publications annotated for our chapter relate to one or more of these components to account for the most prevalent political communication mechanisms in Korea as well as how government-public-media interactions have influenced Koreans' political attitudes and behaviors.

Our bibliography considers each publication's inherent value to political communication research in English centering on Korea.[3] We have primarily focused our attention on communication journals but have also delved into other non-communication journals so long as their content discusses Korea's mechanisms of political communication. Also included are several English-language dissertations on political communication in Korea. The English books, book chapters, journal articles, and PhD dissertations annotated are categorized into five topics: (1) political engagement; (2) national and cultural comparisons; (3) politicians and bureaucrats; (4) media and public opinion; and (5) presidential campaigns and general elections. It should be noted that these categories are not mutually exclusive, and that there is a tendency for ICT-oriented analyses to dominate contemporary political communication research on Korea.

The publications annotated for our chapter show that early political communication research on Korea in English goes back at least four decades. In 1975, University of Georgia PhD student Kenneth Ahn, emphasizing the importance of President Park Chung-hee's political mobilization in his

---

2. Communication Department, Stanford University, "Political Communication," https://comm.stanford.edu/political-communication/ (accessed December 15, 2017).

3. We have searched two scholarly databases, "Communication and Mass Media Complete" and "EBSCOHost for Communication," with keywords, "Korea" and "political communication." Furthermore, another keyword, "civic engagement," was used to get possible academic articles that dealt with political communication. This expanded topical search included additional studies about "social capital," which was directly linked to Koreans' political and civic behaviors. We refined the sources from a communication perspective in terms of theory, conceptual frameworks, content, and implications. After careful crosschecks and reiterations of the process, one hundred publications were ultimately selected.

dissertation,[4] suggested a comprehensive strategy of social group use for political engagement. In 1990, Professor James Larson of the State University of New York published about U.S. diplomacy toward Korea in the television era, detailing the visual portrayal of the Kwangju incident on TV and its impact on President Reagan's visit to Korea in 1983.[5] Beyond these examples, little research was published in English about political communication in Korea from the 1970s through the 1990s. But Korean researchers became active in political communication research in the 2000s. A growing number of Korean and non-Korean communication scholars have been notably prolific in their research on Korean political communication in major English-language communication journals.

The publications we've chosen for annotation present patterns in political attributes, activities, and outcomes. Overall, the current political communication research on Korea published in English shows that media and political institutions play key roles in the Korean public's processing of political information. Our bibliography contextualizes these categories and offers suggestions for future research on political communication in Korea.

POLITICAL ENGAGEMENT

A majority of political communication publications in English examine the role of digital technologies in political participation, providing evidence of the influence of ICTs on political communication in Korea. At the beginning of the "digital politics" era in the early 2000s, Korean scholars focused on Internet-based participation and its impact on an expanding democracy, as broadly defined.[6] The research published in English indicates that political participation is a function of legacy media and civic organizations, but that ICTs are now playing a crucial role. Among the research topics covered are Koreans' use of social media or social network sites (SNS) in discussing issues of public concern, networks, and one's political orientation. Professor Young Min Baek of Yonsei University in Seoul, for instance, speculates on the extent to which SNS use influences users' political behavior.[7] His 2015

4. Kenneth Kunil Ahn, "Mobilization and Participation in Elections: A Study of Korean Voting Behavior" (PhD diss., University of Georgia, 1975).

5. James F. Larson, "Quiet Diplomacy in a Television Era: The Media and U.S. Policy toward the Republic of Korea," *Political Communication & Persuasion* 7, no. 2 (1990): 73–95.

6. Hyeon-Suk Lyu, "The Public's E-Participation Capacity and Motivation in Korea: A Web Survey Analysis from a New Institutional Perspective," *Journal of Information Technology and Politics* 4, no.4 (2007): 65–79.

7. Young Min Baek, "Political Mobilization through Social Network Sites: The Mobilizing Power of Political Messages Received from SNS Friends," *Computers in Human Behavior* 44 (2015): 12–19.

study of SNS and political participation finds that non-voters intend to vote after receiving political messages via SNSs.

Korean political communication covers the characteristics of political protesters and protest leaders in the context of their digital media use, legacy news media coverage, and the power of citizen organizations in political protests.[8] Research on the Korean candlelight vigil in 2008 shows how the traditional media contributed to protesters' identity construction process in public demonstrations against U.S. beef import.[9] In her journal article of 2009 on the Korean candlelight vigils, Professor Jiyeong Kang of the University of Iowa examines how the post-Cold War generation in Korea assigns itself to the task of being the collective enemy of the governing political power.[10] In addition, the political communication literature deals with citizen journalism, online political behavior, participatory democracy, and online activism.

NATIONAL AND CULTURAL COMPARISONS

A second area of research interest to Korea-centered political communication scholars focuses on cross-national and cross-cultural comparisons. In part because many communication scholars in Korea have been trained in the United States, as reflected by the dissertations surveyed for our chapter, several studies are comparatively oriented toward the United States and Korea. Their topics range from ICT-based political communication during the presidential elections, rhetoric during the presidential debates, and the content of relevant videos to political communication and political polarization. Other comparative research revolves around citizen participation in democracies, comparing Korea with the United States on the electoral process and political movements.[11] Particular focus is given to how ICTs are used and how differently cultural factors affect political cultures.

Beyond the United States, Korea has been compared with Asian countries such as Singapore and Taiwan.[12] Unlike Singapore, the political environment in Korea has been influenced by Protestantism and Christianity, engendering

8. Kenneth Kunil Ahn, "Mobilization and Participation in Elections: A Study of Korean Voting Behavior" (PhD diss., University of Georgia, 1975); Taehyun Nam, "Protest Leaders and Their Strategic Choices: A Comparative Analysis of Protests in Korea, 1990–1991" (PhD diss., University of Kansas, 2005).

9. Giovanna Dell'Orto, "The Making of the 2008 Korean Candlelight Vigil: A Study of Politics, Media, and Social Movements" (MA thesis, University of Minnesota, 2012).

10. Jiyeon Kang, "Coming to Terms with 'Unreasonable' Global Power: The 2002 South Korean Candlelight Vigils," *Communication & Critical/Cultural Studies* 6, no. 2 (2009): 171–192.

11. Jongwoo Han, *Networked Information Technologies, Elections, and Politics: Korea and the United States* (Lanham, MD: Lexington Books, 2012).

12. Jonathan Sullivan and Sehun Cheon, "Reconnecting Representatives in Two East Asian Democracies," *East Asia: An International Quarterly* 28, no. 1 (2011): 21–36.

a participatory political culture.[13] Through such comparisons, political communication scholars have been able to provide important insights into political communication among countries. They also offer tailored prescriptions appropriate for the political cultures of specific countries, Korea included.

POLITICIANS AND BUREAUCRATS

Political communication research on Korea also shows that politicians attempt to portray themselves to the public as dedicated and hardworking civil servants. This is largely accomplished by posting policy evaluations and personal stories to various social media, according to Seoul National University Professor Eun-Ju Lee's 2014 co-authored article in *Communication Research*.[14] Focusing on public perceptions of politicians during the Roh Moo-hyun presidency in 2002–2007, research demonstrates that Korean politicians' use of Twitter helps build networks and influence voter attitudes.[15]

Further, Professor Matthew Shapiro of the Illinois Institute of Technology and his co-authors examine the networks that politicians build online in the context of the larger socio-communication system, confirming that politicians have increased their use of ICT to distinguish themselves from their political opponents, and also that their popularity increases with social media use.[16] Elsewhere, a survey of the factors influencing public administrators' acceptance of digital democracy indicates that the perceived usefulness of the Internet, the information quality provided by websites, and positive attitudes toward citizens' civic participation affect public officials' intentions to employ the cyber techniques of digital democracy.[17]

---

13. Marko M. Skoric, "Is Culture Destiny in Asia? A Story of a Tiger and a Lion." *Asian Journal of Communication* 17, no. 4 (2007): 396–415.

14. Eun-Ju Lee and Soo Yun Shin, "When the Medium Is the Message: How Transportability Moderates the Effects of Politicians' Twitter Communication," *Communication Research* 41, no. 8 (2014): 1088–1110.

15. Qian Gong and Gary Rawnsley, "Media Freedom and Responsibility in South Korea: The Perceptions of Journalists and Politicians During the Roh Moo-hyun Presidency," *Journalism* (2017): 1–18.

16. Matthew A. Shapiro et al., "Twitter and Political Communication in Korea: Are Members of the Assembly Doing What They Say?" *Journal of Asia Pacific Studies* 3, no. 3 (2014): 338–357.

17. Chan-Gon Kim, "Public Administrators' Acceptance of the Practices of Digital Democracy: A Model Explaining the Utilization of Online Policy Forums in South Korea" (PhD diss., Rutgers, State University of New Jersey, 2005).

MEDIA AND PUBLIC OPINION

The formation of public opinion as a function of media use has attracted attention from researchers on Korean political communication. In *Media and Democratic Transition in South Korea,* the first of its kind in English, Professor Ki-Sung Kwak at the University of Sydney took special note of the revolutionary change in the government and media relationship in Korea's democratization and public opinion formation processes.[18] And a Northwestern University PhD dissertation on the changing role of the media in Korea's democratization establishes that both traditional and digital media enhance opportunities for the expression of public opinion.[19] Other research finds that news coverage of policy debates and the media's dramatic portrayals help shape public opinion in Korea.[20]

PRESIDENTIAL CAMPAIGNS AND GENERAL ELECTIONS

Publications on elections highlight election campaigns, investigating how the news media cover candidates and what characteristics are featured on candidates' websites and social media. This area of research also examines how the traditional media and ICTs are used for election campaigns, party strategies, and helping build the policy agenda. For instance, in a 2012 *Political Communication* article on the effects of televised presidential debates on viewers' evaluations of candidates, University of California-Davis Professor Jaeho Cho and his co-author conclude that watching the debate on television affects candidates' favorability rating.[21]

In researching political news coverage, communication scholars invoke the traditional and intermedia agenda setting theory to examine how the news media cover Korean presidential candidates. Given that the political orientation of the ruling party affects how the news is framed, news coverage research focuses particularly on framing differences between the conservative and liberal news media.[22] Drawing on the prevalence of ICTs in Korea's

18. Ki-Sung Kwak, *Media and Democratic Transition in South Korea* (Ames, NY: Routledge, 2012).

19. Su Jung Kim, "Emerging Patterns of News Media Use across Multiple Platforms and Their Political Implications in South Korea" (PhD diss., Northwestern University, 2011).

20. Jiso Yoon, "Who Receives Media Attention in South Korea: Analyzing Internal and External Pluralism in the News Coverage of Policy Debates," *Asian Journal of Political Science* 21, no. 2 (2013): 126–147.

21. Jaeho Cho and Yerheen Ha, "On the Communicative Underpinnings of Campaign Effects: Presidential Debates, Citizen Communication, and Polarization in Evaluations of Candidates," *Political Communication* 29, no. 2 (2012): 184–204.

22. Gyotae Ku, "Intermedia Agenda-Setting in the 2000 Presidential Campaign: The Influence of Candidates' Web sites on Traditional News Media" (PhD diss., University of Oklahoma, 2002).

current political communication, comparisons are made between online news and television news. Communication scholars Min Gyu Kim and Joohan Kim at Yonsei University in Seoul have stated that television news is associated with positive evaluations of candidates' morality, while online news is associated with negative evaluations of morality.[23]

THE PATH FORWARD FOR POLITICAL COMMUNICATION RESEARCH

Our annotated bibliography of political communication publications in English establishes that ICT drives political communication research on Korea. ICTs are the main topic for nearly 70 percent of the communication journal articles annotated. It is also notable that only 6 percent were published before the year 2000. Thus, the exponential growth of political communication research on Korea over the past 18 years has been remarkable.

Further English scholarship in political communication on Korea will continue to expand a global understanding of government-media-public relations in Korea. But greater emphasis should be placed on theoretically grounded research that addresses a unique Korean political culture, which will facilitate cross-country comparisons in distinct but interrelated contexts. More political communication research should also employ lab-based experiments and longitudinal panel surveys to establish causal claims. Moreover, future studies should engage in an extensive analysis that may provide policy implications and practical applications for the political system and the general public in Korea and beyond.

The notable increase in the research publications in English over the last two decades should stimulate ongoing scholarship in political communication in Korea among Korean and non-Korean researchers alike. Certainly, the active research program identified in the early years of the twenty-first century provides a clear indication of continued growth, contributing significantly to the enhancement in political communication research and our understanding of democratic institutions in Korea at the national and global levels.

---

23. Min Gyu Kim and Joohan Kim, "Comparing the Effects of Newspaper, TV News, and the Internet News on the Evaluation of a Major Political Candidate: Latent Growth Modeling with Longitudinal Panel Data from the 2007 Presidential Campaign in South Korea," *International Journal of Public Opinion Research* 24 (2012): 62–78.

ANNOTATED BIBLIOGRAPHY

Political Engagement

Baek, Young Min. "Political Mobilization through Social Network Sites: The Mobilizing Power of Political Messages Received from SNS Friends." *Computers in Human Behavior* 44 (2015): 12–19. doi:10.1016/j.chb.2014.11.021.

Baek questions the extent to which social network site (SNS) use interplayed with user characteristics influences political behavior. Relying on a representative, online panel survey in the context of the 2012 Korean general election, his study finds that voting intention is increased when non-voters receive political messages shared from SNS networks.

Baek, Young Min, Irkwon Jeong, and June Woong Rhee. "Political Homophily on Social Network Sites and Users' Poll Skepticism." *Asian Journal of Communication* 25, no. 3 (2015): 271–287. doi:10.1080/01292986.2014.955861.

Can SNS engender political poll skepticism? Baek, Jeong, and Rhee repudiate previous research approaches that viewed Korean citizens' attitude toward political polls. They look into the relationship between perceived SNS opinion environments, poll skepticism, perceived concerns over the negative influence of the polls, and voting intention. Poll skepticism generated by the published polls against voters' political orientation lead to increased voting intent for their supporting candidates.

Chang, Woo-Young. "Online Civic Participation, and Political Empowerment: Online Media and Public Opinion Formation in Korea." *Media, Culture & Society* 27, no. 6 (2005): 925–935.

Chang examines the formation of online media as well as the inability of traditional journalism to foster public discussions. In this way, online media in Korea have the potential to produce democracy-enhancing outcomes. Chang pays particular attention to *Ohmynews* and *Seoprise*, Korea's two online discussion forums. He finds that online media facilitate citizen participation and opinion exchange and, thus, participatory democracy.

Chang, Woo-Young, and Won-Tae Lee. "Cyberactivism and Political Empowerment in Civil Society: A Comparative Analysis of Korean Cases." *Korea Journal* 46, no. 4 (2006): 136–167.

Chang and Lee focus on cyberactivism, i.e., using the Internet to engage in social organizing and movements online. They study how cyberactivism played out in the elections in Korea in the 2000s using Citizens' Alliance for the 2000 General Election (CAGE) and *Nosamo* (Gathering of People Who Love Roh Moo-hyun) as an illustration. The authors conclude that political mobilization has been fostered in a new form and that the examples show that civil society itself may emerge as an independent political force.

Cheon, Yong-Cheol. "Internet Newspapers as Alternative Media: *OhmyNews* in South Korea." *Media Development* 51, no. 1 (2004): 28–32.

The citizen journalism of Korea in the Internet era is reviewed and evaluated. Since the launch of a progressive daily newspaper, *Hankyoreh*, in 1988, there had been limited growth in progressive journalism until *OhMyNews* in 2000. Cheon discusses the trajectory of *Hankyoreh* and *OhMyNews* in terms of participatory journalism.

Cho, Jaeho, and Heejo Keum. "Leveling or Tilting the Playing Field: Social Networking Sites and Offline Political Communication Inequality." *Social Science Journal* 53, no. 2 (2016): 236–246. doi:10.1016/j.soscij.2016.01.002.

Cho and Keum discuss how one's social-economic status (SES) impacts Koreans' communication in offline situations in regard to politics and whether or not their expression can impact their status. They analyze a national survey of Koreans and find that SES is weaker online than offline.

Choi, Doo-Hun, and Dong-Hee Shin. "A Dialectic Perspective on the Interactive Relationship between Social Media and Civic Participation: The Moderating Role of Social Capital." *Information, Communication & Society* 20, no. 2 (2017): 151–166. doi: 10.1080/1369118X.2016.1154586.

Choi and Shin focus on the moderating effects of social capital on the relationship between social media use and civic participation. Relying on data collected through the Korean General Social Survey (KGSS) with a national representative sample, the study finds that civic activities were increased among those who used social media to express opinions with a higher level of social capital.

Choi, Jin-Wook. "Deliberative Democracy, Rational Participation and E-Voting in South Korea." *Asian Journal of Political Science* 14, no. 1 (2006): 64–81. doi: 10 .1080/021853700600832547.

Choi looks at the extent to which information and communication technologies (ICTs) offer the potentials of building an electronic democracy in the 2002 presidential election and the 2000 and 2005 general elections in Korea. Specifically, he discusses how ICTs can help citizens engage in a reason-based, deliberative participation and to increase electronic voting.

Chun, Heasun. "Social Networking Sites and Cyberdemocracy: A New Model of Dialogic Interactivity and Political Mobilization in the Case of South Korea." PhD diss., Buffalo, State University of New York, 2012.

This dissertation assesses the political potential of social networking sites (SNS) and thus provide evidence that SNS and online activities are a valid political mobilizer for individuals in Korea. Overall, SNS increases opportunities for dialogue between citizens and their elected officials and is an outlet for political participation.

Chung, Jong Pil. "Comparing Online Activities in China and South Korea: The Internet and the Political Regime," *Asian Survey* 48, no. 5 (2008): 727–751. doi: 10.1525/as.2008.48.5.727.

This comparative study of the ways that the Internet and political regimes are connected in Korea and China emphasizes the role of each respective government in limiting or allowing the Internet to be used as a political tool. Chung's case study shows the stark differences between the two Asian countries, with censorship in China and aggressive online campaigning in Korea.

Dell'Orto, Giovanna. "The Making of the 2008 Korean Candlelight Vigil: A Study of Politics, Media, and Social Movements." MA thesis, University of Minnesota, 2012.

This M.A. thesis uses the 2008 Korean candlelight vigil to find out how the media contributed to the protesters' identity construction process. Using a discourse analysis of newspaper ads funded by protesters, supplemented with in-depth interviews with protesters, and further supplemented with news frames from two Korean newspapers, Dell'Orto notes that the candlelight vigil attempts to change power relationships through social meanings by highlighting shared norms between the protesters and the average newspaper reader.

Ha, Shang, Seokho Kim, and Se Hee Jo. "Personality Traits and Political Participation: Evidence from South Korea." *Political Psychology* 34, no. 4 (2013): 511–532. doi: 10.1111/pops.12008.

The analysis of a nationally representative survey looks at the relationships between personality traits and various modes of political participation in Korea. The authors' notable finding is that openness is positively linked with protest participation, rally attendance, financial support for politics, and media use for politics.

Han, Jongwoo. "From Indifference to Making the Difference: New Networked Information Technologies (NNITs) and Patterns of Political Participation among Korea's Younger Generations." *Journal of Information Technology & Politics* 4, no. 1 (2007): 57–76. doi:10.1300/J516v04n01_05.

Han explores how the younger generation, new networked information technologies (NNITs) users, who are politically uninterested, got themselves in mainstream Korean political dialogue. He states that NNIT-induced organizations bring on drastic changes in electoral politics. While turnout weakened among groups in general, NNITs play a crucial role in determining the political voting patterns of younger generational groups.

Hauben, Ronda. "Online Grassroots Journalism and Participatory Democracy in South Korea." In *Korea Yearbook*, edited by Rudiger Frank, Jim Hoare, Patrick Kollner, and Susan Press, 61–82. Boston: Brill, 2007.

Korea's grassroots journalism and online participation are emblematic of participatory democracy, and online media have been crucial in a number of political events since 2000, particularly the candlelight protests against the South Korean Status of Forces Agreement (SOFA) in 2002, the presidential election campaign in 2002, and the stem cell research fraud exposure in 2005–2006. Hauben claims that Habermas's public sphere is embodied by both online participation and the Korean "netizens" that exist in that space.

Heo, Yun-Cheol, Ji-Young Park, Ji-Young Kim, and Han-Woo Park. "The Emerging Viewertariat in South Korea: The Seoul Mayoral TV Debate on Twitter, Facebook, and Blogs." *Telematics & Informatics* 33, no. 2 (2014): 570–583. doi:10.1016/j.tele.2015.08.003.

Social networking services (SNSs) are used as a second screening platform for political communication. The authors pay attention to how audiences use SNSs at real time while watching candidate debates. SNS users not only view and interpret political content in TV debates, but also users participate in the production of political views. SNSs are a political participation driver.

Huang, Min-hua, Taehee Whang, and Lei Xuchuan. "The Internet, Social Capital, and Civic Engagement in Asia." *Social Indicators Research* 132, no. 2 (2017): 559–578. doi:10.1007/s11205-016-1319-0.

Huang, Whang, and Zuchuan study how the rise of Internet communication is related to the level of social capital and the role of the internet and social capital in shaping civic engagement in Asia. They use public data from thirteen Asian countries and find that traditional membership in social organizations is still the way social capital is measured.

Hur Suk Jae, and Hyeok Yong Kwon. "The Internet and Inequality in Democratic Engagements: Panel Evidence from South Korea." *International Journal of Communication* 8 (2014): 1174–1194.

Internet use for political communication can affect the interest in politics. Using the data from the 2017 Korean Presidential Election Panel Study, the journal authors assert that the Internet likely reduces the gap in age groups and that the gap is still wide in income groups and groups of different education levels.

Jang, Ahnlee. "Exploration of Communicative Social Capital, Civil and Political Engagement of the Korean Diaspora." PhD diss., University of Maryland, 2012.

Jang targets members of the Korean diaspora in the Washington, DC, area to understand how they have created a community, and how political engagement has emerged as a function of communicative social capital. The author finds that political engagement stems from these religion-based communities.

Jeong, Hoi Ok. "From Civic Participation to Political Participation." *Voluntas: International Journal of Voluntary & Nonprofit Organizations* 24, no. 4 (2013): 1138–1158. doi:10.1007/s11266–012–9316–7.

Jeong studies the Koreans' transition from civic participation to political participation. Unlike the existing literature, this research focuses solely on Korea. It finds that not every civic organization produces political participation. There is a positive impact or more "normal" citizen organizations like art and music and a negative impact in interest-based and political organizations such as professional associations or environmental organizations.

Jin, Bumsub, and Soyoon Kim. "Telethon Viewing, Social Capital, and Community Participation in South Korea." *Communication Quarterly* 62, no. 3 (2014): 253–268. doi: 10.1080/01463373.2014.911762.

What's the mediating role of social capital, which influences the relationship between television-viewing of pro-social campaign program and community participation in Korea? Using an online panel survey, the study finds that telethon viewing enhanced social capital, such as trust in others and neighborliness of social networks, leading to increased civic engagement in altruistic activities.

Kang, Jang-Mook, and Bong-Hwa Hong. "A Political Communication Scheme of Citizen Network System on Disembedding and Embedding Principle." In *Communication and Networking*, edited by Tai-hoon Kim, Hojjat Adeli, Wai-chi Fang, Thanos Vasilakos, Adrian Stoica, Charalampos Z. Patrikakis, Gansen Zhao, Javier Garcia Villalba, and Yang Xiao, 34–42. New York: Springer, 2011.

Disembedding and embedding are the focuses of this book chapter, which occur when there is a restructuring of the structure of communication, namely, from hierarchical to more dispersed communications. This process of dispersion is identified by the authors in Korea as a result of the prolific use of smart devices.

Kang, Jiyeon. "Coming to Terms with 'Unreasonable' Global Power: The 2002 South Korean Candlelight Vigils." *Communication & Critical/Cultural Studies* 6, no. 2 (2009): 171–192. doi:10.1080/14791420902833155.

Kang analyzes the rise of the 2002 candlelight vigils while focusing on how the post-Cold War generation in Korea outlined a national tragedy and pictured themselves as a collective enemy of apparent politics. She calls for attention to the language practices of those who transform the way in which global power relationships influence them within a local context in Korea.

———. "Exuberant Politics on the Internet: Two Forms of Popular Politics in South Korea's 2008 'Beef Protests.'" *International Journal of Communication* 11 (2017): 4118–4137.

A focus is on how young Internet users turn from advocates to critics of President Lee Myung-bak of Korea. Kang explains it as populism. The "Mad Cow Disease" issue captivates public desires, with which politics creates exuberant demonstrations that defy institutional politics. Such conversion fosters mass participation.

———. "Internet Activism Transforming Street Politics: South Korea's 2008 'Mad Cow' Protests and New Democratic Sensibilities." *Media, Culture & Society* 39, no. 5 (2017): 750–761. doi:10.1177/0163443717709444.

Korea's Internet-born candlelight vigils have played a decisive role in Korean democracy. Kang examines the protests against U.S. beef import due to the Mad Cow Disease in 2008. The protests transform civic movements from violent confrontations to festive crowds that directly speak to the authorities with irreverent humor and carnivalesque defiance.

Kang, Seok, Yeojin Julie Kim, and Chang Sup Park. "Political Communication of Korea in the ICT Era: Triadic Interactions among Government, Media, and the Public." In *Communication, Digital Media, and Popular Culture in Korea*, edited by Dal Yong Jin and Nojin Kwak, 105–123. Lanham, MD: Lexington Books (2018).

The tripartite model of government, media, and the public outlines the structure of political communication in Korea. Kang, Kim, and Park elaborate on the interactions among the three components by speculating about the current and past research on political communication studies and civic participation in the information communication technology (ICT) era.

Kern, Thomas, and Sang-hui Nam. "The Making of a Social Movement: Citizen Journalism in South Korea." *Current Sociology* 57, no. 5 (2009): 637–660. doi: 10.1177/0011392109337649.

Kern and Nam situate citizen journalism as a social movement, which emerged due to a newly formed sociocultural environment with the changes in the media system, education, and social movement sector in Korea. They take a multi-sectoral approach to the emergence of citizen journalism where intellectuals, activists, and journalists alike play part in revolutionizing citizen journalism.

Kim, Hyunjung. "Perception and Emotion: The Indirect Effect of Reported Election Poll Results on Political Participation Intention and Support for Restrictions." *Mass Communication & Society* 18, no. 3 (2015): 303–324. https://doi.org/10.1080/152 05436.2014.945650.

Perceived effect and bias of election poll results can be linked with Korean voters' attitudes and political participation. Kim discovers that the hostile media perception accounts for support for restrictions on polling reports. The perception is an igniter of political participation intention.

Kim, Jeong Hee. "Falling into Silence and Fears of Mad Cow Disease in the South Korean Blogosphere." *Cyberpsychology* 3, no. 1 (2009): 1–11.

How can a major opinion in a blog community shape the expression of bloggers? Kim bases his study on the candlelight vigils of 2008 in Korea in 2008 against the import of American beef. The author relates the blogger effect to the spiral of silence and the fragmentation of cyberspace. The study's conclusion: Silence creates a significant part of the planned interaction.

Kim, Jeong-Ho. "The Internet and the Public in South Korea: Online Political Talk and Culture." PhD diss., University of Illinois at Urbana-Champaign, 2012.

In his ethnographic study of the Korean culture of online political discourse, Kim argues that such discourse increases the subjective concept of citizenship. Online citizen polemicists are identified as being morally motivated and must thus contribute to open and common sense-oriented discussions. Political communication online provides ordinary citizens with opportunities to become engaged politically and expand their identities.

Kim, Ji Won, Yonghwan Kim, and Joseph Yoo. "The Public as Active Agents in Social Movement: Facebook and Gangjeong Movement." *Computers in Human Behavior* 37 (2014): 144–151. doi:10.1016/j.chb.2014.04.038.

A social movement Facebook page from Korea is used as a platform for the social movement. The study targets FB posts and comments on the Gangjeong (a town in Jeju Island where public protests against building a new navy base occurred.) movement. The findings show similarities in the posts and comments between the activists and the public. They state that the public with FB use has become more active within the movement.

Kim, Ji-Young. "The Impact of Internet Use Patterns on Political Engagement: A Focus on Online Deliberation and Virtual Social Capital." *Information Polity: The International Journal of Government & Democracy in The Information Age* 11, no. 1 (2006): 35–49.

Optimistic and pessimistic accounts often compete with each other for political engagement. Kim argues that media effects on political engagement are dependent on the way it's used. She finds that the creation of online communities is not a sign of political recovery but could be an essential part to revive civic political life in Korea.

Kim, Jinhee, and Ki Deuk Hyun. "Political Disagreement and Ambivalence in New Information Environment: Exploring Conditional Indirect Effects of Partisan News Use and Heterogeneous Discussion Networks on SNSs on Political Participation." *Telematics & Informatics* 34, no. 8 (2017): 1586–1596. doi: 10.1016/j.tele.2017.07.005.

An influence of political agreement in the news and discussion on political participation in digital media environment is investigated. The exposure to counterattitudinal news likely increases ambivalence and decreases participation. Media contexts plays a key role in a political understanding and participation in Korea.

Kim, Kyun Soo, and Yong-Chan Kim. "New and Old Media Uses and Political Engagement among Korean Adolescents." *Asian Journal of Communication* 17, no. 4 (2007): 342–361. DOI: 10.1080/01292980701636977.

With Korean adolescents' responses to political engagement, Kim and Kim reveal four distinct motivations for political media use: guidance, surveillance, social utility, and entertainment. They confirm the leverage of the Internet in Korean adolescents' media consumption for political communication.

Kim, Sei-Hill. "Media Use, Social Capital, and Civic Participation in South Korea." *Journalism & Mass Communication Quarterly* 84, no. 3 (2007): 477–494.

The civic life in Korea is affected by the interaction of social capital and media use. Using a telephone survey, Kim finds that interpersonal trust and information socializing were related to civic participation. The use of the Internet for entertainment positively predicts social capital. This shows that the production of social capital can be enhanced by the internet.

Kim, Sei-Hill, and Miejeong Han. "Media Use and Participatory Democracy in South Korea." *Mass Communication and Society* 8, no. 2 (2005): 133–153. doi:10.1207/s15327825mcs0802_4.

Kim and Han test the degree to which different types of media content influenced political participation. They find that news media use yields a positive relationship with political participation such as political discussion, voting, and gathering. In contrast, entertainment media use is negatively associated with political participation. Kim and Han confirm the different and distinct effects of media use on political outcomes.

Koo, Ja Hyouk. "A Facilitator of Civic Engagement in Online Group Contexts: The Role of Group Dimensions of Efficacy in Online Political Communities in the Presidential Elections of the United States and South Korea (2007–2008)." PhD diss., University of Virginia, 2011.

Offline and online participation surrounding the presidential elections in the United States and Korea are the focus of this study. Online communications are examined as they are expected to influence offline participation as people pursue shared experiences with individuals sharing similar ideological orientations.

Kwak, Ki-Sung. "From 'Revolutionary Changes' to 'Things as Usual': The Political Role of Online Media in South Korea." *Media International Australia* 141, no. 1 (2011): 87–97.

Kwak studies the role that politics has in the process of democratization in online media. He contends that online media in Korea arose when the institutionalization of political parties is weak, which eventually loses the trust of the public. The impact of online media shows that the great potential of the Internet proves to be less powerful in the 2007 election.

Kwak, Nojin, Scott W. Campbell, Junho Choi, and Soo Young Bae. "Mobile Communication and Public Affairs Engagement in Korea: An Examination of Non-Linear Relationships between Mobile Phone Use and Engagement Across Age Groups." *Asian Journal of Communication* 21, no. 5 (2011): 485–503. doi:10.108 0/01292986.2011.587016.

Kwak and others pay attention to the role of the mobile phone in the political engagement process. Mobile phone use for seeking public affairs plays a significant role in political participation among Koreans. The authors confirm the mobile reinforcement hypothesis, which predicts that mobile phone use adds benefits to the existing use of other media for public affairs and political engagement.

Lee, Aie-Rie. "Value Change and Non-Violent Protest in South Korea: An Empirical Analysis." *Asian Affairs: An American Review* 43, no. 4 (2016): 107–127. doi:10. 1080/00927678.2016.1231549.

Lee uses potential and leftist ideology to analyze the extent to which the mass public's values have changed. She practically discloses that the authoritarian-libertarian scale is related to levels of leftist attitudes. The study reveals that the rise of an authoritarian-libertarian value cleavage plays a dynamic role in the transition of mass political attitudes to actual engagement. The cleavage can be expanded by the media.

Lee, Hoon, and Nojin Kwak. "Mobile Communication and Cross-Cutting Discussion: A Cross-National Study of South Korea and the US." *Telematics & Informatics* 33, no. 2 (May 2016): 534–545. doi:10.1016/j.tele.2015.07.006.

Can mobile communication contribute to deliberative democracy in Korea? Lee and Kwak pay particular attention to how the dynamic interplay between mobile phone uses for social relations and information is associated with an individual's engagement in open dialogue with non-likeminded people (i.e., cross-cutting discussion).

Lee, Hoon, Nojin Kwak, Scott W., Campbell, and Rich Ling. "Mobile Communication and Political Participation in South Korea: Examining the Intersections between Informational and Relational Uses." *Computers in Human Behavior* 38 (2014): 85–92. doi:10.1016/j.chb.2014.05.017.

This study highlights the prediction of enhanced engagement in public life by the fact that multifaceted mobile practices work in coordination with one another. The authors survey adults in Korea and find that political participation is related to informational mobile phone usage. They also determine that two different patterns intermingle with each other to clarify the improved involvement.

Lee, Jinsun. "Net Power in Action: Internet Activism in the Contentious Politics of South Korea." PhD diss., Rutgers, State University of New Jersey, 2009.

Internet activism is the focus of this dissertation, particularly how such activism is distinct from other forms of social organization. Lee concludes that Korean Internet activism is influential and distinct from preexisting social movement organizations, but that it also functions in combination with extant social movement organizations.

Lee, Ji Sue. "Citizens' Political Information Behaviors during Elections on Twitter in South Korea: Information Worlds of Opinion Leaders." PhD diss., Florida State University, 2016.

Employing a mixed-method design of network analysis, tweet content analysis, and interviews, this dissertation attempts to understand how political communication occurred during the 2014 Seoul mayoral election. Bridging the theory of information worlds with Twitter, it is shown that information sharing is driven by, among other factors, perceived political orientations.

Lee, Yeon-Ok. "The Fragile Beauty of Peer-to-Peer Activism: The Public Campaign for the Rights of Media Consumers in South Korea." *New Media & Society* 18, no. 10 (2016): 2254–2270. doi: 10.1177/1461444815582019.

Three conservative media conglomerates have been identified as a hindrance to the country's democratization. Their biased dominance of public discourse is examined. The spatial opportunities and institutional challenges of digital activism are discussed. The study points out the role of peer-to-peer networks of individual citizens in public mobilization.

Lyu, Hyeon-Suk. "The Public's E-Participation and Motivation in Korea: A Web Survey Analysis from a New Institutional Perspective." *Journal of Information Technology and Politics* 4, no. 4 (2007): 65–79. doi: 10.1080/19331680801975789.

Lyu explores institutional and individual factors leading to citizens' electronic participation. Institutional factors embedded in an electronic democracy site played important roles in facilitating public engagement along with individual factors such as motivation and capacity. Thus, his research carries important policy and practical implications for the democratic potential of information and communication technologies (ICTs) in boosting the level of civic participation.

Moon, Seungsook, "The Interplay between the State, the Market, and Culture in Shaping Civil Society: A Case Study of the People's Solidarity for Participatory Democracy in South Korea." *Journal of Asian Studies* 69, no. 2 (2010): 479–505. doi: 10.1017/S0021911810000045.

The power of citizen organizations in progressive social change of South Korea is elaborated. Moon looks at the way the specific social meanings of civil society informed Korean people. The role of class and gender in cultural relativism and debate is speculated.

Na, Eun Kyung, Lee Gang Heong, and Kim Hyun Suk. "'Everything Is Always President Roh's fault?': Emotional Reactions to Politics and Economy as Sources of Presidential Evaluations and the Role of Media Use and Interpersonal Communication." *Asian Journal of Communication* 20, no. 1 (2010): 124–138. doi: 10.1080/01292980903475026.

Na, Lee, and Kim analyze the effects of cognitive and emotional elements on political judgements. Further, the effects of media use and political talk on political participation are emphasized. Emotional reactions are found to have a significant influence on the evaluation of the president's performance.

Nam, Taehyun. "Protest Leaders and Their Strategic Choices: A Comparative Analysis of Protests in Korea, 1990–1991." PhD diss., University of Kansas, 2005.

This dissertation targets the issue of post-democratization protests in Korea to understand how protest leaders structure their protests. There is variation among dissident groups, and spatial concentration plays a particular role in protest formation. Specifically, large populations in small territories help dissidents communicate, helping protest leaders surmount the rebel's dilemma.

Newton, Kim. "The Power of Protest: Images from South Korea's Road to Democracy." *Media, War & Conflict* 3, no. 1 (April 2010): 99–106. doi:10.1177/1750635210356811.

Images in news tell many stories about Korean politics. Newton chronicles the democracy movements of Korea in photos. In 1987, protestors reacted to the ruling government of President Chun Doo Hwan for his refusal to implement constitutional reforms that would lead to direct presidential elections. The photos present historical moments when the Chun government backed down in the face of the Korean people's uprising.

Pang, Huikyoung. "The 2008 Candlelight Protest in South Korea: Articulating the Paradox of Resistance in Neoliberal Globalization." PhD diss., University of South Florida, 2013.

"Articulation" is the primary vehicle for assessing the 2008 candlelight protest against U.S. beef in Korea, building upon political, economic, social, and cultural elements of social resistance. Pang's view on the protests indicates that this social movement focuses on food safety and bridges heterogeneous desires of participants.

Park, Chang Sup. "Pathways to Democratic Citizenship: The Mediating Roles of Deliberation and Political Efficacy in the Effects of Old and New Media Use on Political Participation in South Korea." PhD diss., Southern Illinois University at Carbondale, 2014.

Invoking theories of participatory democracy, this dissertation analyzes the functions of traditional and new media use in Korea, targeting especially the mediating roles of political efficacy and deliberation behaviors during the 2012 Korean presidential election.

Park, Chang Sup, and Kavita Karan. "Unraveling the Relationships between Smartphone Use, Exposure to Heterogeneity, Political Efficacy, and Political Participation: A Mediation Model Approach." *Asian Journal of Communication* 24, no. 4 (2014): 370–389. doi: 10.1080/01292986.2014.892146.

Digital gadgets are becoming an important political tool for engagement. Park and Karan build a mediation model to predict the process. Information use of smartphones predicts political participation mediated by political efficacy. The influence of smartphone use on political participation is also mediated by opinion heterogeneity among the Korean people.

Park, Han Woo, and Nicholas W., Jankowski. "A Hyperlink Network Analysis of Citizen Blogs in South Korean Politics." *Javnost—The Public* 15, no. 2 (2008): 57–74.

Park and Jankowski's study is about how digital communication technologies being embedded into everyday life will positively impact citizen participation in political environments. They find that blogs that are maintained by citizens who openly express a political stance are the preferred target.

Park, Kyungmee, and Sukkyung You. "Media Use Preference: The Mediating Role of Communication on Political Engagement." *Journal of Pacific Rim Psychology* 9, no. 2 (2015): 97–107. doi:10.1017/prp.2015.8.

When it comes to political engagement in Korea, media usage is a medium that has a significant impact. Park and You examine how intense that impactful it is. They focus on communication among media users and its many scopes. The specific age groups are 20–30 years old and 40–50 years old. They discover that online media use influenced political engagement via a mediating factor: online citizen communication.

Qiu, Jack Linchuan. "Mobile Civil Society in Asia: A Comparative Study of People Power II and the Nosamo Movement." *Javnost—The Public* 15, no. 3 (2008): 39–58.

In this comparative study, Qiu analyzes the use of mobile phones and what impact they have on civil society movements in Asian nations including Korea. More specifically, the People Power II and Nosamo movements in Korea were elaborated. By analyzing the entire selection of issues being highlighted, Qiu offers a better understanding of the socio-political features of political communication through mobile phones.

Shin, Wooyeol. "The Making of the 2008 Korean Candlelight Vigil: A Study of Politics, Media, and Social Movements." MA thesis, University of Minnesota, 2012. ProQuest (1520328205).

The candlelight vigils in Korea have created political and social connotations in recent Korean history. Shin explores how the collective identity of protesters is constructed through the 2008 Korean candlelight vigil against U.S. beef import. The social movement is interpreted as symbolic power struggles that impact the change of Korean civic movement.

You, Kyung Han, MiSun Lee, and Sohyun Oh. "Exploring the Relationship between Online Comments Usage and Civic Engagement in South Korea." *Asia-Pacific Social Science Review* 14, no. 1 (2014): 43–58.

You and his colleagues explore the relationship between civic participation and online comments on news stories or so-called daet-geul. Relying on the survey of nearly 800 online news users, their study finds that online news media use is a strong predictor of online commenting behaviors. It also reveals that civic values such as trust in others increase the level of civic and political participation.

National and Cultural Comparisons

Han, Jongwoo. *Networked Information Technologies, Elections, and Politics: Korea and the United States.* Lanham, MD: Lexington Books, 2012.

New networked information technologies have changed the process of elections, politics, and democratic movements. Apolitical citizens, usually younger, have become more involved and are now a cohesive voting bloc, and these new technologies have helped drive change regarding specific issues, such as Korea's beef crisis/protest and President Obama's healthcare reform efforts.

Heo, Mansup, and Jaeyung Park. "Presidential Rhetoric of South Korea and the United States: The Case of Lee and Obama." *Asian Journal of Communication 26*, no. 4 (2016): 301–318. doi:10.1080/01292986.2016.1157616.

Heo and Park highlight a comparison between how the presidents of Korea (Lee Myung-bak) and the United States (Barack Obama) address their people.

The authors find that Lee used more authoritative expressions accentuating his achievements and his position while Obama used more humor and metaphor.

Khang, Hyoungkoo. "A Cross-Cultural Perspective on Video Styles of Presidential Debates in the US and Korea." *Asian Journal of Communication* 18, no. 1 (2008): 47–63. doi:10.1080/01292980701823765.

Khang explores the depiction of cultural values throughout presidential debates of the United States and Korea. The results prove that the nature of debates subdues cultural norms are likely to be rooted in debates. The findings suggest that many countries are switching to media-centered democracies by copying campaign practice changes in the United States.

Kim, Yonghwan. "Does Disagreement Mitigate Polarization? How Selective Exposure and Disagreement Affect Political Polarization." *Journalism & Mass Communication Quarterly* 92, no. 4 (2015): 915–937. doi:10.1177/1077699015596328.

Kim explores what influence selective exposure and interpersonal political disagreement have on political polarization. The study is focused on individuals and how the disagreement can be a moderating variable weakening the relationship between selective exposure and polarization. The data, which come from the United States and Korea, show that disagreements do in fact lead to more divided attitudes.

Kong, Pyungwon. "Change in the Political System of Republic of Korea (ROK) and the United States (U.S.)-ROK Alliance." PhD diss., West Virginia University, 2005.

Kong's dissertation is a broad analysis of socioeconomic and political factors from 1953 to 2003 that have affected Seoul's perception of the U.S.-Republic of Korea alliance. Relevant here is the proliferation and diverse ideological orientations of civic organizations and media outlets, which have increased Koreans' insistence on an "equal partnership" in the U.S.-ROK alliance.

Lee, Shin Haeng. "Digitally Mediated Political Participation: Understanding the Democratic Impact of Internet Diffusion in the Asian Media Systems." PhD diss., University of Washington, 2016.

Lee focuses on political participation in East and Southeast Asia, with particular attention on how Internet use promotes collective action. This form of "unconventional mobilization" across eight Asian countries, based on three cross-national surveys in the mid-2000s and early 2010s, indicates that the "Asian Internet" facilitates communication and political organization, has a greater impact on non-democracies and poorer democracies.

Lee, Soobum, Hyoungkoo Khang, and Yeojin Kim. "A Cross-Cultural Perspective on Televised Political Advertising During the Presidential Election Between the

US and South Korea: 1992–2012." *Asian Journal of Communication* 26, no. 2 (2016): 133–152. doi: 10.1080/01292986.2015.1110605.

What are the common patterns of political ads across cultural boundaries? Lee, Khang, and Kim provide insights into media phenomena are related to cultural orientation between Korea and the United States. The political spots of the two countries demonstrate their unique cultural values exist from the individualist and collectivist orientation perspectives.

Lin, Wan-Ying, Pauline Hope Cheong, Yong-Chan Kim, and Joo-Young Jung. "Becoming Citizens: Youths' Civic Uses of New Media in Five Digital Cities in East Asia." *Journal of Adolescent Research* 25, no. 6 (2010): 839–857. doi: 10.1177/0743558410371125.

The civic potential of Internet uses among youth in five Asian countries is explored. Relying on survey data collected with 1,875 adolescents living in five cities of East Asian countries including Korea, the study reveals that, while Internet penetration rate and use varied across the cities, youngsters increasingly used Internet in general and social networking sites in particular as a civic communication tool in which they participate in public discussion and civic activities.

Otterbacher, Jahna, Libby Hemphill, and Matthew A., Shapiro. "Interacting or Just Acting? A Case Study of European, Korean, and American Politicians' Interactions with the Public on Twitter." *Journal of Contemporary Eastern Asia* 12, no. 1 (2013): 5–20. doi: 10.17477/jcea.2013.12.1.005.

Otterbacher and her co-authors examine how directly citizens can communicate with their elected officials as "interactive media" such as Twitter implies direct engagement between the two groups. The analysis is based on a sample of interactions among officials from the European Union, Korea, and the United States, with American officials being significantly less interactive with constituents relative to their European and Korean counterparts.

Skoric, Marko M. "Is Culture Destiny in Asia? A Story of a Tiger and a Lion." *Asian Journal of Communication* 17, no. 4 (2007): 396–415. doi:10.1080/01292980701637009.

In this article, Skoric compares Singapore and Korea and claims that they have each had an influence on how new communication technologies are used in politics. Skoric also argues that Christianity and Protestantism in Korea have initiated a cultural shift to more participatory and authority-challenging political culture. The evidence of this article comes from the World Values Survey. The findings suggest that two different routes have been found from these cultural differences.

Sullivan, Jonathan, and Sehun Cheon. "Reconnecting Representatives in Two East Asian Democracies." *East Asia: An International Quarterly* 28, no. 1 (2011): 21–36. doi:10.1007/s12140-011-9138-z.

Web-based communication has become popular among democracies all over the world. Politicians have willingly been implementing and adjusting to these new methods. This article focuses on blogging between Taiwan and Korea. These cases have also been compared with the existing literature that has allowed the authors to lay out the findings not just in blogging, but among other media as well. The authors find that blogging has been used to re-establish connections with constituents.

Tak, Jinyoung, and Lynda Lee Kaid. "A Cross-Cultural Study of Political Advertising in the United States and Korea." *Communication Research* 24, no. 4 (1997): 413–430. https://doi.org/10.1177/009365097024004005.

An analysis of advertising messages among politics and what they consist of is conducted. More specifically, it is focused on presidential elections and compares the political communication in the United States and Korea. The authors find that the cultural orientations of each country are vastly reflected in the content and that political advertising is seen as an eye-catching gauge of cultural values due to the evident differences in cultural patterns.

Tak, Jinyoung, Lynda Lee Kaid, and Hyoungkoo Khang. "The Reflection of Cultural Parameters on Videostyles of Televised Political Spots in the US and Korea." *Asian Journal of Communication* 17, no. 1 (2007): 58–77. doi:10.1080/01292980601114570.

Tak and his co-authors compare the video styles of televised political ads between the United States and Korea from the presidential campaigns in 1992. Cultural differences are found in terms of high and low context communication, uncertainty avoidance, non-verbal expression, and the social aspect of *Che-Myun*.

Yang, JungHwan, Hernando Rojas, Magdalena Wojcieszak, Toril Aalberg, Sharon Coen, James Curran, Kaori Hayashi, et al. "Why Are 'Others' So Polarized? Perceived Political Polarization and Media Use in 10 Countries." *Journal of Computer-Mediated Communication* 21, no. 5 (2016): 349–367. doi:10.1111/jcc4.12166.

From the findings of surveys conducted in Korea, Canada, Columbia, Greece, India, Italy, Japan, Norway, the United Kingdom, and the United States, this study investigates how perceived polarization is related to media. The data show that the consumption of news is, in fact, related to perceived polarization but not to attitude polarization which results in the conclusion that the media-polarization relationship is country-dependent.

Politicians and Bureaucrats

Gong, Qian, and Gary Rawnsley. "Media Freedom and Responsibility in South Korea: The Perceptions of Journalists and Politicians during the Roh Moo-hyun Presidency." *Journalism* (2017): online first. doi: 10.1177/1464884916688287.

Gong and Rawnsley analyze the understanding of media freedom from the perspective of journalists and politicians, focusing on the Roh Moo-hyun presidency. Based on interviews with journalists and politicians across the ideological spectrum, the general view is favorable toward Korea's media democratization as the media have greater freedoms. Yet the authors conclude that traditional norms had continued, such as limiting editorial freedom among conservative news outlets.

Hsu, Chien-leng, and Han Woo Park. "Sociology of Hyperlink Networks of Web 1.0, Web 2.0, and Twitter: A Case Study of South Korea." *Social Science Computer Review* 29, no. 3 (2011): 354–368. doi:10.1177/0894439310382517.

Hsu and Park look at how hyperlink networks in Web 1.0 and Web 2.0 are structurally changing. They use data from websites of the Korean National Assembly between 2000 and 2001. They also examine how patterns started to change between 2005 and 2006, when Web 2.0 was initially introduced. Hsu and Park find that through these hyperlinks, individuals, groups, and other beings are connected.

Khan, Gohar Feroz, Ho Young Yoon, Jiyoung Kim, and Han Woo Park. "From E-Government to Social Government: Twitter Use by Korea's Central Government." *Online Information Review* 38, no. 1 (2014): 95–113. https://doi.org/10.1108/OIR-09-2012-0162

This study explores how the central Korean government's Twitter use transforms the configuration of political communication and the relationship between the government and citizens. Using network analyses among tweets for hyperlinks, the study concludes that the government's networking strategy with citizens does not relate to social media activities, but it helps reinforce the government-to-government relationships.

Kim, Chan-Gon. "Public Administrators' Acceptance of the Practices of Digital Democracy: A Model Explaining the Utilization of Online Policy Forums in South Korea." PhD diss., Rutgers, State University of New Jersey, 2005.

What factors determine public officials' acceptance of practices of digital democracy on government websites? In this dissertation, public officials' behavioral intentions to use online policy forums on government websites are studied using a survey administered to Korean officials at various levels of government. Based on 895 responses, perceived usefulness, information quality, and attitudes toward citizen participation predict public officials' intentions.

Lee, Eun-Ju, and Soo Yun Shin. "Are They Talking to Me? Cognitive and Affective Effects of Interactivity in Politicians' Twitter Communication." *Cyberpsychology, Behavior & Social Networking* 15, no. 10 (2012): 515–520. doi:10.1089/cyber.2012.0228.

Lee and Shin study what effects the level of interactivity in politician twitter accounts have on the rational and touching reactions of the public. The higher the interactivity on Twitter, the stronger the sense of social presence with politicians exist. Based on 895 responses, perceived usefulness, information quality, and attitudes toward citizen participation predict public officials' intentions.

———. "When the Medium Is the Message: How Transportability Moderates the Effects of Politicians' Twitter Communication." *Communication Research* 41, no. 8 (2014): 1088–1110. doi:10.1177/0093650212466407.

Do Koreans' Twitter exposure affect someone's evaluation of another person? Lee and Shin look particularly at high profile politician's Twitter accounts in comparison to newspaper interviews and evaluate them and their policies. Lee and Shin view that the people that are shown the newspaper interview were able to recognize discussed issues better and focus less on the candidates.

Park, Han Woo, Chun-Sik Kim, and George A. Barnett. "Socio-Communicational Structure among Political Actors on the Web in South Korea." *New Media & Society* 6, no. 3 (2004): 403–423.

Park and colleagues focus on Korean political parties and politicians on the Internet. They also look at the structure of their socio-communication system and how it changed in the past two years. The authors found that the system has become more solid, united, and collaborative. These results recommend an increased use of the Internet for politics in Korea.

Park, Han Woo, and Randolph Kluver. "Trends in Online Networking among South Korean Politicians: A Mixed-Method Approach." *Government Information Quarterly* 26, no. 3 (2009): 505–515. doi:10.1016/j.giq.2009.02.008.

With blogging as a key political communication tool, Park and Kluver examine how Korean politicians build networks through the blogsphere. There was an increase of using the blog linkages among the Korean National Assembly members of 2005 and 2006, according to their study. But the political communication networks through the blog links became more sporadic, isolated, and decentralized among the politicians.

Park, Se Jung, Yon Soo Lim, Steven Sams, Sang Me Nam, and Han Woo Park. "Networked Politics on Cyworld: The Text and Sentiment of Korean Political Profiles." *Social Science Computer Review* 29, no. 3 (2011): 288–299. doi:10.1177/0894439310382509.

In Korea, a social networking site called "Cyworld" allows politicians to create and maintain an online presence. It also lets them communicate with citizens through their personal Cyworld profiles. The study show that liberalism ruled political speech online and that the opposing party received fewer negative comments.

Shapiro, Matthew A., Libby Hemphill, Jahna Otterbacher, and Han Woo Park. (2014). "Twitter and Political Communication in Korea: Are Members of the Assembly Doing What They Say?" *Journal of Asia Pacific Studies* 3, no. 3 (2014): 338–357.

Instead of focusing on the Twitter content of members of the Korean National Assembly, this study looks at the ways officials communicate and puts the Downsian Spatial model to the test. The study finds the power of information provision on Twitter by liberal members of the Assembly.

Media and Public Opinion

Choi, Myunggoon, Yoonmo Sang, and Han Woo Park. "Exploring Political Discussions by Korean Twitter Users: A Look at Opinion Leadership and Homophily Phenomenon," *Aslib Journal of Information Management* 66, no. 6 (2014): 582–602. doi:10.1108/AJIM-11–2012–0089.

Online discussions of President Lee Myung-bak of Korea via the Twitter platform are analyzed for Koreans' politically oriented commentary. Choi, Sang, and Park analyze data collected from late 2011 to early 2012, totaling more than 26,000 Twitter users and 890,000 relationships across followers, mentions, and retweets. They find that liberal Twitter users with both a strong online and offline presence had the largest influence. The authors also discover homophily regarding Twitter-based political engagement.

Choi, Sujin, and Han Woo Park. "An Exploratory Approach to a Twitter-based Community Centered on a Political Goal in South Korea: Who Organized It, What They Shared, and How They Acted." *New Media & Society* 16, no. 1 (2005): 129–148.

Choi and Park explore the case in which Twitter was used in Korea to call for the elimination of a conservative newspaper. Their mixed-method approach shows that the sustainability of the entire protest group was a function of the group organizers' information provision through Twitter, and that retweeting and "culture jamming" tactics enhanced group solidarity in their newspaper-elimination efforts.

Kim, Daekyung, and Thomas J. Johnson. "A Victory of the Internet over Mass Media? Examining the Effects of Online Media on Political Attitudes in South Korea." *Asian Journal of Communication* 16, no. 1 (2007): 1–18. doi: 10.1080/01292980500467251.

How does online news media use regarding political news and information influence political attitude? To answer this question, Kim and Johnson conduct an online survey of nearly 250 Internet users during the 2004 National Assembly election in Korea. Their survey finds that online news media use vis-à-vis traditional news media use is a stronger factor in predicting political attitude during the election period.

Kim, Sei-Hill, Dietram A. Scheufele, James Shanahan, and Doo-Hun Choi. "Deliberation in spite of Controversy? News Media and the Public's Evaluation of a Controversial Issue in South Korea." *Journalism & Mass Communication Quarterly* 88, no. 2 (2011): 320–336. doi: 10.1177/107769901108800206.

Kim and his colleagues examine the degree to which news media use influences a controversial issue evaluation of the relocating of the Korean administrative capital. Relying on a telephone survey of 527 residents in Seoul, the study reveals that heavy news users are more likely to engage in an informed evaluation of the issue.

Kim, Su Jung. "Emerging Patterns of News Media Use across Multiple Platforms and Their Political Implications in South Korea." PhD diss., Northwestern University, 2011.

By examining TV news consumption in Korea in 2001–2007, this dissertation addresses the lack of research focusing on the effects of ideological polarization and partisan news media outlets. Kim finds that polarization was pre-existing in Korea before cable entered onto the media scene; however, "media repertoires" have been created by Korean TV viewers, watching news from multiple sources.

Kwak, Ki-Sung. *Media and Democratic Transition in South Korea*. Ames, NY: Routledge, 2012.

In this book, Kwak draws attention to the lack of a liberal, individualist culture in Korea, despite the shift away from authoritarian rule in the post-1987 era. However, this book targets the changing role of media in this transition and describes the revolutionary change that has occurred between the state and the media in the democratization process.

Larson, James F. "Quiet Diplomacy in a Television Era: The Media and U.S. Policy toward the Republic of Korea." *Political Communication & Persuasion* 7, no. 2 (1990): 73–95.

James Larson focuses on the Kwangju incident and the visit of the succeeding Korean president, Chun Doo Hwan, to the White House. It explores the role of T.V. coverage in the U.S. policy toward Korea. The study emphasizes what impact television's dramatic visual focus had on politics. The author discovers significantly different interpretations between the Kwangju incident and the President Reagan's first visit.

Lee, Han Soo, and Kae Mook Lee. "Televised Presidential Debates and Learning in the 2012 Korean Presidential Election: Does Political Knowledge Condition Information Acquisition?" *International Journal of Communication* 9 (2015): 2693–2712.

If voters learn about candidates through televised debates is investigated. Lee and Lee find that the effects are dependent on individuals' level of political knowledge.

Televised debates improve constituents' learning in general. Without existing knowledge about political candidates, however, the effect is minimal.

Shin, Doh Chull, Chong-Min Park, Ah-Ran Hwang, Hyeon-Woo Lee, and Jiho Jang. "The Democratization of Mass Political Orientations in South Korea: Ascertaining the Cultural Dimension of Democratic Consolidation." *International Journal of Public Opinion Research* 15, no. 3 (2003): 265–284.

Shin and his co-authors attempt to address Korean citizens' perceptions on democracy as a normative and empirical phenomenon. They contend that Korean citizens still do not detach democracy from authoritarianism. Such perception can be influenced by interpersonal communication and media exposure.

Yoon, Jiso. "Who Receives Media Attention in South Korea: Analyzing Internal and External Pluralism in the News Coverage of Policy Debates." *Asian Journal of Political Science* 21, no. 2 (2013): 126–147. doi:10.1080/02185377.2013.823798.

Mass media has the power to shape how citizens make sense of policy problems. This study takes a look at how diverse the content in the media is and what, if any, side it favors. Yoon finds that the patterns suggest only a limited explanation for declining trust and raise concerns about what side is favored. The Korean newspapers *Dong-A Ilbo* and *Hankyoreh* relatively lacked their ties with political and social organizations on policy debates. As such, the disconnection limits the diversity of voices appearing in the news.

You, Kyung Han. "Entertaining Politics: Exploring Historical Transformation of Production, Distribution, and Consumption of Political Entertainment in Korea." PhD diss., Pennsylvania State University, 2014.

From a historical perspective, this dissertation explores how political entertainment has emerged in Korea given changing social and economic factors as well as shifting power relations. Political institutions as a regulating force of the media industry are given particular attention, and the study shows that both regulation and promotion occur at the policy level. Yet the transformations are ongoing and employ new hybrid formats that blur the lines between news and entertainment.

Presidential Campaigns and General Elections

Ahn, Kenneth Kunil. "Mobilization and Participation in Elections: A Study of Korean Voting Behavior." PhD diss., University of Georgia, 1975.

This analysis of political mobilization in Korea covers the issue broadly, but of relevance here is the proposed connection between urbanization, education, and socio-economic advantage and increased opportunities for political communication, which draw new social groups into the political process.

Cho, Jaeho, and Yerheen Ha. "On the Communicative Underpinnings of Campaign Effects: Presidential Debates, Citizen Communication, and Polarization in Evaluations of Candidates." *Political Communication* 29, no. 2 (2012): 184–204. doi:10.1080/10584609.2012.671233.

Cho and Ha focus on the viewers and what kind of effects presidential debates have on them. More specifically, they describe the indirect impact of debate-induced citizen communication in Korea. He finds that the moderation of debate effects is observed only when predicting one candidate's favorability rating.

Kim, Min Gyu and Joohan Kim. "Comparing the Effects of Newspaper, TV News, and the Internet News on the Evaluation of a Major Political Candidate: Latent Growth Modeling with Longitudinal Panel Data from the 2007 Presidential Campaign in South Korea." *International Journal of Public Opinion Research* 24, no. 1 (2012): 62–78. doi: 10.1093/ijpor/edr046.

The varying degree of news media uses and their differential effects on political outcomes is investigated. Relying on a set of longitudinal data that tracked the 2007 presidential election panel in Korea, the study finds that, while television news use is positively associated with an evaluation of the candidates' morality, the Internet news is the opposite.

Ku, Gyotae. "Intermedia Agenda-Setting in the 2000 Presidential Campaign: The Influence of Candidates' Web sites on Traditional News Media." PhD diss., University of Oklahoma, 2002.

Ku investigates the impact of website campaigning on the traditional news media agenda as well as on public opinion during the 2000 Korean presidential election. He finds that website campaigning is useful as a tool for public relations given that the information is effectively transferred to the traditional media. It should also be noted that the public is affected more by campaign websites that any other media examined by Ku.

Lee, Yeon-Ok, and Han Woo Park. "The Reconfiguration of E-Campaign Practices in Korea." *International Sociology* 25, no. 1 (2010): 29–53. doi: 10.1177/0268580909346705.

The U.S. model of electioneering is tested in the e-campaigning context of Korea. In a case study of the 2007 presidential primaries of the Grand National Party, Lee and Park pay attention to how the online political climate has evolved since 2002. They reveal the dynamic usage of the Internet for political campaigns by candidates.

Shin, Jungsub, and Sungsoo Kim. "Issue Competition and Presidential Debates in Multiparty Systems: Evidence from the 2002, 2007, and 2012 Korean Presidential Elections." *Asian Journal of Communication* 27, no. 3 (2017): 233–249. doi:10.10 80/01292986.2016.1273958.

Shin and Kim examine the Korean presidential elections in 2002, 2007, and 2012 and the issues that each political party focused on. The authors analyze the government parties' strategies for dealing with small or opposition parties. They find that the strategies depend on party size and ideal relationships with opposing parties.

Shin, Eui Hang. "Presidential Elections, Internet Politics, and Citizens' Organizations in South Korea," *Development and Society* 34, no. 1 (2005): 25–47. http://hdl. handle.net/10371/86669.

The democratic transition in Korea, as hypothesized in this study, was a function of citizens' groups and Internet-based news. Through an analysis of the National Election Commission's election results and data collected from Korean newspapers and *Ohmynews*, this hypothesis is tested in the context of the 2002 presidential election in Korea, where Nosamo—a group supporting Roh Moo-hyun—and *Ohmynews* mobilized the citizenry and thus the electorate to support Roh.

Woo, Jisuk. "Television News Discourse in Political Transition: Framing the 1987 and 1992 Korean Presidential Elections." *Political Communication* 13, no. 1 (1996): 63–80.

With framing as a theoretical background, Woo takes a look at how the news media in Korea manipulated the 1987 and 1992 presidential elections of Korea. Woo compares the traditional network with a private network. The research proves that TV news frames several political occurrences in certain aspects. The study concludes that the media continues to be ruled by the government by eliminating dissenting opinions and marginalizing the opposition.

Chapter 3

Journalism and Broadcasting

Hun Shik Kim and John C. Carpenter

News media outlets are thriving in South Korea today with more than 200 newspapers and two dozen network television stations across a country of 50 million people. The prominent "big three" publications—*Chosun Ilbo*, *Dong-A Ilbo*, and *Joongang Ilbo*—are newspapers of record with a combined three million subscribers. Daily newspapers in Korea show a wide range of political spectrum regarding their editorial stance. *Chosun Ilbo* and *Dong-A Ilbo* are known for their right-wing, pro-establishment, and conservative editorial position. *Joongang Ilbo* is a moderately conservative business-friendly newspaper. *Hankyoreh Shinmun* and *Kyunghyang Shinmun* are known as left-leaning, pro-labor union, and progressive newspapers.

There is vibrant competition among numerous online newspapers, including citizen journalism outlet *OhmyNews*. Online news platforms symbolize Korea's digital media revolution and have been credited for helping to revitalize public awareness and participation in social and political discourse.

Korea's broadcast news industry remains subject to the national government's delicate and often unseen influence regardless of the government's political orientation. Although they operate as independent news entities, the credibility of two major public broadcasters—Korean Broadcasting System (KBS) and Munhwa Broadcasting Company (MBC)—regularly comes under fire when they support controversial public policies introduced by the Korean government. Meanwhile, commercial terrestrial TV broadcasters, including the Seoul Broadcasting System (SBS), operate in ten major cities in the country. Cable broadcasters such as JTBC, TV Chosun, and Channel A are competing for audience shares in the niche news market.

METHODS OF SELECTION

In this chapter, we identified and annotated Korean journalism and broadcasting studies published in English. Most studies are scholarly journal articles, books, book chapters, and doctoral dissertations. To locate these publications, we used electronic databases such as EBSCO Host, Education Resources Information Center (ERIC), and ProQuest's Dissertation and Theses finder. To locate additional books and journal articles on the same topic, we used the Google Scholar online search engine, as well as the University of Colorado and the University of Iowa libraries' book title search engines.

The keyword combinations used to locate relevant publications included "Korean journalism," "Korean broadcasting," "Korean press," "Korean news media," "Korean journalism studies," and "Korean journalist." The initial search produced a total of 256 studies using the databases and searching tools. After reviewing the title and the content of each piece of published research, articles that may belong in cognate disciplines in communication such as media law, political communication, communication technologies, public relations, advertising, and health communication were excluded. In addition, we located dozens of English-language books in their entirety or book chapters describing or analyzing Korea's news industry, the status of press freedom in the country, as well as political democratization issues and journalistic practices. Through this selection process, we have identified a total of 106 journalism and broadcasting studies on Korea. The annotated studies in our chapter cover a variety of media platforms: print and online newspapers, magazines, terrestrial and online broadcasting outlets, and alternative news outlets such as podcasts and Twitter.

JOURNALISM RESEARCH TRADITIONS

As an academic discipline, journalism is based on a set of professional practices and skill sets such as the gathering, processing, and distributing of news. Consequently, journalism research utilizes and applies theories and methodologies from different academic disciplines, including communication, media studies, sociology, psychology, political science, and telecommunications. Journalism research has a long history that dates back to the early twentieth century, when one of the first academic publications, *Journalism Bulletin* (later named *Journalism & Mass Communication Quarterly*) was established in 1924. Journalism as a craft and academic discipline has an even longer history. Journalism education first started in France in 1899, and the first journalism program in the United States began at the University of Missouri in 1908. In Korea, the first journalism department was established at Hongik University in 1954. During this early period of Korean journalism research, most journalism educators were journalists-turned-professors, some of whom received advanced educational training in the United States.

English-language publications on Korean journalism appeared in the 1950s as a subfield of international journalism studies conducted by various academics in the United States. One of the first studies of Korean journalism was Pennsylvania State University professor Robert T. Oliver's 1957 *Journalism Quarterly* article, "Present Day Newspapers in the Republic of Korea." Professor Oliver was working for the Korean government as President Syngman Rhee's international affairs advisor and English speechwriter. The following year, the same journal featured Professor Wayne Rowland's article, "The Press in the Korean Republic: Its Status and Problems." Rowland was an American journalism professor who visited Korea to study and advise news media professionals there under U.S. State Department sponsorship. As a newly independent democracy in East Asia undergoing post-Korean War reconstruction, Korea and its press system may have attracted the interest of the American scholars.

Early research foci on Korean journalism during the 1960s and 1970s were the structures of and practices in the newspaper and magazine industries, as well as the professional role conceptions of Korean journalists. In 1962, *International Communication Gazette* published Professor Richard Garver's study on the content of Korean-language daily newspapers. In 1967, the Korean government issued an English-language book titled *History of Korean Journalism* to foster interest in Korean journalism among English-speaking foreign audiences. A handful of journalism studies during this period focused on introducing Korea's post-war period and emerging news industry to the West.

In the 1970s to early 1980s, a group of Korean American scholars in the United States published journalism studies on Korea in English-language publications. Sunwoo Nam at the University of Hawaii, Jae-won Lee at Cleveland State University, and Won H. Chang at the University of Missouri were among those pioneering researchers producing studies on the characteristics of the Korean news media, the status of press freedom, news decision-making processes, and the flow of international news into Korea.[1] Studies during this period contributed to informing international audiences

---

1. See Sunwoo Nam, "The Flow of International News into Korea," *International Communication Gazette* 16, no. 1 (1970): 14–26; Won H. Chang, "Coverage of Unification Issue in North and South Korean Papers," *Journalism Quarterly* 58, no. 4 (1981): 589–593; Jae-won Lee, "South Korea," in *World Press Encyclopedia*, ed. George Thomas Kunan, 2 vols. (New York: Facts on File Inc., 1982), 1:586.

about the press system and the status of press freedom in Korea. Journalism research on Korea may have emphasized government-press relations and press freedom due to the experiences of Korean journalists and their news organizations under authoritarian governments. But theories and research methodologies used during this period were somewhat narrow in nature, relying on philosophical discussions, four theories of the press, journalistic norms, or normative perspectives.

In the late 1980s, the political democratization of Korea contributed to the growth of journalism and mass communication programs at Korean universities as well as to a steady increase in the volume of journalism and broadcasting research appearing in English-language publications. Enrollment in journalism programs grew steadily, and journalism and mass communication became one of the most-popular majors for many university students in Korea. In the United States, Korean-American scholars continued to publish their research on Korean journalism. Then newly joined scholars included media law scholar Kyu Ho Youm (now at the University of Oregon) who produced numerous studies on Korean journalism. According to Professor Seung-Mock Yang at Seoul National University, the 1980s also witnessed an increasing number of journalism studies employing critical media perspectives such as dependency theory and the NWICO (New World Information and Communication Order) debate.[2] As a result, many studies featured qualitative investigations of professional cultures and ideologies of journalism.

In a period of academic pluralism in the 1990s, the introduction of behavioral and social scientific approaches in journalism research increased the number of scholarly publications and expanded the quality of research appearing in many journalism and mass communication journals. As Korean graduate students who earned advanced degrees in journalism and mass communication at various American universities returned to Korea to embark on academic careers, a significant number of journalism studies began reflecting American empirical and social scientific research perspectives. Various scholastic endeavors employed a greater diversity of research methodologies, including content analyses, experiments, and surveys using large sample sizes. The number of scholars in Korea publishing their journalism studies in the English language also increased. The published studies adopted a wide range of theoretical perspectives, including gatekeeping, agenda building, agenda setting, social control in the newsroom, the hierarchy of influence, spiral of silence, diffusion of innovations, third-person effects, rhetorical,

---

2. See Seung-Mock Yang, "A 50-year Survey of Korean Journalism and Communication Research" (Korean) (paper presentation, 15th Korea-Japan International Symposium, Seoul, Sept. 12, 2009).

priming, framing, the knowledge gap, uses and gratification, and electronic colonialism.

In the 2000s, the volume of journalism research increased significantly, and many studies focused on social and political issues using quantitative research methodologies. By this time, social scientific approaches were dominant in journalism research published in the English language. After the rapid transformation of the news media industry following the so-called, disruptive innovations in the newsroom in the 2000s, a growing body of journalism research focused on the changing news industry, adoptions of new media technologies, and the emergence of online digital journalism as favorite topics.

In our research, several keywords have emerged as representing consistent themes for Korean journalism studies: press freedom, roles of journalists, professionalism, and press-government relationship. Keywords such as citizen journalism, Twitter, technology, public sphere, and online media are more frequently found in the recent journalism studies. Areas of inquiry have also switched from mass media (e.g., daily newspapers and terrestrial broadcasting channels) to interactive media (e.g., online newspapers and streaming video news services). For instance, we identified seven journalism studies using *OhmyNews,* which was one of the world's first citizen journalism news outlets.

In the early period of journalism research on Korea, most studies were produced by American or Western scholars interested in Korea and its fledgling news media after the Korean War. Between the 1960s and 1980s, journalism studies on Korea were conducted by either American or Korean scholars. Most studies were single-authored. Over the last two decades, however, we have seen a dramatic increase in the number of co-authored publications, of which many were co-authored by both Korean scholars and non-Korean scholars. The growing number of collaborative and shared authorship between Korean and non-Korean scholars clearly reflects the importance of Korean journalism studies in the global news marketplace as well as in the academic circles. We believe this international cooperation and research collaboration coincide with a transformation of news media in the digital age represented by dissolving national borders, and a blurring of the local and the global boundaries of journalism.

RESEARCH ON THE DISRUPTIVE REALIGNMENT OF TRADITIONAL NEWS MEDIA

Over the last decade, studies of online newspapers and citizen journalism have appeared more frequently in scholarly journals. Most suggest that

Korean news outlets and entrepreneurship have been a driving force in the country's digital media revolution. The crisis in audience decline faced by traditional print and television news media is due to the many alternatives available to Korean news consumers. More and more people are consuming news stories through their mobile devices and laptops, and Twitter and other online news platforms are used to share, distribute, and create news stories and to perform as an interactive public sphere. Since 2014, several studies have incorporated Twitter into journalistic experiments in Korea. The research findings suggest that the new interactive medium does have a significant impact on how Korean news audiences consume, share, and distribute public or private messages, including news. However, a majority of research findings also revealed that Twitter reinforces political partisanship and deepens generational divides over controversial public issues.

RESEARCH ON INTERNATIONAL JOURNALISM

International journalism studies have focused on how Korean journalists and their news media framed and interpreted international incidents such as airline disasters, sports competitions, and diplomatic disputes with other Asian neighbors in which South Korea was deemed to be a critical player. Such studies often revealed that the work of Korean journalists more often than not is dictated by national interests and that their news reporting typically reflected patriotic attitudes. In this context, it is not surprising to find that some researchers are questioning journalistic objectivity in the Korean news media's coverage of international affairs.

In a similar vein, research on the news coverage of North Korea has been a significant topic for scholars who study Korean journalism. Over the last decade, several critical scholarly research articles focusing on the rogue nation's nuclear ambitions and the international community's reactions were published. As defined and noted by Professor Herbert Gans at Columbia University and Professors Tsan Kuo Chang and Jae-won Lee at Cleveland State University, North Korea has two essential characteristics that attract global news media coverage.[3] The totalitarian state has had three generations of a brutal dictatorship that introduces a deviance factor into the news, and the regime has been pursuing a nuclear weapons program that poses security threats to the United States and puts world peace at risk. Hence, it is natural

---

3. See Herbert Gans, *Deciding What's News* (New York: Pantheon, 1979); Tsan Kuo Chang and Jae-won Lee, "Factors Affecting Gatekeepers' Selection of Foreign News: A National Survey of Newspaper Editors," *Journalism Quarterly* 69, no. 3 (1992), 554–561.

that researchers on South Korean journalism display heightened interest in analyzing news coverage and perceptions of North Korea.

RESEARCH ON JOURNALISTIC WORK ENVIRONMENTS

Following the Asian financial crisis and Korea's economic recession in the late-1990s, journalism research has highlighted how newsroom management, including the hiring and firing of journalists, changed the entire media industry. The introduction of digital technologies into the newsroom, as well as newswriting experiments using computer-assisted robot technologies were among the studies published. As the number of female journalists grew significantly during the 2000s, Korean journalism research also focused on gender gaps in the newsroom and professional role conceptions among women in Korean news media.

Beginning in the 2000s, a number of Korean journalism studies published in English have focused on broadcast journalism and new media platforms, including online-based citizen journalism. *OhmyNews*, a pioneering online digital news medium, has been the most-frequently addressed and most-productive topic for international journalism researchers investigating the changing characteristics of Korea's print and multimedia journalism. Research topics in this area ranged from the use of online discussion forums between journalists and readers, to the agenda-setting effects observed in the new digital media. Most findings showed that the new forms of digital media in Korea not only presented an entrepreneurial business model but also enriched political and ideological diversity in the multimedia age.[4]

RESEARCH ON POLITICAL OUTRAGE AND PROTESTS

Recently, journalism research in English started focusing on how news media and journalists framed and reported political outrage and public protests during turbulent news events such as the 2008 candlelight vigil protesting U.S. beef imports, the 2014 Sewol ferry disaster, and presidential elections since 2004. Research findings on these themes suggest that Korean news consumers are beginning to exhibit stark partisan attitudes in their political views, raising concerns that new media are deepening public opinion gaps instead of creating consensus over various political and social issues.

---

4. See Thomas Kern and Sang-hui Nam, "The Making of a Social Movement: Citizen Journalism in South Korea," *Current Sociology* 57, no. 5 (2009), 637–660.

Based on our analysis, it is worth noting that a significant volume of journalism research published in English has focused on specific political or social events, including news coverage of controversial public issues. Given that event-driven journalism research has been a driving force behind developing and confirming new theoretical foundations and perspectives, Korean and non-Korean journalism scholars have yet to catch up with some of the most recent events and issues in Korea by conducting timely research and have their findings published in English-language academic journals. For instance, few, if any, academic studies have investigated topics such as the latest North Korean nuclear crisis since 2016, and the political turmoil over the presidential impeachment in 2017. The same is true for scholarly inquiries into the rapid growth of alternative news media in Korea, including English-language publications and news websites, despite the fact that a robust research program has been produced on the same topic in Korean-language journals. Without a doubt, journalism scholars are expected to explore and produce more research on the interplay and dynamics of Korea's vibrant journalism sector.

ANNOTATED BIBLIOGRAPHY

Press-Government Relations

Chang, Yunshik. "From Ideology to Interest: Government and Press in South Korea, 1945–1979." In *Korean Studies: New Pacific Currents,* edited by Dae-Sook Suh, 249–262. Honolulu: University of Hawaii Press, 1994.

This historical essay traces a journalistic shift away from the people and toward ruling powers in Korea starting with liberation from Japan through the presidencies of Syngman Rhee and Park Chung-hee. At each stage, administrations used laws to control journalists while paying lip service to press freedom. The essay's value lies in information about specific laws that limited the press including the Anti-Communism Law (1961), Public Security Law (1964), Committee on Press Ethics Law (1964), and others.

Heuvel, Jon Vanden, and Everette E. Dennis. *The Unfolding Lotus: East Asia's Changing Media.* Freedom Forum Media Studies Center, Columbia University, 1993.

The Korea chapter (pp. 6–21) of this book focuses on the changing journalism landscape in Korea, particularly after the democratic transition following public protests in 1987. The authors state that the Korean press in the 1990s was living in a golden age by criticizing the government, freely addressing formerly taboo issues, and rapidly expanding in number of outlets.

———. "Trends and Developments in the Media of South Korea." In *Elite Media Amidst Mass Culture*, edited by Chie-woon Kim and Jae-won Lee, 1–26. Seoul, Korea: NANAM Publishing House, 1994.

Heuvel and Everette reiterate the ways industry and journalism practices are changing in Korean news media since the 1987 democratic transition. This book chapter contains very similar discussions found in the two authors' book chapter on Korea in their book titled, *The Unfolding Lotus* (1993).

Kang, Myung Koo. "The Struggle for Press Freedom and Emergence of 'Unelected' Media Power in South Korea." In *Asian Media Studies: Politics of Subjectivities*, edited by John Nguyet Erni and Siew Keng Chua, 75–90. Malden, MA: Blackwell Publishing, 2005. doi:10.1002/9780470774281.ch5.

Kang theorizes a link between the Korean press, conservative government, and business conglomerates in which the press promotes a conservative alliance. He argues that government policies made the press dependent on government and advertisers, making the watchdog role of journalism secondary to pleasing corporations. Kang calls for strict separation between editorial and business sides of news operations and for a rollback of policies that protect media companies from competitors.

Kim, Kyu. "Radio and Television in Korea." *Transactions of the Royal Asiatic Society, Korea Branch* 45 (1969): 97–107.

In this overview of the Korean broadcasting industry, Kim divides the history of radio and television into four stages—Japanese colonial era, post-World War II radio era, free competition era, and the age of early television. As one of the pioneers of Korean broadcasting, Kim suggests that broadcasters should possess a sense of social responsibility. He also points out that most TV broadcasters lack in formal educational training, and thus should strive to acquire professional experience and training in the field.

Kim, Min Gyu, and Joohan Kim. "Comparing the Effects of Newspaper, TV News, and the Internet News on the Evaluation of a Major Political Candidate: Latent Growth Modeling with Longitudinal Panel Data from the 2007 Presidential Campaign in South Korea." *International Journal of Public Opinion Research* 24, no. 1 (2012): 62–78. doi:10.1093/ijpor/edr046

In a study of the 2007 Korean presidential campaign, the authors find that TV news viewing has positive influences on the evaluation of the presidential candidate's morality, while Internet news consumption shows adverse effects. The authors conclude that different types of news media have different effects on political behaviors.

Koh, Myung-shik. "Postwar Development of the Korean Press." *Transactions of the Royal Asiatic Society, Korea Branch* 45 (1969): 37–49.

Koh summarizes the development of the Korean press and the press policies from the U.S. military government in 1945 to President Park Chung-hee's military regime in the late 1960s. Focusing on the development and expansion of the newspaper industry, Koh's article explains how the Korean press has been a medium to reflect Koreans' yearning for democracy and traces the economic growth during the 1960s.

Kwak, Ki-Sung. "Democratization and Changing State-Media Relations in South Korea." In *Journalism and Democracy in Asia*, edited by Michael Bromley and Angela Romano, 123–134. New York: Routledge, 2005.

Kwak addresses critical issues of freedom and journalism in Korea as part of research on several Asian countries. As for the journalism sector in Korea, he states that political and economic liberalization has helped bring about a blooming news media industry while freeing journalists from straitjackets of the authoritarian governments.

———. *Media and Democratic Transition in South Korea*. New York: Routledge, 2012. doi: 10.4324/9780203116173.

Kwak focuses on the changing role of news media in the more democratized political environment in Korea since the 1987 democratic transition. The author discusses the complex interacting forces that still exist and affect the role of the news media under a more delicate form of state control.

Park, Chang Sup. "Korean Media Often Allied with Ruling Political Parties." *Newspaper Research Journal* 36, no. 2 (2015): 265–278. doi: 10.1177/0739532915587297.

Using a framing analysis of Korea's three major newspapers and two television networks, this study suggests the news coverage of presidential election polls was heavily biased toward the ruling party and its candidate. The study also finds that the mainstream news media's election coverage focused mainly on the race between candidates rather than on campaign issues.

Yang, Seung-Mock. "Political Democratization and the News Media." In *Institutional Reform and Democratic Consolidation in Korea*, edited by Larry Diamond and Doh Chull Shin, 149–170. Stanford, CA: Hoover Institution Press, 2000.

Yang describes Korea's political transition from authoritarian regime to a more democratic government after the 1987 democracy movement. The author also concludes that the liberalization under President Roh Tae-woo led the Korean news media industry to change itself from a government-controlled system to an increasingly autonomous entity in line with the radically changing sociopolitical circumstances.

Yin, Jiafei. "Asia and Pacific." In *Global Journalism: Topical Issues and Media Systems*, edited by Arnold S. de Beer and John C. Merrill, 337–399. Boston: Pearson Education, 2009. doi:10.3368/ajs.30.1.107.

Yin's book chapter provides a survey of journalism and news media in countries in the Asia-Pacific region, including Korea. In her description of journalism practices in Korea, Yin characterizes Korean news media as elitist, conservative, pro-establishment, and prone to the practice of self-censorship. Yin also provides highlights of several journalistic practices in the country as late as the early 2000s.

Yoon, Jiso. "Dominating the News: Government Officials in Front-Page News Coverage of Policy Issues in the United States and Korea." *Journal of Public Policy* 34, no. 2 (2014): 207–235. doi: 10.1017/s0143814x14000051.

Yoon examines cross-national variance in government officials' media representation relative to policymaking participation. By comparing front-page news coverage of the *New York Times* of the United States and *Hankyoreh Shinmun* of Korea, the author finds that diverse actors are represented on the front-pages of the *Times* while governmental actors are dominant on the front pages of *Hankyoreh*.

Youm, Kyu Ho. "Press Policy of the U.S. Military Government in Korea: A Case of Failed 'Libertarian' Press Theory?" *American Journalism* 8, no. 2/3 (1991): 160–177. doi:10.1080/08821127.1991.10731337.

Youm investigates how the libertarian press policy was adopted by the U.S. military government in Korea from 1945 to 1948. The author suggests that institutional mechanisms and procedures implemented by the U.S. military government helped develop the Korean press both in quantity and quality. The author also notes that after the termination of U.S. military rule, the Korean government abused some of the regulatory measures against the Korean press.

Freedom of the Press

Chang, Yunshik. "From Ideology to Interest: Government and Press in South Korea, 1945–1979." In *Korean Studies: New Pacific Currents*, edited by Dae-Sook Suh, 243–262. Honolulu: University of Hawaii Press, 1994.

Chang explains the early role of the Korean press as a defender of democracy. However, he argues that the press gradually evolved into protecting its corporate interest rather than its freedom as a public trust. Chang suggests that this strange historical twist was due to the Korean government's "stick-and-carrot" approach to control the media. He states that the authoritarian government as well as the corporate media's self-censorship restricted press freedom even further.

Chong, Chin-Sok. *The Korean Problem in Anglo-Japanese Relations 1904–1910: Ernest Thomas Bethell and His Newspapers: The Daehan Maeil Sinbo and the Korea Daily News.* Seoul, Korea: NANAM Publishing House, 1987.

This book traces the history of one of Korea's first English-language newspapers, the *Korea Daily News.* Because the newspaper was owned by a British citizen, Ernest T. Bethell, it was exempt from the press restrictions imposed by Japanese authorities in Korea in 1905. The *Korea Daily News* and its Korean-language editions became leading voices of dissent as Japan encroached on Korean sovereignty.

Gong, Qian, and Gary Rawnsley. "Media Freedom and Responsibility in South Korea: The Perceptions of Journalists and Politicians during the Roh Moo-hyun Presidency." *Journalism* (2017). doi: 10.1177/1464889916688287.

Drawing from in-depth interviews, the authors analyze the perceptions of media freedom and responsibility by journalists and politicians in Korea during the presidency of Roh Moo-hyun (2003–2008). Findings suggest that both groups had positive appraisals of the country's media democratization. However, the political press remained partially shackled to specific legacies and economic conditions.

Haggard, Stephan, and Jong-Sung You. "Freedom of Expression in South Korea." *Journal of Contemporary Asia* 45, no. 1 (2015): 167–179. doi:10.2139/ssrn. 2505565.

Using New York-based nonprofit Freedom House's world press freedom rankings, the authors find that freedom of expression in Korea has lagged behind that of comparable Asian countries and it has deteriorated since 2008. The authors conclude that the main problems lie in both the political right and left who have placed limits on freedom of expression to contain political opposition.

Kim, Hun Shik. "Media, The Public, and Freedom of the Press." *Social Indicators Research* 62/63 (2003): 345–364. doi: 10.1023/a:1022609620582.

Kim examines the diversification of the news media in Korea since the 1990s as a result of deregulation and democratization. The author also examines the impact of media diversity on the public's use patterns and its trust in the media and evaluates the current state of freedom of the press in Korea. Kim concludes that the Korean press still faces a variety of restraints despite improvements in a few areas.

Kim, Sae-Eun. "Life History of Dismissed Journalists: With a Focus on the Dong-A Committee for Free Press." In *Understanding Journalism in Korea,* edited by Hyung-Cheol Kang, 290–334. Seoul: Communication Books, 2015.

Kim's study positions members of the Dong-A Committee for a Free Press at the forefront of the struggle for journalism unfettered by government or corporate control in Korea. Her study traces members' personal histories from their entry into the field, to their dismissal, to their part in founding *Hankyoreh*. Kim concludes the struggle these journalists experienced provides an example for contemporary media that face similar challenges.

Lee, Jae-kyoung. "Press Freedom and Democratization: South Korea's Experience and Some Lessons." *International Communication Gazette* 59, no. 2 (1997): 135–149. doi: 10.1177/0016549297059002004

Lee found that newsroom visits by Korean secret agents and Ministry of Culture press guidelines in an earlier era were replaced by forces that make reporters hyper-conscious of how government officials will react to their stories. The survival of senior editors with establishment interests, the hierarchical nature of staffing, and a culturally based deference to authority all prolong government influence in media content after official controls have been lifted.

―――. "Anti-Americanism in South Korea: The Media and the Politics of Signification." PhD diss., University of Iowa, 1993. ProQuest (304044408).

Lee analyzes how news media's communication processes constituted an integral element in the generation of anti-Americanism prevalent in Korea during the 1980s. The author argues that the mainstream media's distortion of U.S. foreign policy positions, military regimes' press censorship and systematic control of the encoding of news, and the vehement of anti-American articulation by various dissident publications ultimately resulted in a massive eruption of anti-American sentiments.

Lee, Jae-won. "South Korea: Media System." In *International Encyclopedia of Communication*, edited by Wolfgang Donsbach, 4751–4755. Oxford: Blackwell Publishing, 2008. doi: 10.1002/9781405186407.wbiecs079.pub2.

In this encyclopedia, Lee surveys Korea as a business-friendly and profitable market for the mass media industry. With affluence from the vibrant economy, Lee suggests that the Korean public supports a steady consumption of the traditional media as well as ready experimentation with the rapidly advancing new media.

―――. "The Press of South Korea." In *World Press Encyclopedia: A Survey of Press Systems Worldwide*, edited by Amanda C. Quick, 840–855. Farmington Hills, MI: Gale Group, 2003. doi: 10.5860/choice.40-4389.

Lee describes the press system in Korea focusing on the state of its daily newspapers, broadcasting and electronic media, press laws and censorship, and state-press relations. He suggests that the press and other media industries in Korea have been one major beneficiary of the country's rapid industrialization and liberalization in politics. However, Lee argues that the Korean press has to deal with some legacies that do not align with universal standards.

Nam, Sunwoo. "The Korean Press after Park." *International Communication Gazette* 26, no. 4 (1980): 259–266. doi:10.1177/001654928002600403.

This article describes press conditions as control of the Korean government fell to Chun Doo-hwan after Park Chung-hee's assassination in 1979. After a six-month window of relative freedom, Chun reverted back to the controls employed by his predecessor. Nam speculates that Chun allowed the window of freedom to draw those who were sympathetic to his opposition into the public light so he could eliminate them.

————. "Newspapers under Tribulation: The Present-Day Korean Press?" *International Communication Gazette* 24, no. 2 (1978): 109–120. doi:10.1177/001654927802400201.

Nam's detailed account of Korean journalism under the Park Chung-hee regime describes methods of press control from interrogation of editors and reporters, to closures, to newsroom monitors from the Korean Central Intelligence Agency (KCIA). Highlights include accounts of press activity surrounding the Kim Dae-jung kidnapping in 1973, in which reporters at *Dong-A Ilbo*, *Hankook Ilbo*, and *Chosun Ilbo* protested the government's response.

————. "Editorials as an Indicator of Press Freedom in Three Asian Countries." *Journalism Quarterly* 48, no. 4 (1971): 730–740. doi: 10.1177/107769907104800416.

Comparing newspaper editorials from three Asian countries—the Philippines, Taiwan, and Korea—Nam examines the levels of press freedom in newspapers' political affairs coverage in each country. Nam found that variance in the way the newspapers attacked political leaders during elections: Philippine papers are vitriolic, Korean papers are more cautious whereas Taiwanese papers seldom question the regime.

Sa, Eun Suk. "The Development of Press Freedom in South Korea since Japanese Colonial Rule." *Asian Culture and History* 1, no. 2 (July 2009): 3–17. doi: 10.5539/ach.v1n2p3.

Sa defines and categorizes the four main features of press freedom in Korea since the early twentieth century: severe restriction during the Japanese colonial rule; freedom in an unstable democracy under the American military rule and the First and Second republics; oppression of the military regimes; and the struggle with capital power since the advent of more democratic civilian governments.

Yoon, Youngchul. "Political Transition and Press Ideology in South Korea 1980–1989." PhD diss., University of Minnesota,1989. ProQuest (303801892).

Yoon's dissertation discusses Korea's democratic political transition in 1987 and its contribution in transforming the country's news media industry. The author concludes that the expanding political diversity affected the political and economic environment in which the press operates, the organizational dynamics within the newsroom, and the press's ideological output.

Youm, Kyu Ho. "Korea (North and South), Status of Media in." In *Encyclopedia of International Media and Communications*, edited by Donald H. Johnston, 699–708. Amsterdam: Academic Press, 2003. doi: 10.1016/b0–12–387670–2/00166–7.

In this comprehensive summary of media in North and South Korea, Youm details how the two divided countries have contrastive media systems. He explains North Korean news media are dictated by the state as an instrument of conformity and consensus. Youm also traces the development of South Korea's diverse media as the product of political democratization since 1987. He concludes that the dramatic contrast in media between the two Koreas is shaped by different philosophical and functional approaches.

———. "Press Freedom in 'Democratic' South Korea: Moving from Authoritarian to Libertarian?" *International Communication Gazette* 43, no. 1 (1989): 53–71. doi: 10.1177/00165492804300104.

This article examines the status of press freedom in Korea in times of political liberalization and business deregulation. Youm attributes the ongoing turnabout in the Korean press, from "authoritarian" to "libertarian," to the post-1987 democratization process. However, the author argues that the country continues to confront challenges in terms of legal and political restraints on the press.

Journalism Ethics

Logan, Robert A., and Jaeyung Park. "The Hwang Scandal and Korean News Coverage: Ethical Considerations." *Journal of Mass Media Ethics* 25, no. 3 (2010): 171–191. doi: 10.1080/08900523.2010.498287.

This case study explores the ethical dimensions of the Korean news media's coverage of the Dr. Woo Suk Hwang scandal. The authors find that Korean journalists acted too humanely, overemphasized scientific evidence, and were too culturally sensitive in their news coverage of the Hwang scandal.

Youm, Kyu Ho. "*Chonji* Journalism in Korea: An Issue for Press Ethics." *Media Asia* 20, no. 2 (1993): 100–101. doi:10.1080/01296612.1993.11726412.

Youm points out ethical problems with the practice by some Korean journalists to accept money gifts, or *chonji*, from their news sources. The author says this controversial and unethical journalistic practice should be considered a pressing issue to be resolved.

News Audiences

Wonneberger, Anke, and Su Jung Kim. "TV News Exposure of Young People in Changing Viewing Environments: A Longitudinal, Cross-National Comparison Using People-Meter Data." *International Journal of Communication* 11 (2017): 72–93. doi: 0.1093/ijpor/eds004.

The authors analyze TV news viewing among young people in the Netherlands and Korea during the transition from low- to high-choice viewing environments. Based on people-meter data, the authors found that young adults in both countries spent less time watching the news during the transition period, but that more TV channel choices did not necessarily lead to a decrease in news consumption.

Kim, Sei-Hill. "Testing the Knowledge Gap Hypothesis in South Korea: Traditional News Media, the Internet, and Political Learning." *International Journal of Public Opinion Research* 20, no. 2 (July 2008): 193–210. doi:10.1093/ijpor/edn019.

Kim analyzes the ways Korean newspapers, television stations, and online news portals contribute to or mitigate the knowledge gap between highly educated and less-educated social groups. It found that highly educated users were more likely to find political information online and retain more information from the sites they visit. Kim concludes that the Internet may widen the gap between social classes with regards to political communication, rather than serve as a leveling agent by providing equal access to information.

Kim, Su Jung, and James Webster. "The Impact of a Multichannel Environment on Television News Viewing: A Longitudinal Study of News Audience Polarization in South Korea." *International Journal of Communication* 6 (2012): 838–856.

Using people-meter data on television viewership from 2001 to 2007, Kim and Webster find that Korean TV audiences have become more polarized in their news viewing habits. They also suggest the abundant media channel choices available to TV audiences contributed to deepening the polarized TV viewing patterns.

News Coverage of International Affairs

Choi, Suhi. "The Repertoire, Not the Archive: The 1950 Life and Time Coverage of the Korean War." *Media, War & Conflict* 8, no. 2 (2015): 264–280. doi: 10.1177/1750635215584964.

Based on news coverage of the Korean War in 1950 by *Life* and *Time* newsmagazines, this article identifies five plausible scenarios of how U.S. journalists performed acts of witnessing the unknown battlefield in Korea. Choi concludes that the magazines' journalists performed their roles as memory agents and that their journalistic texts were used as a repertoire in the act of remembrance.

Ha, Jae Sik, and Donghee Shin. "Framing the Arab Spring: Partisanship in the News Stories of Korean Newspapers." *International Communication Gazette* 78, No. 6 (2016): 536–556. doi:10.1177/1748048516640213.

This study uses the hierarchy-of-influences framework to examine the ways ideological orientation informed coverage of Arab Spring uprisings in conservative and liberal newspapers in South Korea. It found that the liberal papers more often framed coverage in terms of economic insecurity, while conservative papers considered what effects the uprisings could have on democratic movements in North Korea and China. The authors concluded that coverage reflected the national security concerns of the papers.

Kim, Hun Shik. "Gatekeeping International News: An Attitudinal Study of Network Broadcasters in Korea." *Sungkok Journalism Review* 11 (2000): 5–24.

In a survey and depth interviews with Korean network television journalists, the author has discovered that three different types of journalist groups exist in their news selection criteria of international news. Kim further finds that Korean TV journalists tend to share similar news selection criteria and demonstrated nationalistic attitudes in selecting news items that involved South Korea as the main actor.

———. "Gatekeeping International News: A Q-Study of Television Journalists in the United States and Korea." PhD diss., University of Missouri at Columbia, 2001. ProQuest (249949459).

Kim explores attitudes of American and Korean television journalists toward international news and their news selection processes. Using a Q-method survey and depth-interviews, he found that national involvement guides international news selection for journalists from both countries. Regardless of nationality and news organization, journalists shared mutual selection criteria for and general attitudes toward international news. Korean journalists, especially, are more driven by national interests and select stories that reflect Korea's ties with specific countries.

Kim, Hun Shik, and Seow Ting Lee. "National Interest, Selective Sourcing and Attribution in Air Disaster Reporting." *Journal of International Communication* 14, no. 1 (2008): 85–103. doi: 10.1080/13216597.2008.9674723.

Kim and Lee find that journalists foreground national interests when covering international air disasters. In an analysis of coverage of the 1997 crash of Korean Air 801 in Guam, the authors conclude that Korean journalists relied heavily on selective sourcing to justify mechanical failures and shutdown of navigational equipment at the airport as the main crash causes. American journalists, meanwhile, relied heavily on the National Transportation Safety Board officials and reported the cause of the crash as pilot error.

Kwon, Kyounghee Hazel, and Shin-Il Moon. "The Bad Guy Is One of Us: Framing Comparison between the U.S. and Korean newspapers and Blogs about the Virginia Tech Shooting." *Asian Journal of Communication* 19, no. 3 (2009): 270–288. doi: 10.1080/01292980903038998.

In this study of news framing of the Virginia Tech shooting reported in U.S. and Korean newspapers and blogs, the author finds that collectivistic storytelling is a common practice of news framing in all newspapers. However, the degree of salience is affected by each nation's orientation toward collectivism.

Nam, Sunwoo. "Flow of International News into Korea." *International Communication Gazette*, 16 (1970): 14–26. doi.org/10.1177/001654927001600102

Nam examines the system of international news flow into Korea and the content of international news in a Korean newspaper. The author concludes that countries involved in the same international event will report actions taken by each other closely.

Pak, Hyeong-Jun. "News Reporting on Comfort Women: Framing, Frame Difference, and Frame Changing in Four South Korean and Japanese Newspapers, 1998–2013." *Journalism & Mass Communication Quarterly* 93, no. 4 (2016): 1006–1025. doi:10.1177/1077699016644560.

The study compares and analyzes 384 news stories by Korean and Japanese newspapers on the "comfort women" who were forced into sexual slavery by the Imperial Japanese Army during World War II. The author finds that news frames for comfort women in all newspapers reflect stereotypical patterns due to each newspaper's political orientation and national affiliation.

Park, Jaeyung, and Jongmin Park. "How Two Korean Newspapers Covered the Starr Report." *Newspaper Research Journal* 21, no. 4 (2000): 83–98. doi:10.1177/073953290002100406.

The authors find that two major Korean daily newspapers, *Joongang Ilbo* and *Chosun Ilbo*, came to opposite conclusions about reporting explicit sexual material in Kenneth Starr's report on U.S. President Bill Clinton in 1998. *Joongang Ilbo* translated and published the report verbatim, whereas *Chosun Ilbo* eliminated or softened the sexual content included in the report. To understand better the different choices made by each newspaper, the authors employ the Potter Box, an ethical decision-making model.

Yan, Yan, and Yeojin Kim. "Framing the Crisis by One's Seat: A Comparative Study of Newspaper Frames of the Asiana Crash in the USA, Korea, and China." *Asian Journal of Communication* 25, no. 5 (2015): 486–506. doi: 10.1080/01292986.2014.990470.

This article compared news frames for the 2013 Asiana Airlines crash in San Francisco in the United States, Korea, and China. The authors find that national interests influenced patterns of news coverage. U.S. newspapers overwhelmingly attributed the crash to pilot error, Korean newspapers framed the crash as a combination of multiple factors, and Chinese newspapers withheld speculation until the official crash investigation became available. The authors conclude that American and Korean news coverage maintained a mutually negative tone.

News Coverage of North Korea

Chang, Won H. "Coverage of Unification Issue in North and South Korean Papers." *Journalism Quarterly* 58, no. 4 (1981): 589–593. doi: 10.1177/107769908105800 410.

In a content analysis of North Korea's *Nodong Shinmun* and South Korea's *Dong-A Ilbo*, Chang found that the two newspapers showed divergent editorial stances on the unification issue. The author found that the South Korean paper advocated a step-by-step solution through dialogue, while the North Korean paper advocated immediate unification without outside interference.

Chong, Miyoung. "A Cross-Cultural Textual Analysis of Western and South Korean Newspaper Coverage of North Korean Women Defectors and Victims of Human Trafficking." Master's thesis, University of North Texas, 2014. ProQuest (1668398958).

This dissertation compares South Korean newspaper coverage of North Korean women defectors as victims of human trafficking with the coverage of the same topic by Western (U.S. and British) newspapers. In a cross-cultural textual analysis, the author found that politics was a crucial factor in the coverage of the issue. The author also argues that all newspapers in the study failed to report on the fundamental causes of the human trafficking, such as gender inequality.

Ha, Jae Sik. "Arab Spring is Wake-up Call for Kim Jong-Il." *Journalism Practice* 9, no. 5 (2015): 741–759. doi:10.1080/17512786.2014.995915.

Ha identifies differences and similarities in how liberal and conservative newspapers in South Korea framed the Arab Spring in their opinion sections. The author finds that ideological orientations of the newspaper outlets have a considerable influence on how each newspaper links the Middle Eastern political upheaval to South Korea's confrontation with North Korea.

Kim, Kyung Hye. "Examining U.S. News Media Discourses about North Korea: A Corpus-Based Critical Discourse Analysis." *Discourse & Society* 25, no. 2 (2014): 221–244. doi: 10.1177/0957926513516043.

Kim compares news coverage of North Korea by three U.S. media outlets: CNN, *Newsweek* and the *New York Times*. Using critical discourse analysis, the author concludes that the three outlets divide the world into certain sets of countries, and that being pro- or anti-U.S. may have an impact on which country is associated with North Korea.

Seo, Hyunjin. "Media and Foreign Policy: A Comparative Study of Journalists' Perceptions of Press-Government Relations during the Six-Party Talks." *Journalism* 12, no. 4 (2011): 467–481. doi: 10.1177/1464884910388227.

Journalists' role conceptions in their coverage of diplomatic issues come to the forefront in this survey-based study. Seo compares results from South Korean, U.S., and European journalists who covered the six-party talks on North Korea's nuclear program. Compared to U.S. and European journalists, the study finds that South Korean journalists considered themselves as part of the negotiation process with North Korea. Seo also concludes that the Korean journalists believe their news sources exert a strong influence over determining the newsworthiness of issues during the talks.

————. "A Comparative Study on Source Credibility and Use in Multinational Nuclear Talks." *Asian Journal of Communication* 20, no. 4 (2010): 440–455. doi: 10.1080/01292986.2010.496861.

Seo's study analyzes the ways U.S. and South Korean journalists used sources and their perceptions of source credibility in reporting the six-party talks on North Korea. The author finds that government officials are dominant sources for both U.S. and Korean journalists. However, the two groups of journalists perceive source credibility of South Korean, North Korean, and Japanese officials very differently.

————. "International Media Coverage of North Korea: Study of Journalists and News Reports on the Six-Party Nuclear Talks." *Asian Journal of Communication* 19, no. 1 (2009): 1–17. doi: 10.1080/01292980802618056.

Using a survey of South Korean and Western journalist who covered North Korea and a content analysis of media reports on North Korea, this study examines what factors influence journalists' perceptions of different attributes of North Korea. The author finds that news sources have a significant influence on journalists' perceptions of North Korea as a rogue state. The author also concludes that journalists' nationality best predicts their perceived importance of North Korea as a dialogue partner.

Yoon, Liv, and Brian Wilson. "Nice Korea, Naughty Korea: Media Framing of North Korea and the Inter-Korean Relationship in the London 2012 Olympic Games." *International Review for the Sociology of Sport* 51, no. 5 (2016): 505–528. doi: 10.1177/1012690214547745.

Differences in how Western media and South Korean news media framed North Korea and the inter-Korean relationship during the London 2012 Summer Olympic Games are the focus of this study. The findings show that the Western representations of North Korea featured discussions of controversies about the North Korean government, and often de-emphasized or dismissed North Korean athletes' efforts. In contrast, South Korean news coverage included few reflections on socio-political problems of North Korea but highlighted athletic accomplishments.

Historical Studies

Kang, Hyeon-Dew. "Development of Early Journalism and Its References to the Outside World in Nineteenth Century in Korea." *Sungkok Journalism Review* 2 (1991): 17–26.

In this study, Kang defines the role of Korea's early newspapers in the late nineteenth century as agents of social change by introducing Western knowledge and culture as well as providing information about the world. In a content analysis of *Hansung Sunbo, Hansung Choobo,* and *Dongnip Sinmum,* Kang examines how the world was reflected in these early Korean newspapers. The findings suggest that the most frequently mentioned countries were China, followed by Japan, the United Kingdom, France, and the United States. The most frequently quoted news sources were politicians/government officials, followed by military officials and ordinary people. Kang concludes that politics was the most significant topic. However, Kang states that as time went by, these newspapers covered domestic issues more than international affairs.

Kim, Bong-Gi. *History of Korean Journalism.* Seoul: Korea Information Service, 1967.

The earliest newspapers in Korean history begin this government-sanctioned account of the Korean press. Written by an editor at the state-run *Korean Republic,* this book is one of the first Korean attempts to present its journalism to a global, English-reading audience. Kim guides the reader through newspaper development in the years leading up to, including, and following the Japanese occupation.

Garver, Richard A. "Content of Korean Language Daily Newspapers." *International Communication Gazette* 8 (1962): 302–316. doi: 10.1177/001654926200800403.

One of the earliest quantitative studies of Korean journalism in English, this content description of nine leading daily newspapers compares journalism in Seoul and provincial cities, using the United States as a baseline. Content is measured in terms of form, style, news origin, and subject.

O'Connor, Peter. *The English-Language Press Networks of East Asia, 1918–1945.* Kent, UK: Global Oriental, 2010.

This book argues that the English-language press of East Asia played a significant role in shaping international perceptions of Japan, Korea, and China in the decades leading up to World War II. O'Connor provides a detailed account of how English-language news outlets in those countries influenced both foreign policy decisions and public opinion in the United States and Great Britain.

Oliver, Robert T. "Present Day Newspapers in the Republic of Korea." *Journalism Quarterly* 34 (1957): 85–86. doi: 10.1177/107769905703400113.

As Korean President Syngman Rhee's policy advisor and speechwriter, Oliver describes the country's news media landscape as well as the government's media policy during the post-Korean War era.

Rowland, Wayne D. "The Press in the Korean Republic: Its Status and Problems." *Journalism Quarterly* 35 (1958): 450–454. doi: 10.1177/107769905803500408.

Rowland wrote this article after a three-month stay in Korea sponsored by the U.S. Department of State. His purpose was to study and advise Korean news outlets. Rowland describes the development of the Korean press after World War II, the logistical and government challenges an emerging press faced, and the state of the country's journalism education.

Media Economics

Jo, Samsup. "Advertising as Payment: Information Transactions in the South Korean Newspaper Market." *Public Relations Review* 37, no. 4 (2011): 399–404. doi: 10.1016/j.pubrev.2011.08.013.

In this study, readers gain insight into the impact market-driven journalism and a declining newspaper readership have on the number and frequency of special purpose advertising revenues from businesses—so-called "information subsidies" between PR practitioners and journalists in Korea. Jo finds that newspaper journalists have relied on the information subsidies more than ever after the economic downturn. The study concludes that advertising revenue from private businesses and government often trade adversarial journalistic role conceptions with cooperative attitudes toward these parties.

Kwak, Ki-Sung. "Corporate Influence on the Media in South Korea: The Case of Samsung." *International Journal of Media & Cultural Politics* 13, no. 1 & 2 (2017): 25–37. doi: 10.1386/macp.13.1-2.25_1.

Kwak examines the editorial approaches of Korean newspapers toward corruption accusations and judicial proceedings against a leading corporation, Samsung. His study finds that there is a complex interplay of ideological inclination and economic interests in the newspapers' reporting on economic corruption. Kwak also argues that the watchdog role of newspapers has been subject to the newspapers' organizational and business interests.

Lee, Na Yeon, and Kanghui Baek. "Squeezing Out Economic News for Business News? Changes in Economic Journalism over the Past 20 Years in South Korea." *Journalism* (2016): 1–19. doi: 10.1177/1464884916665403.

In a content analysis of 2,442 news articles in Korea's three major dailies, the authors find that articles addressing broad public issues such as unemployment and government policies decreased while news about private businesses increased.

The authors conclude that news stories about private business sectors have helped increase advertising revenues for the newspapers.

Park, Chang Sup. "Media Cross-Ownership and Threat to Diversity: A Discourse Analysis of News Coverage on the Permission for Cross-Ownership between Broadcasters and Newspapers in South Korea." *International Journal of Media & Cultural Politics* 10, no. 1 (2014): 43–64. doi: 10.1386/macp.10.1.43_1.

This study analyzes 210 news articles from two ideologically contrastive newspapers in Korea, *Joongang Ilbo* and *Hankyoreh Shinmun,* to compare their editorial and news angles toward the cross-media ownership debate. Park finds that the commercially oriented *Joongang* reported more favorably on the issue by highlighting outlet diversity while the left-leaning, progressive *Hankyoreh* reported critically by emphasizing content diversity.

Working Environment for Journalists

Berkowitz, Dan, and Jonghyuk Lee. "Media Relations in Korea: Cheong between Journalist and Public Relations Practitioner." *Public Relations Review* 30, no. 4 (2004): 431–437. doi: 10.1016/j.pubrev.2004.08.011.

This study considers the ways the Korean concept of *cheong* informs relationships between Korean journalists and public relations practitioners. Based on interviews with news media and public relations professionals, the authors conclude that *cheong* provides a basis for more conciliatory, productive relationships than those found between the same parties in the West.

Choi, Sae-Eun. "Gendered News Production and Women Journalists in Korea: A Historical Approach." In *Understanding Journalism in Korea,* edited by Hyung-Cheol Kang, 335–365. Seoul: Communication Books, 2015.

Choi presents a well-documented history of women journalists in Korea, tracing their involvement in the earliest Korean newspapers through to the present. At each stage of journalism's history, the number of women in news industry has increased, but Choi concludes that a glass ceiling still keeps them out of top positions.

Halvorsen, David. *Confucianism Defies the Computer: The Conflict within the Korean Press.* Honolulu, HI: East-West Center, 1992.

In this essay, Halvorsen traces differences between Korean and Western journalism practices to the influence of Confucianism on Korean media. While the explanations may need to be compared with more contemporary work, the essay explains cultural bases for practices such as the use of anonymous sources, the sprinkling of opinion into pieces that are purportedly "hard news," the acceptance of gifts, and the privilege afforded to Korean press clubs.

Jung, Jaemin, Haeyeop Song, Youngju Kim, Hyunsuk Im, and Sewook Oh. "Intrusion of Software Robots into Journalism: The Public's and Journalists' Perceptions of Newswriting by Algorithms and Human Journalists." *Computers in Human Behavior* 71 (2017): 291–298. doi: 10.1016/j.chb.2017.02.022.

Researchers compare how Koreans rate news articles written by algorithms and human journalists. They find that the public gave higher scores to the algorithm's newswriting work when it was represented as being written by an algorithm, but gave lower scores to the algorithm's work when the author was represented as a human journalist. The authors argue that the findings confirm the public's negative attitude toward journalists' credibility and craving for new information and communication technology services.

Jung, Jaemin. "Causes of Newspaper Firm Employee Burnout in Korea and Its Impact on Organizational Commitment and Turnover Intention." *International Journal of Human Resource Management* 23, no. 17 (2012): 3636–3651. doi: 10.1080/0958 5192.2012.654806.

Work overload is among the leading causes of newsroom burnout, according to this study by Jung. The researcher investigated burnout's causes and consequences among journalists in 10 Korean daily newspapers. Jung finds that employees undergoing burnout also listed a non-autonomous and non-supportive work environment, dissatisfactory levels of income, and troubled relations with coworkers as other main causes.

Kim, Kyung-Hee. "The Influence of Journalists' Gender on Newspaper Stories about Women Cabinet Members in South Korea." *Asian Journal of Communication* 19, no. 3 (2009): 289–301. doi: 10.1080/01292980903039004.

Compared to male reporters, female reporters tend to take a more positive tone in their coverage of certain politicians. They are also less likely to emphasize conflict and use fewer stereotypical references to women cabinet members in Korean government.

———. "Obstacles to the Success of Female Journalists in Korea." *Media, Culture & Society* 28, no. 1 (2006): 123–141. doi: 10.1177/0163443706059578.

Male-dominant newsroom mechanisms and hierarchical corporate cultures in Korea often exclude female journalists from important newsgathering and production processes, deepening further their alienation from the workplace. Kim concludes that the alienation of female journalists exists both at personal and organizational levels.

Kim, Yung Soo, and James D. Kelly. "A Matter of Culture: A Comparative Study of Photojournalism in American and Korean Newspapers." *International Communication Gazette* 70, no. 2 (2008): 155–173. doi: 10.1177/1748048507086910.

In a content analysis of 628 news and feature photographs in 10 elite American and Korean newspapers in composition, subject number, and subject identification, the authors conclude that the Korean approach to photojournalism was purely descriptive, but the American approach was more interpretive. Photographs in the Korean newspapers presented far more news, emphasized the group and maintained a consistent composition. Photographs in the American newspapers ran more features, emphasized individuals, and varied in composition.

Lee, Jae-kyoung. "The Asian Financial Crisis and the Tribulations of the South Korean Media." *International Communication Gazette* 64, no. 3 (2002): 281–297. doi: 10.1177/17480485020640030501.

Lee investigates organizational structural changes in the Korean news media industry during and after the Asian financial crisis in 1997. The author finds that many news organizations downsized or restructured their newsroom operations and fired hundreds of journalists due to financial troubles.

Lee, Min-Kyu, Lydia Frost, and Thomas Hanitzsch. (2016). "Country Report: Journalists in South Korea." *Worlds of Journalism Study*. Updated December 19, 2016. https://epub.ub.uni-muenchen.de/31696/1/Country_Report_South_Korea.pdf.

2014 interviews with Korean journalists provide valuable background for Korean journalism studies. Interviews showed that Korean journalists view accurate reporting, analysis of current affairs, and monitoring government and corporations as their most important roles. Ethics were treated as constant rather than situational, and there was variance in willingness to engage in controversial reporting practices. Fewer than half felt they had autonomy over the processes of story selection.

Lim, Jeongsub. "Representation of Data Journalism Practices in the South Korean and U.S. Television News. *International Communication Gazette* (2018). doi: 10.1177/1748048518759194.

Lim compared data news content from Korean and U.S. television networks using the grounded theory method. The findings suggest that the Korean television networks highlight social issues, politics, and lifestyle; while American television networks cover the economy, social issues, and politics. Both television networks rely on government sources and seldom provide raw data.

Son, Young Jun, Sung Tae Kim, and Jihyang Choi. "Korean Journalists in the 21st Century." In *the Global Journalist in the 21st Century,* edited by David Weaver and Lars Willnat, 66–77. New York: Routledge, 2012. doi: 10.4324/9780203148679.

In a survey of 900 Korean reporters, the authors find that journalistic role conceptions shared by Korean journalists include providing accurate information, verifying information that reaches the public and being a watchdog for government and businesses. Korean journalists also described the biggest barriers to press freedom as interventions from advertisers, government, and newsroom managers.

Yoo, Sang Keon. "Finding a Breakthrough in a Newsroom Labyrinth: Investigating the Work Routines, Professional Challenges, and Future Strategies of Korean Newspaper Sports Journalists." PhD diss., Indiana University, 2015. ProQuest (1655594788).

This dissertation examines the ways sports journalists are adapting to industrial, economic and technological changes in Korea's media environment. The study presents data related to Korean newspaper sports journalists' job satisfaction, work routines, as well as their perceptions of the ways both technological impacts and industry transformations are affecting their work.

Online and Citizen Journalism

Chang, Woo-Young. "Online Civic Participation, and Political Empowerment: Online Media and Public Opinion Formation in Korea." *Media, Culture & Society* 27, no. 6 (2005): 925–935. doi: 10.1177/0163443705057680.

Equipped with new technological possibilities, this study finds that online media in Korea have put themselves forward as new agents of democracy as well as a powerful alternative journalism by challenging the existing conservative media. This study also concludes that the Korean case shows that the electronic online participation of citizens may even develop into off-line social mobilization.

Chung, Deborah S., and Seungahn Nah. "Negotiating Journalistic Professionalism." *Journalism Practice* 8, no. 4 (2014): 390–406. doi: 10.1080/17512786.2013.8131 98.

This article discusses why and how *OhmyNews* has maintained the status of a remarkably successful online news entity in Korea. By analyzing journalistic role conceptions held by the *OhmyNews* staff journalists and the citizen contributors, the authors find that both groups work through collaboration, check and balances, and a negotiation of autonomy. The authors conclude that both groups benefit from the partnership and share similarities in their effort to remain a sustainable news organization.

Hauben, Ronda. "Online Grassroots Journalism and Participatory Democracy in South Korea." In *Korea Yearbook: Politics, Economy and Society,* edited by Rudiger Frank, Jim. Hoare, Patrick Kollner, and Susan Pares, 61–82. Leiden, Netherlands: Brill Online Books and Journals, 2007. doi: 10.1163/ ej.9789004164406.i-306.26.

Hauben traces the development of *OhmyNews*, providing valuable background about the Korean organization's founding, journalistic mission, and role in large-scale events like the 2002 candlelight protests and the 2003 election of Roh

Moo-hyun as president. It ends with an analysis of the role netizens played in uncovering and publicizing the 2005 Hwang stem cell scandal, compared to mainstream media that didn't want to jeopardize relationships with Hwang's laboratory. Hauben treats this episode as evidence of an online public sphere.

Joyce, Mary. *The Citizen Journalism Web Site 'OhmyNews' and the 2002 South Korean Presidential Election*, Cambridge, MA: Berkman Center for Internet & Society, Harvard University, 2007. doi: 10.2139/ssrn.1077920.

Joyce examines the impact of *OhmyNews* during the 2002 Korean Presidential election. The study discusses how real world activism may have contributed to online activism and lays out a narrative of *OhmyNews'* activity during the Presidential election. The author concludes with a discussion of the feasibility of the *OhmyNews* business model.

Kang, Inkyu. "Web 2.0, UGC, and Citizen Journalism: Revisiting South Korea's *OhmyNews* Model in the Age of Social Media." *Telematics & Informatics* 33, no. 2 (2016): 546–556. doi: 10.1016/j.tele.2015.07.007.

Analyzing *OhmyNews'* business model, this study argues that citizen journalism cannot be understood as "user-generated content (UGC)" in general. The author compares dynamics of highly successful *OhmyNews* in Korea with its spinoff *OhmyNews* in Japan and concludes that the same business model can yield completely different results due to social, cultural and symbolic differences in the two countries.

Kern, Thomas, and Sang-hui Nam. "The Making of a Social Movement: Citizen Journalism in South Korea." *Current Sociology* 57, no. 5 (2009): 637–660. doi: 10.1177/0011392109337649.

Citizen journalism in Korea grounds this study of the emergence of innovations in the social movement sector. The author finds that journalists, labor, and unification activists together with progressive intellectuals successfully built coalitions and constituted a sociocultural milieu that promoted reciprocal learning by allowing actors to learn about a social issue and stay active using alternative media.

Kim, Daekyung, and Thomas J. Johnson. "A Victory of the Internet over Mass Media? Examining the Effects of Online Media on Political Attitudes in South Korea." *Asian Journal of Communication*, 16, no. 1 (2006): 1–18. doi: 10.1080/01292980500467251.

Based on an online survey of 249 Internet users during the 2004 National Assembly election in Korea, the authors examine whether reliance on online news media for political news and information influences political attitudes after controlling for demographics and use of the traditional media. The findings suggest that the reliance on independent online newspapers is a stronger predictor than traditional media and their online counterparts.

Kim, Eun-Gyoo, and James W. Hamilton. "Capitulation to Capital? *OhmyNews* as Alternative Media." *Media, Culture & Society* 28, no. 4 (2006): 541–560. doi:10.1177/0163443706065028.

Kim and Hamilton investigate the emergence, structure, and operation of *OhmyNews* in Korea, which hybridizes features of both commercial and ostensibly "alternative" media. The authors conclude that *OhmyNews* is a unique response to unique enabling conditions, and that its commercial features are inextricably a part of its progressive nature.

Kim, Kyungmo, Young Min Baek, and Narae Kim. "Online News Diffusion Dynamics and Public Opinion Formation: A Case Study of the Controversy over Judges' Personal Opinion Expression on SNS in Korea." *Social Science Journal* 52, no. 2 (2015): 205–216. doi: 10.1016/j.soscij.2015.02.001.

A controversial tweet by a Korean judge about the government's attempt to regulate messages on social networking services provides a basis for this study of the processes of news diffusion and online public opinion formation on the Internet. The study traces citation patterns from one news/opinion to another news/opinion as it follows the formation of dominant frames surrounding the issue. The results show that public discourse on the Internet is extremely polarized and fragmented along political ideological lines.

Kim, Sei-Hill, Dietram A Scheufele, James Shanahan, and Doo-Hun Choi. "Deliberation in Spite of Controversy? News Media and the Public's Evaluation of a Controversial Issue in South Korea." *Journalism & Mass Communication Quarterly* 88, no. 2 (2011): 320–336. doi: 10.1177/107769901108800206.

Using a controversial government plan to relocate the administrative capital of Korea, this study examines the role of news media use in facilitating the public's informed evaluation of the issue. The study finds that respondents who used news media frequently were more able to articulate a specific reason why relocation would be a good or a bad idea. Heavy users of news media were also more firmly opinionated on key issue attributes and tended to think about the issue more carefully.

Lee, Byoungkwan, Karen Lancendorfer, and Ki Jung Lee. "Agenda-Setting and the Internet: The Intermedia Influence of Internet Bulletin Boards on Newspaper Coverage of the 2000 General Election in South Korea." *Asian Journal of Communication* 15, no. 1 (2005): 57–71. doi: 10.1080/0129298042000329793.

The influence of Internet bulletin boards on newspaper coverage of the 2000 general election in Korea is this article's focus. The authors find that newspapers influenced Internet bulletin boards at the first level of agenda-setting. Then the authors find the Internet bulletin boards influenced newspaper coverage at the second level of agenda-setting. Based on the findings, the authors suggest that the

Internet funnels and leads public opinion as well as affecting the coverage of other news media.

Lim, Jeongsub. "The Mythological Status of the Immediacy of the Most Important Online News." *Journalism Studies* 13, no. 1 (2012): 71–89. doi: 10.1080/146167 0x.2011.605596.

Online news media's strength over other news media includes almost real-time updates of their news content. This study finds such an immediacy of online news content is a myth among journalists and the public in Korea. The author argues that frequent updates of the online news stories merely reflect the medium's institutional news production practices.

Nah, Seungahn, and Deborah S. Chung. "Communicative Action and Citizen Journalism: A Case Study of *OhmyNews* in South Korea." *International Journal of Communication* 10 (2016): 2297–2317.

Through in-depth interviews with citizen journalists in Korea, the authors find that citizen journalism can be well understood at the intersection between the lifeworld and systems. Specifically, the study identifies a coexistence mechanism by which citizen journalism competes, collaborates, coordinates, and compromises with professional journalism through communicative action, such as mutual understanding, reason-based discussion, and consensus building.

Park, Chang Sup. "Citizen News Podcasts and Journalistic Role Conceptions in the United States and South Korea." *Journalism Practice* 11, no. 9 (2017): 1158–1177. doi: 10.1080/17512786.2016.1224682.

This study compares audience perceptions of citizen news podcasts in the United States and Korea. Drawing evidence from different journalistic role conceptions and media systems theory, the author finds that American audiences view citizen podcasts as performing the role of interpreters of social issues, while Koreans consider the podcasts as carrying out the role of critical commentator against the government and businesses.

———. "Citizen News Podcasts and Engaging Journalism: The Formation of a Counter-Public Sphere in South Korea." *Pacific Journalism Review* 23, no. 1 (2017): 245–262. doi: 10.24135/pjr.v23i1.49.

By analyzing the content of 11 popular citizen news podcasts in Korea, the author finds that the discourse of citizen podcasts transgresses existing social and cultural hierarchies and subverts a range of authoritative discourse by mainstream media. The study also reveals that these podcasts typically rely on humor, parody, and satire in delivering their messages to the audiences.

Shin, Wooyeol. "Being a Truth-teller Who Serves Only the Citizens: A Case Study of Newstapa." *Journalism* 16, no. 5 (2015): 688–704. doi: 10.1177/1464884914525565.

This journal article, which has been expanded into Shin's PhD dissertation (ProQuest ID: 1835113538), chronicles ways the online citizen-participatory news outlet Newstapa in Korea has transformed the traditional news media landscape. Shin concludes that Newstapa has challenged established mainstream broadcast news media and prompted Korean journalists to work closely with ordinary citizens by encouraging them to participate in the newsgathering and producing processes.

Song, Yonghoi. "Internet News Media and Issue Development: A Case Study on the Roles of Independent Online News Services as Agenda-Builders for Anti-US Protests in South Korea." *New Media and Society* 9, no. 1 (2007): 71–92. doi: 10.1177/1461444807072222.

Song examines the agenda-setting potential of online news media in Korea by comparing online and traditional news coverage of the 2002 deaths of two Korean schoolgirls who were run over by a U.S. military vehicle. Song concludes that, through their choice of alternative sources to those cited in conservative, mainstream media, online news media contributed to anti-American sentiment after a U.S. military court found the drivers innocent of any crime.

You, Kyung Han, Seoyeon Allison Lee, Jeong Kyu Lee, and Hyunjin Kang. "Why Read Online News? The Structural Relationship among Motivations, Behaviors, and Consumption in South Korea." *Information, Communication & Society* 16, no. 10 (2013): 1574–1595. doi: 10.1080/1369118X.2012.724435.

This study measures the effects that motivations for reading online news had on more than 800 online users in Korea. The authors find that the users' motivations are closely associated with in-depth reading, which leads to the actual use of the online news knowledge.

Social Media and Journalism

Cho, Seong Eun, and Dong-Hee Shin. "Media Discourse in a Hyper-Connected Society: A Comparison between Media Frame and Twitter Discourse during Media Strike." *Info* 16, no. 2 (2014): 67–79. doi: 10.1108/info-02-2013-0004.

This study argues that traditional news media in Korea tend to report media labor union strikes superficially with a neutral tone, while Twitter represents the media workers' arguments and demands more positively. The authors suggest the changing media environment has reinforced partiality of news in both traditional and alternative media.

Hahn, Kyu S., Seungjin Ryu, and Sungjin Park. "Fragmentation in the Twitter Following of News Outlets: The Representation of South Korean Users' Ideological and Generational Cleavage." *Journalism & Mass Communication Quarterly* 92, no. 1 (2015): 56–76. doi: 10.1177/1077699014559499.

In a survey of 1,811 respondents in Korea and analysis of more than 700,000 Twitter co-following patterns, this study finds that partisan and generational selectivity polarizes news following on Twitter. The authors suggest that Twitter is likely to reinforce existing political divisions in society by reducing the likelihood of chance encounters with disagreeable views.

Kim, Yonghwan. "Understanding J-blog Adoption: Factors Influencing Korean Journalists' Blog Adoption." *Asian Journal of Communication* 21, no. 1 (2011): 25–46. doi: 10.1080/01292986.2010.524229.

In exploring factors affecting journalists' adoption of weblogs in Korea, this study finds that organizational and social pressures have a greater influence than personal and psychological reasons on journalists' decisions to adopt and continue their j-blogs.

Kim, Yonghwan, Youngju Kim, Yuan Wang, and Na Yeon Lee. "Uses and Gratifications, Journalists' Twitter Use, and Relational Satisfaction with the Public." *Journal of Broadcasting & Electronic Media* 60, no. 3 (2016): 503–526. doi: 10.1080/08838 151.2016.1164171.

Through a survey of Korean journalists, this study revealed that journalists' motivations for Twitter use are positively related to their job-related activities on Twitter (e.g., posting/sharing their news and interacting with audience), which consequently influences perceived relational satisfaction with the public.

Lee, Na Yeon, and Younghwan Kim. "The Spiral of Silence and Journalists' Outspokenness on Twitter." *Asian Journal of Communication* 24, no. 3 (2014): 262–278. doi: 10.1080/01292986.2014.885536.

Twitter can serve as a public sphere when journalists speak up about politically controversial issues? That's the conclusion of this study, based on a survey of 118 Korean journalists from nine newspapers and two network television stations. They also find that journalists who are politically conservative are less likely than politically liberal journalists to discuss their opinions on Twitter. The authors conclude that journalists' ideology is a significant factor in expressing their opinions on Twitter in South Korea.

Lee, Na Yeon, Yonghwan Kim, and Jiwon Kim. "Tweeting Public Affairs or Personal Affairs? Journalists' Tweets, Interactivity, and Ideology." *Journalism* 17, no. 7 (2016): 845–864. doi: 10.1177/1464884915585954.

By combining a content analysis and a survey with Korean journalists, this study examines to what extent journalists talk about public affairs on Twitter and interact with others. The authors find that more than 60 percent of the tweets were topics related to public affairs and more than half were related to journalists' interaction with the public. The study also finds that Twitter use is closely related to journalists' political ideology and that journalists from liberal newspapers are more likely to interact with their readers on Twitter.

Public Controversies and Political Outrage

Cho, SeungHo, and Sook-Yeong Hong. "Journalists' Evaluation of the South Korean Government's Crisis Management in the *Cheonan* Incident." *Journal of Contingencies & Crisis Management* 24, no. 4 (2016): 221–229. doi: 10.1111/1468–5973.12117.

This study considers ways journalists judge and react to the withholding of information by the Korean government during the sinking of the naval vessel *Cheonan* in 2010. Using depth-interviews with 11 journalists who covered the incident, the authors find that all journalists believe that the government mismanaged information about the cause of the sinking. Half of the journalists were critical of the government's restrictive information policy during the crisis, while the other half considered it to be in the best interest of national security.

Durham, Frank D., and John C. Carpenter. "The Face of Multiculturalism in South Korea: Media Ritual as Framing in News Coverage of Jasmine Lee." *Journalism* 16, No. 8 (2015): 975–992. doi: 10.1177/1464884914550137.

Intersections of the government's multicultural policy and processes of media framing in the appointment of Jasmine Lee, a naturalized Korean citizen, to the National Assembly are the foundation of this study. Using Turner's social drama theory, analysis traces coverage through the stages of breach, crisis, redress and reintegration, finding that the press ultimately defines multiculturalism in Korea in assimilationist terms according to the domestic cultural status quo.

Kwak, Nojin. "The Roles of the Media and Mediated Opinion Leadership in the Public Opinion Process." *International Communication Gazette* 61, no. 2 (1999): 175–191. doi: 10.1177/0016549299061002005.

Kwak analyzes newspaper content regarding the government's decision to prosecute two ex-presidents responsible for the Kwangju massacre in Korea. The prosecution was a reversal from the government's initial policy position and reflected popular demands. By comparing news coverage of the mainstream *Chosun Ilbo* and alternative *Hankyoreh Shinmun*, the author concludes that the alternative newspaper produced a greater variety of information and presented opinions that supported public positions.

Lee, Sangwon, and Jihyun Esther Paik. "How Partisan Newspapers Represented a Pandemic: The Case of the Middle East Respiratory Syndrome in South Korea." *Asian Journal of Communication* 27, no. 1 (2017): 82–96. doi: 10.1080/0129298 6.2016.1235592.

This study documents news framing of the Middle East Respiratory Syndrome (MERS) pandemic at two partisan Korean newspapers. In a content analysis of news stories, the authors find that the left-wing progressive *Hankyoreh Shinmun* placed more emphasis on attributing responsibility to the government and society, while the right-wing conservative *Chosun Ilbo* attributed responsibility to the individuals affected by the disease.

Shin, Wooyeol. "Conservative Journalists' Myth-Making in South Korea: Use of the Past in News Coverage of the 2008 Korean Candlelight Vigil." *Asian Studies Review* 40, no. 1 (2016): 120–136. doi: 10.1080/10357823.2015.1126221.

A study of how three Korean newspapers covered the 2008 candlelight vigil protesting a beef import deal with the United States concludes that journalists emphasized "anti-U.S.," "leftist-led," and violent images from past protests. This provided a means to construct revisionist rhetoric and language in reporting the latest candlelight vigils.

You, Myoungsoon, and Youngkee Ju. "The Influence of Outrage Factors on Journalists' Gatekeeping of Health Risks." *Journalism & Mass Communication Quarterly* 92, no. 4 (2015): 959–969. doi: 10.1177/1077699015596339.

In a survey of 200 Korean journalists, this study finds that journalists' perceptions of the "outrage factors" posed by health risks are influential in their determining newsworthiness across the five public health hazards under investigation.

Chapter 4

Communication and Technology

Namkee Park, Seungyoon Lee, and Jae Eun Chung

Our Communication and Technology chapter covers the past few decades' studies in English on communication and technology in South Korea. Communication and technology as a topic for research is encompassing for two reasons: (1) an ongoing advancement in communication technology encourages communication researchers to keep up with the technologies' role, effects, and implications in society, and (2) the boundaries of communication technology range from the ancient time's rudimentary drawings and characters to today's smartphones and social media.[1] Hence, the theories on communication technologies are diverse, and the methods employed to develop and test the theories are multifaceted. For our focused discussion, communication technology can be broadly defined as any technological or electronic system of communication among individuals and groups or between individuals and groups.[2]

The study of communication and technology in Korea is relatively recent and oriented toward electronic media. It has blossomed since the late 1980s and the early 1990s, when an array of new technologies such as cable or satellite television were introduced and diffused. Shortly afterward, the Internet, which has tremendously transformed our daily life, has ignited the study of communication technology both in its quantity and diversity. Moreover, the rapid development of the Internet infrastructure and accompanying Web 2.0 applications has facilitated numerous empirical studies.[3]

---

1. Namkee Park, "Communication and Technology," in *Korean Communication, Media, and Culture*, ed. Dal Yong Jin and Nojin Kwak, 153–172 (Lanham, MD: Lexington Books, 2018).
2. Park, "Communication and Technology."
3. Oh Myung and James Larson, *Digital Development in Korea: Building an Information Society* (New York: Routledge, 2011).

It is interesting to note that the number of Koreans who studied in the United States had significantly increased since the middle of the 1990s, when new communication technologies were dramatically developed. Many of those U.S.-educated scholars in Korea and abroad started researching communication technology relating to Korea, and they published their research as books, journal articles, and conference papers in English. Since the late 1990s, voluminous studies have appeared in major international scholarly journals.

The following criteria and methods have informed our selection of English-language studies on Korean communication and technology.

First, we have searched Google Scholar for studies published in communication-related English journals. We have used the following search terms in combination with the keyword *Korea*: *communication technology, Internet communication, online communication, mobile communication, social network site communication, computer-mediated communication, human-computer interaction, communication policy,* and *technology policy.*

Second, we have first selected specific *scholarly* journals and then searched for all studies that have included the keyword *Korea*. We have narrowed the search to the articles focusing on the Korean context. A total of 12 journals have been selected.[4]

Finally, we have paid attention to books published in English by searching through the keywords *communication* and *Korea* in Google Books and Amazon Books. We have chosen the books dealing with the key themes of this chapter.

Through this keyword search process, we have identified 97 journal articles, two books, seven book chapters, and one doctoral dissertation that are worthy enough for inclusion in our chapter.[5]

AN OVERVIEW

The selected communication and technology studies have been divided into nine subareas:

---

4. These journals selected for our chapter include: *Journal of Communication; Communication Research; Human Communication Research; Communication Theory; Journal of Computer-Mediated Communication; New Media and Society; Computers in Human Behavior; Cyberpsychology, Behavior, and Social Networking; International Journal of Human-Computer Interaction; International Journal of Human-Computer Studies; Telecommunications Policy;* and *Asian Journal of Communication.*

5. Korean scholars have written voluminous studies of communication and technology in English. If their studies do not relate to the Korean context or use a Korean sample as study participants, however, we have not included them in our bibliography.

- user studies (15);
- technology diffusion and acceptance (13);
- computer-mediated communication (17);
- human-computer interaction (9);
- mobile communication (7);
- technology use and political participation (18),
- game studies (7),
- technology addiction and problematic use (11), and
- and communication technology policy and economics (10).

As indicated by the number in the parentheses, the subrea of technology use and political communication stands out from other areas for research. It is followed by those about computer-mediated communication, user studies, and technology diffusion and acceptance. It is especially noteworthy that the majority of communication and technology studies center on the socio-psychological aspects of communication technology.

Numerous English-language studies on social psychological analyses of communication technology have focused on variables like personality traits of Big-Five Factors,[6] belongingness, life satisfaction, self-efficacy, social norms, subjective well-being, ethical orientations, and parasocial interaction. These studies have investigated the socio-psychological antecedents for the use of communication technologies, including the Internet, electronic bulletin boards, social networking sites (SNSs), and smartphones, as well as consequences from the use. Likewise, those on computer-mediated communication have examined the role of socio-psychological variables relating to communication technology, for example, social comparison orientations, perceived self, self-construal, self-consciousness, and their effects on self-presentation. Similarly, studies on human-computer interaction have more often revolved around technology-centered concepts, such as interactivity, social presence, transportability, screen size, and presentation mode, and their impacts on technology use or satisfaction.

Another line of research in English has centered on diffusion and adoption of new communication technologies. The continuous development of new technologies since the late 1980s has led a number of studies to examine various factors that affect adoption and use. These studies have investigated a wide range of socio-psychological antecedents that account for specific communication technology's adoption and use in Korea, the global leader in communication technology use and information infrastructure.[7] Notably,

---

6. Big-Five personality traits are openness, conscientiousness, extraversion, agreeableness, and neuroticism.
7. Oh and Larson. *Digital Development in Korea.*

however, a significant number of studies in this area of research have drawn on the technology acceptance model (TAM) or its extensions as a theoretical framework.

Countless studies in English on Korean communication technologies have highlighted the role of communication technology in the process of political participation and civic engagement in Korean society. These studies have examined the impacts of new communication technologies such as the Internet, mobile devices, and SNSs on technology users' political attitudes, public opinion formation, engagement, and participation. Furthermore, this type of research has paid attention to social capital and its contributions to participatory democracy in a liberalized Korea since the mid-1980s.[8]

Communication technologies do not necessarily bring positive effects to Koreans. Scores of studies have concentrated on the negative aspects of new communication technologies, including depressive symptoms, cyberbullying, and addiction. Those studies on addiction occupy the largest portion, since the continuous introduction of new technologies has the possibility of attracting users who are psychologically vulnerable. Among such technologies and devices are the Internet, computer/online games, mobile/smartphones, and SNSs. In addition, the issues of cyberbullying and privacy infringement have received particular attention. The effect of computer/online games on game players' aggressiveness was also constantly examined as a hot topic on television and radio.[9] From a broader sociological perspective, the issue of digital divide in Korea has been noted by some scholars, particularly during the late 1990s and the early 2000s.[10] Whereas the early years' studies on digital divide primarily examined the disparity issue of Internet access, the emphasis has recently shifted to the digital divide in the use of SNSs.[11]

A considerable number of studies address policy and economic issues, which has been a relatively minor area in communication. This can be attributed to the participation by scholars in law, public administration, and economics in researching communication and technology. These non-communication scholars were interested in the role of government and its intervention in the emerging new media industries, political and economic

---

8. Hoon Lee et al., "Mobile Communication and Political Participation in South Korea: Examining the Intersections between Informational and Relational Uses," *Computers in Human Behavior* 38 (2014): 85–92.

9. Ki Joon Kim and S. Shyam Sundar, "Can Interface Features Affect Aggression Resulting from Violent Video Game Play? An Examination of Realistic Controller and Large Screen-Size," *Cyberpsychology, Behavior, and Social Networking* 16, no. 5 (2013): 329–334.

10. Joo-Seong Hwang, "Digital Divide in Internet Use within the Urban Hierarchy: The Case of South Korea," *Urban Geography* 25, no. 4 (2004): 372–389.

11. Yoosun Hwang and Namkee Park, "Digital Divide in Social Networking Sites," *International Journal of Mobile Communications* 11, no. 5 (2013): 446–464.

forces affecting the market structure, and the interplay among various stakeholders.[12]

Furthermore, considering the unique history of Korea, where bureaucrats and technocrats have been deeply involved in their country's industrialization and liberalization,[13] the crucial role of government officials in the information and communication sector and their impact on the construction of the industry landscape do not come as a surprise. Thus, the research on policy and economics covers a broad spectrum, ranging from the Internet infrastructure, Internet standardization, broadband Internet to the convergence of telecommunication, broadcasting, and Internet services.

CONTRIBUTIONS AND FUTURE DIRECTIONS

The study of communication and technology in Korea since the 1990s has contributed to the overall growth of communication research.[14] With the rapid innovation and wide diffusion of communication technologies in Korea, English-language studies based on Korean data offered reflection on, and implications from, various technologies in their relatively early stages. Accompanying social problems such as addiction and bullying in Korea have also provided an outlook for the future. In addition, with studies of communication technology use, as they are closely linked to issues in political communication (e.g., diffusion of protests), health communication (e.g., addiction and well-being), and journalism (e.g., agenda-setting and framing) in Korean society, the amassed number of studies on communication and technology have facilitated conceptual exploration and theoretical explications in other disciplines. While these contributions should deserve their due global recognition, there is room for further growth in several aspects.[15]

First, most studies in English on Korean communication and technology are limited to quantitative methods and analyses. Studies of the sociopsychological features of communication and technology use methods such as experiments and surveys, and consequently, statistical analyses are employed to derive findings. In the future, however, qualitative methods and mixed-methods would enable scholars and readers to explain in depth the unique ways in which Korea's communication technology has been evolving.

---

12. See James F. Larson and Jaemin Park, "From Developmental to Network State: Government Restructuring and ICT-led Innovation in Korea," *Telecommunications Policy* 38, no. 4 (2014): 1–16.

13. Jyoti Choudrie and Heejin Lee, "Broadband Development in South Korea: Institutional and Cultural Factors," *European Journal of Information Systems* 13, no. 2 (2004): 103–114.

14. Park, "Communication and Technology."

15. Park, "Communication and Technology."

Second, more effort needs to be put to translating the increase in the number of English-language studies into theoretical progress. The relatively short history of the scope and diversity of subareas has led numerous studies to explore a variety of concepts, characteristics, and impacts related to communication technologies. As paradoxical as it may seem, however, few theoretical models or theories have originated from these studies. Although the communication technology landscape is rapidly evolving in Korea, communication scholars ought to theorize broader issues observed across various platforms and technologies that could inform our fundamental understanding of human communication and technologies. An unending replication and reproduction of research using the same theoretical models or an atheoretical approach should be cautioned against.

Third, comparative studies in English of Korea and the Unites States that take advantage of a relatively easy data access should be reassessed. The number of data-collection sites itself does not automatically contribute to a theoretical development. Furthermore, a simple comparison of technology use with speculations about cultural differences across the two countries offers limited insights on their implications. The value of comparative studies could be enhanced only by their convincing theoretical framework.

Finally, the study of communication and technology is expected to flourish with many publications in books and academic journals in English, since many Korean and non-Korean scholars in communication are paying discerning attention to the emerging technologies, including big data platforms and applications, virtual reality (VR), augmented reality (AR), or artificial intelligence (AI).[16]

Korea has been one of the leading countries in exploring the potentials and consequences of these new technologies. The communication and technology research in English has always been a frontrunner to discover new research fields and pave the way for later studies globally. Considering the rapidly changing technology environment, English-language publications on communication and technology will most likely play a key role in inviting next-generation studies that will delineate new theoretical concepts and models.

ANNOTATED BIBLIOGRAPHY

User Studies

Bae, Hyuhn-Suhck, and Byoungkwan Lee. "Audience Involvement and Its Antecedents: An Analysis of the Electronic Bulletin Board Messages about

---

16. Steve Jones, "People, Things, Memory and Human-Machine Communication," *International Journal of Media and Cultural Politics* 10 (2014): 245–258.

an Entertainment-Education Drama on Divorce in Korea." *Asian Journal of Communication* 14, no. 1 (2004): 6–21. https://doi.org/10.1080/01292980420001 95125.

Through content analysis of electronic bulletin board messages about an entertainment-education (EE) program in Korea, Bae and Lee find two antecedents—episode topic and issue controversy—to be associated with audience involvement with media content. Their study has implications regarding how EE can be effectively designed and can utilize program websites.

Choi, Yong Jun, and Mazharul Haque. "Internet Use Patterns and Motivations of Koreans." *Asian Journal of Communication* 12, no. 1 (2002): 126–140. https://doi.org/10.1080/01292980209364817.

Choi and Haque offer a glimpse into the motivations and patterns of Internet use in Korea in its early stages. Entertainment, sexuality, online transaction, and social interaction are correlated with Koreans' Internet use. In addition, the authors also pay attention to traditional media use, noting the negative correlations between Internet use and TV viewing.

Chung, Byung Do, Jae Heon Park, Yoon Jeon Koh, and Sangwon Lee. "User Satisfaction and Retention of Mobile Telecommunications Services in Korea." *International Journal of Human–Computer Interaction* 32, no. 7 (2016): 532–543. doi: https://doi.org/10.1080/10447318.2016.1179083.

Smartphone users in Korea are segmented according to two key factors underlying the perceived benefits from mobile services—basic services and functions as well as cost and monetary benefits from mobile service providers. User demographics are considered in the segmentation to understand which aspects of mobile services are important for each segment's overall satisfaction.

Hwang, Joo-Seong. "Digital Divide in Internet Use within the Urban Hierarchy: The Case of South Korea." *Urban Geography* 25, no. 4 (2004): 372–389. https://doi.org/10.2747/0272–3638.25.4.372.

The digital divide of the Internet use from a geographical perspective is explored. It is found that meaningful use of the Internet divides the urban hierarchy in Korea into two layers, Seoul and other areas. Also, the regional setting plays a significant role in explaining how to determine the variation of engagement rates.

Hwang, Yoosun, and Namkee Park. "Digital Divide in Social Networking Sites." *International Journal of Mobile Communications* 11 no. 5 (2013): 446–464. https://doi.org/10.1504/IJMC.2013.056955.

The effects of demographic variables on the use of social networking sites (SNSs) and SNS users' Internet skills to expand the scope of digital divide are investigated. Survey data collected from Korea show that for both SNS use and Internet skills, education, monthly income and smartphone use affect SNS use positively, whereas age affects negatively.

Kang, Seok, and Jaemin Jung. "Mobile Communication for Human Needs: A Comparison of Smartphone Use between the US and Korea." *Computers in Human Behavior* 35 (2014): 376–387. https://doi.org/10.1016/j.chb.2014.03.024.

The authors link smartphone basic needs, smartphone use, and life satisfaction based on samples of college students in the United States and Korea. Safety needs and self-actualization needs best account for smartphone use. Overall, the prevalent approach of utilizing individualistic versus collectivistic cultural dimension to explain media use may need to be reconsidered.

Kim, Hyondong, and Yang Woon Chung. "The Use of Social Networking Services and Their Relationship with the Big Five Personality Model and Job Satisfaction in Korea." *Cyberpsychology, Behavior, and Social Networking* 17, no. 10 (2014): 658–663. http://doi.org/10.1089/cyber.2014.0109.

Social networking service (SNS) use in Korea is found to be positively related to job satisfaction and also to moderate the association between Big Five personality traits and job satisfaction. Individuals with high extroversion show higher job satisfaction when they use SNS services. Further, individuals with low agreeableness, when they use SNS, have higher job satisfaction.

Kim, Yeolib, Daniel A. Briley, and Melissa G. Ocepek. "Differential Innovation of Smartphone and Application Use by Sociodemographics and Personality." *Computers in Human Behavior* 44 (2015): 141–147. https://doi.org/10.1016/j.chb.2014.11.059.

Moving beyond well-established findings on the role of sociodemographic characteristics on smartphone and application use, personality is worth considering. Findings from a representative Korean sample show that personality influences different patterns of use. For example, extraversion is associated with an increased relational application use, while conscientiousness is associated with a decreased use of e-commerce applications.

Lee, Sujin. "Analysis of College Students' Online Life-Styles and Their Psychological Profiles in South Korea." *Cyberpsychology, Behavior, and Social Networking* 13, no. 6 (2010): 701–704. https://doi.org/10.1089/cyber.2009.0443.

How can we better understand problematic Internet use? The authors examine individuals' level of cyber ethics based on their online lifestyle profile, Internet use patterns, and tendency toward Internet addiction among Korean college students. A segment of users labeled Individualistic Group (IG), which have higher sensation seeking and independence factors in terms of online experience, show the lowest level of cyber ethics.

Park, Cheol. "Hedonic and Utilitarian Values of Mobile Internet in Korea." *International Journal of Mobile Communications* 4, no. 5 (2006): 497–508. https://doi.org/10.1504/IJMC.2006.009256.

Two contrasting values related to mobile Internet use in Korea are studied. The hedonic value of mobile Internet is positively associated with the importance of use convenience and information quality, while negatively associated with service cost. The utilitarian value is positively associated with the importance of service cost and connection stability.

Park, Namkee, Hyun Sook Oh, and Naewon Kang. "Factors Influencing Intention to Upload Content on Wikipedia in South Korea: The Effects of Social Norms and Individual Differences." *Computers in Human Behavior* 28, no. 3 (2012): 898–905. https://doi.org/10.1016/j.chb.2011.12.010.

What are the factors that influence individuals' intention to voluntarily contribute content to Wikipedia? A study of Korean Wikipedia users shows that self-efficacy is positively associated with the intention for both users and non-users of Wikipedia. Individual attributes such as issue involvement and ego involvement are also important. The authors conclude that individual influences have a larger impact on individuals' contribution to Wikipedia than social influences do.

————. "Idiocentrism versus Allocentrism and Ethical Evaluations on Illegal Downloading Intention between the United States and South Korea." *Journal of Global Information Technology Management* 19, no. 4 (2016): 250–266. https://doi.org/10.1080/1097198X.2016.1246933.

The effects of the personality dimension of idiocentrism and allocentrism, individual experiences, and ethical evaluations on illegal downloading intention are explored. The study finds that the personal trait of self-reliance affects illegal downloading intention for U.S. students, while that of interdependence affects the intention of Korean students.

Sang, Yoonmo, Jeong-Ki Lee, Yeora Kim, and Hyung-Jin Woo. "Understanding the Intentions Behind Illegal Downloading: A Comparative Study of American and Korean College Students." *Telematics and Informatics* 32, no. 2 (2015): 333–343. https://doi.org/10.1016/j.tele.2014.09.007.

The factors that predict college students' intentions to download digital content through unauthorized peer-to-peer (P2P) file-sharing sites are examined. This study also explores how cultural contexts are related to those intentions among college students in the United States and Korea. The findings show that cultural differences may play an important role with respect to people's intentions to engage in illegal downloading.

Yoon, Kyongwon. "The Making of Neo-Confucian Cyberkids: Representations of Young Mobile Phone Users in South Korea." *New Media & Society* 8, no. 5 (2006): 753–771. https://doi.org/10.1177/1461444806067587.

Young mobile phone users are represented in popular discourses in various ways. By analyzing discourses shown in government policy documents, major newspapers, and advertisements in Korea, the author shows that there are concerns about young generations' mobile phone use and their vulnerability to global consumer culture and materialism.

You, Kyung Han, Seoyeon Allison Lee, Jeong Kyu Lee, and Hyunjin Kang. "Why Read Online News? The Structural Relationships among Motivations, Behaviors, and Consumption in South Korea." *Information, Communication & Society* 16, no. 10 (2013): 1574–1595. https://doi.org/10.1080/1369118X.2012.724435.

The motivations behind online news usage and their relationships with news consumption in Korea are analyzed. Three motivations including information-seeking, entertainment, and social utility are associated with in-depth online news reading behavior, which subsequently are associated with actual online news consumption.

Technology Diffusion and Acceptance

Ahn, Dohyun, and Dong-Hee Shin. "Differential Effect of Excitement versus Contentment, and Excitement Versus Relaxation: Examining the Influence of Positive Affects on Adoption of New Technology with a Korean Sample." *Computers in Human Behavior* 50 (2015): 283–290. https://doi.org/10.1016/j.chb.2015.03.072.

Users' cognitive and motivational factors in the adoption of new technology in Korea are examined. Users' interest and excitement are found to have positive associations with new technology adoption, while contentment and relaxation have negative associations.

Chun, Heasun, Hyunjoo Lee, and Daejoong Kim. "The Integrated Model of Smartphone Adoption: Hedonic and Utilitarian Value Perceptions of Smartphones among Korean College Students." *Cyberpsychology, Behavior, and Social Networking* 15, no. 9 (2012): 473–479. https://doi.org/10.1089/cyber.2012.0140.

An integrated model of smartphone adoption in Korea is suggested in incorporating social influences (SIs), perceived technicality, as well as hedonic and utilitarian attitudes. Users' attitudes and their intention are highly influenced by SI and positive self-image, while hedonic enjoyment is equally important as utilitarian usefulness in predicting the adoption intention.

Im, Yung-Ho, Eun-mee Kim, Kyungmo Kim, and Yeran Kim. "The Emerging Mediascape, Same Old Theories? A Case Study of Online News Diffusion in Korea." *New Media & Society* 13, no. 4 (2011): 605–625. https://doi. org/10.1177/1461444810377916.

The main ideas of traditional diffusion study are re-examined in the context of the Internet in Korea. Two news stories, one initiated by an established news organization and the other uploaded by an individual Internet user, are selected for a case study. The study finds that the original stories undergo transformations in terms of content and form over time in the diffusion process.

Joo, Jihyuk, and Yoonmo Sang. "Exploring Koreans' Smartphone Usage: An Integrated Model of the Technology Acceptance Model and Uses and Gratifications Theory." *Computers in Human Behavior* 29, no. 6 (2013): 2512–2518. https://doi. org/10.1016/j.chb.2013.06.002.

Two theoretical approaches, the technology acceptance model (TAM) and the uses and gratifications approach, are sought to be integrated, in order to look at adoption and use of smartphones among Koreans. The authors claim that to spread information system with innovative and active features, developers should pay attention to users' intrinsic motivations as well as to their extrinsic perceptions.

Kim, Ki Joon, and S. Shyam Sundar. "Does Screen Size Matter for Smartphones? Utilitarian and Hedonic Effects of Screen Size on Smartphone Adoption." *Cyberpsychology, Behavior, and Social Networking* 17, no. 7 (2014): 466–473. https://doi.org/10.1089/cyber.2013.0492.

The psychological effects of screen size on smartphone adoption in Korea are investigated. A large screen, compared with a small screen, is likely to lead to higher smartphone adoption by simultaneously promoting both the utilitarian and hedonic qualities of smartphones, which in turn positively influence perceived ease of use of—and attitude toward—the device, respectively.

Kwon, Hyosun Stella, and Laku Chidambaram. "A Cross-Cultural Study of Communication Technology Acceptance: Comparison of Cellular Phone Adoption in South Korea and the United States." *Journal of Global Information Technology Management* 1, no. 3 (1998): 43–58. https://doi.org/10.1080/10971 98X.1998.10856236.

Why and how are cellular phones adopted and used by people in two different cultures, the United States and Korea? The findings indicate that Korea has a smaller, but more active user base of cellular phone subscribers compared with the United States, which has a larger, but less active user base.

Kwon, Kyunghee Hazel, and Bum Soo Chon. "Social Influences on Terrestrial and Satellite Mobile-TV Adoption in Korea: Affiliation, Positive Self-Image, and Perceived Popularity." *International Journal on Media Management* 11, no. 2 (2009): 49–60. https://doi.org/10.1080/14241270902756419.

The association between the social influence, adopters' individual factors, and the adoption of two different forms of mobile TV, terrestrial and satellite in Korea, is examined. Three dimensions of social influences, defined respectively as "affiliation," "positive self-display," and "perceived popularity," are identified. These three social influences differ in degree in relation to the adopters' demographic characteristics and innovativeness.

Lee, Sungjoon. "An Integrated Adoption Model for E-Books in a Mobile Environment: Evidence from South Korea." *Telematics and Informatics* 30, no. 2 (2013): 165–176. https://doi.org/10.1016/j.tele.2012.01.006.

Given that adoption of mobile e-book systems is relatively retarded in Korea, the factors that facilitate its adoption need to be examined. Individual innovativeness are found to have a significant influence on perceived usefulness and perceived ease of use. In addition, both perceived usefulness and perceived ease of use affect not only intention to use but also the innovation resistance.

Lee, Hyunjoo, Daejoong Kim, Jungho Ryu, and Sungjoon Lee. "Acceptance and Rejection of Mobile TV among Young Adults: A Case of College Students in South Korea." *Telematics and Informatics* 28, no. 4 (2011): 239–250. https://doi.org/10.1016/j.tele.2010.04.002.

What are the factors influencing Korean young people's mobile TV adoption behaviors ranging from non- and discontinuous to actual adoption? The study indicates that information needs and newspaper reading are negatively associated with mobile TV adoption, while entertainment needs are a significant positive predictor of the adoption likelihood.

Nam, Yoonjae, and George A. Barnett. "Communication Media Diffusion and Substitutions: Longitudinal Trends from 1980 to 2005 in Korea." *New Media & Society* 12, no. 7 (2010): 1137–1155. https://doi.org/10.1177/1461444809356334.

Longitudinal trends in Korean use of eight communication technologies are analyzed in order to examine the media's displacement or supplementary effects. The results indicate that international mail, domestic telephone and telex can be best described by a quadratic, suggesting that they are undergoing non-adoption, while the trends for domestic mail and international telephone calls show exponential growth.

Park, Namkee, Yong-Chan Kim, Hae Young Shon, and Hongjin Shim. "Factors Influencing Smartphone Use and Dependency in South Korea." *Computers in Human Behavior* 29, no. 4 (2013): 1763–1770. https://doi.org/10.1016/j.chb.2013.02.008.

The factors affecting the Korean people's use of smartphones are investigated. Results show that motivations and innovativeness affect the use of smartphones, while behavioral activation system (BAS) and locus of control demonstrate their unique contributions to explaining smartphone use.

Rhee, Kyung Yong, and Wang-Bae Kim "The Adoption and Use of the Internet in South Korea." *Journal of Computer-Mediated Communication* 9, no. 4 (2004). https://doi.org/10.1111/j.1083–6101.2004.tb00299.x.

The issue of adoption of the Internet and the digital divide in Korea is investigated. Socio-demographic factors, attitudes toward the Internet, social supports, and the influence that Internet access had on Korean people, are included for this study. The study finds that Internet adoption in Korea is influenced more by family support than by other characteristics.

Yu, Eun, Ahreum Hong, and Junseok Hwang. "A Socio-Technical Analysis of Factors Affecting the Adoption of Smart TV in Korea." *Computers in Human Behavior* 61 (2016): 89–102. https://doi.org/10.1016/j.chb.2016.02.099.

Three aspects related to smart TV in Korea are examined: (1) bundling as a market competition strategy, (2) services using technological features represented by N-screen, and (3) consumer attributes from the socio-technical perspective. Bundling by communications service providers is found to be a more effective strategy to keep market share away from new entrants.

Computer-Mediated Communication

Chang, Woo-Young, and Han Woo Park. "The Network Structure of the Korean Blogosphere." *Journal of Computer-Mediated Communication* 17, no. 2 (2012): 216–230. https://doi.org/10.1111/j.1083–6101.2011.01567.x.

Koreans' protests against U.S. beef imports are examined by deconstructing online dynamics of news diffusion between May and June 2008. Korean bloggers' political positions on U.S. beef imports were polarized, which ultimately influenced their network positions and the way news was diffused to them.

Choi, Jaz Hee-jeong. "Living in Cyworld: Contextualising Cy-Ties in South Korea." In *Uses of Blogs*, edited by Joanne Jacobs, 173–186. New York: Peter Lang, 2006.

A contextualization of Cyworld in Korean society is provided. The chapter shows that, Cyworld, whose number of members equated approximately to one quarter of the nation's entire population in the middle of 2000, clearly leads the blog league within Korea.

Ha, Young Wook, Jimin Kim, Christian Fernando Libaque-Saenz, Younghoon Chang, and Myeong-Cheol Park. "Use and Gratifications of Mobile SNSs: Facebook and KakaoTalk in Korea." *Telematics and Informatics* 32, no. 3 (2015): 425–438. https://doi.org/10.1016/j.tele.2014.10.006.

Gratifications driving mobile social network site (SNS) use in Korea are identified. Gratifications are divided into "obtained"—cognitive, hedonic, integrative, social interactive—and "opportunities"—mobile convenience. Social interactive gratification exerts a significant effect on all other gratifications-obtained variables, whereas mobile convenience has a significant impact on all other gratifications.

Hjorth, Larissa. "Cybercute politics: The Internet Cyworld and Gender Performativity in Korea." In *Media Consumption and Everyday Life in Asia,* edited by Youna Kim, 203–216. London: Routledge, 2008.

A discussion of how the conventional forms of gender performativity are being contested in a Korean social networking service, Cyworld, is provided. The chapter details the feminized practices that govern the presentation and upkeep of online identities in the online venue.

Ishii, Kenichi, and Morihiro Ogasahara. "Links between Real and Virtual Networks: A Comparative Study of Online Communities in Japan and Korea." *CyberPsychology & Behavior* 10, no. 2 (2007): 252–257. https://doi.org/10.1089/cpb.2006.9961.

The extent to which online communities affect real-world personal relations is explored based on a cross-cultural survey conducted in Japan and Korea. The study finds that Japanese users prefer more virtual-network-based online communities, while their Korean counterparts prefer real-group-based online communities.

Jang, Kyungeun, Namkee Park, and Hayeon Song. "Social Comparison on Facebook: Its Antecedents and Psychological Outcomes." *Computers in Human Behavior* 62 (2016): 147–154. https://doi.org/10.1016/j.chb.2016.03.082.

The associations among Facebook use, social comparison orientation on Facebook (SCOF), and psychological outcomes among Korean college students are examined. Also, the roles of self-esteem and impression management are explored as antecedents of SCOF. Facebook use are positively associated with perceived social support, yet it is not significantly associated with mental health.

Jung, Taejin, Hyunsook Youn, and Steven McClung. "Motivations and Self-Presentation Strategies on Korean-Based "Cyworld" Weblog Format Personal Homepages." *CyberPsychology & Behavior* 10, no. 1 (2007): 24–31. https://doi.org/10.1089/cpb.2006.9996.

Individuals' motives and interpersonal self-presentation strategies on constructing a Korean SNS, Cyworld mini-homepage, is examined. Entertainment and personal income factors are major predictors in explaining homepage maintenance expenditures and frequencies of updating.

Kang, Seok. "The Elderly Population and Community Engagement in the Republic of Korea: The Role of Community Storytelling Network." *Asian Journal of*

Communication 23, no. 3 (2013): 302–321. https://doi.org/10.1080/01292986.20 12.725176.

The associations among Korean elders' use of local media, connections to local organizations, communication with neighbors, length of residence, and homeownership, and their contributions to the development of neighborhood belonging, collective efficacy, and volunteering behaviors in the community, are examined. Korean elders who use media frequently, connect with local organizations, and have conversations with neighbors often are actively involved in neighborhood activities.

Khang, Hyoungkoo, and Irkwon Jeong. "Perceived Self and Behavioral Traits as Antecedents of an Online Empathic Experience and Prosocial Behavior: Evidence from South Korea." *Computers in Human Behavior* 64 (2016): 888–897. https://doi.org/10.1016/j.chb.2016.08.010.

Perceived self-traits and behavioral traits as antecedents of online empathic experiences and prosocial behavior are examined. In the Korean context, perceived self-traits are strongly associated with both empathic experiences and prosocial behavior. Further, bonding networking is positively associated with prosocial behavior, while bridging networking shows a negative association with prosocial behavior.

Kim, Yoojung, Dongyoung Sohn, and Sejung Marina Choi. "Cultural Difference in Motivations for Using Social Network Sites: A Comparative Study of American and Korean College Students." *Computers in Human Behavior* 27, no. 1 (2011): 365–372. https://doi.org/10.1016/j.chb.2010.08.015.

Cultural contexts are compared in shaping the use of communication technology. The study's findings suggest that Korean college students put more weight on obtaining social support from existing social relationships, while American counterparts place relatively greater emphasis on seeking entertainment.

Kim, Kyung-Hee, and Haejin Yun. "Cying for Me, Cying for Us: Relational Dialectics in a Korean Social Network Site." *Journal of Computer-Mediated Communication* 13, no. 1 (2007): 298–318. https://doi.org/10.1111/j.1083–6101.2007.00397.x.

A relational dialectics approach to gain insights into the nature of relational communication via Cyworld, a Korean social networking service, is utilized. Qualitative analysis of in-depth interview data from 49 Korean users suggests that Cyworld users routinely negotiate multiple dialectical tensions that are created within the online world, transferred from face-to-face contexts, or imposed by interpersonal principles that relate to Korea's collectivistic culture.

Lee, Dong-Hoo. "Smartphones, Mobile Social Space, and New Sociality in Korea." *Mobile Media & Communication* 1, no. 3 (2013): 269–284. https://doi.org/10.1177/2050157913486790.

The emerging mobile communication practices in Korea that resulted from smartphones are examined. The study pays particular attention to the use of Twitter via smartphones. Based on qualitative interview data, the author discusses how mobile social media forms a pseudo-aural space for volatile but self-expediential social networks and how it shapes a new sociality.

Lee, Gyudong, Jaeeun Lee, and Soonjae Kwon. "Use of Social-Networking Sites and Subjective Well-Being: A Study in South Korea." *Cyberpsychology, Behavior, and Social Networking* 14, no. 3 (2010): 151–155. https://doi.org/10.1089/cyber.2009.0382.

The use of SNSs and users' subjective well-being in Korea are investigated. The results demonstrate that the amount of self-disclosure on SNSs is positively associated with subjective well-being. In addition, an individual's socioeconomic status is negatively associated with self-disclosing behavior.

Lee-Won, Roselyn J., Minsun Shim, Yeon Kyoung Joo, and Sung Gwan Park. "Who Puts the Best 'Face' Forward on Facebook?: Positive Self-Presentation in Online Social Networking and the Role of Self-Consciousness, Actual-to-Total Friends Ratio, and Culture." *Computers in Human Behavior* 39 (2014): 413–423. https://doi.org/10.1016/j.chb.2014.08.007.

How do individual, interpersonal, and cultural variables influence positive self-presentation in online social networking in Korea? Self-consciousness and actual-to-total "friends" ratio are not significantly associated with positive self-presentation on Facebook; however, culture shows a significant association with positive self-presentation on Facebook.

Park, Namsu, and Hyunjoo Lee. "Social Implications of Smartphone Use: Korean College Students' Smartphone Use and Psychological Well-Being." *Cyberpsychology, Behavior, and Social Networking* 15, no. 9 (2012): 491–497. https://doi.org/10.1089/cyber.2011.0580.

The association between motives of smartphone use, social relation, and psychological well-being among Korean college students is explored. The motives of smartphone use are positively associated with bonding relations but negatively associated with bridging relations. The results also indicate that needs for caring for others are negatively associated with loneliness and depression and positively associated with self-esteem.

Shim, Minsun, Min Ju Lee, and Sang Hee Park. "Photograph Use on Social Network Sites among South Korean College Students: The Role of Public and Private Self-Consciousness." *CyberPsychology & Behavior* 11, no. 4 (2008): 489–493. https://doi.org/10.1089/cpb.2007.0104.

Individual differences in photo use on social network sites (SNSs) among Korean college students are examined. Findings suggest that public self-consciousness is positively associated with the higher frequency of posting photos, replying to comments on the photos, and scrapping photos on their mini-homepages. The frequency of posting photos is also determined by participants' public self-consciousness but not by private self-consciousness.

Shim, Minsun, Roselyn J. Lee-Won, and Sang Hee Park. "The Self on the Net: The Joint Effect of Self-Construal and Public Self-Consciousness on Positive Self-Presentation in Online Social Networking among South Korean College Students." *Computers in Human Behavior* 63 (2016): 530–539. https://doi.org/10.1016/j.chb.2016.05.054.

How do self-construal and public self-consciousness jointly influence positive self-presentation in online social networking among Korean college students? The negative association between interdependent self-construal and positive self-presentation on Facebook is significant among those low in public self-consciousness; the association becomes less prominent for those higher in public self-consciousness.

Human-Computer Interaction

Kim, Ki Joon, Eunil Park, and S. Shyam Sundar. "Caregiving Role in Human–Robot Interaction: A Study of the Mediating Effects of Perceived Benefit and Social Presence." *Computers in Human Behavior* 29, no. 4 (2013): 1799–1806. https://doi.org/10.1016/j.chb.2013.02.009.

Whether assigning a caregiving role to a robot or to its human interactant has psychological effects on the quality of human–robot interaction (HRI) is examined. Using a Korean sample, the study finds that being a recipient of caregiving acts leads users to form more positive perceptions of the robot than being an ostensible caregiver to the robot.

Kim, Ki Joon, and S. Shyam Sundar. "Can Interface Features Affect Aggression Resulting from Violent Video Game Play? An Examination of Realistic Controller and Large Screen-Size." *Cyberpsychology, Behavior, and Social Networking* 16, no. 5 (2013): 329–334. https://doi.org/10.1089/cyber.2012.0500.

Guided by the General Aggression Model (GAM), the authors examine the controller type (gun replica vs. mouse) and screen size (large vs. small) as key technological aspects, with spatial presence and arousal as potential mediators. Results from a Korean sample show that a realistic controller and a large-screen display induce greater aggression, presence, and arousal. Contrary to GAM, however, arousal shows no effects on aggression.

———. "Mobile Persuasion: Can Screen Size and Presentation Mode Make a Difference to Trust?" *Human Communication Research* 42, no. 1 (2016): 45–70. https://doi.org/10.1111/hcre.12064.

The extent to which variations in screen size (large vs. small) and presentation mode (video vs. text) contribute to user perceptions of media content on their smartphones in the Korean context is explored. Results indicate that large screen size and video mode promote heuristic processing, while small screen size and text mode encourage systematic processing.

Lee, Kwan Min, Eui Jun Jeong, Namkee Park, and Seoungho Ryu. "Effects of Interactivity in Educational Games: A Mediating Role of Social Presence on Learning Outcomes." *International Journal of Human-Computer Interaction* 27 no. 7 (2011): 620–633. https://doi.org/10.1080/10447318.2011.555302.

The effects of networked interactivity on game users' learning outcomes among Korean college students are tested by comparing three groups (online educational quiz game vs. off-line educational quiz game vs. traditional classroom lecture). Networked interactivity in the online educational quiz game condition enhances game users' positive evaluation of learning, test performance, and feelings of social presence. However, there is no significant difference between the off-line educational quiz game and the lecture-based conditions.

Lee, Eun-Ju, and Soo Yun Shin. "Are They Talking to Me? Cognitive and Affective Effects of Interactivity in Politicians' Twitter Communication." *Cyberpsychology, Behavior, and Social Networking* 15, no. 10 (2012): 515–520. https://doi.org/10.1089/cyber.2012.0228.

When and how does the level of interactivity in politicians' Twitter communication affect the public's cognitive and affective reactions in the Korean context? Exposure to the high-interactivity Twitter page induces a stronger sense of direct conversation with the politician, but only among less affiliative participants who usually avoid social interaction.

———. "When the Medium Is the Message: How Transportability Moderates the Effects of Politicians' Twitter Communication." *Communication Research* 41, no. 8 (2014): 1088–1110. https://doi.org/10.1177/0093650212466407.

Whether exposure to a high profile politician's Twitter page (vs. newspaper interview) affects the participants' evaluations of him and his policies in the Korean context is examined. Exposure to the politician's Twitter page heightens the sense of direct conversation with him (i.e., social presence), which in turn induces more favorable impressions of and a stronger intention to vote for him.

Park, Han Woo, Chun-Sik Kim, and George A. Barnett. "Socio-Communicational Structure among Political Actors on the Web in South Korea: The Dynamics of Digital Presence in Cyberspace." *New Media & Society* 6, no. 3 (2004): 403–423. https://doi.org/10.1177/1461444804042522.

The structure of the socio-communication network among Korean political parties and politicians on the World Wide Web is explored. Also, the study looks into how the structure changed over the last two years. The network became denser, more highly integrated, centralized, and interactive over time. It indicates an increased use of World Wide Web for political discourse in Korea.

Sams, Steven, and Han Woo Park. "The Presence of Hyperlinks on Social Network Sites: A Case Study of Cyworld in Korea." *Journal of Computer-Mediated Communication* 19, no. 2 (2014): 294–307. https://doi.org/10.1111/jcc4.12053.

The extent to which hyperlinks appear within user-submitted comments on Korean social network service Cyworld is examined. Links to social movements are common as is news stories regarding the bleak economic forecast. The findings show the ways in which the presence of hyperlinks and short messages within online dialogs provides an insight into public perception as a whole.

Shin, Dong-Hee, Yongsuk Hwang, and Hyunseung Choo. "Smart TV: Are They Really Smart in Interacting with People? Understanding the Interactivity of Korean Smart TV." *Behaviour & Information Technology* 32, no. 2 (2013): 156–172. https://doi.org/10.1080/0144929X.2011.603360.

The effects of perceived interactivity on the motivations and attitudes toward smart TV in Korea are examined. Further, the mediating roles of perceived interactivity in the effect of performance on attitude toward smart TV are investigated. The findings provide practical insights into how to develop a user-centered smart TV interface.

Mobile Communication

Hjorth, Larissa. "Being Real in the Mobile Reel: A Case Study on Convergent Mobile Media as Domesticated New Media in Seoul." *Convergence: The International Journal of Research into New Media Technologies* 14, no. 1 (2008): 91–104. https://doi.org/10.1177/1354856507084421.

The rise of mobile communication studies and the role of locality in Seoul, one of the mobile innovation centers in Korea, are discussed. It also touches on the role of mobile media as a domestic new medium in Korea.

Joo, Nam-Seok, and Bom-Taeck Kim. "Mobile Phone Short Message Service Messaging for Behavior Modification in a Community-Based Control Programme in Korea." *Journal of Telemedicine and Telecare* 13, no. 8 (2007): 416–420.

A community-based anti-obesity program using mobile phone short message service (SMS) messaging is assessed. A total of 927 Korean participants are recruited and visit a public health center for initial assessment. Findings show that SMS messaging may be an effective method of behavior modification in weight control and anti-obesity health education programs when promoted by community health centers.

Kim, Shin Dong. "Korea: Personal Meanings." In *Perpetual Contact: Mobile Communication, Private Talk, Public Performance*, edited by James E. Katz and Mark A. Aakhus, 63–79. New York: Cambridge University Press, 2002.

The unique social and cultural conditions in Korea that accelerated the speed and range of mobile phone diffusion are explored. Based on observations and some statistical evidence, the author suggests that hierarchical and collective characteristics facilitated the conditions for fast diffusion of the technology.

Kim, Hyo, Gwang Jae Kim, Han Woo Park, and Ronald E. Rice, R. E. "Configurations of Relationships in Different Media: FtF, Email, Instant Messenger, Mobile Phone, and SMS." *Journal of Computer-Mediated Communication* 12, no. 4 (2007): 1183–1207. https://doi.org/10.1111/j.1083–6101.2007.00369.

The configurations of communication relationships in Korea through face-to-face, email, instant messaging (IM), mobile phone, and short message service (SMS), are analyzed. IM, SMS, and mobile phone are distinctive media for students, mobile phone for homeworkers, and email for organizational workers. Moreover, mobile phones tend to be used in reinforcing strong social ties.

Lee, Seoyeon, and S. Shyam Sundar. "Cosmetic Customization of Mobile Phones: Cultural Antecedents, Psychological Correlates." *Media Psychology* 18, no. 1 (2015): 1–23. https://doi.org/10.1080/15213269.2013.853618.

A Korea–U.S. comparison survey examines the degree to which aspects of cultural psychology predict aesthetic motivations for mobile-phone customization. Culture predicts other-directedness, which is associated with aesthetic motivations for cosmetic customization of mobile phones, which in turn is related to product attachment.

Park, Namkee, and Hyunjoo Noh. "Effects of Mobile Instant Messenger Use on Acculturative Stress among International Students in South Korea." *Computers in Human Behavior* 82 (2018): 34–43. https://doi.org/10.1016/j.chb.2017.12.033.

The effects of KakaoTalk use, a mobile instant messenger (MIM) in Korea, and home-country originated social networking site (SNS) use, on international students' acculturative stress, satisfaction with life in Korea, and perceived social support, are tested. The study finds that the use of KakaoTalk helps foreign students reduce their acculturative stress and enhance their satisfaction with Korean life.

Yoon, Kyongwon. "Retraditionalizing the Mobile." *European Journal of Cultural Studies* 6, no. 3 (2003): 327–343.

With ethnographic research in Seoul, Korea, a "peripheral" and local perspective on teenage mobile phone users and sociality is proposed. The mobile phone is found to be appropriated in localized ways in which the traditional form of sociality, *cheong*, is rearticulated. The study suggests that there is no clear-cut evidence that young people have become disembedded from local sociality; rather, they are reimagining the local through mobile technology.

Technology Use and Political Participation

Bhuiyan, Serajul. "Use of Internet in Political Participation in South Korea." *Asia Pacific Media Educator* 1, no. 15 (2004): 9.

A qualitative review of secondary documents and research findings is conducted to assess the role of Internet in political participation in Korea. The review points out the role of various channels used including email, text messages, and interest-group websites as sources of information, and the increasing importance of online political activities in voter participation and decision making.

Chang, Woo-Young. "Online Civic Participation, and Political Empowerment: Online Media and Public Opinion Formation in Korea." *Media, Culture & Society* 27, no. 6 (2005): 925–935. https://doi.org/10.1177/0163443705057680.

Chang offers an examination of Korea's online political media, focusing on two alternative citizen-participatory media. These media emphasize the interactivity between news providers and consumers through devices such as bulletin boards that allow opinion exchange. These media also play a role as a platform for participatory democracy and for challenging the power of conservative media.

Choi, Sujin, and Han Woo Park. "An Exploratory Approach to a Twitter-Based Community Centered on a Political Goal in South Korea: Who Organized It, What They Shared, and How They Acted." *New Media & Society* 16, no. 1 (2014): 129–148. https://doi.org/10.1177/1461444813487956.

A case study of online community aimed for political mobilization and collective activism is offered. A mixed-method analysis of a Twitter community in Korea shows that retweeting practices, cultural tactics, the framing process of discourses, and the organizer's communication effort strengthen group solidarity and collective identity, ultimately contributing to the sustainability of the group.

Chun, Heasun. "Social Networking Sites and Cyberdemocracy: A New Model of Dialogic Interactivity and Political Mobilization in the Case of South Korea." PhD diss., State University of New York at Buffalo (2013). ProQuest (1317011935).

This dissertation suggests that dialogic interactions on social network site (SNS) contribute to online and offline political engagement. A case of Twitter communication between citizens and politicians in Korea shows that interpersonal interactivity is associated with citizen's feedback. Further, those with stronger engagement with SNSs and stronger perception of interactivity on SNSs show more active political participation.

Hur, Suk Jae, and Hyeok Yong Kwon. "The Internet and Inequality in Democratic Engagements: Panel Evidence from South Korea." *International Journal of Communication* 8 (2014): 21.

Using a Korean panel study, the authors show that Internet use for political information is associated with enhancement in interest in politics in general, and also reduces the gap in political interest between older and younger individuals. However, the effect is not found in terms of reducing the gap across people with different income or educational attainment.

Hyun, Ki Deuk, and Jinhee Kim. "Differential and Interactive Influences on Political Participation by Different Types of News Activities and Political Conversation through Social Media." *Computers in Human Behavior* 45 (2015): 328–334. https://doi.org/10.1016/j.chb.2014.12.031.

Do news activities and conversation on social network site (SNS) play an interactive role in political participation? Three types of news activities on Facebook and Twitter—reception, following, and dissemination—are examined based on a sample of social media users in Korea. News activities themselves do not influence political participation, but political conversation do. Further, political conversation moderates the association between the three news activities and political participation.

Kim, Daekyung, and Thomas J. Johnson. "A Victory of the Internet over Mass Media? Examining the Effects of Online Media on Political Attitudes in South Korea." *Asian Journal of Communication* 16, no. 1 (2006): 1–18. https://doi.org/10.1080/01292980500467251.

An online survey of 249 politically interested Internet users during the 2004 national Assembly election in Korea examines whether reliance on online news media for political news and information influences political attitudes. Reliance on independent Web-based newspapers is a stronger predictor than traditional media and their online counterparts.

Kim, Sei-Hill. "Testing the Knowledge Gap Hypothesis in South Korea: Traditional News Media, the Internet, and Political Learning." *International Journal of Public Opinion Research* 20, no. 2 (2008): 193–210. https://doi.org/10.1093/ijpor/edn019.

The author finds that the gap in political knowledge between people with different education levels in Korea is greater among heavy newspaper readers and users of political web. Those with higher education display greater learning when exposed to newspaper or when using the Internet than those with a lower education level. The effect is not shown in the case of television news.

Kim, Sei-Hill, and Miejeong Han. "Media Use and Participatory Democracy in South Korea." *Mass Communication and Society* 8, no. 2 (2005): 133–153. https://doi.org/10.1207/s15327825mcs0802_4.

The key argument of this study is that the effects of mass media use on political participation depend on the specific content offered by the media. Data from Korea show that news media use is associated with participatory behaviors, while entertainment media use has a negative association. News media use is also linked with political interests, perceived knowledge, and political participation.

Kim, Kyun Soo, and Yong-Chan Kim. "New and Old Media Uses and Political Engagement among Korean Adolescents." *Asian Journal of Communication* 17, no. 4 (2007): 342–361. https://doi.org/10.1080/01292980701636977.

How are motivations of political media use linked with political engagement? The authors study Korean adolescents and show that Internet use has become the dominant channel for political engagement rather than traditional media use. Further, the different motivations behind media use make differences to the outcomes: two motivations—guidance and social utility needs—of new and old media use are associated with adolescents' political engagement.

Kwak, Nojin, Scott W. Campbell, Junho Choi, and Soo Young Bae. "Mobile Communication and Public Affairs Engagement in Korea: An Examination of Non-Linear Relationships between Mobile Phone Use and Engagement across Age Groups." *Asian Journal of Communication* 21, no. 5 (2011): 485–503. https://doi.org/10.1080/01292986.2011.587016.

Mobile reinforcement hypothesis is supported in this study of Korean mobile phone users, where the effects of mobile phone use on public affairs participation is stronger for those who are already interested and involved in public affairs. How the three dimensions of mobile phone use—informational, relational, and social recreational—are differentially associated with community engagement and political participation is also examined.

Lee, Hoon, Nojin Kwak, Scott W. Campbell, Rich Ling. "Mobile Communication and Political Participation in South Korea: Examining the Intersections between Informational and Relational Uses." *Computers in Human Behavior* 38 (2014): 85–92. https://doi.org/10.1016/j.chb.2014.05.017.

The role of mobile communication in public discourse in Korea is examined. Results show that informational mobile use and relational mobile use interact to predict higher political participation. In addition, the role of political self-efficacy is noteworthy, where it produces a three-way interaction with the two types of mobile use to produce higher political participation.

Lee, Byoungkwan, Karen M. Lancendorfer, and Ki Jung Lee. "Agenda-Setting and the Internet: The Intermedia Influence of Internet Bulletin Boards on Newspaper Coverage of the 2000 General Election in South Korea." *Asian Journal of Communication* 15, no. 1 (2005): 57–71. https://doi.org/10.1080/0129298042000 329793.

Content analysis and cross-lagged comparisons of major newspapers and Internet bulletin boards during the 2000 election in Korea are conducted. Findings show reciprocity in agenda-setting mechanisms in which newspapers influence bulletin boards at the first level of agenda-setting, which in turn influences newspapers at the second level of agenda-setting.

Lim, Jeongsub. "A Cross-Lagged Analysis of Agenda Setting among Online News Media." *Journalism & Mass Communication Quarterly* 83, no. 2 (2006): 298–312. https://doi.org/10.1177/107769900608300205.

The causal relationships among the issue agendas of three online news media in Korea during two time periods are investigated. The study finds that the issue agendas of the two online newspapers at Time 1 influenced the issue agendas of the online wire service at Time 2. The online wire service did not influence the issue agendas of the two newspapers during the same time periods.

Lim, Yon Soo, and Han Woo Park. "How Do Congressional Members Appear on the Web? Tracking the Web Visibility of South Korean Politicians." *Government Information Quarterly* 28, no. 4 (2011): 514–521. https://doi.org/10.1016/j.giq.2011.02.003.

The web visibility of Korea's 18th National Assembly members is examined. The most visible politicians in the Korean webosphere have highly qualified political careers and prominence, and the difference in politicians' web visibility depends on their political attributes (their term, constituency, and party), not on their demographic attributes (their gender and age).

Lin, Yang, and Sunhee Lim. "Relationships of Media Use to Political Cynicism and Efficacy: A Preliminary Study of Young South Korean Voters." *Asian Journal of Communication* 12, no. 1 (2002): 25–39. https://doi.org/0.1080/01292980209364812.

The association between media use, political distrust, and efficacy is examined through data collected from college students in Korea. Use of radio is negatively associated with feelings of political efficacy, while newspaper use has a positive association. Further, negative feelings toward media campaign coverage are linked with feelings of efficacy, possibly through promoting the desire of change.

Park, Se Jung, and Yon Soo Lim. "Information Networks and Social Media Use in Public Diplomacy: A Comparative Analysis of South Korea and Japan." *Asian Journal of Communication* 24, no. 1 (2014): 79–98. https://doi.org/10.1080/0129 2986.2013.851724.

Park and Lim compare online public diplomacy efforts of Korean and Japanese organizations through a network analysis of organizational website links and a content analysis of Facebook content. The two countries' communication strategies are shown to differ in multiple aspects: Korea demonstrates more centralized networks among key public diplomacy organizations and engage in a two-way communication with audiences through social network site postings.

Song, Yonghoi. "Internet News Media and Issue Development: A Case Study on the Roles of Independent Online News Services as Agenda-Builders for Anti-US Protests in South Korea." *New Media & Society* 9, no. 1 (2007): 71–92. https://doi.org/10.1177/1461444807072222.

The author provides a contrast between mainstream newspaper and online news services in their coverage and frame use around a political protest during 2002 in Korea. The study challenges inter-media agenda-setting model, claiming that beyond simple counts of the number of news stories across news organizations, the content of coverage and the frames used need to be carefully examined.

Game Studies

Chang, Byeng-Hee, Seung-Eun Lee, and Byoung-Sun Kim. "Exploring Factors Affecting the Adoption and Continuance of Online Games among College Students in South Korea Integrating Uses and Gratification and Diffusion of Innovation Approaches." *New Media & Society* 8, no. 2 (2006): 295–319. https://doi.org/10.1177/1461444806059888.

Various factors affecting adoption and continuance of online game playing among college students in Korea are investigated. The study also looks at the factors that differentiate online game players from non-players, examining variables that set apart those who continue playing online games from those who discontinue and those who have potentials for playing online games in the future.

Cho, Hyun, Sang-Kyu Lee, Jung-Seok Choi, Sam-Wook Choi, and Dai-Jin Kim. "An Exploratory Study on Association between Internet Game Contents and Aggression in Korean Adolescents." *Computers in Human Behavior* 73 (2017): 257–262. https://doi.org/10.1016/j.chb.2016.12.077.

Cho and colleagues survey Internet game players in Korea to investigate the influence of game playing on aggressive behaviors. The influence of Internet game is examined depending on the level of game genres and game age ratings.

Jin, Dal Yong. *Korea's Online Gaming Empire*. Cambridge, MA: MIT Press. 2010.

Jin's book offers an overview of Korea's online gaming industry. It touches on various aspects of the online gaming industry, such as regulatory framework that fastened and facilitated its development, the emergence of eSport as a youth culture, the working conditions of professional online gamers, the role of game fans, and its connection to the global market.

Jin, Dal Yong, Florence Chee, and Seah Kim. "Transformative Mobile Game Culture: A Sociocultural Analysis of Korean Mobile Gaming in the Era of

Smartphones." *International Journal of Cultural Studies* 18, no. 4 (2015): 413–429. https://doi.org/10.1177/1367877913507473.

Jin, Chee, and Kim discusses sociocultural factors that are specific to Korea (e.g., community-based social environment, distinctive commuting patterns) to explain the explosion of mobile gaming in the country. By employing socio-historical and institutional analyses as methodological frameworks, it offers an in-depth perspective into how Korea has made a transition from computer-based to mobile phone-based game culture.

Rea, Stephen C. "Mobilizing Games, Disrupting Culture: Digital Gaming in South Korea." In *Mobile Gaming in Asia,* edited by Dal Yong Jin, 73–89. Dordrecht, Netherlands: Springer, 2017.

How does mobile game culture complement the past of PC-based online gaming in Korea? Rea details the unique spatio-temporal characteristics of mobile games, compared with PC-based games, and their implications for the evaluation of mobile gaming and its players in the unique setting of Korean culture.

Sang, Yoonmo, Sora Park, and Hogeun Seo. "Mobile Game Regulation in South Korea: A Case Study of the Shutdown Law." In *Mobile Gaming in Asia,* edited by Dal Yong Jin, 55–72. Dordrecht, Netherlands: Springer, 2017.

Sang, Park, and Seo highlight regulatory framework, sociocultural norms, economic market forces, and the architecture of mobile online games, in relation to the application of the Shutdown Law enacted in 2011 in the context of mobile gaming. It raises the need to re-consider the Korean government's paternalistic approach to regulate online games and re-evaluate the meanings of game playing among the youth.

Seok, Soonhwa, and Boaventura Dacosta. "The World's Most Intense Online Gaming Culture: Addiction and High-Engagement Prevalence Rates among South Korean Adolescents and Young Adults." *Computers in Human Behavior* 28, no. 6 (2012): 2143–2151. https://doi.org/10.1016/j.chb.2012.06.019.

Surveying adolescents and young adults in Korea, Seok and Dacosta identify the magnitude of pathological online video game addiction by differentiating those who are addicted and those who are highly engaged. The authors emphasize the importance of distinguishing between non-pathological and pathological game play so as not to overestimate the prevalence of online game addiction.

Technology Addiction and Problematic Use

Choi, Suk Bong, and Myung Suh Lim. "Effects of Social and Technology Overload on Psychological Well-Being in Young South Korean Adults: The Mediatory Role of Social Network Service Addiction." *Computers in Human Behavior* 61 (2016): 245–254. https://doi.org/10.1016/j.chb.2016.03.032.

Does social network site (SNS) overload influence psychological well-being of individuals? Findings from a Korean sample show that social overload, which refers to the burden of dealing with a large number of relationships, and technology overload, which is similar to technostress, leads to SNS addiction. Subsequently, SNS addiction is negatively associated with psychological well-being.

Ha, Jee Hyun, Bumsu Chin, Doo-Heum Park, Seung-Ho Ryu, and Jaehak Yu. "Characteristics of Excessive Cellular Phone Use in Korean Adolescents." *CyberPsychology & Behavior* 11, no. 6 (2008): 783–784. https://doi.org/10.1089/cpb.2008.0096.

What are the psychological problems associated with Korean adolescents' excessive cell phone use? Adolescents have a strong attachment to their cell phone and show depressive symptoms, higher interpersonal anxiety, lower self-esteem, and higher Internet addiction tendencies.

Hur, Mann Hyung. "Demographic, Habitual, and Socioeconomic Determinants of Internet Addiction Disorder: An Empirical Study of Korean Teenagers." *CyberPsychology & Behavior* 9, no. 5 (2006): 514–525. https://doi.org/10.1089/cpb.2006.9.514.

A holistic approach is offered that considers demographic, socioeconomic, and usage characteristics for understanding Korean teenagers' Internet addiction disorder. The author also suggests multiple dimensions of Internet addiction including self-control, Internet dependency, psychological distress, and abnormal behavior. Therefore, interventions for addiction disorder need to incorporate the interplay between individual and social factors.

Jun, Sangmin. "The Reciprocal Longitudinal Relationships between Mobile Phone Addiction and Depressive Symptoms among Korean Adolescents." *Computers in Human Behavior* 58 (2016): 179–186. https://doi.org/10.1016/j.chb.2015.12.061.

Jun warns a possible vicious cycle of mobile phone addiction and depression among adolescents. A three-year longitudinal dataset of Korean adolescents shows that there is a bidirectional relationship between mobile phone addiction and depressive symptoms over time.

Kim, Jung Eun, and Jinhee Kim. "International Note: Teen Users' Problematic Online Behavior: Using Panel Data from South Korea." *Journal of Adolescence* 40 (2015): 48–53. https://doi.org/10.1016/j.adolescence.2015.01.001.

What are the predictors of teens' delinquent online behaviors? Unauthorized ID use, disguised gender or age in chatting, and cursing or insulting behaviors of Korean teens are studied. Individual factors such as self-control, problematic offline behavior, and time spent on computer as well as peer-level factors such as association with deviant peers explain delinquent online behaviors.

Lee, Soojung. "Analyzing Negative SNS Behaviors of Elementary and Middle School Students in Korea." *Computers in Human Behavior* 43 (2015): 15–27. https://doi.org/10.1016/j.chb.2014.10.014.

Using data from Korea, the author examines the patterns and predictors of children's and young adolescents' engagement in negative social network site (SNS) behaviors. The most frequently engaged negative behavior is stealing others' private information. Several predictors including grade and SNS usage time explain the different levels of negative behaviors. The findings provide implications for education efforts to nurture positive SNS use among children.

Lee, Changho, and Namin Shin. "Prevalence of Cyberbullying and Predictors of Cyberbullying Perpetration among Korean Adolescents." *Computers in Human Behavior* 68 (2017): 352–358. https://doi.org/10.1016/j.chb.2016.11.047.

An in-depth look is provided into the current state of cyberbullying in the context of Korean adolescents, where 34 percent of respondents identified themselves as being bullies and/or victims. The experience of being cyberbullied, bullying offline, and time spent on chat and social network service media positively predict cyberbullying perpetration.

Lee, Ju Young, Kyoung Min Shin, Sun-Mi Cho and Yun Mi Shin. "Psychosocial Risk Factors Associated with Internet Addiction in Korea." *Psychiatry Investigation* 11, no. 4 (2014): 380–386. https://doi.org/10.4306/pi.2014.11.4.380.

Internet addiction can be explained based on various socio-demographic and psychological variables. Data from middle school students in Korea show that being male, older age, and being younger at the time of first Internet use are predictive of addiction. Internet addition is correlated with depressive symptoms, social problems, attention problems, and delinquency.

Park, Seungmin, Minchul Kang, and Eunha Kim. "Social Relationship on Problematic Internet Use (PIU) among Adolescents in South Korea: A Moderated Mediation Model of Self-Esteem and Self-Control." *Computers in Human Behavior* 38 (2014): 349–357. https://doi.org/10.1016/j.chb.2014.06.005.

Korean adolescents' social relationships with peers and mother are highlighted in examining their problematic Internet use (PIU). Social relationships were associated with PIU. Further, self-esteem mediated the effects of peer relationship on PIU, and self-control moderated the indirect effects of both types of social relationships on PIU via self-esteem.

Shin, Sang-Eun, Nam-Seok Kim, and Eun-Young Jang. "Comparison of Problematic Internet and Alcohol Use and Attachment Styles among Industrial Workers in Korea." *Cyberpsychology, Behavior, and Social Networking* 14, no. 11 (2011): 665–672. https://doi.org/10.1089/cyber.2010.0470.

How do the predictors of problematic Internet use compare with those of problematic alcohol use? Data collected from Korea show that depression is a common predictor of both, while problematic Internet use is predicted by several additional variables including both anxious and avoidant attachment and phobia. Further, depression moderates the relationship between avoidant attachment and problematic Internet use.

Tippett, Neil, and Keumjoo Kwak. "Cyberbullying in South Korea." In *Cyberbullying in the Global Playground: Research from International Perspectives*, edited by Qing Li, Donna Cross, and Peter K. Smith, 202–219. West Sussex, UK: John Wiley & Sons, 2011.

A comprehensive overview of cyberbullying among teens in Korea is presented. Issues including age and gender correlates, common responses and reported feelings by victims, the overlap between bullies and victims, and the association between traditional bullying and cyberbullying are discussed.

Communication Technology Policy and Economics

Bae, Young. "Diffusion and Usage Patterns of the Internet in Korea and Japan: A Comparison of Policy and Cultural Factors." *Development and Society* 33, no. 2 (2004): 229–250.

Bae compares Korea and Japan in their adoption and use of the Internet among the youth. The analysis reveals that Koreans, compared with Japanese, use the Internet more as a communication conduit as opposed to a tool for information and entertainment. The study speculates that such a difference originates from cultural difference.

Bae, Hyuhn-Suhck, and Thomas F. Baldwin. "Policy Issues for Cable Startup in Smaller Countries: The Case in South Korea." *Telecommunications Policy* 22, no. 4 (1998): 371–381. https://doi.org/10.1016/S0308–5961(98)00016–0.

The start of cable development in Korea is analyzed with a focus on policy, industry structure, and programming. The study finds that Korea faced the hurdles of introducing the cable industry to a country with a small audience size and thus, the country needed flexible policies.

Choi, Young Soo, and Liz Ross. "Policy and Power: The Impact of the Internet on the Younger Generation in South Korea." *Social Policy and Society* 5, no. 3 (2006): 421–429. https://doi.org/10.1017/S1474746406003095.

Based on the analysis of narratives of young people aged between 13 and 18 in Korea, Choi and Ross present the implications of Internet use among the youth and the changes in power dynamics that the Internet has brought within family relationships and within public policy making and private sectors.

Choudrie, Jyoti, Anastasia Papazafeiropoulou, and Heejin Lee. "A Web of Stakeholders and Strategies: a Case of Broadband Diffusion in South Korea." *Journal of Information Technology* 18, no. 4 (2003): 281–290. https://doi.org/10.1 080/0268396032000150816.

The process of broadband diffusion in Korea is analyzed with a focus on major stakeholders and their roles. Particular attention is paid to a discussion of how the government acts as a key player affecting the diffusion of broadband services. The authors also offer implications for other countries that look for strategies for broadband diffusion.

Contreras, Jorge L. "Divergent Patterns of Engagement in Internet Standardization: Japan, Korea and China." *Telecommunications Policy* 38, no. 10 (2014): 914–932. https://doi.org/10.1016/j.telpol.2014.09.005.

What are the differences among Korea, Japan, and China in their development of Internet standards and participation in the Internet Engineering Task Force (IETF)? Korea is different from Japan and China in that its involvement in IETF is significant but still below that of Japan and China.

Han, Gwang-Jub, and Woo-Hyun Won. "Building a Telecommunications Infrastructure for the 21st Century: Public Policy Implications of the Cable Television Development Plan in Korea." *Asian Journal of Communication* 5, no. 1 (1995): 1–51. https://doi.org/10.1080/01292989509364712.

How does the development of the cable television industry vary in countries such as the United States, Germany, France, and Japan? Han and Won apply the lessons from these countries to make suggestions for regulatory changes for Korea, where the cable industry was still in an early stage.

Hong, Areum, Changi Nam, and Seongcheol Kim. "Estimating the Potential Increase in Consumer Welfare from the Introduction of Super Wi-Fi Services in Korea." *Telecommunications Policy* 40, no. 10–11 (2016): 935–944. https://doi. org/10.1016/j.telpol.2015.05.004.

Hong, Nam, and Kim assess consumers' willingness to pay for a Super Wi-Fi service by using a conjoint analysis in the context of Korea. In particular, the willingness to pay is found to be greater among consumers in non-urban areas compared with those residing in urban areas.

Kim, Hongbum, Dong-Hee Shin, and Daeho Lee. "A Socio-Technical Analysis of Software Policy in Korea: Towards a Central Role for Building ICT Ecosystems." *Telecommunications Policy* 39, no. 11 (2015): 944–956. https://doi.org/10.1016/j. telpol.2015.09.001.

The fundamental issues in governmental regulations and policies pertaining to the software industry in Korea are addressed. For the continued growth of the software industry in Korea, the authors suggest the need to understand the critical role software plays in a social context and recommend investing more in the core technology of software.

Oh, Myung, and James Larson. *Digital Development in Korea: Building an Information Society*. New York: Routledge, 2011.

Digital development in Korea started during the 1980s. This book details deregulatory changes and their impacts on diverse aspects of information and communication technology in Korea, including the broadband and mobile industry as well as smart cities. The book also includes discussion of social and cultural infrastructure, which has enabled evolution of Korea's digital industry.

Ueki, Yasushi. "Jumping Up to the Internet-Based Society: Lessons from South Korea." In *Information Technology Policy and the Digital Divide: Lessons for Developing Countries*, edited by Mitsuhiro Kagami, Masatsugu Tsuji, and Emanuele Giovannetti, 114–134. Cheltenhan, UK: Edward Elgar, 2004.

What are various factors that facilitated the rapid expansion of broadband Internet in Korea? Ueki writes that they include strong governed-led policy, densely populated urban areas coupled with an emphasis on education, and the culture of homogenous mentality and collectivists. The author also discusses the dark sides of Internet use and penetration.

Chapter 5

Health Communication

Hye-ryeon Lee, Hye-Jin Paek, Minsun Shim, and Peter J. Schulz

Health communication is a rapidly growing field within the discipline of communication. The U.S. National Cancer Institute and the Centers for Disease Control and Prevention defines health communication as the study and use of communication strategies to inform and influence individual and community decisions that enhance health.[1] Coupled with the increased availability of grant funding for health issues, health communication has grown enormously as a research field in the past two decades,[2] and the scope of research has broadened to address a wide variety of health issues.

HEALTH COMMUNICATION SCHOLARSHIP

Health communication scholarship has been expanding in Korea and globally.[3] Many Korean students with advanced degrees in communication from American universities have founded the Korea Health Communication Association. This Korean health communication scholarly organization has published its flagship journal, *Health Communication Research* since 2009. In addition, Korean communication scholars in the United States study Korean immigrants, and others research Korea in a comparative context. Hence, a considerable body of health communication research has been published in English on Koreans in Korea or Korean immigrants abroad. We

---

1. U.S. Dept. of Health and Human Services, *Making Health Communication Programs Work: A Planner's Guide* (Bethesda, MD: U.S. Department of Health and Human Services, National Institutes of Health, 2002).
2. U.S. Dept. of Health and Human Services, *Making Health Communication Programs Work*, 2.
3. Hye-Jin Paek et al., "The Emerging Landscape of Health Communication," *Health Communication* 25, no. 6–7 (2010). 552.

provide an overview of existing English-language publications on Korea-related health communication.[4]

HEALTH COMMUNICATION STUDIES IN ENGLISH

Health communication research on Korea has a short history. The first Korea-related health communication work in English was the 2003 dissertation by Professor Yang Soo Kim at the University of Oklahoma comparing psychological health of Korean expatriates in America and American expatriates in Korea.[5] Nine studies were published between 2004 and 2010, and 50 studies after 2011. Communication journals were the dominant publication outlet for 41 studies, while a significant minority of 13 studies was published in non-communication journals. There were 4 dissertations and 2 theses. To date, Korean health communication has been the topic of one book-length monograph in English.

The topics for published health communication research covered were quite diverse, ranging from various diseases to public health and other social issues. Smoking and cancer have been the two most frequently studied topics. Quantitative research methodology has dominated Korean health communication scholarship in English, with 55 out of 60 studies using quantitative methods alone. Only one study has applied qualitative methods alone. Nearly 50 studies have used individuals as the unit of analysis while slightly more than 10 studies have used messages as the unit of analysis. Koreans were the only study population for two-thirds of the studies. Meanwhile, Koreans were compared with other ethnic groups or Korean immigrants in 17 studies, and 3 studies focused on Korean immigrants alone.

---

4. We identified 60 Korean health communication studies that were published in English as of January 2017, through a systematic search process using six electronic databases: Communication and Mass Media Complete (CMMC), PsycINFO, MEDLINE, EBSCO Host Cumulative Index to Nursing and Allied Health Literature (CINAHL), Educational Resources Information Center (ERIC), and ProQuest's Dissertation and Theses database. Given the explosive growth of health-related research, it is not possible to succinctly survey research on health communication broadly defined, and the included studies represent publications that fit the narrow definition of health communication research as accepted by communication discipline. For more detailed description of the search procedure and expanded review of the studies, see Hye-ryeon Lee, Hye-Jin Paek, and Minsun Shim, "A Survey of Health Communication Scholarship on Korea: Breadth, Depth, and Trends of Published Research" in Communication, Digital Media, and Popular Culture in Korea: Contemporary Research and Future Prospects, ed. Dal Yong Jin and Nojin Kwak (Lanham, MD: Lexington Books, 2018), 175–214.

5. Yang Soo Kim, "A Study of Cross-Cultural Adaptation" (PhD diss., University of Oklahoma, 2003).

HEALTH COMMUNICATION STUDIES: FOUR RESEARCH AREAS

A brief overview of health communication research on Korea in four research areas (messages, audience characteristics and processes, new media, and culture) is in order. This classification is based on communication scholarship at large to provide a meaningful overview for major communication elements (message, audience, and media) and to stimulate future research within the unique Korean context.

Study of Messages

A total of 12 of studies investigated messages in health communication. One of the most notable features of this group of studies is that all studies focused on messages in the media. None of the studies concerned messages exchanged in non-mediated contexts of interpersonal dyads or group interactions. So the scope of messages studied in Korean health communication research is narrow, only including messages created by authorities and available in the media.

The primary focus was placed on studying news media, including newspapers, television news, and online news. Other media outlets examined were television advertising and government press releases. Most studies on news stories reflect scholarly interests in content analyses of messages already available in the media. Relatively little attention has been paid to message design and construction for health campaign and intervention in Korea.

Another notable pattern in Korean health communication research in English was that the results of the content analysis were often linked to existing statistical or archived data, speculating on the possible outcomes or implications of media coverage. Such efforts to connect findings from media messages with other statistical data help researchers address what implications the media messages may have for real life at a macro or society level.

The most dominant set of research samples were messages written in Korean and available in Korean media. Only three were cross-national; two studies compared the U.S. and Korean news media, and one study analyzed data from three Asian countries. One study examined Korean-American community newspapers.

Study of Audience Characteristics and Processes

Study of Audience Characteristics

Another significant body of health communication publications (11 studies) centered on the impact of audience characteristics in the context of diverse health issues. Audience characteristics studied included demographics, personality traits, other personal factors, and social factors as well as communication behaviors.

A majority of studies examined the role of different communication behaviors such as traditional media use, Internet and web-based media use, and interpersonal communication in influencing health behaviors across different contexts. The emerging consensus among these studies is that interpersonal communication and Internet and web-based media use influence audience health behaviors consistently, while traditional media use has rather sporadic impact. This may reflect that these studies were all conducted in the twenty-first century when the influence of traditional media waned.

Many studies investigated how personal trait factors including trait anxiety, self-monitoring and sensation seeking influence health behavior. But a few studies examined social factors like perceived peer pressure, social capital, and perceived opinion congruence. A study by Ohio State University Professor Hyunyi Cho and others, for example, examined a cultural factor, self-construal in combination with other personal and social factors.[6]

A great number of publications investigated how different audience characteristics impacted cognitive variables such as information overload, health consciousness, acceptance of nuclear power plants, self-efficacy and risk perceptions. Several studies examined (self-reported) actual behaviors while others focused on behavioral intention.

Study of Audience Processes

While studies of audience characteristics ask *what* antecedents predict, explain, or influence health-related outcomes, studies of audience processes attempt to answer *how* they do so. In other words, audience process studies explore how and why people seek and process health information, and they do so by explicating underlying mechanisms based on theoretical frameworks that employ audience perceptions.

Among 15 audience process studies, the majority focused on risk perceptions in the context of various health and risk issues. Risk perception is an important concept in risk communication because it affects subsequent

---

6. Hyunyi Cho, Jinro Lee, and Jiyeon So, "Personal, Social, and Cultural Correlates of Self-Efficacy Beliefs," *Health Communication* 24, no. 4 (2009), doi: 10.1080/10410230902889381.

preventive and recommended behaviors. All but one of the studies examined media effects on risk perceptions—that is, how different types of media play a role in forming and changing risk perceptions, which are also related to communicative behavior and behavioral intention. The one exception in media effects research analyzed the message construction side of the risk communication process by asking Korean journalists which risk characteristics affect their decisions about the newsworthiness of various risk issues.[7] A prevailing number of studies on risk perception suggest that there is increased interest in risk issues in Korea, and that risk and health communication, which developed independently from each other, are becoming integrated.

Another major area of research on audience process is health information seeking employing both cross-sectional and longitudinal survey data collected both in the United States and Korea. In particular, two dissertations by Wonsun Kim at George Mason University and Joung Hwa Koo at Florida State University examined why Korean immigrants in the United States sought health information, and what predicted their health information seeking. These two studies are valuable considering that qualitative research on Korean immigrants is lacking in Korean health communication research. A research team that includes the prominent health communication scholar Gary Kreps published two studies on Korean Americans living near Washington, DC, examining the associations among audience characteristics, information sources, and information seeking behaviors using survey and focus group data.

Study of New Communication Media

The development of the Internet, social media, and other communication technologies has enabled the unique applications of technology to health communication contexts. Twelve studies have investigated how new communication media are used in Korean health contexts and its impact on health outcomes. Eleven studies have focused on the Internet or social media, while one study centered on mobile applications.

A major area of research on new communication media is online health information seeking or more general health-related online activities. The effects of online information seeking was studied either in the context of a particular topic (e.g., cancer, body image) or in a broader context of general health information. Online health information seeking has been examined not only as a predictor but also as an outcome or a mediator in health communication process.

---

7. Myoungsoon You and Youngkee Ju, "The Influence of Outrage Factors on Journalists," *Journalism & Mass Communication Quarterly* 92, no. 4 (2015), doi: 10.1177/1077699015596339.

A salient feature in this line of research is its great concern on adolescent groups. Three studies examined online activities among adolescents in Korea, with a particular interest in misbehaviors with health implications. Specific topics include the associations of Internet overuse and addiction with aggression among high school students, the role of aggression in predicting Internet addiction, as mediated through anxiety, depression, and impulsivity among middle school students, and the relationship between levels of online activities and cyberbullying behavior among 12 to 15-year-old adolescents. Considering the high rates of Internet and SNS use in Korea, studies speculating on the ways in which adolescents engage in online activities deserve scholarly attention in Korean health communication research.

Study of Culture

Ten publications specifically focused on studying culture. All are cross-national and include the United States. By far the most popular cultural concept referred to is the dichotomy of collectivistic and individualistic cultures as delineated by the renowned culture scholar Geert Hofstede.[8] This is often complemented by other cultural concepts and social science approaches such as the University of Michigan social psychologist Richard Nisbett's holistic and analytic thinking styles,[9] self-construals, the message framing, theories of behavioral intentions, the third-person effect, and Edward Hall's concept of cultural contexts.[10] In fact, findings from several studies cast doubt on the validity of claims that East Asian cultures can be described as collectivistic and Western cultures as individualistic. Perhaps the days of this popular distinction are over.

In terms of health subjects, the effect of anti-smoking campaigns is the most popular health communication topic in the studies of culture. Hyung-seok Lee's thesis at California State University at Fullerton examined the effects of individualistic and collectivistic fear appeals in anti-tobacco campaigns and found no differences.[11] The prominent health communication scholar Hye-Jin Paek at Hanyang University in Korea and others have published studies on the topic as well.[12,13]

---

8. Geert Hofstede, *International Differences in Work-related Values* (Beverly Hills, CA: Sage, 1980).

9. Richard Nisbett, *The Geography of Thought* (New York: Free Press, 2003).

10. Edward Hall, *Beyond Culture* (New York: Anchor Press, 1976).

11. Hyung-seok Lee, "Cultural Considerations: In Anti-Smoking Health" (M.A. thesis, California State University, Fullerton, 2004).

12. Hyegyu Lee and Hye-Jin Paek, "Roles of Guilt and Culture in Normative Influence," *Psychology, Health & Medicine* 19, no. 1 (2014), doi: 10.1080/13548506.2013.772303.

13. Hye-Jin Paek, Hyegyu Lee, and Thomas Hove, "The Role of Collectivism Orientation in Differential Normative Mechanisms," *Asian Journal of Social Psychology* 17, no. 3 (2014), doi: 10.1111/ajsp.12065.

Sang-Yeon Kim, an intercultural communication scholar at the University Wisconsin-Milwaukee, and others have researched the influence of culture on the related topic of body weight perception, weight reduction, and nutritional behavior.[14,15] Professors Kyoo-Hoon Han and Samsup Jo at Sookmyung University in Seoul have traced collectivistic versus individualistic appeal on the outcomes of cancer screening.[16] A productive health communication scholar, Hyunyi Cho's co-authored journal article has tested and confirmed hypotheses about the third-person effect in the context of cultural orientations.[17] Yang Soo Kim's University of Oklahoma dissertation found a positive relationship between communication competence in their host culture and mental health among Korean immigrants.[18] Echoing the nineteenth century great observer of political culture, Alexis de Tocqueville, Americans were found to exert stronger pressure to conform, and Koreans in the United States were less welcome than Americans in Korea.

Summary and Conclusions

While still in the early stages of development, health communication scholarship on Korea in English is growing steadily. Judging from its publication trend, we expect the pace of growth will speed up in the coming years. Indeed, Korea seems to provide an interesting context for global health communication research because of the high frequency in contemporary Korean society of diverse human-made, natural, environmental, and public health risks, along with its unique cultural and social characteristics.

Existing English-language health communication research on Korea shows diversity in some areas but homogeneity in other areas. A wide spectrum of health issues has served as study contexts for a variety of variables, concepts, and theories for scholars. The diversity clearly suggests a rapid expansion of breadth of English-language scholarship on health communication about Korea in recent years. On the other hand, it shows a lack of depth in research for each topical context.

In contrast to the diversity of topic and theory, research methodology and study populations are quite homogeneous. Quantitative research methodology, specifically survey methods, dominate the field. With survey being

14. Sang-Yeon Kim et al., "Cultural Differences in Women's Body Weight Perception," *Health Care for Women International* 33, no. 11 (2016), doi: 10.1080/07399332.2015.1107070.

15. Sang-Yeon Kim et al., "Healthy Food and Cultural Holism," *International Journal of Intercultural Relations* 52 (2016), doi: 10.1016/j.ijintrel.2016.03.002.

16. Kyoo-Hoon Han and Samsup Jo, "Women's Responses to Cancer Prevention Campaigns," *Health Care for Women International* 33, no. 1 (2012), doi: 10.1080/07399332.2011.630117.

17. Hyunyi Cho and Miejeong Han, "Perceived effect of the mass media on self vs. other," *Journal of Asian Pacific Communication* 14, no. 2 (2004), doi: 10.1075/japc.14.2.06cho.

18. Kim, "Host Environment, Communication, and Psychological Health."

dominant, most studies are conducted at an individual level, and nearly all studies are based on self-report data. Similarly, a large majority of studies focus on messages and study participants in Korea.

As more scholars from various parts of the world study health communication relating to Korea, diversification of research methods and more studies using organizational and societal level analysis may benefit the discipline. Finally, more comparative studies are needed since health and risk issues are not limited within a national boundary. We can gain better insight on how health issues are influenced by genetic as well as cultural and environmental factors through comparative studies involving more diverse populations in and outside of Korea.

ANNOTATED BIBLIOGRAPHY

Study of Messages

Ha, Jin Hong, Debashis Deb Aikat, and Eun Hwa Jung. "Theories and Messages in South Korean Antismoking Advertising." *Health Communication* 30, no. 10 (2015): 1022–1031. doi: 10.1080/10410236.2014.915075.

This study examines the theories and messages in Korean antismoking advertisements. Results show that Korean antismoking advertisements primarily target adults, normally using statistical evidence; the most prevalent persuasive health message used social norms, whereas the most prevalent affective appeal use fear appeals; the advertisements mention more benefits of not smoking than barriers to not smoking.

Fu, King-Wa, and Paul S. F. Yip. "Estimating the Risk for Suicide Following the Suicide Deaths of 3 Asian Entertainment Celebrities: A Meta-Analytic Approach." *Journal of Clinical Psychiatry* 70, no. 6 (2009): 869–878. doi: 10.4088/JCP.08m04240.

Fu and Yip estimate the risk for suicide after the suicide deaths of entertainment celebrities in Asia. A retrospective time-series analysis of the suicide deaths in Hong Kong (2001–2003), Taiwan, and Korea (both from 2003–2005) show that there was overall 25 percent increase in the risk for suicide during the first four weeks following celebrity suicides compared with the reference period. The same-gender and same-method specific increases suggest that as people identify more with the celebrity, their risk for suicide rises.

Ju, Youngkee, Jeongsub Lim, Minsun Shim, and Myoungsoon You. "Outrage Factors in Government Press Releases of Food Risk and Their Influence on News Media Coverage." *Journal of Health Communication* 20, no. 8 (2015): 879–887. doi: 10.1080/10810730.2015.1018602

This 2015 study investigates whether outrage factors of food risks intensify journalistic attention. Using content analysis method, press releases issued by the Ministry of Food and Drug Safety in Korea in 2012 are linked to the number of news stories covering the given risk. Results show that controllability was the most salient outrage factor, followed by trust, voluntariness, familiarity, and human origin; the greater the outrage score of a risk, the more news stories of the risk.

Jun, Jungmi, and Kyeung Mi Oh. "Framing Risks and Benefits of Medical Tourism: A Content Analysis of Medical Tourism Coverage in Korean American Community Newspapers." *Journal of Health Communication* 20, no. 6 (2015): 720–727. doi: 1 0.1080/10810730.2015.1018574.

The focus of this study is to examine Korean-American community newspapers' representation of risks and benefits involved with medical tourism offered in Korea. According to content analyses of Korean-American community newspapers from 2007–2012, based on the framing theory, the newspapers are rarely engaged in risk communication and lack sufficient information about potential risks of Korean medical tourism, while emphasizing diverse benefits.

Jung, Heeyoung Jenni. "Framing Health Care: The Exposure of Postnatal Care in the U.S. and South Korean Media." PhD diss., Indiana University, 2014. ProQuest (1571088).

In this dissertation, Jung studies how news media in the U.S. and Korea frame the postnatal care subject differently. Results suggest that U.S. media emphasizes the health care benefits of new health insurance plans or policies regarding postnatal care, whereas Korean media stresses the risk of not receiving proper postnatal care and its possible symptoms. Based on these results, the researcher explains how the different news frame creates different thematic structures and public opinions in the two countries.

Lee, Hannah, and Soontae An. "Social Stigma Toward Suicide: Effects of Group Categorization and Attributions in Korean Health News." *Health Communication* 31, no. 4 (2016): 468–477. doi: 10.1080/10410236.2014.966894.

The purpose of this study is to examine the influence of health news content on the stigma of suicide. Stigma scores were lower for those who read an article explaining the causes of suicide as uncontrollable than for those reading the causes as controllable, and lower for those who read an article depicting suicidal people as the in-group than the out-group categorization. Furthermore, stigma scores were the highest when the out-group categorization was combined with the controllable causes of suicide.

Lee, Na Yeon. "The Influence of Business Strategies on the Frames of Health News: A Comparison of Health News in Two Korean Newspapers." *Asian Journal of Communication* 24, no. 2 (2014): 173–188. doi: 10.1080/01292986.2013.8581 72.

This study examines how an adoption of a spin-off publication, which is a subsidiary of a parent company, might be associated with changes in the frames of health news. A content analysis of two Korean newspapers shows that reporters at the spin-off relied more on health news sources from potential advertisers and that the frames emphasized medical treatments rather than the promotion of healthy lifestyles, which was the focus of frames before the spin-off.

Logan, Robert A., Jaeyung Park, and Jae-Hwa Shin. "Elite Sources, Context, and News Topics." *Science Communication* 25, no. 4 (2004): 364–398. doi: 10.1177/1075547004265580.

Using content analysis, this study documents the coverage of a public health crisis in Korea. The findings suggest that two Korean daily newspapers (*Chosun Ilbo* and *Hankyoreh*) from 1999–2000 emphasized governmental officials and physicians as news sources in favor of elite news sources, underemphasized other news sources, and limited in-depth reporting. However, these newspapers also made some efforts to use a range of sources and provide some multidimensional news coverage during the public health crisis.

Moon, Miri. "Cosmetic Surgery as a Commodity for 'Sale' in Online News." *Asian Journal of Communication* 25, no. 1 (2015): 102–113. doi: 10.1080/01292986.20 14.996167.

Moon analyzes the online news content on cosmetic surgery procedures in Korea. According to a content analysis of news content from 2007 to 2013, the number of articles that pertain to plastic surgery has dramatically increased each year, and more than 60 percent of the articles portrayed plastic surgery in a positive light. News articles also used strategic patterns to include promotional content, suggesting that amid journalism in a highly market-driven environment, plastic surgery has become a commodity.

Oh, Hyun Jung, Thomas Hove, Hye-Jin Paek, Byoungkwan Lee, Hyegyu Lee, and Sun Kyu Song. "Attention Cycles and the H1N1 Pandemic: A Cross-National Study of US and Korean Newspaper Coverage." *Asian Journal of Communication* 22, no. 2 (2012): 214–232. doi: 10.1080/01292986.2011.642395.

This 2012 study analyzes U.S. and Korean news coverage of the H1N1 pandemic to examine cross-cultural variations in attention cycle patterns, cited sources, and news frames on this transnational issue. A content analysis during the period of April to October 2009 reveals that attention cycle patterns, news frames, and sources varied across the two countries according to professional norms, cultural values, social ideologies, and occurrences of relevant events.

Shim, Minsun, Yong-Chan Kim, Su Yeon Kye, and Keeho Park. "News Portrayal of Cancer: Content Analysis of Threat and Efficacy by Cancer Type and Comparison with Incidence and Mortality in Korea." *Journal of Korean Medical Science* 31, no. 8 (2016): 1231–1238. doi: 10.3346/jkms.2016.31.8.1231.

News portrayal of specific cancer types with respect to threat and efficacy is examined in this study. The study also looks into whether news portrayal corresponds to actual cancer statistics. A content analysis of cancer news stories in Korea from 2008 to 2012 shows that threat was overall more prominent than efficacy information, and there were discrepancies between news portrayal and actual statistics, e.g., over-reported threat of pancreatic and liver cancers and underreported threat of stomach and prostate cancers.

Moon, Young Sook. "How Food Ads Communicate 'Health' with Children: A Content Analysis of Korean Television Commercials." *Asian Journal of Communication* 20, no: 4 (2010): 456–476. doi: 10.1080/01292986.2010.496858.

Moon explores the current practice of television food advertising targeted at children in Korea and extends previous content analyses by examining the content and presentation manner of health-related claims as well as persuasive appeals and food types. The results of the analysis of 403 television commercials show children in Korea are still mainly targeted with advertising messages that urge the consumption of unhealthy foods heavily emphasizing sensory and emotional appeals.

Study of Audience Characteristics and Processes

Study of Audience Characteristics

Cho, Hichang, Jae-Shin Lee, and Seungjo Lee. "Optimistic Bias about H1N1 Flu: Testing the Links between Risk Communication, Optimistic Bias, and Self-Protection Behavior." *Health Communication* 28, no. 2 (2013): 146–158. doi: 10.1 080/10410236.2012.664805.

Using data from Korea, this study examines the relationship between optimistic bias, indirect risk experience, mass media and interpersonal communication, and self-protection behavior in the context of H1N1 flu. Its authors document that there is indeed optimistic bias about one's vulnerability for H1N1 flu, optimistic bias is rather enduring and resilient. While optimistic bias had a nonsignificant association with self-protection behavior, it plays an important moderating role by reducing the effect of interpersonal communication on self-protection behavior.

Cho, Hyunyi, Jinro Lee, and Jiyeon So. "Personal, Social, and Cultural Correlates of Self-Efficacy Beliefs among South Korean College Smokers." *Health Communication* 24, no. 4 (2009): 337–345. doi: 10.1080/10410230902889381.

This 2009 study investigates how various personal social and cultural characteristics of college smokers are related to their self-efficacy beliefs to refrain from smoking under difficult circumstances. Results show that perceived success of the latest quit trial and interpersonal communication with friends positively predicted self-efficacy. The cultural orientation of independent self-construal was also positively associated with self-efficacy.

Hong, Hyehyun, and Minjung Sung. "The Influence of Risk Perception on South Korean Mothers' Use of Infant Formula." *Health, Risk & Society* 17, no. 5–6 (2015): 368–387. doi: 10.1080/13698575.2015.1112879.

Hong and Sung explore what audience factors influence Korean mothers' use of infant formula. Demographic factors and perceptions about different aspects of formula were included. Results show that those with a job, and those with higher income are more likely to use formula. Perception about the safety of formula's raw materials was a key factor for formula feeding. Perceptions about economic benefit or the safety of the manufacturing facilities and the distribution system did not influence formula use.

Kang, Soo Jin, Tae Wha Lee, Michael K. Paasche-Orlow, Gwang Suk Kim, and Hee Kwan Won. "Development and Evaluation of the Korean Health Literacy Instrument." *Journal of Health Communication* 19, no. 2 (2014): 254–266. Doi: 1 0.1080/10810730.2014.946113.

The main focus of this study is to develop and evaluate the Korean Health Literacy Instrument that is designed to measure the capacity to understand and use health-related information and make informed health decisions. Through a series of validation studies, the authors successfully create an 18-item Korean Health Literacy Instrument with a high level of reliability. The instrument is deemed to be suitable for screening Korean adults who have limited health literacy skills.

Kim, Kwang Sik, and Jun-Hong Kim. "The Role of Sensation Seeking, Perceived Peer Pressure, and Harmful Alcohol Use in Riding with an Alcohol-Impaired Driver." *Accident Analysis and Prevention* 48 (2012): 326–334. doi: 10.1016/j. aap.2012.01.033.

This study investigates how sensation seeking, perceived peer pressure, alcohol use and gender influence the behavior of riding with an alcohol-impaired driver (RAID) among Korean adults. Results show that indeed sensation seeking propensity, perceived peer pressure, and frequent harmful drinking were significantly related to RAID behavior. Gender did not have direct influence on RAID, and exerted indirect influence through sensation seeking and harmful drinking.

Kim, Sei-Hill. "Testing Fear of Isolation as a Causal Mechanism: Spiral of Silence and Genetically Modified (GM) Foods in South Korea." *International Journal of Public Opinion Research* 24, no. 3 (2012): 306–324. doi: 10.1093/ijpor/eds017.

Kim examines if two key concepts from the spiral of silence theory, fear of isolation and perception of opinion climate influence people's willingness to speak out about genetically modified foods in Korea. Results support the idea that fear of isolation is a causal mechanism that links perceived opinion climates to opinion expression. An individual's fear of isolation, as a personality trait, was related negatively to his or her willingness to speak out, and the influence of opinion climates was greater among those who had a greater fear of isolation in general.

Lee, Chul-joo, Jakob D. Jensen, and Jiyoung Chae. "Correlates of Cancer Information Overload: Focusing on Individual Ability and Motivation." *Health Communication* 31, no. 5 (2016): 626–634. doi: 10.1080/10410236.2014.986026.

The focus of this study is to identify audience factors that influence cancer information overload (CIO) defined as an aversive disposition wherein a person is confused and overwhelmed by cancer information. Education level, trait anxiety, cancer history, and the use of active media channels were examined using three samples from the United States and one from Korea. Tait anxiety was found to be positively associated with CIO, while health information use from active media channels was negatively associated with CIO.

Quick, Brian L., and Jiyoung Chae. "An Examination of the Relationship between Health Information Use and Health Orientation in Korean Mothers: Focusing on the Type of Health Information." *Journal of Health Communication* 20, no. 3 (2015): 275–284. doi: 10.1080/10810730.2014.925016.

This study investigates how health information use influences overall health information orientation and consciousness regarding their children's health among Korean mothers. Different types of information use were found to influence health orientation differently. The use of mothering community for informal information was associated with health information orientation, but not with health consciousness. Education level moderated the relationship between interpersonal communication and health consciousness, and between print media use and health information orientation.

Oh, Sang-Hwa. "Am I in Danger?: Predictors and Behavioral Outcomes of Public Perception of Risk Associated with Food Hazards." PhD diss., University of South Carolina, 2014. ProQuest (3634877).

In this dissertation, Oh explores possible factors that may affect the way Koreans perceive personal and societal risks of food hazards and their intention to take preventive actions. Factors such as scientific knowledge, trust in information sources, news media use, and engaging in interpersonal communication was examined. Results show that many of the examined audience factors were related to risk perceptions, and personal-level risk perception was significantly associated with the intention to take preventive actions.

Park, Keeho, Ji Young Lim, and Yong-Chan Kim. "Effects of Health Literacy and Social Capital on Health Information Behavior." *Journal of Health Communication* 20, no. 9 (2015): 1084–1094. doi: 10.1080/10810730.2015.1018636.

This 2015 study addresses the question of whether social capital attenuates the effect of low functional health literacy on health information resources, efficacy, and behavior using in-person interviews data from Korea. Results show that respondents' social capital had positive effects on the scope of health information sources, health information efficacy, and health information-seeking intention. A significant moderation effect of bridging social capital and bonding social capitals were also found in relation to other variables.

Song, Yosep, Daewook Kim, and Dongsub Han. "Risk Communication in South Korea: Social Acceptance of Nuclear Power Plants (NPPs)." *Public Relations Review* 39, no. 1 (2013): 55–56. doi: 10.1016/j.pubrev.2012.10.002.

The focus of this study is to examine the effects of perceived efficacy, perceived risk, communication quality, and trust on social acceptance of nuclear power plants (NPPs) in Korea. Results show that perceived efficacy was most strongly related to social acceptance of NPPs, but communication quality and trust also mediated relationships among perceived efficacy, perceived risk, and social acceptance of NPPs.

Study of Audience Processes

Bae, Hyuhn-Suhck, William J. Brown, and Seok Kang. "Social Influence of a Religious Hero: The Late Cardinal Stephen Kim Sou-hwan's Effect on Cornea Donation and Volunteerism." *Journal of Health Communication* 16, no. 1 (2011): 62–78. doi: 10 .1080/10810730.2010.529489.

This study analyzes how the news media diffused the death of Cardinal Stephen Kim and how this news affected people's intention toward cornea donation and volunteerism. Results show that the multistep social influence process through which parasocial interaction with Kim affected intention toward cornea donation and volunteerism through identification with him.

Chae, Jiyoung. "A Three-Factor Cancer-Related Mental Condition Model and its Relationship with Cancer Information Use, Cancer Information Avoidance, and Screening Intention." *Journal of Health Communication* 20 (2015): 1133–1142. doi: 10.1080/10810730.2015.1018633.

Using three sets of data, the study develops a 3-factor cancer-related mental condition model encompassing affective (cancer fear), cognitive (cancer risk perception), and affective-cognitive (cancer worry) conditions. Analysis of two-wave data in the stomach cancer context finds that, although the three components of the model are positively related to one another, they are differentially related to cancer information use, screening intention, and cancer information avoidance.

———. "Who Avoids Cancer Information?: Examining a Psychological Process Leading to Cancer Information Avoidance." *Journal of Health Communication* 21 (2016): 837–844. doi: 10.1080/10810730.2016.1177144.

Chae carefully examines a psychological path to cancer information avoidance (CIA) with a focus on information processing (cancer information overload, CIO) and personal traits. Analyzing both U.S. and Korean samples, the study finds that CIA was predicted by trait anxiety by way of CIO. It concludes that some people are inherently inclined to avoid cancer information due to their trait anxiety, which results in confusion about cancer information.

Chang, Jeongheon J., Sei-Hill Kim, Jae Chul Shim, and Dong Hoon Ma. "Who Is Responsible for Climate Change?: Attribution of Responsibility, News Media, and South Koreans' Perceived Risk of Climate Change." *Mass Communication and Society* 19 (2016): 566–584. doi: 10.1080/15205436.2016.1180395.

This survey study deals with whether the way people attribute responsibility can affect their perceived risks and whether media use can influence the way the audiences attribute responsibility. The results show that respondents who attributed the negative consequences of climate change to the government or large corporations perceived a greater risk. Television news and online bulletin boards and blogs were differentially related to blaming the government and corporations.

Kim, Wonsun. "The Role of Social Support and Social Networks in Health Information Seeking Behavior Among Korean Americans." PhD diss., George Mason University, 2013. ProQuest (1428746728).

With an intramethod approach, this dissertation investigates the influences of social support networks on health information seeking behaviors among Korean immigrants. The quantitative data show the positive relationship between access to social support and online health information seeking activities. The qualitative data explain reasons why social networks are important channels for health information.

Koo, Joung Hwa. "Adolescents' Information Behavior when Isolated from Peer Groups: Lessons from New Immigrant Adolescents' Everyday Life Information Seeking." PhD diss., Florida State University, 2013. ProQuest (1448279745).

Using a mixed method approach, this dissertation examines how 16 newly immigrated Korean adolescents seek and use necessary information. The results reveal the participants' everyday life information seeking behaviors and main information needs. Five main themes emerge from the data: Parents attachment in information seeking and uses, dependence on interpersonal information sources, information ground, two-step flow, and passive information-seeking, information-avoiding and ignorance.

Oh, Kyeung Mi, Gary L. Kreps, Jungmi Jun, Elizabeth Chong, and Lolita Ramsey. "Examining the Health Information–Seeking Behaviors of Korean Americans." *Journal of Health Communication* 17 (2012): 779–801. doi: 10.1080/10810730.2011.650830.

The analysis of a cross-sectional survey among 254 Korean Americans in the Washington, D.C., area finds that Korean ethnic media sources and Internet are important sources used regularly. Age, years of education completed, and English proficiency levels significantly predicted the likelihood of their Internet use. Low-income Korean Americans with less education were more likely to seek health information in Korean ethnic magazines and newspapers, whereas Korean Americans with higher education and English proficiency were more likely to seek information online.

Oh, Kyeung Mi, Jungmi Jun, Xiaoquan Zhao, Gary L. Kreps, and Eunice E. Lee. "Cancer Information Seeking Behaviors of Korean American Women: A Mixed-Methods Study Using Surveys and Focus Group Interviews." *Journal of Health Communication* 20 (2015):1143–1154. doi: 10.1080/10810730.2015.1018578.

This mixed-methods study uses focus group interviews and surveys to find that Korean-American women viewed health care professionals as the most trusted cancer information source but used the Internet and Korean ethnic media more often for cancer information because of language, cultural, and economic barriers. When seeking cancer information, important factors for Korean-American women were accessibility, affordability, and language proficiency, cultural sensitivity, meeting immediate needs, understandability, convenience, and reliability of cancer information sources.

Oh, Sang-Hwa, Hye-Jin Paek, and Thomas Hove. "Cognitive and Emotional Dimensions of Perceived Risk Characteristics, Genre-Specific Media Effects, and Risk Perceptions: The Case of H1N1 Influenza in South Korea." *Asian Journal of Communication* 25 (2015): 14–32.

Their investigation expands the impersonal- and differential-impact hypotheses by explicating their underlying mechanisms and incorporating arguments from the psychometric paradigm. Analysis of an online survey among adults in Korea in the context of H1N1 influenza indicates the differential roles of the cognitive and emotional dimensions of people's perceived risk characteristics in risk perceptions and highlights a more salient mediating role of emotional aspects of perceived risk characteristics in risk perceptions.

Paek, Hye-Jin, Sang-Hwa Oh, and Thomas Hove. "How Fear-Arousing News Messages Affect Risk Perceptions and Intention to Talk about Risk." *Health Communication* 31, no. 9 (2016): 1051–1062. doi: 10.1080/10410236.2015.1037 419.

The survey data were collected among Korean adults in two risk issues—carcinogens and mad cow disease—to explore how personal- and societal-level mediate the relationship between fear-arousing media messages and intention to talk about the risk. The results of structural equation modeling show that fear-arousing news messages are positively related to personal-level risk perception, as well as to societal-level risk perception. Fear arousing news messages lead to intention to talk about the risk directly and indirectly through risk perceptions.

Shim, Minsun, and Myoungsoon You. "Cognitive and Affective Risk Perceptions toward Food Safety Outbreaks: Mediating the Relation between News Use and Food Consumption Intention." *Asian Journal of Communication* 25, no: 1 (2015): 48–64, doi: 10.1080/01292986.2014.989242.

The roles that cognitive risk perception (perceived risk of susceptibility and severity) and affective risk perception (worry) play in predicting intention to consume outbreak-associated food products is the focus of this study. Nationwide survey data in Korea show that both perceived risk and worry were negatively associated with food consumption intention and that perceived risk and worry mediated the associations between news use and food consumption intention.

So, Jiyeon, Hyunyi Cho, and Jinro Lee. "Genre-Specific Media and Perceptions of Personal and Social Risk of Smoking among South Korean College Students." *Journal of Health Communication* 16 (2011): 523–549. doi: 10.1080/10810730.2 010.546488.

The authors collected survey data among 558 Korean college students to examine the association between genre-specific media exposure and personal and social risk perceptions of smokers and nonsmokers. Results show that news media exposure predicted smokers' personal risk perceptions, whereas entertainment media exposure predicted nonsmokers' personal risk perceptions. Exposure to health infotainment predicted social risk perceptions, but not personal risk perceptions, of both smokers and nonsmokers.

Song, Hayeon, Hochang Shin, and Youngmi Kim. "Perceived Stigma of Alcohol Dependency: Comparative Influence on Patients and Family Members." *Journal of Substance Use* 20, no: 3 (2015): 155–161. doi: 10.3109/14659891.2013.878761.

This study investigates the stigma associated with alcohol dependency and its influence on patients and their family members. Analysis of data collected among 106 patients related to alcohol dependency and 60 family members of the patients finds that both patients and family members perceive high levels of stigma associated with alcohol dependency. Being female and perceived importance about the social role of drinking was positively related to feelings of stigma among patients.

You, Myoungsoon, and Youngkee Ju. "A Comprehensive Examination of the Determinants for Food Risk Perception: Focusing on Psychometric Factors, Perceivers' Characteristics, and Media Use." *Health Communication* 32 (2017): 82–91. doi: 10.1080/10410236.2015.1110003.

A nationwide survey of Korean adults in the context of Chinese processed foods and Japanese seafood imported to Korea was analyzed to compare the effects of psychometric factors of risks, risk attitudes, trust, favorability of the country of origin, and media use on people's food risk perceptions. Results show that psychometric factors had the greatest influence on food risk perception, followed by perceivers' characteristics and media use. Some interaction effects between media use and psychometric factors were reported.

————. "The Influence of Outrage Factors on Journalists' Gatekeeping of Health Risks." *Journalism & Mass Communication Quarterly* 92 (2015): 959–969. doi: 10.1177/1077699015596339.

This paper documents the effects of Peter Sandman's "outrage" factors on journalistic risk gatekeeping. Analysis of the survey data among 200 Korean journalists reveals that the average outrage factors perceived by the reporters were influential in determining the degree of newsworthiness in all five risk issues. Among 15 outrage factors, "catastrophic potential" was the most salient influence.

Study of New Communication Media

Chae, Jiyoung. "Online Cancer Information Seeking Increases Cancer Worry." *Computers in Human Behavior* 52 (2015): 144–150. doi: 10.1016/j.chb.2015.05.019.

Chae explores the effects of online cancer information seeking on cancer worry, which has been found to promote cancer screening. Study 1, a cross-sectional survey with U.S. participants, found a positive association between online cancer information seeking from professional health-related websites and cancer worry. To establish the causality, Study 2, conducting a two-wave survey in Korea, found that online cancer information seeking from online news at Wave 1 increased cancer worry at Wave 2.

Cho, Jaehee, Dongjin Park, and Herim Erin Lee. "Cognitive Factors of Using Health Apps: Systematic Analysis of Relationships Among Health Consciousness, Health Information Orientation, eHealth Literacy, and Health App Use Efficacy." *Journal of Medical Internet Research* 16, no. 5 (2014): e125. doi: 10.2196/jmir.3283.

The authors examine the effects of four cognitive factors (health consciousness, health information orientation, eHealth literacy, and health app use efficacy) on the extent of health app use. They also explore the influence of two different use patterns with regard to the relationships among the main study variables. The results from the path analysis show a significant direct effect of health consciousness as well as strong mediating effects of health app use efficacy.

Kim, Kitai. "Association between Internet Overuse and Aggression in Korean Adolescents." *Pediatrics International: Official Journal of the Japan Pediatric Society* 55, no. 6 (2013): 703–709. doi: 10.1111/ped.12171.

This study examines the association between Internet overuse and aggression among Korean adolescents. The proportions of boys who were classified as severe addicts and moderate addicts were 2.5 percent and 52.7 percent, respectively. For girls, the corresponding proportions were 1.9 percent and 38.9 percent, respectively. Findings show that smoking, alcohol, and level of Internet addiction were independently associated with all aggressive characteristics.

Kim, Sei-Hill, Hwalbin Kim, and Sang-Hwa Oh. "Talking about Genetically Modified (GM) Foods in South Korea: The Role of the Internet in the Spiral of Silence Process." *Mass Communication & Society* 17, no. 5, (2014): 713–732. doi : 10.1080/15205436.2013.847460.

Using the issue of genetically modified foods, this study examines how the Internet may affect the spiral of silence phenomenon in Korea. Findings suggest that the Internet may play an important role in shaping people's perceptions of opinion climates. Perceived opinion congruence with other people were significantly associated with one's willingness to participate in an online forum, indicating that expressing an opinion on the Internet may be subject to the spiral of silence effect.

Lee, Hye-ryeon, Hye Eun Lee, Jounghwa Choi, Jang Hyun Kim, and Hae Lin Han. "Social Media Use, Body Image, and Psychological Well-being: A Cross-cultural Comparison of Korea and the United States." *Journal of Health Communication* 19, no. 12 (2014): 1343–1358.

This study investigates the relationships among social media use for information, self-status seeking and socializing, body image, self-esteem, and psychological well-being, and some cultural effects moderating these relationships. Using online survey data, the authors found that body satisfaction had positive effects on psychological well-being in both American and Korean samples. However, they found different patterns of relationship between various forms of social media use and body satisfaction for Americans compared to Koreans.

Lee, Sun Young, Jounghwa Choi, and Ghee-Young Noh. "Factors Influencing Health-Related Internet Activities and their Outcomes." *Journal of Health Communication* 22, no. 11 (2016): 1179–1186. doi: 10.1080/10810730.2016.1236852.

Using data from a Web-based survey in Korea, the authors explore why people participate in health-related Internet activities and what the potential impacts of such activities are. Results indicated that trust in health information from doctors decreased communication activities, whereas trust in online health information increased both communication and information activities. Both communication and information activities increased discussions with doctors about online health information, which subsequently led to satisfaction with health care.

Lim, Jae-A, Ah Reum Gwak, Su Mi Park, Jun-Gun Kwon, Jun-Young Lee, Hee Yeon Jung, Bo Kyung Sohn, Jae-Won Kim, Dai Jin Kim, and Jung-Seok Choi. "Are Adolescents with Internet Addiction Prone to Aggressive Behavior?: The Mediating Effect of Clinical Comorbidities on the Predictability of Aggression in Adolescents with Internet Addiction." *Cyberpsychology, Behavior, and Social Networking* 18, no. 5 (2015): 260–267. doi: 10.1089/cyber.2014.0568.

The authors investigate the association between aggression and Internet addiction disorder (IAD), as well as the mediating effects of anxiety, depression, and impulsivity in cases in which IAD predicts aggression or aggression predicts IAD. A survey was conducted with middle school students in Seoul. The data revealed a linear association between aggression and IAD. The hypothesized mediators had partial or full mediating effects when aggression predicted IAD, but they had no mediating effect when IAD predicting aggression.

Lin, Wan-Ying, Xinzhi Zhang, Hayeon Song, and Kikuko Omori. "Health Information Seeking in the Web 2.0 Age: Trust in Social Media, Uncertainty Reduction, and Self-Disclosure." *Computers in Human Behavior* 56 (2016): 289–294. doi: 10.1016/j.chb.2015.11.055.

This 2016 study examines how self-disclosure is driven by the level of trust in social media and uncertainty reduction actions in three countries. Compared to their counterparts in Korea and the United States, youths in Hong Kong were significantly more likely to disclose personal health issues with peers online, and held a higher level of trust toward health information on social media. Meanwhile, both the level of trust in social media and uncertainty reduction actions were positively associated with online self-disclosure.

Oh, Hyun Jung, and Byoungkwan Lee. "The Effect of Computer-Mediated Social Support in Online Communities on Patient Empowerment and Doctor–Patient Communication." *Health Communication* 27, no. 1 (2012): 30–41. doi: 10.1080/1 0410236.2011.567449.

Oh and Lee test a mechanism through which Korean diabetes patients' exchange of computer-mediated social support (CMSS) in diabetes online communities influences their sense of empowerment and intention to actively communicate with the doctor. Data indicate significant relationships among patients' online community activities, perceived CMSS, sense of empowerment, and intention to actively communicate with the doctor. Sense of empowerment was an underlying mechanism for the influence of perceived CMSS on intention to communicate with the doctor.

Park, Sora, Eun-Yeong Na, and Eun-mee Kim. "The Relationship between Online Activities, Netiquette and Cyberbullying." *Children and Youth Services Review* 42 (2014): 74–81. doi: 10.1016/j.childyouth.2014.04.002.

The relationship between levels of online activities and cyberbullying behavior and the moderating impact of netiquette is studied. A face-to-face survey was conducted on a nationally representative sample of 12 to 15 year-old adolescents in Korea. The results show that frequent users of the Internet and SNS are more likely to engage in, become victims of and witness cyberbullying behavior. On the other hand, studying online, netiquette, and communication time with parents were negatively correlated to cyberbullying behavior.

Song, Hayeon, Kikuko Omori, Jihyun Kim, Kelly E Tenzek, Jennifer Morey Hawkins, Wan-Ying Lin, Yong-Chan Kim, and Joo-Young Jung. "Trusting Social Media as a Source of Health Information: Online Surveys Comparing the United States, Korea, and Hong Kong." *Journal of Medical Internet Research* 18, no. 3 (2016): e25. doi: 10.2196/jmir.4193.

The goal of this study is to investigate if cultural variations exist in patterns of online health information seeking, specifically in perceptions of online health information sources, in the United States, Korea, and Hong Kong. The findings support significant cultural differences in information processing preferences (experience-based versus expertise-based) for online health information.

Yoo, Woohyun, Doo-Hun Choi, and Keeho Park. "The Effects of SNS Communication: How Expressing and Receiving Information Predict MERS-Preventive Behavioral Intentions in South Korea." *Computers in Human Behavior* 62 (2016): 34–43. doi: 10.1016/j.chb.2016.03.058.

In the context of Middle East respiratory syndrome (MERS) in Korea, this study investigates how two communicative behaviors (message expression and reception) in SNSs affected the communicators' intentions to engage in MERS-preventive behaviors. Survey results support the presence of effects from expressing and receiving MERS-related information via SNSs and their underlying mechanism through self-efficacy and perceived threat.

Study of Culture

Bresnahan, Mary, Sun Young Lee, Sandi W. Smith, Sachiyo Shearman, Reiko Nebashi, Cheong Yi Park, and Jina Yoo. "A Theory of Planned Behavior Study of College Students' Intention to Register as Organ Donors in Japan, Korea, and the United States." *Health Communication* 21 (2007): 201–211. doi: 10.1080/10410230701307436.

Based on the Theory of Planned Behavior (TPB), this study investigated how the TPB factors contributed to intention to register as an organ donor among college students in Japan, Korea, and the United States. Path analyses resulted cultural differences in factors predicting behavioral intention: Subjective norm was a significant predictor only among U.S. samples; the relationship between perceived behavioral control and behavioral intention was positive among Japanese, negative among Koreans, and insignificant among Americans.

Cho, Hyunyi, and Miejeong Han. "Perceived Effect of the Mass Media on Self vs. Other: A Cross-Cultural Investigation of the Third Person Effect Hypothesis." *Journal of Asian Pacific Communication* 14, no. 2 (2004): 299–318. doi: 10.1075/ japc.14.2.06cho.

Cho and Han refer to the observation that people tend to assume communication has strong effects on others and clearly weaker effects on themselves. Based on surveys among 351 Korean and 320 U.S. college students about their perception of beer and liquor advertisements and television news on AIDS and smoking, the authors find a difference between the self and the other in both cultures, but a wider gap, as hypothesized, in the United States as an individualistic culture, where the difference between self and other is believed to be larger.

Han, Kyoo-Hoon, and Samsup Jo. "Does Culture Matter?: A Cross-National Investigation of Women's Responses to Cancer Prevention Campaigns." *Health Care for Women International* 33, no. 1 (2012): 75–94. doi: 10.1080/07399332.2 011.630117.

This study provides a look into the effects of individualistic and collective appeal and gain- and loss-framing in a cancer screening educational intervention but did not show any main effect. Interactions of collectivistic appeal and gain framing, respectively of individualistic appeal and loss framing (not in Japan) were, however shown to have effects. The results are based on 955 participants in an experiment, coming from Korea, Japan, and the United States.

Kim, Sang-Yeon, Tae-Seop Lim, Hayeon Song, Emily M. Cramer, Seokhoon Ahn, Jihyun Kim, Nathan England, Hyun-Joo Kim, and Junghyun Kim. "Healthy Food and Cultural Holism." *International Journal of Intercultural Relations* 52 (2016): 49–59. doi: 10.1016/j.ijintrel.2016.03.002.

It is hypothesized that a person with the holistic style would value natural food as a whole and for what it does to oneself, while an analytic style would appreciate a food item for its ingredients, for what is in it, and what it contributes to a healthy diet. Using data from small samples of elderly citizens, 84 in Korea and 61 in the United States, and a follow-up survey of 284 U.S. college students, the study found that the concrete orientations with regard to food are grounded in more abstract thinking styles. Findings are based on small samples of elderly citizens.

Kim, Sang-Yeon, Anna Herrman, Hayeon Song, Tae-Seop Lim, Emily Cramer, Seokhoon Ahn, Jihyun Kim, Hiroshi Ota, Hyun-Joo Kim, and Junghyun Kim. "Exploring Cultural Differences in Women's Body Weight Perception: The Impact of Self-Construal on Perceived Overweight and Engagement in Health Activities." *Health Care for Women International* 33, no. 11 (2016): 1203–1220. doi: 10.1080 /07399332.2015.1107070.

This study traces the influence of culture on the perception of body weight and the likelihood of taking corrective measures. Based on surveys of 277 female college students from Korea, Japan, and the United States, the study found that Japanese more than Korean and American women overestimate their body weight. Perception of overweight was associated with the interdependent rather than independent self-construal. Taking the measures against overweight is strongly dependent on the mediation of the relationship between construal and perception by self-criticism.

Kim, Yang Soo. "Host Environment, Communication, and Psychological Health: A Study of Cross-Cultural Adaptation Comparing Korean Expatriates in the United States with American Expatriates in South Korea." PhD diss., University of Oklahoma, 2003. ProQuest (305303556).

In this dissertation, Kim addresses the effect of cultural competence and communication on mental health among Korean immigrants to the United States as well as U.S. immigrants to Korea. It found that mental health among expatriates was higher if they had a higher communicative competence in their host culture. Mental health was also higher the more the participant communicated, in person or via the mass media. Results are based on convenience samples of 105 Americans and 106 Koreans.

Lee, Hyung-seok. "Cultural Considerations: In Anti-Smoking Health Appeals Effects of Individualistic versus Collective Appeals in the United States and Korea." M.A. thesis, California State University, Fullerton, 2004. ProQuest (305035981).

Lee's study looks into the role of cultural considerations in relative effectiveness of different appeal types. This study found no differences in the effects of individualistic and collectivistic fear appeals in anti-tobacco campaigns, and the fundamental assumptions that Korean students were more collectivistically oriented while U.S. students show more of an individualistic orientation was not confirmed either. Data come from a controlled experiment conducted in both countries.

Lee, Hyegyu, and Hye-Jin Paek,. "Roles of Guilt and Culture in Normative Influence: Testing Moderated Mediation in the Anti-Secondhand Smoking Context." *Psychology, Health & Medicine* 19, no. 1 (2014): 14–23. doi: 10.1080/13548506.2013.772303.

Lee and Paek pursue the question about how, in terms of mediation and moderation, norm messages (descriptive, injunctive, subjective) affect smokers' behavioral intentions with regard to passive smoking. Guilt arousal is expected to be more effective in collectivistic East Asian than in Western cultures. Results find no direct effect of norm messages, but guilt arousal affected behavioral intention, and more so in Korea than in the United States Sample consisted of 310 college students from both countries.

Paek, Hye-Jin, Jay (Hyunjae) Yu, and Beom Jun Bae. "Is On-Line Health Promotion Culture-Bound?: Cultural Characteristics Manifested in U.S. and South Korean Antismoking Web Sites." *Journal of Advertising* 38, no. 1 (2009): 35–47. doi: 10.2752/JOA0091–3367380103.

This study examines three aspects of cultural characteristics manifested in U.S. and Korean antismoking Web sites: cultural values (individualism and collectivism), high and low cultural contexts, and culture-bound health promotion strategies drawn from existing theories in other disciplines. Findings seem to partially support Edward Hall's cultural context framework, but not Geert Hofstede's cultural value framework. Results are based on 22 Korean and 67 U.S. anti-smoking web sites.

Paek, Hye-Jin, Hyegyu Lee, and Thomas Hove. "The Role of Collectivism Orientation in Differential Normative Mechanisms: A Cross-National Study of Anti-Smoking Public Service Announcement Effectiveness." *Asian Journal of Social Psychology* 17, no. 3 (2014): 173–183. doi: 10.1111/ajsp.12065.

This research finds that collectivism orientation is significantly related to the perception of injunctive norms only among Korean respondents, that perception of descriptive and injunctive norms lead to behavioral intention through different mechanisms, and that the normative mechanism was more rigorous and consistent among Koreans than Americans. These results are based on a survey among 464 Korean and American college students.

Chapter 6

Advertising

Chang-Dae Ham, Yongick Jeong, and Jacqueline Hitchon

Historically, economic developments have driven the evolution of an advertising industry. The South Korean advertising industry is no exception. It has shown a similar evolutionary pattern since the first advertisement appeared in *Hansung Chubo*, a government weekly gazette, in 1886 for a German trading company, Edward Meyer & Co.[1]

The United States has influenced Korean advertising since the late nineteenth century. Two Korean advertising scholars have characterized the American impact on advertising in Korea as "noticeable" after *The Independent,* a bilingual newspaper in Seoul, was founded in 1896.[2] However, given that the Japanese colonial rule of 1910–1945 was followed by the Korean War in 1950–1953, there was little opportunity for advertising to grow into a business to be reckoned with in Korea until the 1970s. The phenomenal economic growth that started in the 1970s catapulted the Korean advertising industry to a new level of global relevance. In 2011, Professors Kie-hyuk Shin and In-sup Shin wrote: "Advertising as we understand it today had to wait until the 'Miracle on the Han River' materialized."[3] By the late 1970s, the economy of Korea took off and joined the oft-touted club of Asia's "four little tigers"—Hong Kong, Korea, Singapore, and Taiwan. Koreans' per capita GNP jumped from less than $100 in the early 1960s to more than $1,600 at the end of the 1970s. Shin and Shin continued: "With

---

1. "South Korea," *AdAge* September 15, 2003, accessed May 14, 2018, http://adage.com/article/adage-encyclopedia/south-korea/98887/

2. Kie-Hyuk Shin and In-Sup Shin, "American Influence on the Development of Advertising in Korea, 1896–2010," *Journal of Practical Research in Advertising and Public Relations* 4, no. 2 (2011): 9.

3. Shin and Shin, "American Influence on the Development of Advertising in Korea, 1896–2010," 10.

such a remarkable economic growth in place, the stage had now been set for competition necessitating professional advertising agency services."[4]

In 2016, Korea became the world's eleventh largest economy with $9.4 billion in total media advertising expenditure.[5] Its status as an economic powerhouse and as a vibrant political democracy was reflected in several notable international events, including the Seoul Olympic Games in 1988 and the Korea-Japan World Cup in 2002.

THE PURPOSE AND FINDINGS OF OUR CHAPTER

As a rapidly emerging group of advertising researchers, Korean and non-Korean scholars have shown a great deal of interest in Korean advertising and its unique culture. More often than ever, Korea-related advertising research appears in scholarly publications in English.

Our chapter attempts to systematically classify and analyze Korean advertising research in major English books, journals, and dissertations. Also, our bibliography of key Korean advertising research publications in English should help identify Korean and non-Korean advertising research trends and provide a topical guideline for future research on Korean advertising.

For our bibliographical search, we identified 24 major scholarly journals in advertising, marketing, and communication,[6] employing the same criteria as previous researchers have applied in leading advertising trend analysis.[7] We also searched books, book chapters, and dissertations that center on Korean advertising. Using the three keywords, "advertising," "Korea," and "Korean," in four research databases (i.e., Business Source Complete; Academic Search Complete; Communication & Mass Media Complete; Google Scholar),

---

4. Shin and Shin, "American Influence on the Development of Advertising in Korea, 1896–2010," 10.

5. Young-woon Kang, "Mobile Ad Spending in Korea Soar 36% on Year in 2016," *Pulse*, March 7, 2017, accessed March 23, 2018, http://pulsenews.co.kr/view.php?sc=30800021&year=2017&no=156650.

6. Among the notable major advertising and related journals in English that we have checked for our bibliography are the *Journal of Advertising, Journal of Advertising Research, International Journal of Advertising, Journal of Current Issues and Research in Advertising, Journal of Interactive Advertising, Journal of Consumer Research, Journal of Marketing; Journal of Marketing Research, Journal of Retailing, Journal of the Academy of Marketing Science, Marketing Science, Communication Research.* We have also searched several leading general communication journals: *Journal of Communication, Human Communication Research, Journal of Broadcasting and Electronic Media, Journalism and Mass Communication Quarterly, Asian Journal of Communication,* and *International Journal of Communication.*

7. Kyongseok Kim et al., "Trends in Advertising Research: A Longitudinal Analysis of Leading Advertising, Marketing, and Communication Journals, 1980 to 2010," *Journal of Advertising* 43 no. 3 (2014): 296–316; Hyoungkoo Khang et al., "A Retrospective on the State of International Advertising Research in Advertising, Communication, and Marketing Journals: 1963–2014," *International Journal of Advertising* 35, no.3 (2016): 540–568.

we initially identified a total of 191 Korea-related advertising research publications in English. After reviewing each publication, we selected 110 that fit the focus of our chapter and classified them into six main topical categories with 12 subcategory groups.

Our bibliographical research has found a few non-U.S. publications, including an English-language book on Korean advertising. *Advertising in Korea* is the first book of its kind in English on advertising in Korea.[8] The 10-chapter book discusses the past and present of Korean advertising. Among the notable topics examined in the book are the Korean advertising industry, advertising laws and regulations, advertising organizations and publications, and advertising education.

Equally noteworthy is a rare study of American influence on adverting in Korea from the late nineteenth century to 2010. Korean advertising educators Kie-Hyuk Shin and In-Sup Shin analyzed the lasting impact of the United States on advertising in Korea from the late 1890s to 2010.[9] Probably this is one of the few English-language research papers that examine the history of Korean advertising as enduringly influenced by Americans.

ADVERTISING SCHOLARSHIP AS AN ACADEMIC DISCIPLINE

Over the last few decades, Korea has boomed as an economy, which led a vibrant advertising industry to quickly emerge, together with scholars interested in studying advertising. As advertising has evolved as an academic discipline, its scholarship has become more self-reflective and a stronger influencer of its own direction.[10] As Korean advertising research has attained the stature of a mature discipline globally, it has come to incorporate important research implications for the practice of advertising in Korea. The question then becomes: To what extent can we identify key trends reflected in the nearly 30 years of English-language advertising research in Korea?

Advertising research trends provide a larger context for us to interpret our annotated bibliography of major English books, book chapters, journal articles, theses and dissertations on Korean advertising. How to impact the advertising industry remains an important goal of much academic research,

8. Kie Hyuk Shin and In Sup Shin, *Advertising in Korea*, 5th ed. (Seoul: Communication Books, 2013).

9. Shin and Shin, "American Influence on the Development of Advertising in Korea, 1896–2010," 10.

10. Michelle R. Nelson, Chang-Dae Ham, and Regina Ahn. "Knowledge Flows between Advertising and Other Disciplines: A Social Exchange Perspective," *Journal of Advertising* 46, no. 2 (2017): 309–322.

which requires familiarity with the industry practice. Most research will be empirical and quantitative if Korean advertising is progressing along similar lines as in the United States. Theoretical explorations of advertising research tend to rely heavily on theories that explain individual and cognitive effects such as the dual process models, whereas cross-cultural theories have been applied to investigate Korea-related advertising in English, such as the dimensions of national culture[11] identified by Dutch cross-cultural psychologist Geert Hofstede and his colleagues in their influential book of 2010, *Cultures and Organizations,*

We can anticipate that message content and consumer research have been dominant topics, with adult consumers and students the most prevalent populations of subjects and respondents. Given the emergence of digital and social media in recent years, more English-language articles on Korean advertising research may increasingly incorporate new media, social and cause-related marketing, the role of data, and consequent changes in consumer behavior, including sharing and co-branding.

As its economy is experiencing unprecedented growth, Korea should serve as an insightful lens on advertising developments as a relatively young market with its own unique culture. Our chapter assesses Korea's ties to advertising in the United States and other countries.

ADVERTISING RESEARCH IN ENGLISH PUBLICATIONS

Against the growing economic values of international markets, Koreans' cultural values and identities have been widely spotlighted in advertising research. The cultural value studies, referred to as "Cultural Influence on Ad Content and Reponses," have examined how consumers' cultural values and identities are associated with their responses to advertising, looking at Koreans or Korean immigrants, or comparing them with Americans and other ethnic groups. Included in this body of research is how Korean consumers' cultural values and national identities are reflected by advertising content. Most studies of this type have examined cultural differences between the countries based on psychological theories, concepts, and dimensions like collectivistic versus individualistic characteristics.

A unique area of research in advertising deals with the perceptions by advertising clients, agencies, and industry practitioners regarding how advertising actually works. Called "Industry Issue and Practitioner Perspectives," such studies address how clients select ad agencies, how they evaluate agency

---

11. Geert Hofstede, Gert Jan Hofstede, and Michael Minkov, *Cultures and Organizations: Software of the Mind: Intercultural Cooperation and Its Importance for Survival* (New York: McGraw-Hill, 2010).

services, and how agency practitioners perceive work ethics, from the perspective of cultural and national differences.

Advertising effects have been the focus of the largest corpus of Korean research. Named as "Advertising Effect in Specific Contexts," researchers have investigated advertising effects in various contexts. This body of research has tested various advertising message effect in Korean and cross-cultural contexts. Findings have revealed that the same ad message cues, formats, and contexts have diverse impacts on advertising effects depending on the cultural characteristics involved. In "Celebrity Endorsement Effect," scholars analyze the effect of celebrity use across different cultures, including Korea and the United States. "Corporate Social Responsibility and Cause-Related Marketing" have been highlighted as well, examining how the general public perceives corporate social responsible (CSR) activities in Korea in comparison with other countries. Scholars have also probed "Advertising Effect in the Health Context" that relates to anti-smoking, cosmetic surgery, beauty image, nudity, and gay-themed ads. "Advertising Effect in the Political Context" has analyzed the effect of political advertising in Korean and cross-cultural contexts. "Product Placement and Sponsorships," a niche topic in advertising research, compares Korea with other countries, including the United States, in product placement and sponsorships.

Another salient topic for Korean advertising research is to investigate diverse audiences' social and psychological characteristics and their impact on advertising. Studies test how and why TV viewers and other audience groups respond to advertising, similarly or differently from other segments or from general audiences across countries. A focal audience group comprises children, proceeding from the assumption that children are more vulnerable than adults to commercial messages.

As in other communication areas, the Internet or media digitalization has brought about dramatic change in the advertising industry. Such changes significantly influence advertising research on Korea. On the one hand, advertising effects have been tested on diverse digital platforms like Search, Social, Mobile, and Web. On the other hand, this line of research has delved into the other side of digital advertising, known as "consumers' digital privacy." Consumers disclose their personal information on digital platforms to more conveniently use the platforms or their services. But such informational disclosure entails serious personal privacy concerns. Such digital phenomena in Korea or within the cross-cultural context were investigated in this research.

Employing various social and cultural psychological theories and concepts, many Korean advertising studies in English have paid critical attention to the similar but different effects of advertising content and contexts on consumers in Korea and other culturally distinguished countries. The dominant theory underlying these studies is cultural dimensions developed by Edward T. Hall, author of *Beyond Culture*[12] and Dutch social psychologist Geert Hofstede, a pioneer researcher on cross-cultural groups and organizations. Scholars have also turned to other psychological and sociological theories in explaining cultural difference (e.g., self-construal theory). Their findings suggest that cultural and national differences should be considered across diverse topics in Korea and in a cross-cultural context.

SUMMARY AND CONCLUSIONS

Advertising scholars examine a variety of research topics on Korea, Korean, and Korean-American consumers. In addition, they take note of the unique Korean culture, particularly focusing on the cross-cultural contexts advertising. Their research has ranged from audiences, messages, and media to industry perspectives. Most Korea-related advertising studies in English have employed diverse theories, while cross-cultural theories have played the most important role. The majority of studies have used quantitative approaches.

But Korean advertising law and policy issues have rarely been examined. Only one book chapter addresses the topic. This is rather surprising since advertising is subject to more than 100 laws and regulations, including the pre-clearance of advertisements by the Korea Advertising Review Board (KARB) as a self-regulatory institution. Indeed, a section of the Korea chapter in *Media, Advertising & Entertainment Law throughout the World* (2018 ed.) is devoted to Korean advertising law, which recognizes the significance of advertising law in Korean media and related laws.

Although its history is relatively short, English-written Korean advertising research has dealt with a wide range of topics. Our 100-plus annotations of Korean advertising publications in English should serve as an unmistakable evidence that advertising research on Korea will continue with its upward trajectory in the global twenty-first century. No doubt this confirms Korean advertising as a worthy research topic for scholars around the world.

ANNOTATED BIBLIOGRAPHY

American Influence on Advertising

Shin, Kie-Hyuk, and In-Sup Shin. "American Influence on the Development of Advertising in Korea, 1896–2010." *Journal of Practical Research in Advertising and Public Relations* 4, no. 2 (2011): 7–24.

---

12. Edward T. Hall, *Beyond Culture* (New York: Anchor Book, 1976).

Korean advertising educators Shin and Shin's journal article examines the enduring impact of the United States on advertising in Korea for more than a century since the late 1890s. Probably this is one of the few English-language research papers that focus on the history of Korean advertising as it was indelibly influenced by Americans.

Cultural Influence on Advertising Content and Reponses

Cultural Influence on Advertising Context

Cho, Bongjin, Up Kwon, James W. Gentry, Sunyu Jun, and Fredric Kropp. "Cultural Values Reflected in Theme and Execution: A Comparative Study of U.S. and Korean Television Commercials." *Journal of Advertising* 28, no. 4 (1999): 59–73.

The authors conduct a cultural content analysis of commercials from Korea and the United States to identify a number of underlying cultural dimensions of East Asian and North American culture. The authors develop a framework for practitioners and scholars in measuring cultural values inherent to a country.

Cutler, Bobby Dean. "International Advertising: A Content Analysis of Cross-Cultural Differences." PhD diss., University of North Texas, 1991. ProQuest (303936659).

Cutler analyzes 1,983 magazine advertisements from United States, United Kingdom, France, India, and Korea to examine the degree to which cross-national standardization of advertising. The results reveal that cross-national differences are significant in most executional factors, such as use of direct response technique, comparative product appeal, and literal versus symbolic appeal.

Kim, Kwangmi Ko, "The Globalization of the Korean Advertising Industry: History of Early Penetration of TNAAs and Their Effects on Korean Society." PhD diss., Pennsylvania State University, 1994. ProQuest (304114622).

The author uses an institutional level of analysis in examining the transnational advertising agencies' (TNAAs) expansion into the Korean advertising market. TNAAs' operations result in many changes in Korean advertising, such as the beginning of cigarette advertising, increase of commercial time, and the growing usage of foreign-made advertisements in broadcast and print media.

Lee, Soobum. "Colonizing Consumer Culture: A Semiotic Analysis of the Korean Advertising." PhD diss., University of Oklahoma, 1997. ProQuest (304368171).

Lee looks into the theoretical foundations for analyzing advertising as a consumer culture, Korean advertisements in magazines and TV. His study shows that Korean culture creates its own uniqueness in advertising by combining Western and traditional components.

Moon, Seung-Jun, and Michelle R. Nelson. "Exploring the Influence of Media Exposure and Cultural Values on Korean Immigrants' Advertising Evaluations." *International Journal of Advertising* 27, no. 2 (2008): 299–330.

Exposure to American mass media leads immigrants to accept American cultural values. If immigrants have an affinity toward American cultural values, however, this does not mean they feel negatively toward Korean cultural values, and vice versa. But the acceptance of these cultural values indirectly influences preference for models in print advertising (Caucasian versus Asian).

Tak, Jinyoung, "A Cross-Cultural Comparative Study on Political Advertising between America and Korea: A Content Analysis of Presidential Campaign Ads from 1963 to 1992." PhD diss., University of Oklahoma, 1993. ProQuest (304061844).

Tak analyzes 784 newspaper political advertisements and 110 television campaign commercials in Korea and the United States. Cultural orientations are significantly reflected in political advertising messages about American and Korean candidates. Political advertising is a conspicuous indicator of cultural values, representing clear differences between U.S. and Korean cultural patterns.

Yoo, Jinnie Jinyoung, and Wei-Na Lee. "Calling It Out: The Impact of National Identity on Consumer Response to Ads with a Patriotic Theme." *Journal of Advertising* 45, no. 2 (2016): 244–255. doi: 10.1080/00913367.2015. ProQuest (1065778).

The study finds that Korean Americans can have their patriotism "primed" to increase attitudes and purchase intention toward brands with a patriotic messaging. There is a similar but unequal effect on Caucasian Americans; Korean-American attitudes increase at a much greater degree.

Yoon, Kak. "Content Analysis of the Cultural Values Reflected in 1987 and 1997 Korean Magazine Advertisements." *Asian Journal of Communication* 12, no. 1 (2002): 40–57.

Yoon examines the use of individualistic appeals in Korean magazine advertisements. He identifies four individualistic appeals (efficiency and performance; sensuous; individuality and independence; intellect). He proposes that Korea can be a candidate for standardized marketing, but agencies remain hesitant on such an approach.

Yoon, Tae-Il, and Doyle Yoon. "Cultural Influences on Consumers' Processing of Advertising: A Structural Equation Approach." *Asian Journal of Communication* 13, no. 1 (2003): 55–78.

Advertising content is positively associated with attitudes in Korean consumers but is negatively associated with Caucasian Americans. For Koreans and Korean Americans, prior attitude toward the brand affects emotional responses, but no link for Caucasian Americans. Demographic subgroups further affect attitudes toward advertising. It is important to consider cultural as well as demographic variables when constructing advertisements.

Cultural Influence on Consumers' Responses to Advertisements

Bu, Kyunghee, Kim Donghoon, and Lee Seung-Yon. "Determinants of Visual Forms Used in Print Advertising." *International Journal of Advertising* 28, no. 1 (2009): 13–47. doi: 10.2501/S0265048709090453.

Researchers add a third level to the traditionally dichotomous measure of visual directness to expose the relevance of traditional marketing variables when gauging the preferences of Korean consumers. The traditional idea that Korean consumers value high-context and indirect advertisements is challenged when considering what is being advertised. Namely, the researchers identify brand familiarity as probably the most important variable.

Cho, Young Dae, "The Role of Culture and Advertising Industry Environment in Shaping Advertising Messages in Korea: A Cross-National Analysis." Master's thesis, California State University, Fullerton, 1993. ProQuest (304109024).

Using TV commercials from eight countries, including Korea, Cho examines how advertising industry environment, in combination with culture, is associated with television message production, analyzing advertising messages' creative strategy, informativeness, and cultural form with advertising environment. The results reveal cross-cultural differences in creative strategy, information content and form, which also closely related to advertising environment.

Choi, Sejung Marina, and Carrie La Ferle. "Convergence across American and Korean Young Adults: Socialisation Variables Indicate the Verdict Is Still Out." *International Journal of Advertising* 23, no. 4 (2004): 479–506.

A study of 275 Korean and 245 American college students addresses the idea of a growing consumer culture and the possibility of cross-cultural advertisements. While the results display that the groups are using the same media, the value of each medium differs between the two groups. While American students spend more time on the radio, Koreans students are more interested in their friends' opinion when considering a purchase.

Choi, Yung Kyun, and Gordon E. Miracle. "The Effectiveness of Comparative Advertising in Korea and the United States." *Journal of Advertising* 33, no. 4 (2004): 75–87.

The cultural differences of Korea and the United States are examined in the context of comparative advertising. The results show that direct comparative advertising (DCA) and indirect comparative advertising (ICA) campaigns are more successful in the less collectivistic culture of the United States, but there is no significant effect on purchase intent in either culture.

Chung, Girl-Jin, "Attitudes toward Advertising: A Q-Methodological Study of Consumers and Advertising Practitioners in Korea," PhD diss., University of Missouri-Columbia 1990. ProQuest (303898447).

How do consumers and advertising practitioners perceive each other? Using Q-methodology, Chung identifies three types of consumers (control agents; rational supporters; critical realists) and two types of advertising practitioners (advocators; self-regulators). Results show that each group has distinctive perception about other groups.

Han, Sang-Pil, "Individualism and Collectivism: Its Implications for Cross-Cultural Advertising," PhD diss., University of Illinois at Urbana-Champaign, 1990. ProQuest (303856301).

How is individualism-collectivism, a core dimension of cultural variability, reflected in the advertising appeals in Korea and the United States? Using a content analysis and two experiments, Han demonstrates that advertisements in the United States utilize individualistic appeals to a greater extent, and collectivistic appeals to a lesser extent, than do Korean advertisements.

Keown, Charles F., Laurence W. Jacobs, Richard W. Schmidt, and Kyung-Il Ghymn. "Information Content of Advertising in the United States, Japan, South Korea, and the People's Republic of China." *International Journal of Advertising* 11, no. 3 (1992): 257–267.

Information cues vary in number across four countries studied, including Korea, United States, Japan, and China. Across all the countries, advertisements in print media contain more information cues than advertisement on television or radio. These ratios, however, vary from country to country. This study provides evidence for a think-global, act-local approach to international advertising.

Kim, Byoung Hee, Sangpil Han, and Suki Yoon. "Advertising Creativity in Korea." *Journal of Advertising* 39, no. 2 (2010): 93–108. doi: 10.2753/JOA0091–3367390207.

Kim develops advertising creativity scale that fits Korea, the Confucian culture of the East. Four dimensions are identified: originality, considerateness, clarity, and product relevance. The second dimension is unique to Eastern values while the other three borrow from previously established dimensions.

Kim, Dong Hoo, and Yongjun Sung. "'Where I Come From' Determines, 'How I Construe My Future': The Fit Effect of Culture, Temporal Distance, and Construal Level." *International Journal of Advertising* 37, no. 2 (2018): 270–288. doi: 10.1080/02650487.2016.1238661.

By testing students from Korea and the United States, the authors conduct two studies to investigate whether individuals' cultural orientations influence the relationship between their construal level and temporal distance. Overall results indicate that individuals' evaluations of ads are moderated by their cultural orientations.

Kim, Yoo-Kyung. "The Impact of Cultural and Market Distance on International Advertising: A Content Analysis of Magazine Advertising from the United States, Japan and Korea." PhD diss., Syracuse University, 1996. ProQuest (304293496).

How does Korean magazine advertising employ standardized versus localized approaches? Using content analysis, Kim finds that 6 out of 10 creative strategies are different across Korea, Japan, and the United States. Combinations of cultural and market distance are related to advertising distance, which in turn, is associated with degree of advertising standardization.

Lee, Chunsik, Youngtae Choi, and Junga Kim. "Testing a Cultural Orientation Model of Electronic Word-of-Mouth Communication: A Comparative Study of U.S. And Korean Social Media Users." *Asian Journal of Communication* 28, no.1 (2018): 74–92. doi: 10.1080/01292986.2017.1334075.

The authors propose and examine the horizontal–vertical dimensions of individualism and collectivism (HVIC)-eWOM model by determining social media users in the United States and Korea. Findings indicate that, regardless of individualistic-collectivistic cultural values, vertical aspects play a salient factor in driving opinion-leadership as well as opinion-seeking behaviors for the two countries.

Myers, Matthew B., Roger J. Calantone, Thomas J. Page Jr., and Charles R. Taylor. "Academic Insights: An Application of Multiple-Group Causal Models in Assessing Cross-Cultural Measurement Equivalence." *Journal of International Marketing* 8, no. 4 (2000): 108–121.

The researchers use three constructs (attitude toward the ad, attitude toward the brand, and purchase intent) to test measurement equivalence in the United States and Korea. Results support the argument that multiple-group structural equivalence measurement is a useful tool in determining the model fit in cross-cultural research.

Shim, Sung Wook. "Advertising Appeals and Culture: The Difference between Culturally Congruent and Culturally Deviant Individuals in Korea." PhD diss., University of Florida, 2002. ProQuest (276185250).

How does self-concept affect persuasiveness of individualistic and collectivistic appeal advertisements with product use condition? Shim finds that culturally congruent individuals have a more positive attitude than culturally deviant individuals, but the effect of the self-concept varies by a personal versus shared product.

Taylor, Charles R., Gordon E. Miracle, and R. Dale Wilson. "The Impact of Information Level on the Effectiveness of U.S. and Korean Television Commercials." *Journal of Advertising* 26, no. 1 (1997): 1–18.

Korea is compared with the United States on the relationship between ad preference and the levels of information in the advertisement. Taylor, Miracle, and
Wilson conclude that the subjects respond differently to information level congruent with the differences in cultural context and values. Americans prefer high
levels of information and Koreans prefer low levels of information.

Yoo, Chan Yun, and Hyo-Gyoo Kim. "An Analysis of Prediction Error for New
Prime-Time Television Programmes: A Comparative Study between the USA and
Korea." *International Journal of Advertising* 21, no. 4 (2002): 525–546.

This study proposes culturally unique factors that return the least levels of prediction error for television programs. For instance, drama is the most popular type of
TV program in Korea. Also, returning lead-ins and lead-outs are not effective in
Korean audiences. Program length is of little significance in the United States, but,
in Korea, as the program length grows longer, the prediction error grows greater.

Yoo, Changjo, Bang Hae-Kyong, and Kim Youngchan. "The Effects of a Consistent
Ad Series on Consumer Evaluations." *International Journal of Advertising* 28,
no. 1 (2009): 105–123. doi: 10.2501/S0265048709090465.

A dual-experiment study conducted in Korea shows that consistency in
advertisements returns a greater positive attitude toward the brand and purchase
intention. Researchers also discover that a series of different, but consistent ads,
results in greater brand attitudes as opposed to repetition of the same ad, although
purchase intention is relatively unaffected by the consistency of ads.

Industry Issues and Practitioner Perspectives

Chang, Dae Ryun. "Advertising in South Korea." In *More Advertising Worldwide*,
edited by Ingomar Kloss, 165–188. Berlin: Springer, 2002.

Chang's overview of the Korean advertising industry includes the history of
Korean advertising, advertising spending, advertising industry structure and
characteristics, and the traditional and online Korea media.

Cho, Dong-Sung, Jinah Choi, and Youjae Yi. "International Advertising Strategies
by NIC Multinationals: The Case of a Korean Firm." *International Journal of
Advertising* 13, no. 1 (1994): 77–92.

There are distinct and unique characteristics of advertising strategies as firms move
from an export-oriented and multinationally oriented stage toward the globally
oriented stage. Multinational stage objectives seem to build from export stage
objectives. But then global advertising objectives shift drastically. Korean firms
are just starting to go global, but the authors believe that as more firms make the
switch, they will follow this model.

Hwang, Jang-Sun, and Hyun-Jae Yu. "Korea's Advertising Education." In *Advertising Education around the World*, edited by Jef I. Richards and Billy I. Ross, 160–168, N.p.: American Academy of Advertising, 2014.

Hwang and Yu's Korea chapter for the American Academy of Advertising (AAA) book on advertising education in 27 countries is a highly informative and readable overview of Korean advertising education. The Korean advertising industry is concisely introduced before advertising education in Korean colleges and universities is analyzed through its three stages: early era (1974–1988); blooming era (1989–mid-1990s); and restructuring era (mid-1990s-to date). Various academic and professional educational programs are introduced.

Kim, Ilchul, Dongsub Han, and Don E. Schultz. "Understanding the Diffusion of Integrated Marketing Communications." *Journal of Advertising Research* 44, no. 1 (2004): 31–45.

Integrated marketing communications (IMC) has become prevalent in advertising agency and client relations in Korea. Increasing amounts of firms agree on its benefits. However, a few things are inhibiting the universal spread of IMC. A majority of the agency respondents would agree to change their compensation programs if the clients would agree to implement IMC.

Kitchen, Philip J., Ilchul Kim, and Don E. Schultz. "Integrated Marketing Communications: Practice Leads Theory." *Journal of Advertising Research* 48, no. 4 (2008): 531–546. doi: 10.2501/S0021849908080513.

Integrated Marketing Communication (IMC) is an increasingly embraced concept globally. Korean firms focus IMC efforts particularly on more large-scale clients and much of their IMC initiatives are borne from PR departments. Also, in Korea, client demand for IMC is growing and diversifying. Over half of Korean clients seek out IMC. The authors claim that IMC, on a global scale, is stuck in the realm of tactical implementation.

Lee, Dong Hwan, and Chan Wook Park. "Conceptualization and Measurement of Multidimensionality of Integrated Marketing Communications." *Journal of Advertising Research* 47, no. 3 (2007): 222–236. doi: 10.2501/S0021849907070274.

A review of existing IMC literature produces a four-dimension model (unified communications for consistent message and image; differentiated communications to multiple consumer groups; database-centered communications for tangible results; and relationship fostering communications with existing customer dimensions) for the practice of IMC. A review of Korean companies exposes a previously undiscovered essential part to IMC—long-term relationships with customers.

Moon, Young Sook, and George R. Franke. "Cultural Influences on Agency Practitioners' Ethical Perceptions: A Comparison of Korea and the U.S." *Journal of Advertising* 29, no. 1 (2000): 51–65.

This study attempts to display the cultural influences on feelings toward ethics. Koreans show a particular disfavor for situations that involve company loyalty (i.e., hiring someone from a competitor). But they approve of scenarios involving fees and favors. American participants respond opposite in both of those scenarios.

Na, Woonbong, and Roger Marshall. "A Cross-Cultural Assessment of the Advertising Agency Selection Process: An Empirical Test in Korea and New Zealand." *International Journal of Advertising* 20, no. 1 (2001): 49–66.

Researchers mimic a study performed in New Zealand to expose structural and cultural differences in advertising agency selection. Despite some similarities, the selection process is greatly different in the different cultures. In Korea, chief executive officers (CEOs) hold a lot more power in selection committees than in New Zealand. The key election criteria are the same, but the variables are weighted differently.

Na, Woonbong, Roger Marshall, and Youngseok Son. "How Businesses Buy Advertising Agency Services: A Way to Segment Advertising Agencies' Markets?" *Journal of Advertising Research* 43, no. 1 (2003): 86–95.

Researchers survey Korean-based firms and offer a universal basis for the segmentation of advertising agency customers. Segmentation is based on a customer's market orientation. This is a top-down quality for a business and permeates through the organization. The researchers suggest that advertising agencies can tailor their public relations efforts depending on how market-driven a senior manager appears to be.

———. "An Assessment of Advertising Agency Service Quality." *Journal of Advertising Research* 39, no. 3 (1999): 33–41.

A study of Korea-based practitioners measures the service quality of advertising agencies based on "top-of-the-mind" recall by agency clients. Results suggest that Korean companies evaluate advertising agencies based on six individual dimensions of service. Korean firms also consider these dimensions at different levels of importance.

Shin, Kie Hyuk, and In Sup Shin. *Advertising in Korea.* 5th ed. Seoul: Communication Books, 2013.

This book is the first of its kind, and it remains the only English-language book on advertising in Korea. The 10-chapter book of 168 pages discusses the past and present of Korean advertising. Among the notable topics addressed by Shin and Shin are the Korean advertising industry, advertising laws and regulations, advertising organizations and publications, and advertising education.

Advertising Effect in Specific Contexts

Advertising Effect in General

Ahn, Jungsun, Carrie La Ferle, and Doohwang Lee. "Language and Advertising Effectiveness: Code-Switching in the Korean Marketplace." *International Journal of Advertising* 36, no. 3 (2017): 477–495. doi: 10.1080/02650487.2015.1128869.

The authors test the impact of code-switching on advertising effectiveness when two languages are used in an ad in the Korean market. Generally Korean-English code-switching and transliterated Korean-English code-switching are more effective than English-Korean code-switching for attitude toward the slogan and product evaluation. But different results emerge when the perceived difficulty of English words come in to play.

Choi, Jieun, Charles R. Taylor, and Doo-Hee Lee. "Do Resonant Advertisements Resonate with Consumers?" *Journal of Advertising Research* 57, no. 1 (2017): 82–93. doi: 10.2501/JAR-2017–007.

Using Korean college students, the authors investigate if resonant advertisements that can be interpreted in multiple ways are more persuasive than their non-resonant counterparts. Results show that resonant advertisements have an advantage over non-resonant advertisements in terms of cutting through ad clutter and message persuasion, but have limited impact on attitudinal and behavioral measures.

Choi, Yung Kyun, Sung Mi Lee, and Hairong Li. "Audio and Visual Distractions and Implicit Brand Memory: A Study of Video Game Players." *Journal of Advertising* 42, no. 2–3 (2013): 219–227. doi: 10.1080/00913367.2013.775798.

What are the effects of sensory distractions on the memory of brands presented in video games in Korea? Kim, Lee, and Li's study finds that auditory stimuli have a more negative effect on brand memory than visual stimuli. They note that unfamiliar brands receive more direct attention than a common, internalized brand.

Hwang, Jang-Sun. "How to Manage the Intensity of Comparison in Comparative Advertising over Time." *International Journal of Advertising* 21, no. 4 (2002): 481–503.

The authors test comparative advertising (CA) on Korean consumers. Results show a gradual increase in comparison with the greatest positive impacts on ad effectiveness. Findings suggest that it is best to begin a CA campaign with indirect comparison. Comparisons between products can become gradually more direct.

Jun, Sunkyu, Yoojeong Jeong, James W. Gentry, and Yong J. Hyun. "The Moderating Effect of Self-Esteem on Consumer Responses to Global Positioning in Advertising."

International Journal of Advertising 36, no. 2 (2017): 272–292. doi: 10.1080/026 50487.2015.1094859.

The authors conduct two studies to examine the interplay among perceived self-esteem, the effectiveness of brands advertised through global positioning, and cosmopolitan orientations within the Korean advertising context. Results show that the degree of perceived self-esteem plays a moderating role in determining ad performance.

Kim, Jooyoung, Eun Sook Kwon, and Bongchul Kim. "Personality Structure of Brands on Social Networking Sites and Its Effects on Brand Affect and Trust: Evidence of Brand Anthropomorphization." *Asian Journal of Communication* 28, no.1 (2018): 93–113. doi: 10.1080/01292986.2017.1363794.

Using Korean samples, the authors investigate the personality dimensions of brands promoted on social networking sites (SNSs). The brands advertising on SNSs contain more human-assimilated personalities than the brands that are not promoted on SNSs. In addition, the authors discuss six characteristics of brands with SNS presence.

Kwak, Hyokjin, George M. Zinkhan, and Denise E. DeLorme. "Effects of Compulsive Buying Tendencies on Attitudes toward Advertising: The Moderating Role of Exposure to TV Commercials and TV Shows." *Journal of Current Issues & Research in Advertising* 24, no. 2 (2002): 17.

Compulsive buying tendency(s) (CBT) is an individual phenomenon that is present in both high context and low context cultures. CBT effectively causes negative attitudes toward advertising in audiences in Korea and the United States. In Korea, heavy exposure to TV shows and TV commercials reduces negative attitudes toward advertising. In the United States, these attitudes are relatively unaffected regardless of TV exposure.

Park, Hyunsoo. "Forecasting Advertising Communication Effects Using Media Exposure Distribution Models: Test Market Results in South Korea." PhD diss., University of Florida, 1998. ProQuest (304445508).

Park examines how to predict Korean advertising effect using beta nominal exposure distribution (BBD) model. The result shows that BBD and normative framework, in combination with calibrating procedure, are useful tools to estimate target audience awareness, preference, and willingness of the campaign message.

Seo, Won Jae. "Understanding the Impact of Visual Image and Communication Style on Consumers' Response to Sport Advertising and Brand: A Cross-Cultural Comparison." PhD diss., University of Texas at Austin, 2010. ProQuest (760115360).

Seo determines the factors influencing ad and brand attitudes, purchase intentions as well as consumers' thoughts and feelings toward visual images and communication styles of sport print advertising in Korea and the United States. Seo finds that while Americans show overall positive attitudes toward ads and brands, the complex visual image, high-context verbal communication, and the presence of both individualistic and collectivistic characteristics induce more favorable attitudes toward advertising and brand in Korea.

Taylor, Charles R., R. Dale Wilson, and Gordon E. Miracle. "The Impact of Brand Differentiating Messages on the Effectiveness of Korean Advertising." *Journal of International Marketing* 2, no. 4 (1994): 31–52.

Brand differentiating messages (BDM) are common in U.S. advertising. This study shows that these techniques can be successful in the collectivist culture of Korea as well. Results show that attitudes toward the brand and purchase intention of the brand and product rise when commercials implement BDMs.

Whang, Haesung, Eunju Ko, Ting Zhang, and Pekka Mattila. "Brand Popularity as an Advertising Cue Affecting Consumer Evaluation on Sustainable Brands: A Comparison Study of Korea, China, and Russia." *International Journal of Advertising* 34, no. 5 (2015): 789–811. doi: 10.1080/02650487.2015.1057381.

The authors explore the relationship between brand popularity and brand sustainability in three countries. Results show that each culture reacts differently to brand popularity in a variety of categories. Highly involved Koreans are more novelty-conscious, hedonic and habitual. While both Chinese and Russians are also brand perfectionists, only Chinese are considered brand-conscious and impulsive.

Celebrity Endorsement Effect

Choi, Sejung Marina, Wei-Na Lee, and Hee-Jung Kim. "Lessons from the Rich and Famous." *Journal of Advertising* 34, no. 2 (2005): 85–98.

A content analysis of commercials in Korea and the United States shows the similarities and differences in each country's use of celebrities for advertising. Both countries predominantly use celebrities to promote food and beverage items, personal care products, and services. Korean advertisers, however, tend to have celebrities playing a character in the commercial.

Kim, Bongchul, Jooyoung Kim, Hana Kim, and Myungil Choi. "Practitioners' Celebrity Endorser Selection Criteria in South Korea: An Empirical Analysis Using the Analytic Hierarchy Process." *Asian Journal of Communication* 27, no.3 (2018): 285–303. doi: 10.1080/01292986.2017.1284247.

What are the similarities and dissimilarities between clients and advertising agencies in Korea in selecting celebrity endorsers? Research findings suggest that clients and advertising agencies use different selection criteria on celebrity selection although both rate the brand-centered factor (match-up) as the most significant criterion.

Lee, Wei-Na, and Sejung Marina Choi, "Celebrity Advertising: The Asian Perspective." In *Advertising & Reality: A Global Study of Representation and Content*, edited by Amir Hetsroni, 165–188. New York: Continuum International Publishing Group, 2012.

How are celebrities used in advertising in Korea and Japan? The two Asian countries, which share similar cultural factors, show a similar pattern in celebrity endorsement with a small number of fine differences. In both counties, a limited number of domestic celebrities are used for multiple different commercials.

Paek, Hye-Jin. "Understanding Celebrity Endorsers in Cross-Cultural Contexts: A Content Analysis of South Korean and US Newspaper Advertising." *Asian Journal of Communication* 15, no. 2 (2005): 133–153. doi: 10.1080/01292980500118292.

Paek proposes that in a high-power distance, high-trend pursuing culture like Korea, cultural celebrities are more quickly considered experts regardless of the product they are endorsing. Also important to note is that in certain markets, like fashion and cosmetics, Korean audiences react well to foreign celebrities.

Um, Nan-Hyun, and Wei-Na Lee. "Does Culture Influence How Consumers Process Negative Celebrity Information? Impact of Culture in Evaluation of Negative Celebrity Information." *Asian Journal of Communication* 25, no. 3 (2015): 327–347. doi: 10.1080/01292986.2014.955860.

Using a survey method, Um and Lee explore trends in attribution inconsistent with traditional fundamental attribution error assumptions in Korea and the United States. While Korean consumers are more affected by other-oriented negative information, American consumers show no difference between other-oriented and self-oriented negative information.

Yoo, Jae-woong, and Young-Ju Jin. "Effects of Celebrity-Organization Congruence on Audience Attitudes, Preferences, and Credibility Ratings for Goodwill Ambassadors." *Asian Journal of Communication* 23, no. 6 (2013): 620–636. doi: 10.1080/01292986.2013.790912.

Korean participants evaluate Korean organizations lower in three credibility categories when congruence between the organization, and their goodwill ambassador is low. These three categories are attractiveness, trustworthiness, and expertise. This effect is bilateral; the ambassador's image is also at stake. When an organization is considering a goodwill ambassador, it needs to select for maximal image-congruence.

Corporate Social Responsibility and Cause-Related Marketing

Kim, Hyo-Sook. "A Reputational Approach Examining Publics' Attributions on Corporate Social Responsibility Motives." *Asian Journal of Communication* 21, no. 1 (2011): 84–101. doi: 10.1080/01292986.2010.524230.

Using 200 Korean college students, Kim identifies factors that influence a public's opinion of two firms participating in the same corporate social responsibility (CSR) activity. Research shows that publics prefer a low-congruence activity by an organization and information via third parties. In addition, prior reputation plays a significant moderating role on public perception of a company's CSR effort.

Kim, Yeonshin, Tae Hyun Baek, Sukki Yoon, Sangdo Oh, and Yung Kyun Choi. "Assertive Environmental Advertising and Reactance: Differences between South Koreans and Americans." *Journal of Advertising* 46, no. 4 (2017): 550–564. doi: 1 0.1080/00913367.2017.1361878.

What are the cultural differences between Korea and the United States in response to assertive messages used in environmental advertising campaigns? Kim and others demonstrate that Korean and Americans react differently to assertive messages in recycling and energy-saving environmental campaigns as well as online magazines.

Minton, Elizabeth, Christopher Lee, Ulrich Orth, Chung-Hyun Kim, and Lynn Kahle. "Sustainable Marketing and Social Media: A Cross-Country Analysis of Motives for Sustainable Behaviors." *Journal of Advertising* 41, no. 4 (2012): 69–84. doi: 10.2753/JOA0091–3367410405.

Using online surveys, the authors examine the impact of sustainability motives on social media use in Korea, Germany, and the United States. They find that the involvement motives lead to recycling behaviors and green transportation use in all the three countries. Only in the United States and Germany, involvement motives result in anti-materialistic views and organic food purchase. Interestingly, Koreans show the largest amount of sustainable motivations and activities.

Moon, Sun-Jung, John P. Costello, and Dong-Mo Koo. "The Impact of Consumer Confusion from Eco-Labels on Negative WOM, Distrust, and Dissatisfaction." *International Journal of Advertising* 36, no. 2 (2017): 246–271. doi: 10.1080/026 50487.2016.1158223.

Using the Korean food and detergent industry, Moon, Costello, and Koo conduct a quasi-experimental field study to test the impact of ecolabels on negative consumer confusions. Results indicate that negative emotion induced by ecolabel confusions mediates the effect of negative word-of-mouth, distrust, and dissatisfaction.

Ryoo, Yuhosua, Na Kyong Hyun, and Yongjun Sung. "The Effect of Descriptive Norms and Construal Level on Consumers' Sustainable Behaviors." *Journal of Advertising* 46, no. 4 (2017): 536–549. doi: 10.1080/00913367.2017.1396514.

Using a popular Korean coffee brand, the authors conduct two studies to examine if the relationship between two types of descriptive norms (provincial and general norms) and consumers' sustainable behaviors can be influenced by construal level messages. Results suggest that the degree of similarities between descriptive norms and construal level message determines the attitudinal and behavioral changes.

Sohn, Yong Seok, Han Jin K., and Lee Sung-Hack. "Communication Strategies for Enhancing Perceived Fit in the CSR Sponsorship Context." *International Journal of Advertising* 31, no. 1, (2012): 133–146. doi: 10.2501/IJA-31-1-133-146.

The authors find that explanatory links within corporate social responsibility (CSR) advertisements are beneficial to both high-fit and low-fit cases in Korea. Advertisements, however, benefit from different types of information depending on the perceived level of fit. High-fit situations benefit through a relational advertisement strategy. On the other hand, low-fit situations benefit by an elaborational advertisement strategy.

Yoon, Sukki., Yeonshin Kim, and Tae Hyun Baek. "Effort Investment in Persuasiveness: A Comparative Study of Environmental Advertising in the United States and Korea." *International Journal of Advertising* 35, no. 1 (2016): 93–105. doi: 10.1080/02650487.2015.1061963.

By testing energy conservation and recycling advertisements, this study shows that people in the United States are more likely than Koreans to adopt habits from environmental advertisements that propose high effort. Results suggest that persuasion is based on two factors: amount of effort and sociocultural background, regardless of the pledge content.

Advertising in the Health Context

Baek, Tae Hyun, and Hyunjae Yu. "Online Health Promotion Strategies and Appeals in the USA and South Korea: A Content Analysis of Weight-Loss Websites." *Asian Journal of Communication* 19, no. 1 (2009): 18–38. doi: 10.1080/01292980802618064.

What are the health-related communications in weight-loss websites in Korea and the United States? Baek and Yu find that Korean and U.S. sites use some of the same appeals. But they are at different percentages. While Korean sites have more social support and personal appearance appeals, U.S. sites promote health as opposed to appearance in their weight loss appeals.

Huh, Jisu, Denise E. DeLorme, and Leonard N. Reid. "Scepticism towards DTC Advertising: A Comparative Study of Korean and Caucasian Americans." *International Journal of Advertising* 31, no. 1 (2012): 147–168. doi: 10.2501/IJA-31-1-147-168.

Korean Americans with more collectivistic values view direct-to-consumer advertising (DTCA) less skeptically while individualistic-oriented respondents have stronger DTCA skepticism. The authors advise marketing managers to recognize different within-country cultural factors when considering DTCA campaigns.

Huh, Jisu, Denise E. Delorme, Leonard N. Reid, and Junga Kim. "Do Korean-Americans View Drug Advertisements Differently Than Non-Hispanic White Americans?" *Journal of Advertising Research* 54, no. 3 (2014): 332–345. doi: 10.2501/JAR-54-3-332-345.

White Americans are more active users of different direct-to-consumer advertising (DTCA) media than Korean Americans, according to Huh and others. Television, Internet, and newspaper are the most effective DTCA media for the Korean-American consumers.

Kim, Kwangmi K. "Selling Smoke to Asia: An Historical Analysis of Conflicting US Policies on Cigarette Advertising and Promotions." *Asian Journal of Communication* 12, no. 2 (2002): 120–140. doi: 10.1080/01292980209364826.

Kim analyzes the history of the liberalization of Asian cigarette markets (Japan, Taiwan, Korea, and Thailand) driven by the U.S. government and cigarette companies. She finds that the U.S. government uses its global economic and political influences to liberalize the monopolized Asian cigarette markets, and this market liberalization has resulted in changes in cigarette advertising and promotional environments.

Kim, Yeung-Jo. "The Role of Regulatory Focus in Message Framing in Antismoking Advertisements for Adolescents." *Journal of Advertising* 35, no. 1 (2006): 143–151.

Using Korean high school students, the author finds that anti-smoking campaign effectiveness is highest when the frame and focus of a campaign are congruent (promotion frame—promotion focus; prevention frame—prevention focus). The results also indicate that the impact of congruency is moderated by self-views and self-monitoring.

Moon, Miri. "Cosmetic Surgery as a Commodity for 'Sale' in Online News." *Asian Journal of Communication* 25, no. 1 (2015): 102–113. doi: 10.1080/01292986.2014.996167.

According to content analysis of Korean online news of 2007–2013, there was a dramatic increase in news articles on plastic surgery. Sixty percent of the articles portray cosmetic surgery positively. Within these positive portrayals, articles are increasingly using cosmetic surgery practitioners for quotes, citing their full name. Moon reports that articles on cosmetic surgery in Korea use more native advertising techniques.

Morris, Pamela K. "Comparing Portrayals of Beauty in Outdoor Advertisements across Six Cultures: Bulgaria, Hong Kong, Japan, Poland, South Korea, and Turkey." *Asian Journal of Communication* 24, no. 3 (2014): 242–261. doi: 10.108 0/01292986.2014.885535.

Using a holistic perspective to include physical and affective notions of attractiveness, Morris examines outdoor advertisements featuring women in six countries, including Korea. Results indicate that images portraying women are based on the culture they are presented in and represent public ideals. This finding provides meaningful implications to practitioners to identify, develop and plan based on culture-specific habits, preferences, and styles.

Nelson, Michelle R., and Hye-Jin Paek. "Nudity of Female and Male Models in Primetime TV Advertising across Seven Countries." *International Journal of Advertising* 27, no.5 (2008): 715–744. doi: 10.2501/S0265048708080281.

A content analysis of TV commercials across seven countries, including Korea, examines the level and prevalence of male and female models' nudity. Accepted nudity correlates with product congruence in all countries, and there are general differences between the East and West in these categories. Korea displays a much more conservative attitude toward nudity than its Eastern counterpart, Thailand.

Paek, Hye-Jin, Jay Hyunjae Yu, and Beom Jun Bae. "Is On-Line Health Promotion Culture-Bound?: Cultural Characteristics Manifested in US and South Korean Antismoking Web Sites." *Journal of Advertising* 38, no. 1 (2009): 35–48. doi:10.2753/JOA0091–3367380103.

Paek and others attempt to add to the cross-cultural advertising literature by addressing cultural characteristics in health related websites. Their study concludes that culture-bound health-related strategies are used differently in the contrasting cultures. Korean advertisements in health-related websites show more individualistic indicators than their U.S. counterparts. The authors propose a "cultural value paradox."

Um, Nam-Hyun, Jong Min Kim, and Sojung Kim. "Korea out of the Closet: Effects of Gay-Themed Ads on Young Korean Consumers." *Asian Journal of Communication* 26, no. 3 (2016): 240–261. doi: 10.1080/01292986.2016.1144774.

The authors study the effectiveness of gay-themed ads in Korea. Results show that young Korean consumers have moderate tolerance levels for homosexuality. In terms of effectiveness, while gender does not show a significant impact, an individual's level of homophobia is a primary mediating factor in the evaluation of gay-themed ads.

Wilcox, Gary B., Marye Tharp, and Yang Ki-Tae. "Cigarette Advertising and Consumption in South Korea, 1988–1992." *International Journal of Advertising* 13, no. 4 (1994): 333–346.

A look at aggregate foreign cigarette advertising in Korea establishes a correlation with cigarette consumption by Koreans. Overall, however, advertising has no significant effect on consumption. Instead, cigarette advertising has an influence on what types of cigarettes Koreans are smoking.

Zhang, Juyan. "The Foods of the Worlds: Mapping and Comparing Contemporary Gastrodiplomacy Campaigns." *International Journal of Communication* 9 (2015): 568–591.

Are approaches to different nations' advertisement of culinary culture dynamic and unique? Zhang's content analysis answers in the affirmative. Healthiness and diversity are the main factors in all countries' gastrodiplomacy campaigns. There is also great emphasis on food safety. Overall, nations are becoming increasingly innovative in promoting their foods. Korea includes the connection between the East and the West in their marketing.

Advertising in the Political Context

Lee, Soobum, Lynda Lee Kaid, and Jinyoung Tak. "Americanization of Korean Political Advertising." *Asian Journal of Communication* 8, no. 1 (1998): 73–86.

What do Korean political television spots show? A content analysis finds a growth in individualistic, American themes. But this trend is not fully penetrating. There is a rise of negative tone, though it remains reserved, and a growing emphasis on candidate image in Korean political advertisements. There is also clear "Americanization" in the categories of logical, emotional, and fear appeals.

Lee, Soobum, Hyungkoo Khang, and Yeojin Kim. "A Cross-Cultural Perspective on Televised Political Advertising during the Presidential Election between the US and South Korea: 1992–2012." *Asian Journal of Communication* 26, no. 2 (2016): 133–152. doi: 10.1080/01292986.2015.1110605.

Korea is compared with the United States on political ads used in presidential elections. Lee and others state that Korean and U.S. presidential candidates use more high-context communication where U.S. candidates use low-context. U.S. political ads focus more on issues and policy while Korean ads emphasize personal characteristics. But advertisements in both cultures rely on emotional appeals in their political advertisements.

Tak, Jinyong, Lynda Lee Kaid, and Hyoungkoo Khang. "The Reflection of Cultural Parameters on Videostyles of Televised Political Spots in the US and Korea." *Asian Journal of Communication* 17, no. 1 (2007): 58–77. doi: 10.1080/01292980601114570.

What are the video characteristics of political advertisements in Korea and the United States? U.S. video ads focus on policy and issues where Korean ads pay particular attention to personal image and their viability, as well as importance, as a leader. Korean candidates show more conservatism addressing their opponents than Americans.

Tak, Jinyong, Lynda Lee Kaid, and Soobum Lee. "A Cross-Cultural Study of Political Advertising in the United States and Korea." *Communication Research* 24, no. 4 (1997): 413–430.

Political advertisements mirror the distinct cultures, according to a content analysis of political television commercials from the 1992 presidential election campaigns in the United States and Korea. Cultural orientations are clearly reflected in the commercial messages, indicating that political advertising is a conspicuous indicator of cultural values.

Product Placement and Sponsorships

Han, Sangpil, Jiwon Choi, Hyunchil Kim, John A. Davis, and Ki-Young Lee. "The Effectiveness of Image Congruence and the Moderating Effects of Sponsor Motive and Cheering Event Fit in Sponsorship." *International Journal of Advertising* 32, no. 2 (2013): 301–317. doi: 10.2501/IJA-32-2-301-317.

This study uses a case study of sponsorship campaigns in Korea during the 2002 and 2006 World Cup. The authors collect survey responses from 300 Korea residents to provide evidence for the effectiveness of a "created fit" between sponsor and event. Results indicate that "cheering event fit" moderates negative image congruence.

Lee, Taejun David, Yongjun Sung, and Sejung Marina Choi. "Young Adults' Responses to Product Placement in Movies and Television Shows: A Comparative Study of the United States and South Korea." *International Journal of Advertising* 30, no. 3 (2011): 479–507. doi: 10.2501/IJA-30-3-479-507.

Korean and American young adult consumers perceive product placement in TV and movies in similar ways. Lee and others' findings indicate that materialism, attitude toward advertising, and realism enhancement are significant factors of brand attention. In the United States, materialism and realism enhancement are the most powerful predictors of cognitive response to product placement. In Korea, however, the strongest predictors are attitude toward advertising and materialism.

Liu, Honglei, Kyung Hoon Kim, Yung Kyun Choi, Sang Jin Kim, and Siqing Peng. "Sports Sponsorship Effects on Customer Equity: An Asian Market Application." *International Journal of Advertising* 34, no. 2 (2015): 307–326. doi: 10.1080/026 50487.2014.994801.

The authors determine an appropriate fit between a sponsor and an event enhances brand loyalty in China and Korea. While attitude toward the brand positively influences brand preference in Korea, brand attitude has little impact on brand preference in China. The authors conclude that although sport sponsorships can achieve global representation for brands and products, there are still boundaries to consider.

Na, Jeonghee, and Junghyun Kim. "Does 'Articulation' Matter in Sponsorship?: The Type of Articulation and the Degree of Congruence as Determinants of Corporate Sponsorship Effects." *Asian Journal of Communication* 23, no. 3 (2013): 268–283. doi: 10.1080/01292986.2012.731606.

Na and Kim examine the importance of articulation in successful corporate sponsorship using Korean high school students. When there is a low degree of congruence between the sponsor and the event, non-commercial articulation can help to downplay the extrinsic motives of sponsorship. In a situation of high congruence, however, both commercial and non-commercial articulation can strengthen sponsorship effects.

Nebenzahl, Israel D., and Eugene D. Jaffe. "The Effectiveness of Sponsored Events in Promoting a Country's Image." *International Journal of Advertising* 10, no. 3 (1991): 223–237.

This study focuses on the 1988 Olympic Games hosted in Seoul. It finds that exposure to the games leads to greater purchase intention of Korean products. But the impact is limited to self-selected audiences who watch sports. Nebenzahl and Jaffe argue that purchase intention could be opposite in a less stable country where there is a greater possibility for catastrophes.

Research on Particular Audience Segments

Advertising Targeting Children

An, Soontae, Hyun Seung Jin, and Eun Hae Park. "Children's Advertising Literacy for Advergames: Perception of the Game as Advertising." *Journal of Advertising* 43, no. 1 (2014): 63–72. doi: 10.1080/00913367.2013.795123.

Using public elementary school students in Korea, the authors find that a simple educational video can greatly impact a child's evaluation of advertisements embedded in video games and advertisements in general. Results suggest that when children are exposed to short videos focused on enhancing their advertising literacy, they are able to readily identify advertisements.

Cho, Eunji, and Seung-Chul Yoo. "Effects of Violent Television Programmes on Advertising Effectiveness among Young Children: Findings from a Field Experiment of Kindergarten Samples in South Korea." *International Journal of Advertising* 33, no. 3 (2014): 557–578. doi: 10.2501/IJA-33-3-557-578.

Cho and Yoo examine the association between violent TV watching and advertising effectiveness using 6-year-old children in Korea. They conclude that brands are better memorized when they are placed in violent programs. Cho and Yoo theorize that the excitement of the violence lowers the child's processing of the ad itself and causes a positive increase in attitude toward the brand and advertisements as well as purchase intent.

Han, Kyoo-Hoon, and Jieun Kim. "Utility of Advertising for Creativity Education: An Experimental Study Targeting School Children." *International Journal of Advertising* 36, no. 3 (2017): 439–456. doi: 10.1080/02650487.2016.1139484.

Using a field experimental research approach, Han and Kim examine the impact of the Advertising-in-Education (AIE) program on creativity development among Korean elementary school students. They state that the AIE program has a positive impact on developing creative ability and creative personality of elementary school students.

Moon, Young Sook. "How Food Ads Communicate 'Health' with Children: A Content Analysis of Korean Television Commercials." *Asian Journal of Communication* 20, no. 4 (2010), 456–476. doi: 10.1080/01292986.2010.496858.

Advertisements for unhealthy foods account for about three quarters of food advertisements in Korea, and the appeals used in these commercials (sensory and emotional) are targeting children. Healthfulness claims tend to be empty, and nutritional content is not a priority. As childhood obesity in Korea climbs, the researchers urge more research in this area so healthier foods and habits can be more effectively advertised to children.

Shin, Wonsun, Jisu Huh, and Ronald J. Faber. "Developmental Antecedents to Children's Responses to Online Advertising." *International Journal of Advertising* 31, no. 4 (2012): 719–740. doi: 10.2501/IJA-31-4-719-740.

According to a study of Korean elementary school, children with higher level ad-skepticism are likely to have a more negative attitude toward online-advertising. But these attitudinal responses do not necessarily correlate to behavioral responses. Instead, the level of perceived Internet competency has a greater effect on behavioral response. Children who are more confident in their abilities on the Internet is more likely to disclose personal information.

Audience Segmentation Strategy

Kim, Choogn-Ryuhn. "Identifying Viewer Segments for Television Programs." *Journal of Advertising Research* 42, no. 1 (2002): 51–66.

The study proposes a three-step segmentation scheme that identifies segments of Korean viewers who view similar program sets. Viewers in each segment represent different demographic profiles, program viewing patterns, and commercial viewing times. The authors acknowledge the possibility of competition through program co-occurrence, since certain segments of viewers may choose to watch related but different programs.

Koo, Wanmo. "Generation Y Attitudes toward Mobile Advertising: Impacts of Modality and Culture." PhD diss., University of North Texas, 2010. ProQuest (818327520).

Koo compares Korea with the United States on what determines attitudes toward mobile advertising in an apparel context and its subsequent impact on behavior intention. He also investigates the effects of modality and culture on attitudes toward apparel mobile advertising. Koo's study indicates that entertainment, informativeness, irritation, and credibility determine the attitudes toward apparel mobile advertising, and attitudes can explain behavioral intention. Koreans are different from Americans on the perceived entertainment, irritation, and credibility.

Kwak, Hyokjin, Trina Larsen Andras, and George M. Zinkhan. "Advertising to 'Active' Viewers: Consumer Attitudes in the US and South Korea." *International Journal of Advertising* 28, no. 1 (2009): 49–75. doi: 10.2501/S0265048709090428.

Testing of the uses and gratifications model finds that more active exposure to TV content increases the positive relationship between favorable attitudes toward advertisements and products in both the United States and Korea. But more goal-directed exposure leads to more favorable attitudes toward ads and products in Korea but not in the United States.

Digital Interactive Advertising

Digital Interactive Advertising Strategies and Effects

An, Daechun. "Advertising Visuals in Global Brands' Local Websites: A Six-Country Comparison." *International Journal of Advertising* 26, no. 3 (2007): 303–332.

An's study highlights the presumption of the differences between high and low-context cultures. Global companies tend to represent their products based on assumed cultural values in the East (Korea, Japan, and China) and the West (United States, England, Germany). Western culture's visual ads include less celebrities, more photographs, and a higher frequency of direct shots of a product. Eastern culture's visual ads display higher frequencies of symbolic visuals, more celebrities, more illustrations, and a lower frequency of direct product portrayals.

Cho, Chang-Hoan, and Hongsik John Cheon. "Cross-Cultural Comparisons of Interactivity on Corporate Web Sites: The United States, the United Kingdom, Japan, and South Korea." *Journal of Advertising* 34, no. 2 (2005): 99–115.

What are the cross-cultural differences on web interactivity between Western (United States and United Kingdom) and Eastern (Korea and Japan) corporate websites. Focusing primarily on consumer-message and consumer-marketer interactivity, Cho and Cheon find that consumer-message and consumer-marketer interactivity are more popular on Western websites while consumer-consumer interactivity is more prevalent on Eastern websites.

Choi, Yung Kyun, Juran Kim, and Sally J. McMillan. "Motivators for the Intention to Use Mobile TV: A Comparison of South Korean Males and Females." *International Journal of Advertising* 28, no. 1 (2009): 147–167. doi:10.2501/S0265048709090477.

A sample of 256 undergraduate students in Korea is examined to determine motivations, attitudes and intentions to use mobile TV services. Males are more influenced by entertainment and status motivation. Females are motivated by social interaction influences. Both genders respond positively to a permanent access motivator.

Jerath, Kinshuk, Liye Ma, and Young-Hoon Park. "Consumer Click Behavior at a Search Engine: The Role of Keyword Popularity." *Journal of Marketing Research* 51, no. 4 (2014): 480–486. doi: 10.1509/jmr.13.0099.

The authors categorize Internet users of a Korean search engine into two groups based on their keyword searches: low-involvement consumers (those who usually search more popular keywords) and high-involvement consumers (those who usually search for less popular key words). Results suggest that less popular keywords see a greater ratio of sponsored clicks to total clicks.

Jerath, Kinshuk, Liye Ma, Young-Hoon Park, and Kannan Srinivasan. "A 'Position Paradox' in Sponsored Search Auctions." *Marketing Science* 30, no. 4 (2011): 612–627. doi: 10.1287/mksc.1110.0645.

Through analysis of a data set from a popular Korean search engine, the authors identify a "position paradox." This paradox addresses the relation to where firms are placed in search engine results. While high-quality firms tend to be placed lower on a list of results, low-quality firms, on a per click basis, benefit from the exposure of superior positioning on the list.

Jung, Jaemin, Sung Wook Shim, Hyun Seung Jin, and Hyoungkoo Khang. "Factors Affecting Attitudes and Behavioural Intention towards Social Networking Advertising: A Case of Facebook Users in South Korea." *International Journal of Advertising* 35, no. 2 (2016): 248–265. doi: 10.1080/02650487.2015.1014777.

Does peer influence have the strongest positive effect on Korean Facebook users' attitudes toward social networking advertisements (SNAs)? Jung and others state Yes. As invasiveness of the ad and concern for privacy grow, however, particularly simultaneously, positive effects are proportionally negated. These two variables increase in likelihood if the consumer is not fully comfortable on the social networking site.

Ju-Pak, Kuen-Hee. "Content Dimensions of Web Advertising: A Cross-National Comparison." *International Journal of Advertising* 18, no. 2 (1999): 207–231.

Ju-Pak's content analysis of web advertisements of Korea, England, and the United States shows that the web medium is ripe with desirable advertising features but it is not being used to its potential. Interestingly, the research finds a level of similarity in the creativity of the ads when they are advertising a service. But product advertisements are unique to their country, not just their region.

Kim, Ki Joon, and S. Shyam Sundar. "Mobile Persuasion: Can Screen Size and Presentation Mode Make a Difference to Trust?" *Human Communication Research* 42, no. 1 (2016): 45–70. doi: 10.1111/hcre.12064.

Consistent with the Modality, Agency, Interactivity and Navigability (MAIN) model, a study of 120 undergraduate Korean students reveals that large screen video format advertisements promote heuristic information processing while small screen textual advertisements promote systematic information processing. These two modes of processing have great effects on a customer's type and level of trust which can directly affect purchase intention.

Ko, Hanjun, Chang-Hoan Cho, and Marilyn S. Roberts. "Internet Uses and Gratifications." *Journal of Advertising* 34, no. 2 (2005): 57–70.

This study of American and Korean college students demonstrates that a user's motivations on the Internet affects attitudes toward brands, sites, and their overall purchase intention. Koreans tend to have social motivations on the Internet and prefer human-human interactions. Satisfying any motivation leads to positive brand attitudes and purchase intention.

Ko, Hanjun, Marilyn S. Roberts, and Cho Chang-Hoan. "Cross-Cultural Differences in Motivations and Perceived Interactivity: A Comparative Study of American and Korean Internet Users." *Journal of Current Issues & Research in Advertising* 28, no. 2 (2006): 93–104.

A study of American and Korean Internet users examines cultural differences existing on the Internet, which is often thought of as a globally relevant and universally applicable medium. Results indicate that U.S. users are more information-driven in their Internet usage and respond better to human-message interactions. Korean users, on the other hand, are more socially motivated and tend to respond well to human-human interactions.

Lee, Joowon, and Dong-Hee Shin. "Positive Side Effects of In-App Reward Advertising: Free Items Boost Sales: A Focus on Sampling Effects." *Journal of Advertising Research* 57, no. 3 (2017): 272–282. doi: 10.2501/JAR-2017-036.

By analyzing the user-level field data from a Korean network company, Lee and Shin investigate the impact of free game items offering through in-app reward advertisements on in-app purchases. Findings suggest that gamers who receive free game items are likely to purchase more game items than those who do not receive free game items.

Muk, Alexander. "Consumers' Intentions to Opt in to SMS Advertising: A Cross-National Study of Young Americans and Koreans." *International Journal of Advertising* 26, no. 2 (2007): 177–198.

A cross-national survey provides preliminary evidence that both Korean and American consumer attitudes and beliefs influence intentions to accept short message service (SMS) ad messages. Individual attitudes toward technological innovation and particularly the SMS medium greatly affects attitude toward SMS ads. Koreans are more receptive toward, and more likely to accept, SMS advertisements than Americans.

Park, Hee Sun, Hye Eun Lee, and Jeong An Song. "I Am Sorry to Send You SPAM." *Human Communication Research* 31, no. 3 (2005): 365–398.

A cross-cultural study on the use and acceptance of apologies in the United States begins with the discovery that Korean advertisements in unsolicited emails carry more apologies than U.S. advertisements of the same nature. Park and others find that Korean consumers find this to be more normal than American consumers.

Pashupati, Kartik, and Jeng Hoon Lee. "Web Banner Ads in Online Newspapers: A Cross-National Comparison of India and Korea." *International Journal of Advertising* 22, no. 4 (2003): 531–564.

The authors conduct a cross-national content analysis of web-banner ads in India and Korea. Findings indicate the differences in the types of products advertised, the presence and positioning of price cues, and the type of appeal (rational versus emotional) used. The researchers argue that the differences may have been caused by the level of technology advance rather than by a difference in cultural value.

Rodgers, Shelly, Jin Yan, Ruth Rettie, Frank Alpert, and Doyle Yoon. "Internet Motives of Users in the United States, United Kingdom, Australia, and Korea: A Cross-Cultural Replication of the WMI." *Journal of Interactive Advertising* 6, no. 1 (2005): 79–89.

The authors test the web motivation inventory (WMI) to determine the motivations to use the Internet in Korea, Australia, the United States, and the United Kingdom. They demonstrate the stability of the WMI test in the global setting, although four motives (research, communicate, surf, and shop) differ among the countries.

Seo, Yuri, Xiaozhu Li, Yung Kyun Choi, and Sukki Yoon. "Narrative Transportation and Paratextual Features of Social Media in Viral Advertising." *Journal of Advertising* 47, no. 1 (2018): 83–95. doi: 10.1080/00913367.2017.1405752.

The authors study the possible impact of narrative transportation on the success of viral advertising on social networking services in Korea and China. Results show that the influence of narrative transportation is moderated by the personal ties between the senders and the receivers, advertising disclosure, and the social proof for viral ads.

Yeu, Minsun, Hee-Sook Yoon, Charles R. Taylor, and Doo-Hee Lee. "Are Banner Advertisements in Online Games Effective?" *Journal of Advertising* 42, no. 2–3 (2013): 241–250. doi: 10.1080/00913367.2013.774604.

What's the effectiveness of banner ads on explicit and implicit memory? Using Korean college students, the authors find that recognition is independent of involvement and achievement in the game. Thus, banner ads in games can be effective even in a high level of concentration on the game.

Consumer Privacy Issues

Im, Seunghee, Doo-Hee Lee, Charles R. Taylor, and Catherine D'Orazio. "The Influence of Consumer Self-Disclosure on Web Sites on Advertising Response." *Journal of Interactive Advertising* 9, no. 1 (2008): 87–106.

What's the transference effect of self-disclosure on online advertising? Using Korean college students, Im and others discover that consumers are more likely to positively respond to advertisements on a website after they have entered their personal information onto that website.

Ko, Hanjun, Jaemin Jung, JooYoung Kim, and Sung Wook Shim. "Cross-Cultural Differences in Perceived Risk of Online Shopping." *Journal of Interactive Advertising* 4, no. 2 (2004): 20–29.

What's the difference in perceived risk of online shopping in Korea and the United States? Ko and others' study concludes that Koreans are more concerned with the social risk of online purchasing, whereas Americans are concerned with factors such as time, financial, and psychological risk.

Shin, Wonsun, Jisu Huh, and Ronald J. Faber. "Tweens' Online Privacy Risks and the Role of Parental Mediation." *Journal of Broadcasting & Electronic Media* 56, no. 4 (2012): 632–649. doi: 10.1080/08838151.2012.732135.

Using elementary students and their parents in Korea, the authors examine the role of parental influence in tweens' online information disclosures from the privacy perspective. They find that parent-tween disagreement has a significant impact on the disclosure of personal information online while parental mediation is not closely associated with the online information disclosure.

Chapter 7

Public Relations

Jae-Hwa Shin, Eyun-Jung Ki, and Arunima Krishna

A great deal of public relations scholarship relating to the South Korean context has appeared in Korean publications over the years. But much of the cutting-edge PR research on Korea has been published in English, situating Korean public relations in a global setting. The pioneering English-language research on public relations in Korea can be credited to the growing body of U.S.-educated Korean scholars teaching at American and Korean universities since the early 2000s. Many Korean scholars have closely collaborated with non-Korean scholars across the countries and in particular the United States. Equally noteworthy is the increasing emphasis on English research publications as a Korean institutional priority and Korean scholars' efforts to keep abreast of global advancements since the early 2000s. The growing impact of Korean public relations scholarship in and outside Korea has contributed to public relations as a major academic discipline that covers a wide range of specialized areas.

Hong Bo, the Korean term for "public relations," which literally means "broadly informing," has grown exponentially since the late 1980s, when the emergence of a liberal democratic regime entailed a robust free market economy in Korea.[1] The promotion of economic growth tied with flourishing corporate public relations produced a rich body of scholarship in public relations. Yet a heavy emphasis on media relations practice and research in Korea prior to the 1990s is not much different from public relations in other countries. By the late 1990s, Korean PR scholars embraced the changing emphasis in practice on relationship management, crisis and reputation management, international public relations and public diplomacy, ethics

---

1. Jongmin Park, "Images of 'Hong Bo' (Public Relations)' and PR in Korean Newspapers," *Public Relations*<This space is dropped from the PDF>*Review* 27, no. 4 (2001): 403–420.

and corporate social responsibility, and professionalism and leadership. This diverse and sophisticated set of scholarly and professional endeavors emerged in Korea as public relations began to mirror PR practices in the United States, Europe, and other developed democratic capitalist countries.[2]

For the past 20 years, public relations scholars have been prolific in publishing their Korea-related research in English. An increasing number of Korean academics have hit their stride in the global PR scholarship. This is evident from the fact that almost all of the English publications annotated for our chapter have been published since 2000, and about 60 percent of them have appeared since 2010. Not only the amount but also the diversity of Korea PR scholarship represent the growth in a global scholarship.

Our chapter provides an overview of Korean public relations scholarship published in English books, book chapters, journals, and unpublished dissertations and theses.[3] It showcases Korean PR research in English, and at the same time it suggests productive avenues for future scholarly endeavors. It traces the development of public relations practice within the unique Korean context. Moreover, it captures the robust research approach that Korean and non-Korean scholars have taken since 2000 to develop the practice and theory of Korean public relations. The common themes that have emerged from Korean public relations scholarship in English are consonant with the development and trends of global public relations scholarship.[4]

UNDERSTANDING PUBLIC RELATIONS PRACTICE THROUGH RESEARCH SCHOLARSHIP

Understanding the public relations profession and its practice in Korea has been a key area of scholarly attention, and the scholarly publications have been considerable since 2000. A number of PR research efforts over the years have demonstrated that Korean PR practice has evolved from its focus on relations between PR professionals and journalists[5] to an increased focus on

---

2. Yungwook Kim, "Professionalism and Diversification: The Evolution of Public Relations in South Korea," In *The Global Public Relations Handbook: Theory, Research, and Practice,* ed. Krishnamurth Sriramesh and Dejan Verčič (Mahwah, NJ: Lawrence Erlbaum Associates, 2003), 106.

3. Our bibliography centers on English-language publications of journalism and communication, widely circulated across the countries including the United States, with a focus on Korean public relations. Also annotated for our chapter are unpublished U.S. dissertations and theses written in English. The three authors have used their institutional databases and library systems for their comprehensive bibliographical search.

4. Jae-Hwa Shin, "The Development and Trends of Public Relations Research, Theory and Practice," In *Communication, Digital Media, and Popular Culture in Korea: Contemporary Research and Future Prospects,* ed. Dal Yong Jin and Nojin Kwak (Lanham, MD: Lexington Books, 2018), 245–280.

5. Jae-Hwa Shin and Glen T. Cameron, "Informal Relations: A Look at Personal Influence in Media Relations,"*Journal of Communication Management* 7, no. 3 (2003): 239–253.

strategic relationship management. The advent of sophisticated models of public relations in Korea has moved public relations from a technical to a management function, with organization-public relationships (OPR) cultivation being a persistent theme.

Ethical Concerns and Calls for Corporate Social Responsibility

Public relations ethics and its influence on PR practitioners have formed a major topic of research, and a majority of PR ethics studies have been published in English since 2010. Scholars have focused on the impact of organizational and personal factors on ethical public relations practice in Korea. They have examined the ethical standards among Korean PR practitioners[6] and the relationship between PR practitioners' personal ethics and their professional commitment. This line of research encompasses the sub-theme of corporate social responsibility (CSR), particularly in connection with the relationship between the perceptions and outcomes of corporate CSR activities.

Survey of Public Relations Identity, Roles, and Professionalism

Along with ethical practice, Korean public relations scholarship in English has paid growing attention to the identity, roles, functions, and professionalism of the field, with particular focus on understanding perceived discrepancies between public relations professionals and other professionals such as marketing professionals or government officials. Among those is the investigation of the disparities in professional standards among government and corporate PR professionals.[7] This scholarly trend reflects the evolving process of the public relations profession from the publicity model to a strategic management approach in Korea. Recent scholarship in the Korean PR profession has gravitated toward understanding the perceptual discrepancies between PR and non-PR professionals, including marketing professionals and the government.

6. Yungwook Kim, "Ethical Standards and Ideology among Korean Public Relations Practitioners," *Journal of Business Ethics* 42, no. 3 (2003): 209–223.

7. Jongmin Park, "Discrepancy between Korean Government and Corporate Practitioners Regarding Professional Standards in Public Relations: A Co-Orientation Approach," *Journal of Public Relations Research* 15, no. 3 (2003): 249–275.

THEORIZING PUBLIC RELATIONS SCHOLARSHIP AS A FORCE IN ENGLISH PUBLICATIONS

Korean public relations research published in English has been much informed by two major strains of public relations theory—the excellence theory and the contingency theory. Theories such as rhetorical theory and critical theory have been less prominent in Korea PR scholarship, though the image restoration theory associated with the rhetorical approach has been examined in crisis communication research in the Korean context. While the excellence theory has generated several organization-public relationship studies, the contingency theory has revolved around strategic conflict management research associated with crisis, risk, issue, conflict or reputation management. PR scholars have tested how the generic principles of the excellence theory are applied to public relations practice in Korea.[8] They have analyzed contingency factors that influence public relations practice at individual, organizational, or social levels.[9] Crisis, risk, issue, reputation, and conflict management research, along with the contingency approach, has generated the greatest volume of Korean public relations publications in English, which parallels the global public relations scholarship trends over the last decades.

Increasing Emphasis on Studies of Organization-Public Relationships

The emphasis on media relations research until the early 2000s has slowly shifted to organization-public relationship (OPR) research in Korea-related public relations. These studies can be categorized into two groups: (1) studies applying OPR developed in the United States to the Korean context to improve the external validity, and (2) studies attempting to find the cultural or Korea-specific elements of OPR. They have identified a few unique characteristics of relationship-building in Korea, for example, personal network (face and favor) as a specific measure of relationship in Korea[10] or the concept of *chemyon* (i.e., Korean for "face") as an essential factor in Korean relationship-building.[11]

---

8. Yunna Rhee, "Global Public Relations: A Cross-Cultural Study of the Excellence Theory in South Korea," *Journal of Public Relations Research* 14, no.3 (2002): 159–184.

9. Jae-Hwa Shin, Jongmin Park, and Glen T. Cameron, "Contingent Factors: Modeling Generic Public Relations Practice in South Korea," *Public Relations Review* 32, no. 2 (2006): 184–185.

10. Samsup Jo, "Measurement of Organization–Public Relationships: Validation of Measurement Using a Manufacturer–Retailer Relationship," *Journal of Public Relations Research* 18, no. 3 (2006): 225–248.

11. Yungwook Kim and Jungeun Yang, "Chemyon, Relationship Building, and Conflicts," in *Relations as Relationship Management: Relational Approach to the Study and Practice of Public*

Prevalence of Crisis, Issue, Risk, Conflict, and Reputation Management Research

Crisis communication has emerged as a major area in PR scholarship globally and locally. The volume of crisis communication research in English publications suggests its significance in Korean PR scholarship over the last twenty years. Some published studies have examined crisis communication strategies using image restoration strategies or the situational crisis communication theory,[12] while others have looked into the conflict management styles with cultural variables[13] or reputation management as an organizational outcome.[14] With the dominant influence of crisis, issue, and conflict management research, the role of stakeholder activism in controversial issues or crises and segmentation of the publics has attracted scholarly attention of Korea public relations since 2010.[15] The cross-cultural applicability of the Situational Theory of Problem Solving (STOPS) has been tested to understand the communication behaviors of the publics relating to a cross-cultural issue while the Issues of Processes Model has been applied to investigate how a politically inactive public became active.[16] The rise of social media has empowered the diverse publics, which has enabled an important area of scholarly investigation, yet the technological advancements have not much been explored as the trend of global scholarship.

Public Relations Research with Localization and Globalization

South Korea's ascendency in the global economy of the twenty-first century has led scholars to look into Korean public relations research from an international perspective. A number of studies published in English have investigated cultural variables and suggested a unique characteristic

Relations, ed. Eyun-Jung Ki, Jeong-Nam Kim, and John Ledingham, 2nd ed. (New York: Routledge Press, 2015), 240–257.

12. Sooyoung Cho and Glen T. Cameron, "Public Nudity on Cell Phones: Managing Conflict in Crisis Situations," *Public Relations Review* 32, no. 2 (2006): 199–201.

13. Emma K. Wertz and Sora Kim, "Cultural Issues in Crisis Communication: A Comparative Study of Messages Chosen by South Korean and US Print Media," *Journal of Communication Management* 14, no. 1 (2010): 81–94.

14. Sung-Un Yang and James E. Grunig, "Decomposing Organisational Reputation: The Effects of Organisation-Public Relationship Outcomes on Cognitive Representations of Organisations and Evaluations of Organisational Performance," *Journal of Communication Management* 9, no. 4 (2005): 305–325.

15. Jeong-Nam Kim, Lan Ni, and Bey-Ling Sha, "Breaking Down the Stakeholder Environment: A Review of Approaches to the Segmentation of Publics," *Journalism & Mass Communication Quarterly* 85, no. 4 (2008): 751–768.

16. Jinsoo Kim and Moonhee Cho, "When the 'Stroller Moms' Take Hold of the Street: A Case Study of How Social Influence Made the Inactive Publics Active in Anti-US Beef Protest in Seoul— An Issues Processes Model Perspective," *International Journal of Strategic Communication* 5, no. 1 (2011): 1–25.

of Korean PR.[17] With an emphasis on globalization, several studies have centered on public diplomacy and the strategic positioning of Korea in the world economy and its international reputation.[18] Comparative studies have been used as a common approach to understanding cultural differences or testing the applicability of a theory developed in one country to another across various topics, including crisis, issue, ethics, and corporate social responsibility.

ANNOTATED BIBLIOGRAPHY

Media Relations, Source-Reporter Relationship, and Agenda-Building[19]

Berkowitz, Dan, and Jonghyuk Lee. "Media Relations in Korea: Cheong between Journalist and Public Relations Practitioner."*Public Relations Review* 30, no. 4 (2004): 431–437. doi: 10.1016/j.pubrev.2004.08.011.

This study uses interviews to understand how the unique Korean concept of *cheong* has conditioned the relationship between PR professionals and journalists in Korea. Results suggest that *cheong* has a positive influence on media relations and lessens the potential for the adversarial and mistrustful stances traditionally adopted by both professions.

Jo, Samsup. "Advertising as Payment: Information Transactions in the South Korean Newspaper Market." *Public Relations Review* 37, no. 4 (2011): 399–404. doi: 10.1016/j.pubrev.2011.08.013.

Through in-depth interviews with PR professionals in Korea, Jo finds that the transformation from print to digital journalism and changes in funding have made newspapers increasingly dependent on news subsidies. The practice of rewarding the placement of news stories with advertising as payment plays a significant role in defining relationships between journalists and PR practitioners as news sources.

---

17. Eyun-Jung Ki and Lan Ye, "An Assessment of Progress in Research on Global Public Relations from 2001 to 2014," *Public Relations Review* 43, no. 1 (2017): 235–245.

18. Seong-Hun Yun, "Toward Public Relations Theory-Based Study of Public Diplomacy: Testing The Applicability of the Excellence Study," *Journal of Public Relations Research* 18, no.4 (2006): 287–312; Sung-Un Yang, Hochang Shin, Jong-Hyuk Lee, and Brenda Wrigley, "Country Reputation in Multi-Dimensions: Predictors, Effects, and Communication Channels," *Journal of Public Relations Research* 20, no. 4 (2008): 421–440.

19. For the thematic categories of public relations research, see Jae-Hwa Shin, "The Development and Trends of Public Relations Research, Theory and Practice," in *Communication, Digital Media, and Popular Culture in Korea: Contemporary Research and Future Prospects*, ed. Dal Yong Jin and Nojin Kwak (Lanham, MD: Lexington Books, 2018). Each publication is placed in each thematic category based on its dominant theme.

Jo, Samsup, and Yungwook Kim. "Media or Personal Relations? Exploring Media Relations Dimensions in South Korea." *Journalism & Mass Communication Quarterly* 81, no. 2 (2004): 292–306. doi: 10.1177/107769900408100205.

Jo and Kim's study centers on PR practitioners in Korea and finds that personal relationships with journalists are crucial in getting media coverage and minimizing negative media coverage.

Kang, Hyun Jin. "South Korean Public Relations Practitioners' and Journalists' Perceptions: A Gap Analysis." Master's thesis, Michigan State University, 2007.

Using the coorientation model, Kang investigates the relationship between journalists and PR practitioners in Korea. The findings suggest that the two professionals perceive their relationship quality as neutral, while their estimation of the other profession's perceptions about the relations are inaccurate.

Kim, Yungwook, and Jiyang Bae. "Korean Practitioners and Journalists: Relational Influences in News Selection." *Public Relations Review* 32, no. 3 (2006): 241–245. doi: 10.1016/j.pubrev.2006.05.016.

Korean PR practitioners' perceptions provide insight into the ways that source-reporter relationships influence news story selection. Findings show that PR practitioners believe that in formal situations, media routine principles condition the selection of news stories while personal relationship or the giving of gifts are influential in journalists' selection of stories in informal media relations.

Lee, Jonghyuk, and Dan Berkowitz. "Third Gatekeeping in Korea: The Screening of First-Edition Newspapers by Public Relations Practitioners." *Public Relations Review* 30, no. 3 (2004): 313–325. doi: 10.1016/j.pubrev.2004.05.004.

In-depth interviews with Korean corporate and government public relations practitioners are used to examine the "third gatekeeping" process by which PR professionals review news stories and suggest revisions prior to publication. The practice raises ethical questions related to the potential for manipulating news coverage.

Min, Sungick. "An Analysis of Sport Reporters' Perceptions of the Effectiveness of Sport Public Relations Practitioners' Influence Practices in South Korea." PhD diss., University of Northern Colorado, 2009. ProQuest (304963993).

Min investigates effective PR influence tactics through interviews with Korean sports reporters. Sports journalists report that reciprocation affects their writing, indicating the importance of PR practitioners' maintaining a strong relationship with sports reporters.

Shin, Jae-Hwa, and Glen T. Cameron. "The Interplay of Professional and Cultural Factors in the Online Source-Reporter Relationship." *Journalism Studies* 4, no. 2 (2003): 253–272. doi: 10.1080/1461670032000074829a.

Shin and Cameron compare cultural and professional factors marking source-reporter relationships in Korea and the United States. Twenty types of offline and online interactions are assessed as useful, influential, credible, ethical, and professional. The online media transforms the source-reporter relationships, yet cultural values are interplayed in the professional relationships.

———. "Informal Relations: A Look at Personal Influence in Media Relations." *Journal of Communication Management* 7, no. 3 (2003): 239–253. doi: 10.1108/13632540310807395.

Surveys among Korean PR practitioners and journalists show that PR practitioners perceive informal relations to influence media coverage more than journalists do. While journalists perceive a gap between their own and PR practitioners' ethics, PR practitioners misunderstand journalists' ethical values greater than their counterpart.

———. "The Potential of Online Media: A Coorientational Analysis of Conflict between PR Professionals and Journalists in South Korea." *Journalism & Mass Communication Quarterly* 80, no. 3 (2003): 583–602. doi: 10.1177/1077699003 08000307.

The coorientational analysis of Korean PR practitioners and journalists indicates that online source-reporter relationships generate fewer perceived discrepancies of the relationships among PR practitioners than do offline source-reporter relationships. The online interactions are perceived as less conflicting than the offline interactions.

Shin, Jae-Hwa, Jaesub Lee, and Jongmin Park. "Perceptual Dynamics of Pluralistic Ignorance and Social Distance: Public Relations Practitioners and Journalists in South Korea." *Asian Journal of Communication* 22, no. 1 (2012): 19–43. doi: 10. 1080/01292986.2011.622773.

Using correlational theory and third-person effects, the social and professional distance perceived by PR practitioners and journalists is investigated on the two dimensions of conflict and strategy. Each group has similar differences in their perceptions of the other's value, as well as the other's perceived value among the general public. Results show that journalists predict PR practitioners' views and their value less accurately than the PR practitioners predict journalists' views, in comparison to the general publics.

Verhoeven, Piet. "The Co-Production of Business News and Its Effects: The Corporate Framing Mediated-Moderation Model." *Public Relations Review* 42, no. 4 (2016): 509–521. doi: 10.1016/j.pubrev.2016.03.006.

Verhoeven conducts a meta-analysis of the relationships between corporations and journalists. Results confirm the moderating effect of culture, such as the practice of *Cheong*, and the mediating impact of interpersonal relations specific to individual countries, including Korea.

Yun, Seong-Hun, and Heesang Yoon, "Are Journalists' Own Problems Aggravating Their Hostility toward Public Relations?" *Public Relations Review* 37, no. 3 (2011): 305–313. doi: 10.1016/j.pubrev.2011.03.004.

Surveys of Korean journalists about their job satisfaction and relationship with PR professionals suggest that Korean journalists do not tend to hold negative views of PR nor do they believe that PR professionals have a higher status than do journalists.

Public Relations Theory Building: Excellence versus Contingency

Choi, Yoonhyeung, and Glen T. Cameron. "Overcoming Ethnocentrism: The Role of Identity in Contingent Practice of International Public Relations." *Journal of Public Relations Research* 17, no.2 (2005): 171–189. doi: 10.1207/s1532754xjprr1702_6.

The authors interview heads of PR agencies with multinational corporations (MNCs) as clients to understand how such clients practice PR in Korea, particularly in conflict situations. PR agency heads report "fear factor" as a key contributor to MNCs' adopting accommodative stances during crises.

Hwang, Sungwook. "The Estimation of the South Korean Government's Diplomacy for Its Opposing Public North Korea." *Journal of Public Relations Research* 24, no. 4 (2012): 338–352. doi: 10.1080/1062726X.2012.689900.

Hwang surveys Koreans to understand their perception of contingency factors and evaluation of the Korean government's stance toward North Koreans, confirming the generalizability of the contingency model and identifying the strongest contingency factors in international conflict.

Hwang, Sungwook, and Glen T. Cameron. "The Elephant in the Room Is Awake and Takes Things Personally: The North Korean Nuclear Threat and the General Public's Estimation of American Diplomacy." *Public Relations Review* 34, no. 1 (2008): 41–48. doi: 10.1016/j.pubrev.2007.11.001.

The authors examine the role of leadership style and perception of situational factors on the North Korean nuclear crisis. Such factors as dominant coalition characteristics, external threats, and external public characteristics emerge as strong predictors of the public assessment of the crisis. They suggest that threat perception and public characteristics help guide PR practitioners in developing messages that match the public's assessment of threats.

Kim, Yungwook, and Linda Childers Hon. "Public Relations in South Korea: Applying Theories and Exploring Opportunities." *Journal of Asian Pacific Communication* 11, no. 2 (2001): 263–286. doi: 10.1075/japc.11.2.09kim.

Kim and Hon evaluate the extent to which theories of PR developed in the West are applied in Korea. Using interviews with CEOs and PR practitioners, the authors pinpoint roadblocks associated with how PR practitioners adopt models of practice developed in the West and cultural norms that guide PR practice in Korea.

Rhee, Yunna. "Global Public Relations: A Cross-Cultural Study of the Excellence Theory in South Korea." *Journal of Public Relations Research* 14, no. 3 (2002): 159–184. doi: 10.1207/S1532754XJPRR1403_1.

Rhee appraises the applicability of the excellence theory and generic principles in Korea, showing that the excellence theory explains PR practice in Korea in conjunction with culture-specific elements including collectivism and dynamic elements of Confucianism.

Shin, Jae-Hwa "The Development and Trends of Public Relations Research, Theory and Practice." In *Communication, Digital Media, and Popular Culture in Korea: Contemporary Research and Future Prospects*, edited by Dal Yong Jin and Nojin Kwak, 245–280. Lanham, MD: Lexington Books, 2018.

The author reviews the history, development, and trends of Korea public relations research tied with the evolution of Korea PR practice. The thematic analysis shows a general pattern of Korea public relations research in the Korean context as well as international settings. Further research directions are suggested in global scholarship.

Shin, Jae-Hwa, Jongmin Park, and Glen T. Cameron. "Contingent Factors: Modeling Generic Public Relations Practice in South Korea." *Public Relations Review* 32, no. 2 (2006): 184–185. doi: 10.1016/j.pubrev.2006.02.015.

The authors survey Korean PR practitioners to assess the relative influence of contingent variables. At the management level, respondents report the salience of organizational-level variables. At the staff level, departmental variables are perceived as dominant. PR professionals in general note the release of negative information and conflict as major constraining variables.

Shin, Jae-Hwa, Robert L. Heath, and Jaesub Lee. "A Contingency Explanation of Public Relations Practitioner Leadership Styles: Situation and Culture." *Journal of Public Relations Research* 23, no. 2 (2011): 167–190. doi: 10.1080/1062726X. 2010.505121.

This study compares the preferred leadership styles of PR professionals in the United States and Korea. The results show that U.S. professionals consider strategic communication or problem-solving activities to be important, while Korean professionals emphasize leadership characteristics and functions related to practical and resourceful capabilities.

Yun, Seong-Hun. "Toward Public Relations Theory-Based Study of Public Diplomacy: Testing the Applicability of the Excellence Study." *Journal of Public Relations Research* 18, no. 4 (2006): 287–312. doi: 10.1207/s1532754xjprr1804_1.

Yun integrates the excellence theory and public diplomacy and identifies two models of public relations behavior and excellence in public relations. The findings support the applicability of the conceptual and measurement frameworks developed.

Publics and Activism

Jo, Samsup. "Factors Shaping Activists' Perceptions of Corporate Organizations: An Empirical Case from South Korea." *Public Relations Review* 37, no. 2 (2011): 178–180. doi: 10.1016/j.pubrev.2011.01.002.

Surveys of activists demonstrate that while Korean activists have a positive evaluation of the essential functions of corporate culture, they oppose and distrust corporate communications. They most strongly object to corporations' influence on the media through their superior power and financial resources.

Kim, Jeong-Nam, Lan Ni, Sei-Hill Kim, and Jangyul Robert Kim. "What Makes People Hot? Applying the Situational Theory of Problem Solving to Hot-Issue Publics." *Journal of Public Relations Research* 24, no. 2 (2012): 144–164. doi:10.1080/1062726X.2012.626133.

The authors test the cross-cultural applicability of the Situational Theory of Problem Solving (STOPS) to the rise of a hot-issue public and investigate the perceptual, cognitive, and motivational predecessors of Koreans' active information behaviors.

Kim, Jinsoo, and Moonhee Cho. "When the 'Stroller Moms' Take Hold of the Street: A Case Study of How Social Influence Made the Inactive Publics Active in Anti-US Beef Protest in Seoul—An Issues Processes Model Perspective." *International Journal of Strategic Communication* 5, no. 1 (2011): 1–25. doi: 10.1080/1553118X.2010.515544.

Kim and Cho illustrate the process of issue creation and transforming inactive publics into active ones by applying the Issues Processes Model. In-depth interviews explain why Korean stroller moms participated in the protest; these moms' knowledge and involvement are enhanced through online social community sites, a primary player in transforming them from an inactive to an active public.

Kim, Soojin, and Arunima Krishna. "Unpacking Public Sentiment toward the Government: How Citizens' Perceptions of Government Communication Strategies

Impact Public Engagement, Cynicism, and Communication Behaviors in South Korea." *International Journal of Strategic Communication* (forthcoming).

Government public relations is central to this study as the authors examine how Korean citizens' perception of the communication strategy adopted by their government affects their sentiment toward it. Bridging strategy is recommended as the optimal communication strategy to increase public engagement and decrease cynicism.

Kim, Soojin, and Jeong-Nam Kim. "Bridge or Buffer: Two Ideas of Effective Corporate Governance and Public Engagement." *Journal of Public Affairs* 16, no. 2 (2016): 118–127. doi: 10.1002/pa.1555.

Kim and Kim evaluate the relationship between public relations strategy adoption and organizational factors. Interviews with Korean communication consultants show that bridging and buffering strategies are associated with organizational factors.

Krishna, Arunima. "New Food Technology and Public Fear: Testing Motivated Information Behaviors and the Problem Chain Recognition Effect Between Lay and Educated Publics." Master's thesis, Purdue University, 2013.

Krishna explores differences between lay and expert publics' perceptions of new food technology in Korea. Using the Situational Theory of Problem Solving (STOPS) as the theoretical framework, she identifies the interrelatedness of new food-related perceptions and attendant communication behaviors among Koreans.

Laufer, Daniel, and Jae Min Jung. "Incorporating Regulatory Focus Theory in Product Recall Communications to Increase Compliance with a Product Recall." *Public Relations Review* 36, no. 2 (2010): 147–151. doi: 10.1016/j.pubrev.2010.03.004.

Laufer and Jung survey Korean students to understand whether product recall messages have the desired effect on their target audiences. The authors find that while purchase intentions are affected by the negative aspect of a product recall, there is the benefit of increased compliance resulting from recall messages that had a regulatory focus.

Moon, Bitt Beach, Yunna Rhee, and Sung-Un Yang. "Developing Public's Information Transmitting Behavior (ITB) Model in Public Relations: A Cross-National Study." *Journal of Public Relations Research* 28, no. 1 (2016): 4–18. doi: 10.1080/10627 26X.2015.1107482.

The authors use surveys conducted in Korea and the United States to develop and validate a six-dimensional model of publics' information transmitting behavior (ITB). The six dimensions are positive-proactive megaphoning, positive-reactive megaphoning, negative-proactive megaphoning, negative-reactive megaphoning, avoiding, and no commenting.

Park, Nohil, and JiYeon Jeong. "Finding Publics within the Blogosphere: The Blogger Public Segmentation Model." *Asian Journal of Communication* 21, no. 4 (2011): 389–408. doi:10.1080/01292986.2011.581299.

Park and Jeong advance a model to segment bloggers based on their issue involvement and self-efficacy. Based on the survey results, bloggers are categorized in four ways (active bloggers, constrained bloggers, routine bloggers, and active bloggers), and the results suggest that active bloggers show more journalistic behavior.

Shin, Kyung-Ah, and Miejeong Han. "The Role of Negative Emotions on Motivation and Communicative Action: Testing the Validity of Situational Theory of Problem Solving in the Context of South Korea." *Asian Journal of Communication* 26, no. 1 (2016): 76–93. doi: 10.1080/01292986.2015.1083597.

The authors examine the impact of negative emotions on publics' situational perceptions and communicative actions. Surveys of Korean students support the applicability of the Situational Theory of Problem Solving (STOPS) in understanding people's perceptions about a key social issue, as well as the role of emotions as a mediator in the model.

Organization-Public Relationships and Measurement

Hwang, Sungwook. "The Effect of Charitable Giving by Celebrities on the Personal Public Relations." *Public Relations Review* 36, no. 3 (2010): 313–315. doi:10.1016/j.pubrev.2010.04.010.

A survey of college students shows a positive correlation between charitable giving and credibility perception, which is a positive overall assessment of the celebrity. In a public relations context, positive assessment correlates to perception of the celebrity's credibility, attitude toward the celebrity, and intention to attend performance by, or purchase products endorsed by, the celebrity.

Jin, Bumsub, and Soobum Lee. "Enhancing Community Capacity: Roles of Perceived Bonding and Bridging Social Capital and Public Relations in Community Building." *Public Relations Review* 39, no. 4 (2013): 290–292. doi: 10.1016/j.pubrev.2013.08.009.

Jin and Lee test community capacity in rural Korea by surveying 385 adults across Korea to understand the role of bonding and bridging social capital in community building and enhancing community capacity. The authors find that corporations' PR efforts could serve as important bridges, empowering local residents to resolve conflicts and find solutions.

Jo, Samsup. "Measurement of Organization-Public Relationships: Validation of Measurement Using a Manufacturer-Retailer Relationship." *Journal of Public Relations Research* 18, no. 3 (2006): 225–248. doi: 10.1207/s1532754xjprr1803_2.

Jo examines five relational dimensions (satisfaction, trust, commitment, control mutuality, and face and favor) and personal network in the context of Samsung Electronics in Korea and its retailers. He proposes that satisfaction, trust, and commitment are global measures, while personal network is a specific measure to Eastern culture.

Jo, Samsup, and Jae-Woong Yoo. "How Does the Corporate Sector Perceive Non-profit Organizations? Evidence from South Korea." *Journal of Communication Management* 19, no. 4 (2015): 324–334. doi: 10.1108/JCOM-11–2013–0077.

Surveys of 260 corporate executives suggest that they believe that non-profits have more power than corporations in building a media agenda, but do not necessarily see non-profits as inherently trustworthy. Four broad factors to evaluate non-profits include whether the non-profits are positive functions of activists, any negative aspects of organizational culture, their trustworthy characteristics, and expected ethical management practices.

Jo, Samsup, and Sung Wook Shim. "Paradigm Shift of Employee Communication: The Effect of Management Communication on Trusting Relationships." *Public Relations Review* 31, no. 2 (2005): 277–280. doi: 10.1016/j.pubrev.2005.02.012.

Surveys of Korean corporate employees serve to assess if supportive oral communication is linked to perceptions of trust and support by management. Positive communication is associated with the building of trusting relationships. Direct communication from immediate supervisors is more useful than mediated communication through official channels.

Kim, Hyo-Sook. "A Multilevel Study of Antecedents and a Mediator of Employee-Organization Relationships." *Journal of Public Relations Research* 19, no. 2 (2007): 167–197. doi: 10.1080/10627260701290695.

Kim surveys Korean employees to develop and examine the dimensions of employee relationship antecedents and test the impact of organizational structure and internal communication on organization-employee relationship quality using organizational justice as a relationship mediator.

———. "Examining the Role of Informational Justice in the Wake of Downsizing from an Organizational Relationship Management Perspective." *Journal of Business Ethics* 88, no. 2 (2009): 297–312. doi: 10.1007/s10551–008–9964–0.

Kim studies how companies effectively communicate with employees during downsizing. In the setting of a Korean company undergoing downsizing, she finds that employees' perception that the company is enacting informational justice affects their perceived organization-employee relationship and their turnover intentions.

Kim, Jarim, and Minjung Sung. "The Value of Public Relations: Different Impacts of Communal and Exchange Relationships on Perceptions and Communicative Behavior." *Journal of Public Relations Research* 28, no. 2 (2016): 87–101. doi: 10 .1080/1062726X.2016.1191014.

Kim and Sung explore (1) relationship quality between a university in Korea and its students and (2) how relationship quality and relationship type affect students' perceptions and communication behaviors around an issue of a tuition increase. The two relationship types—communal and exchange—are found to differently influence problem recognition, constraint recognition and involvement recognition.

Kim, Jeong-Nam, and Yunna Rhee. "Strategic Thinking about Employee Communication Behavior (ECB) in Public Relations: Testing the Models of Megaphoning and Scouting Effects in Korea." *Journal of Public Relations Research* 23, no. 3 (2011): 243–268. doi: 10.1080/1062726X.2011.582204.

The authors conceptualize dimensions of employees' communication behavior (ECB) applicable for theory and practice in public relations in the Korean context. They introduce two distinctive dimensions of ECB: megaphoning and scouting, which together form micro-boundary spanning.

Kim, Soojin. "Strategic Predisposition in Communication Management: Understanding Organizational Propensity towards Bridging Strategy." *Journal of Communication Management* 20, no. 3 (2016): 232–254. doi: 10.1108/JCOM-06–2015–0050.

Kim inspects factors influencing companies' predisposition toward certain communication strategies. Surveys of communication/PR managers in Korea show that the complexity of the external environment, corporate culture, analytical orientation, and leadership's attitude toward stakeholders all affect which communication strategies a company is likely to adopt.

_____. "Determinants of Employee Turnover Intention: Understanding the Roles of Organizational Justice, Supervisory Justice, Authoritarian Organizational Culture and Organization-Employee Relationship Quality." *Corporate Communications: An International Journal* 22, no. 3 (2017): 308–328. doi: 10.1108/CCIJ-11–2016–0074.

Kim analyzes the relationships between organizational justice, supervisory justice, authoritarian culture, organization-employee relationship quality and employee turnover intention in Korean companies. The results reveal that organizational justice and supervisory justice have positive associations with organization-employee relationship quality.

Kim, Soojin, and Arunima Krishna. "Bridging Strategy versus Buffering Strategy: Enhancing Crisis Management Capability in Public Management for Relational and Reputational Improvement, and Conflict Avoidance." *Asian Journal of Communication* 27, no. 5 (2017). doi: 10.1080/01292986.2017.1313876.

Kim and Krishna examine how communication and PR managers' reports of adoption of bridging or buffering strategy affect their crisis management capability, conflict avoidance, and attendant relational and reputational outcomes in the Korean context. Findings support predictions of adoption of the bridging strategy and positive organizational outcomes.

————. "Communication or Action? Strategies Fostering Ethical Organizational Conduct and Relational Outcomes." *Public Relations Review* 43, no. 3 (2017): 560–567. doi: 10.1016/j.pubrev.2017.03.009.

The authors examine the impact of bridging and buffering on an organization's ethical conduct and on organization-public relationships based on a survey of Korean communication managers. Findings show that bridging is correlated with better relationship and results in lower instances of conflict in strategic communications, while buffering is not.

Kim, Yungwook, and Jungeun Yang. "Chemyon, Relationship Building, and Conflicts." In *Relations as Relationship Management: Relational Approach to the Study and Practice of Public Relations*, 2nd ed., edited by Eyun-Jung Ki, Jeong-Nam Kim, and John Ledingham, 240–257. New York: Routledge Press, 2015.

This chapter discusses *chemyon*, the Korean face, as a key cultural concept in a relationship-building context. In Korean culture, maintaining harmony among group members is essential, and communication behaviors to resolve conflict are likely to have several consequences for harmonious relationship building. Examining *chemyon*'s effect on relationship building is suggested for future study.

Moon, Bitt Beach, and Yunna Rhee. "Exploring Negative Dimensions of Organization-Public Relationships (NOPR) in Public Relations." *Journalism & Mass Communication Quarterly* 90, no. 4 (2013): 691–714. doi:10.1177/1077699013503161.

Moon and Rhee develop a measure of negative organization-public relationships that includes dissatisfaction, distrust, control dominance, and dissolution. The authors test the scale among Koreans to operationalize negative organization-public relationships.

Moon, Bitt Beach, and Sung-Un Yang. "Why Publics Terminate Their Relationship with Organizations: Exploring Antecedents of Relationship Dissolution in South Korea." *Asian Journal of Communication* 25, no. 3 (2015): 288–306. doi: 10.108 0/01292986.2014.960876.

Moon and Yang examine why Korean consumers may dissolve consumer-corporate relationships. Individuals terminating their relationship with an organization do so due to relational distrust and dissatisfaction and may be motivated to engage in negative communication behaviors about the organization in question.

Rhee, Yunna, and Beach Moon. "Organizational Culture and Strategic Communication Practice: Testing the Competing Values Model (CVM) and Employee Communication Strategies (ECS) Model in Korea." *International Journal of Strategic Communication* 3, no.1 (2009): 52–67. doi: 10.1080/15531180802608386.

The authors construct a scale of organizational culture and employee communication based on the Competing Values Model (CVM). Survey data from Korea confirm the reliability and validity of CVM measures that effectively test the relationship between organizational culture and employee communication strategies.

Suh, Taewon, and Hochang Shin. "When Working Hard Pays Off: Testing Creativity Hypotheses." *Corporate Communications: An International Journal* 13, no. 4 (2008): 407–417. doi: 10.1108/13563280810914838.

Suh and Shin assess organizational encouragement as an effective moderator between working hard and creativity and performance. Responses from Korean PR practitioners indicate that organizational encouragement of creativity may significantly increase hard work among employees.

Yang, Sung-Un. "An Integrated Model for Organization-Public Relational Outcomes, Organizational Reputation, and Their Antecedents." *Journal of Public Relations Research* 19, no. 2 (2007): 91–121. doi: 10.1080/10627260701290612.

Yang tests the impact of organization-public relationship outcomes on organizational reputation by controlling perceptions of communication behaviors (familiarity and experience). Data collected from Korea show the positive impact of relational outcome. Corporate executives surveyed acknowledge non-profits as having agenda-building power, but not necessarily as being inherently trustworthy.

Crisis, Issue, Risk, Conflict, and Reputation Management

An, Seon-Kyoung, Dong-Jin Park, Seungho Cho, and Bruce Berger. "A Cross-Cultural Study of Effective Organizational Crisis Response Strategy in the United States and South Korea." *International Journal of Strategic Communication* 4, no. 4 (2010): 225–243. doi: 10.1080/1553118X.2010.515543.

The authors investigate publics' evaluation of organizational response strategies using a between-subjects experiment across two countries (United States vs. Korea). Respondents in a collectivistic culture show more negative attitudes, emotions, and impressions toward the organizational responses than their individualistic counterparts.

Cha, Heewon, and Yang, Sung-Un. "Corporate Reputation and Global News Media: South Korean Cases of Agenda-Setting." In *Corporate Reputation and the News Media: Agenda-Setting within Business News Coverage in Developed, Emerging, and Frontier Markets*, edited by Craig Carroll, 340–362. New York: Routledge Press, 2010.

The authors focus on the first and second levels of agenda-setting to understand variables affecting corporate reputation. Surveys of residents in Seoul illuminate the interconnections between aided and unaided awareness of five companies, corporate reputation, media credibility, and issue-related information.

Cha, Heewon, Jee Won Suh, and Jangyul Robert Kim. "The Effect of Issue Obtrusiveness, Issue Congruence, and Response Strategies on the Acceptance of Crisis Communication Messages." *Asian Journal of Communication* 25, no. 3 (2015): 307–326. doi: 10.1016/j.pubrev.2010.03.001.

The authors study the impact of crisis response strategy, issue congruence, and issue obtrusiveness on the public's acceptance of organizations' crisis communication messages by using two large Korean business groups (Hyundai and SK). Results indicate that publics' acceptance of messages depends on the type of strategy adopted by the organization.

Cha, Heewon, Yeonhee Song, and Jangyul Robert Kim. "Effects of Issue Ownership and Issue Obtrusiveness on Corporate Reputation at Two Korean Corporations." *Public Relations Review* 36, no. 3 (2010): 289–291. doi: 10.1016/j.pubrev.2010.03.001.

The authors examine the effect of issue obtrusiveness and issue ownership on the reputations of two prominent Korean corporations (Hyundai and SK) through a survey of Koreans. Perception of positive issue ownership (North Korea and employment in the case of Hyundai and education, employment, and environment in the case of SK) has a positive effect on corporate reputation.

Cho, Sooyoung, and Glen T. Cameron. "Public Nudity on Cell Phones: Managing Conflict in Crisis Situations." *Public Relations Review* 32, no. 2 (2006): 199–201. doi: 10.1016/j.pubrev.2006.02.021.

This study analyzes the stances taken by Korean netizens and an organization behind allegedly offensive images, netian Entertainment. The authors argue for the salience of a new contingent variable, netizen, and that it should be added to the matrix of contingent variables.

Ha, Jin Hong. "The Role of Relationships in Crisis Communication: The Impact of Agency-Client Relationships and Perception of Crisis Strategies on Crisis-Related Task Conflict, Performance, and Satisfaction." PhD diss., University of North Carolina at Chapel Hill, 2013. ProQuest (1377305783).

Ha researches the impact of PR agency-client relationship on the effectiveness of crisis communication. The results of surveys of PR practitioners illustrate the impact of trust and mutuality on crisis communication and that commitment is not a distinct concept among Korean practitioners. Practitioners do not differentiate between crisis stages to determine strategies.

Jeong, Se-Hoon. "Public's Responses to an Oil Spill Accident: A Test of the Attribution Theory and Situational Crisis Communication Theory." *Public Relations Review* 35, no. 3 (2009): 307–309. doi: 10.1016/j.pubrev.2009.03.010.

Jeong tests the Situational Crisis Communication Theory in the wake of an oil spill that occurred after a barge owned by Samsung hit an oil tanker in 2007. Results indicate that with little information about distinctiveness, Koreans are likely to make a higher internal attribution of responsibility.

———. "Public Support for Haitian Earthquake Victims: Role of Attributions and Emotions." *Public Relations Review* 36, no. 4 (2010): 325–328. doi: 10.1016/j.pubrev.2010.08.003.

Jeong surveys Koreans to assess factors influencing support for earthquake victims. The role of emotion and attribution of responsibility are tested as moderating variables. He finds that uncontrollable attribution messages tend to increase the likelihood that individuals would support victims of the Haitian earthquake.

Kang, Minjeong, and Sung Un Yang, "Comparing Effects of a Country on International Consumers' Product Attitudes and Purchase Intentions." *Corporate Reputation Review* 13, no. 1 (2010): 52–62. doi: 10.1057/crr.2010.1.

Kang and Yang evaluate the extent to which individuals' perceptions of Korea influence their perceptions of Korean companies and products and their attendant purchase intentions. Surveys of U.S. respondents demonstrate that both country reputation and company reputation contribute to individuals' attitudes and purchase intentions. Overall, corporate reputation positively affects country reputation.

Kim, Yungwook. "Negotiating with Terrorists: The Iterated Game of the Taliban Korean Hostage Case." *Public Relations Review* 34, no. 3 (2008): 263–268. doi: 10.1016/j.pubrev.2008.04.007.

Kim examines the dimensions of the Taliban Korean hostage situation from the perspective of game theory and concludes that the Korean government was too focused on avoiding conflict and makes too many concessions, which increases the likelihood of future incidents of terrorism.

Kim, Yungwook, Heewon Cha, and Jangyul Robert Kim. "Developing a Crisis Management Index: Applications in South Korea." *Journal of Public Relations Research* 20, no. 3 (2008): 328–355. doi: 10.1080/10627260801962962.

The authors validate a crisis management index as an integrated crisis management tool in Korea. The index consists of three dimensions: organizational strategy, organization system and culture, and execution and communication.

Kim, Yungwook, and Jungeun Yang. "The Influence of *Chemyon* on Facework and Conflict Styles: Searching for the Korean Face and Its Impact." *Public Relations Review* 37, no. 1 (2011): 60–67. doi: 10.1016/j.pubrev.2010.09.007.

Kim and Yang highlight the role of *chemyon*, or the concept of face, as it relates to both personal and social characteristics such as status, recognition, and social pride. A survey of Koreans shows people's preference for cooperative facework, conflict styles, and the positive and negative impacts of *chemyon* on crisis and conflict situations.

Kim, Jarim. "Elaborating the Halo Effect of SCCT: How and Why Performance History Affects Crisis Responsibility and Organizational Reputation." *Journal of Public Relations Research* (2017): 1–18. doi: 10.1080/1062726X.2017.1405812.

Based on the Situational Crisis Communication Theory (SCCT), Kim conducts interviews to understand why and how a halo effect takes place in a food crisis in Korea. The findings indicate that good performance history of the company involved in the crisis contributes to lower crisis responsibility attribution and less threat to the company.

Moon, Bitt Beach, and Yunna Rhee. "Message Strategies and Forgiveness during Crises: Effects of Causal Attributions and Apology Appeal Types on Forgiveness." *Journalism & Mass Communication Quarterly* 89, no. 4 (2012). doi: 10.1177/1077699012455388.

This experimental study among Korean college students investigates the impact of message appeals and crisis attributions on forgiveness. The two types of causal attributions have a main effect on forgiveness, while attributions and message appeals have an interaction effect on publics' forgiving the offending company.

Song, Yosep, Daewook Kim, and Dongsub Han. "Risk Communication in South Korea: Social Acceptance of Nuclear Power Plants (NPPs)." *Public Relations Review* 39, no. 1 (2013): 55–56. doi: 10.1016/j.pubrev.2012.10.002.

The authors test the effects of perceived efficacy, perceived risk, communication quality, and trust on social acceptance of nuclear power plants (NPPs) in Korea. Surveys show the social acceptance of NPPs to be more strongly associated with acceptance of nuclear power as a viable energy source, communication quality, and trust than with perception of risk.

Sung, Minjeong, and Sung-Un Yang. "Toward the Model of University Image: The Influence of Brand Personality, External Prestige, and Reputation." *Journal of Public Relations Research, 20,* no. 4 (2008): 357–376. doi: 10.1080/10627260802153207.

Sung and Yang survey Korean college students to explore the impact of perceived organizational personality, reputation, and external prestige of a university on the students' supportive attitude toward the university. Analyses indicate that all tested constructs positively affect students' supportive attitudes toward the university.

Wertz, Emma K., and Sora Kim. "Cultural Issues in Crisis Communication: A Comparative Study of Messages Chosen by South Korean and US Print Media." *Journal of Communication Management* 14, no. 1 (2010): 81–94. doi: 10.1108/13632541011017825.

Wertz and Kim compare coverage of food-borne illnesses in Korean media with U.S. media. Content analyses show that uncertainty avoidance played a role in denial, justification, and excusing strategies is being used more in Korea than in the United States.

Yang, Sung-Un, Hochang Shin, Jong-Hyuk Lee, and Brenda Wrigley. "Country Reputation in Multidimensions: Predictors, Effects, and Communication Channels." *Journal of Public Relations Research* 20, no. 4 (2008): 421–440. doi: 10.1080/10627260802153579.

Yang and others establish a multi-dimensional measure of country reputation and test the impact of Americans' experience with Korea and awareness of Korea's reputation on foreign publics' supportive behavioral intention toward the country. They find a positive relationship between individual experience and country reputation, with public awareness as a strong mediator.

Yang, Sung-Un, and James E. Grunig. "Decomposing Organisational Reputation: The Effects of Organisation-Public Relationship Outcomes on Cognitive Representations of Organisations and Evaluations of Organisational Performance." *Journal of Communication Management* 9, no. 4 (2005): 305–325. doi: 10.1108/13632540510621623.

Yang and Grunig investigate the impact of four relational outcomes on individuals' evaluations of five Korean companies' performance and their cognitive representations of the organization. The findings demonstrate that active communication behaviors and familiarity with the organization positively affect individuals' evaluations of their relationship with the organization.

Ethics and Corporate Social Responsibility

Bae, Jiyang, and Soojung Kim. "The Influence of Cultural Aspects on Public Perception of the Importance of CSR Activity and Purchase Intention in Korea." *Asian Journal of Communication* 23, no. 1 (2013): 68–85. doi: 10.1080/0129298 6.2012.725174.

Bae and Kim unpack the impact of Geert Hofstede's four cultural dimensions on publics' perceptions of and relative importance given to different types of corporate social responsibility (CSR) activities and their purchase intentions. Surveys of Koreans reveal that collectivism and long-term orientation were both associated positively with all the CSR dimensions.

Bae, Jiyang, and Sun-A Park. "Socio-Contextual Influences on the Korean News Media's Interpretation of Samsung's $847.6 Million Donation." *Journal of Public Relations Research* 23, no. 2 (2011): 141–166. doi: 10.1080/1062726X.2010.504 794.

A content analysis of news stories about Samsung's large donation after a series of misconduct scandals illustrates how news media in Korea interpreted Samsung's corporate social responsibility. Findings show that the media are not satisfied unless the company fulfills its legal responsibility and interpret such a large donation as an excuse or justification to diminish negative outcomes.

Cho, Sooyoung, and Youngshin Hong. "Netizens' Evaluations of Corporate Social Responsibility: Content Analysis of CSR News Stories and Online Readers' Comments." *Public Relations Review* 35, no. 2 (2009): 147–149. doi: 10.1016/j. pubrev.2008.09.012.

The authors examine stories about corporate social responsibility on Korean websites and in two Korean newspapers along with reader comments to explore how the public conceives and evaluates corporate social responsibility. Findings indicate that readers express cynicism and are suspicious of motives after a crisis and when monetary donations are involved.

Han, Ji Yeon, Hyun Soon Park, and Hyeonju Jeong. "Individual and Organizational Antecedents of Professional Ethics of Public Relations Practitioners in Korea." *Journal of Business Ethics* 116, no. 3 (2013): 553–566. doi: 10.1007/ s10551–012–1480–6.

The authors analyze how personal ethics and organizational factors affect Korean PR practitioners' ethics and find that practitioners working in agencies display higher levels of commitment to the profession than in-house practitioners, who display more commitment to their organization.

Jeong, JiYeon. "Practitioners' Perceptions of Their Ethics in Korean Global Firms." *Public Relations Review* 37, no. 1 (2011): 99–102. doi: 10.1016/j. pubrev.2010.09.004.

Interviews show that while practitioners strongly advocate for a strong ethical foundation, they lack consensus about universal ethical standards. Each interviewee working at the Korean branches of global PR firms notes the strong relationship between high ethical standards and enhanced professionalism. The author identifies nine elements of ethical standards.

Kang, Jin-Ae, Bruce K. Berger, and Hochang Shin. "Comparative Study of American and Korean Practitioners' Dissent with Perceived Unethical Management

Decisions." *Public Relations Review* 38, no. 1 (2012): 147–149. doi: 10.1016/j. pubrev.2011.12.006.

Responses of Korean PR practitioners and PRSA members demonstrate the use of dissent tactics in situations of unethical organizational decisions. "Assertive confrontation" is most commonly used among all practitioners, although Koreans are inhibited from making unethical decisions and leaking information to external sources.

Ki, Eyun-Jung, Hong-Lim Choi, and Jang Hyuk Lee. "Does Ethics Statement of a Public Relations Firm Make a Difference? Yes, It Does!" *Journal of Business Ethics* 105, no. 2 (2012): 267–276. doi: 10.1007/s10551–011–0971–1.

Ki and colleagues address the effectiveness of PR agencies' ethics statements using surveys of Korean PR agency employees. They report that firms with ethics statements and educational programs about the ethics statements have employees who report more ethical public relations practice.

Ki, Eyun-Jung, and Soo-Yeon Kim. "Ethics Codes of Public Relations Firms in the United States and South Korea." *Journalism & Mass Communication Quarterly* 87, no. 2 (2010): 363–377. doi: 10.1177/107769901008700209.

Ki and Kim compare Korean- and U.S.-based PR firms' ethics codes. Analyses demonstrate similar patterns of language use and client-oriented content in both samples, with limited focus on ethical values.

Ki, Eyun-Jung, William J. Gonzenbach, Hong-Lim Choi, and Junghyuk Lee. "Determinants of Ethical Practices of Public Relations Practitioners in Korea." *Asian Journal of Communication* 22, no. 2 (2012): 140–159. doi: 10.1080/01292 986.2011.642398.

Using results of surveys with Korean PR agency employees to explore ethical public relations practice in Korea, the authors find that the existence and awareness of an ethics code and relativism are directly associated with ethical practices, and relativism mediated the relationship between age and ethical practice.

Kim, Daewook, and Myung-Il Choi. "A Comparison of Young Publics' Evaluations of Corporate Social Responsibility Practices of Multinational Corporations in the United States and South Korea." *Journal of Business Ethics* 113, no. 1 (2013): 105–118. doi: 10.1007/s10551–012–1285–7.

The authors examine young individuals' perceptions of corporate social responsibility (CSR) and attendant evaluations of organization-public relationships (OPRs). Surveys of U.S. and Korean college students show that U.S. students evaluate CSR practices more favorably than do Korean students. The two sets of young adults also differ in how they evaluate OPRs in light of CSR.

Kim, Hyo-Sook. "A Reputational Approach Examining Publics' Attributions on Corporate Social Responsibility Motives." *Asian Journal of Communication* 21, no. 1 (2011): 84–101. doi:10.1080/01292986.2010.524230.

Kim examines the role of prior corporate reputation, congruence of corporate social responsibility activities, and source of CSR information on publics' attributions of the sincerity of CSR activities. Surveys of Korean college students show that prior corporate reputation moderates the role of congruence and source on publics' perception of the sincerity of CSR activities.

Kim, Yeon Soo, and Youjin Choi. "College Students' Perception of Philip Morris's Tobacco-Related Smoking Prevention and Tobacco-Unrelated Social Responsibility." *Journal of Public Relations Research* 24, no. 2 (2012): 184–199. doi: 10.1080/1062726X.2012.626138.

Kim and Choi survey U.S. and Korean college students to understand the effects of two tobacco companies' corporate social responsibility (CSR) programs—a tobacco-related smoking prevention versus not-tobacco-related program. They find that the not-tobacco-related program and a positive CSR motive stimulate more positive outcomes including CSR values, positive attitude toward CSR activities, and behavioral intention toward the company.

Kim, Yungwook. "Ethical Standards and Ideology among Korean Public Relations Practitioners." *Journal of Business Ethics* 42, no. 3 (2003): 209–223. doi: 10.1023/A:1022281507601.

Kim uses an experimental design to examine the relationship between ethical ideology and Korean PR practitioners' perceptions about ethical decision-making. Results imply that ethical ideology significantly affects ethical decision-making.

Kim, Yungwook, and Soo-Yeon Kim. "The Influence of Cultural Values on Perceptions of Corporate Social Responsibility: Application of Hofstede's Dimensions to Korean Public Relations Practitioners." *Journal of Business Ethics* 91, no. 4 (2010): 485–500. doi: 10.1007/s10551–009–0095-z.

The authors probe how Korean PR practitioners perceive corporate social responsibility (CSR) based on Geert Hofstede's cultural dimensions. Results indicate that social traditionalism explains practitioners' attitudes toward CSR most strongly, although all cultural dimensions are significantly related to CSR attitudes.

Lee, Ki-Hoon, and Dongyoung Shin. "Consumers' Responses to CSR Activities: The Linkage between Increased Awareness and Purchase Intention." *Public Relations Review* 36, no. 2 (2010): 193–195. doi: 10.1016/j.pubrev.2009.10.014.

Lee and Shin assess the relationship between corporate social responsibility (CSR) and purchase intention, specifically focusing on Korean consumers' awareness and understanding of companies' CSR. They reveal a positive relationship between perceptions of "good" CSR activities and the likelihood of buying products.

Oh, Hyun Jee, Regina Chen, and Chun-ju Flora Hung-Baesecke. "Exploring Effects of CSR Initiatives in Strategic Postcrisis Communication among Millennials in China and South Korea." *International Journal of Strategic Communication* 11, no. 5 (2017): 379–394. doi: 10.1080/1553118X.2017.1360892.

The authors investigate the effectiveness of different post-crisis corporate social responsibility (CSR) activities. Interviews with Chinese and Korean millennials uncover positive evaluations of post-crisis CSR activities despite awareness of underlying self-serving motive. CSR fit with the organization's business and crisis influences the CSR's impact, continuity, and transparency in evaluation of post-crisis CSR initiatives.

Oh, Won Yong, Young Kyun Chang, and Aleksey Martynov. "The Effect of Ownership Structure on Corporate Social Responsibility: Empirical Evidence from Korea." *Journal of Business Ethics* 104, no. 2 (2011): 283–297. doi: 10.1007/s10551-011-0912-z.

The authors probe the impact of companies' ownership structures on their engagement in corporate social responsibility (CSR). Analyses of large Korean companies show that companies with institutional or foreign investors had better CSR ratings, while top management ownership is negatively associated with CSR ratings.

Shim, Kyujin, Myojung Chung, and Young Kim. "Does Ethical Orientation Matter?: Determinants of Public Reaction to CSR Communication." *Public Relations Review* 43, no. 4 (2017): 817–828. doi: 10.1016/j.pubrev.2017.05.001.

The authors survey Koreans to understand the impact of individuals' ethical orientation on their perceptions of companies' corporate social responsibility (CSR) communication intentions. Deontological ethical orientation and strategic CSR frame are associated with negative communication intention.

Professionalism, Leadership, Role, and Identity of Public Relations

Choi, Jounghwa. "Elaborating the Concept of Public Relations Roles and a Test of Its Utility." PhD diss., Michigan State University, 2007. ProQuest (304843732).

The author identifies roles played by Korean PR practitioners and explicates the PR models followed by different organizations. Surveys of PR practitioners reveal seven roles: activist, advocate, advisor, expert prescriber, liaison, monitor, and coordinator.

Ha, Jin Hong, and Mary Ann Ferguson. "Perception Discrepancy of Public Relations Functions and Conflict among Disciplines: South Korean Public Relations versus Marketing Professionals." *Journal of Public Relations Research* 27, no. 1 (2015): 1–21. doi: 10.1080/1062726X.2014.924838.

This study discusses how PR and marketing professionals in Korea differently perceive the PR function and how the discrepancies in perception affect the conflicts between them. Results reveal discrepancies in each department's perceived function as a significant contributor to conflict.

Jang, Ahnlee, and Hyunhee Kim. "Cultural Identity, Social Capital, and Social Control of Young Korean Americans: Extending the Theory of Intercultural Public Relations." *Journal of Public Relations Research* 25, no. 3 (2013): 225–245. doi: 10.1080/1062726X.2013.788444.

Using interviews and focus groups, Jang and Kim seek to understand young Korean Americans' perceptions of their cultural identity, their use of social capital, and identification of conflicts between themselves and their significant others. The authors articulate multifaceted, situational identities that are beyond cultural stereotypes.

Jo, Samsup, and Jooho Kim. "In Search of Professional Public Relations: *Hong Bo* and Public Relations in South Korea." In *Public Relations in Asia: An anthology,* edited by Krishnamurthy Sriramesh, 239–260. Singapore: Thomson, 2004.

This chapter discusses a specific feature of Korea public relations, *Hong Bo*. It indicates specific cultural, political, and economic variables as well as media environments operating in Korea public relations. It suggests consideration of such unique variables in implementing public relations strategies and techniques for future communication professionals in a Korean context.

Kim, Yungwook. "Professionalism and Diversification: The Evolution of Public Relations in South Korea." In *The Global Public Relations Handbook: Theory, Research, and Practice*, edited by Krishnamurthy Sriramesh and Dejan Verčič, 106–120. Mahwah, NJ: Lawrence Erlbaum Associates, 2003.

Kim traces the evolution of public relations practice and scholarship in Korea, focusing on how social, economic, cultural, and political factors characterizing the nation have influenced public relations.

Kim, Yungwook, and Linda Childers Hon. "Craft and Professional Models of Public Relations and Their Relation to Job Satisfaction among Korean Public Relations Practitioners." *Journal of Public Relations Research* 10, no.3 (1998): 155–175. doi: 10.1207/s1532754xjprr1003_01.

A survey of 167 Korean public relations practitioners confirms that the craft models of press agentry and public information are prevalently used while practitioners' desire is to use professional public relations models. Practitioners who are more professionally oriented display higher job satisfaction

Park, Jongmin. "Images of '*Hong Bo*' (Public Relations) and PR in Korean Newspapers." *Public Relations Review* 27, no. 4 (2001): 403–420. doi: 10.1016/ S0363–8111(01)00097–2.

Analyzing the terms *Hong Bo* and PR in three major Korean newspapers, Park explicates the meaning of each term in context. *Hong Bo* is used more often in a neutral or positive manner than the term PR, which is often described as hype. The author encourages PR professionals to redefine the term "PR" positively.

————. "Discrepancy between Korean Government and Corporate Practitioners Regarding Professional Standards in Public Relations: A Co-Orientation Approach." *Journal of Public Relations Research* 15, no. 3 (2003): 249–275. doi: 10.1207/ S1532754XJPRR1503_3.

Using surveys of Korean PR professionals and a co-orientation approach, Park interprets the extent of incongruence between government and corporate public relations practitioners regarding professional standards. Findings confirm the existence of multiple disparities and point to cultural perspectives as a factor in the discrepancies.

Shin, Jae-Hwa, Jaesub Lee, Jongmin Park, and Kwang Hee Kim. "Past, Present and Future Relations in South Korea: Issues, Work Environments, and Leadership." In *Public Relations Leaders as Sensemakers: A Global Study of Leadership in Public Relations and Communication Management*, edited by Bruce K. Berger and Juan Meng, 171–185. New York: Routledge Press, 2014.

Surveys show that Korean practitioners reference two-way communication, shared power, and using appropriate plans, messages, and strategies as important leadership characteristics. Korean PR professionals note that the PR profession in Korea needs to build task competencies and professionalization.

Yoo, Jae-Woong, and Samsup Jo. "A Comparative Analysis of the Perception of Public Relations in Chinese and South Korean Newspapers." *Public Relations Review* 40, no. 3 (2014): 503–505. doi: 10.1016/j.pubrev.2014.01.010.

Yoo and Jo compare Chinese and Korean newspapers' framing of PR and find that news articles often associate PR with government persuasion in China and PR with private industry in Korea. *Hong Bo*, a Korean term for public relations, is often correlated with for-profit organizations and image management.

New Media and Technology

Hong, Hyehyun. "The Internet, Transparency, and Government-Public Relationships in Seoul, South Korea." *Public Relations Review* 40, no. 3 (2014): 500–502. doi: 10.1016/j.pubrev.2014.01.011.

This article examines public perceptions of transparency in the government's Internet communications. Surveys of residents in Seoul reveal that those who consider the Internet a useful information source perceive greater transparency and assess the government positively in general.

Hwang, Sungwook. "The Strategic Use of Twitter to Manage Personal Public Relations." *Public Relations Review* 38, no. 1 (March 2012): 159–161. doi: 10.1016/j.pubrev.2011.12.004.

Hwang uses responses from Korean students to assess their evaluations of CEOs' leadership. Most students report associating CEOs' Twitter use with positive evaluations of the CEO and the organization. Twitter's association with cutting-edge technology and candidness of dialogue is perceived as appealing and is associated with a positive organizational image.

———. "The Effect of Twitter Use on Politicians' Credibility and Attitudes toward Politicians." *Journal of Public Relations Research* 25, no. 3 (2013): 246–258. doi: 10.1080/1062726X.2013.788445.

Hwang investigates how Koreans evaluate Korean politicians' Twitter use their perception of politicians' credibility, and their evaluation of Twitter-using politicians. He finds that young adults' attitudes toward politicians' Twitter use have a positive impact on perceived credibility, which also has a positive effect on attitudes toward Twitter-using politicians.

Jo, Samsup, and Jaemin Jung. "A Cross-Cultural Study of the World Wide Web and Public Relations." *Corporate Communications: An International Journal* 10, no. 1 (2005): 24–40. doi:10.1108/13563280510578187.

Jo and Jung compare the websites of large companies in the United States and Korea to understand the differences in features posted and investigate the relationship between these features and James Grunig's public relations model. The authors note that press agentry and public information are dominantly used features in the websites in both countries.

Jun, Min-Chul. "Internet Usage in Korea: A Survey of Public Relations Practitioners." Master's thesis, University of South Alabama, 2003.

Jun describes how PR practitioners in Korea use the Internet to conduct their practice. Surveys of 1,200 members of a Korean PR organization reveal a strong impact of the Internet on PR practice, particularly through the fostering of two-way communication.

Park, In Soon. "The Influence of New Media Marketing Public Relations on the South Korean Film Industry in Relation to the United States Film Industry." PhD diss., University of Southern California, 2007. ProQuest (304843732).

Park analyzes film marketing PR in Korea to understand the success of "sleeper hits" at the box office. The author concludes that many sleeper hits achieved extraordinary success at the box office in the United States and Korea due to new media.

Shim, Hye Rin. "The Internet as a Public Relations Tool: Study of Korean Practitioners' Perception." Master's thesis, University of Florida, 2002.

The author examines the relationship between practitioners' Internet use and the models of PR practice they utilize. Surveys of Korean PR practitioners demonstrate a significant positive relationship between Internet usage and the adoption of two-way communication model of PR.

International Public Relations, National Image, and Public Diplomacy

Choi, Hong-Lim. "PR Meets *Hong Bo*: An Alternative Approach to International Public Relations." PhD diss., University of Iowa, 2007. ProQuest (304860962).

Choi examines how PR practitioners working for multi-national corporations in Korea perceive their roles within the organization as well as in the broader social setting. Using case study analyses and interviews with PR practitioners, the author explicates an alternative approach to PR practice in Korea.

Choi, Jinbong. "The Representation of North Korean National Image in National Newspapers in the United States." *Public Relations Review* 36, no. 4 (2010): 392–394. doi: 10.1016/j.pubrev.2010.08.001.

This study focuses on how *The New York Times* and *The Washington Post* framed the national image of North Korea. While the *Times* covered North Korea more frequently, the *Post*'s coverage is evaluated as more in depth. Both newspapers presented negative images of the country using predominant words associated with North Korea including evil, enemy, and blackmailer.

Halff, Gregor, and Anne Gregory. "Toward an Historically Informed Asian Model of Public Relations." *Public Relations Review* 40, no. 3 (2014): 397–407. doi: 10.1016/j.pubrev.2014.02.028.

Results of a survey of PR professionals in Asian countries identify commonalities. The authors devote significant discussion to scholarship characterizing Korean PR in relation to the unique system of *Chaebols* and the development of *Hong Bo*.

Han, Jiyoon. "National Reputation by a Non-Profit Organization: How Voluntary Agency Network of Korea (VANK) Affects the National Reputation of South Korea." Master's thesis, Syracuse University, 2012.

This study examines the role of a non-profit, the Voluntary Agency Network of Korea (VANK), in influencing Korea's nation branding. Interviews conducted with both employees of VANK and the government reveals that participants believe VANK to be filling gaps left by the government's own practice of nation branding, particularly in using social media to convey positive messages about Korea to its strategic publics.

Han, Jiyoon Karen, and Sung-Un Yang. "Investigating the Role of Non-Governmental Organizations in New Public Diplomacy." *Journal of Asian Pacific Communication* 27, no. 2 (2017): 196–212. doi: 10.1075/japc.27.2.03han.

Han and Yang explore the role of a non-profit, the Voluntary Agency Network of Korea (VANK), in influencing Korea's national branding. Interviews with employees of VANK and the government show that VANK is filling gaps left by the government's own practice of nation branding, particularly in using social media to convey positive messages about Korea to its strategic publics.

Han, Miejeong, and Sei-Hill Kim. "South Koreans' Perceptions of North Koreans and Implications for Public Relations Campaigns." *Public Relations Review* 30, no. 3 (2004): 327–333. doi: 10.1016/j.pubrev.2004.04.004.

The authors survey Anyang, South Korea, residents to understand their perception of North Koreans and the potential for establishing stronger relations. Media portrayals of North Koreans as less educated and more narrow-minded affect opinions. The authors assert that more positive media impressions of North Koreans would facilitate building favorable relationships with North Korea.

Hong, Yeonjin. "Influence of Culture on Public Relations Practitioner Roles: A Cross-National Comparative Study, the United States and South Korea." Master's thesis, California State University, Fullerton, 2003.

Hong compares how organizational culture influences PR practitioners' role enactment in the United States and Korea. Surveys of PR practitioners in both countries show that enactment of either manager or technician role depend on the levels of Geert Hofstede's dimensions of culture within the organization.

Jo, Samsup, Sung Wook Shim, and Jaemin Jung. "Propaganda or Public Relations Campaign? International Communication on the War against Iraq." *Public Relations Review* 34, no. 1 (2008): 63–65. doi: 10.1016/j.pubrev.2007.11.006.

By comparing evaluations of the success of Iraq War-related PR campaigns in the United States, United Kingdom, and Korea, the authors assess governments' public relations. Results illustrate that the war is perceived positively in the United States and the United Kingdom, but negatively in Korea, suggesting that Koreans may perceive war-related PR efforts as propaganda.

Kim, Hyo-Sook. "Exploring Global Public Relations in a Korean Multinational Organization in the Context of Confucian Culture." *Asian Journal of Communication* 13, no. 2 (2003): 65–95. doi: 10.1080/01292980309364839.

This case study of a Korean multinational corporation examines the cultural variables that play a role in determining the corporation's PR practice. Findings showed that Confucianism played a significant role in the company's culture. However, interviews with employees indicate that PR practice varies over different regions where the corporation was based, shedding light on home country culture versus globalization dynamics.

Kim, Induk. "Voices from the Margin: A Culture-Centered Look at Public Relations." PhD diss., Purdue University, 2008. ProQuest (304519941).

Using interviews, Kim documents the voices of Korean peasant activists and their communicative acts of resistance against neoliberal globalization based on the culture-centered approach. Peasant activists organize different communicative acts of resistance because they have difficulty presenting their voice and influencing policy discourse.

Kim, Ji Young, and Sung-Un Yang. "Effects of Government Public Relations on International News Coverage." *Public Relations Review* 34, no. 1 (2008): 51–53. doi: 10.1016/j.pubrev.2007.11.010.

Focusing on 105 events described in 11 Korean newspapers and one government publication, Kim and Yang assess the relationships among three variables: newsworthiness, public relations involvement, and international news coverage. Using grounded gatekeeping theory, they imply that gatekeeping influences internal news routines and the use of press releases submitted by government PR professionals.

Kim, Yungwook. "Do South Korean Companies Need to Obscure Their Country-of-Origin Image?: A Case of Samsung." *Corporate Communications: An International Journal* 11, no. 2 (2006): 126–137. doi: 10.1108/13563280610661660.

Kim examines the disparate effects of country image on consumers' brand image and purchase intention through differently perceived nationality groups (i.e., Japan, Korea, and Taiwan). Surveys of U.S. residents show that country image has no effect on brand image and purchase intention.

Lee, Hyung Min, and Jong Woo Jun. "Explicating Public Diplomacy as Organization-Public Relationship (OPR): An Empirical Investigation of OPRs between the US Embassy in Seoul and South Korean College Students." *Journal of Public Relations Research* 25, no. 5 (2013): 411–425. doi: 10.1080/1062726X.2013.795863.

Lee and Jun use responses from Korean college students to explore the relationship quality between the U.S. embassy and Korean college students in the context of public diplomacy. Students' perception of their relationship with the U.S. embassy are related to their attitudes and behavioral intentions toward the United States and its citizens. This study identifies the association between public diplomacy outcomes and organization-public relationship.

Li, Weidong, Qinghua Wang, Jing Li, and Kun Zhang. "National Image of World Major Countries in Chinese Undergraduates' Minds: An Evaluation Based on Components of a Nation." *Public Relations Review* 42, no. 3 (2016): 476–478. doi: 10.1016/j.pubrev.2014.05.001.

The authors explore Chinese citizens' perceptions of foreign countries, including Korea. Chinese undergraduate students' perceptions of countries rest on comparisons of global competitiveness rather than economic performance. They assess the United States as having the strongest national image, followed respectively by Germany, United Kingdom, France, Russia, China, Korea, Japan, and India.

Oh, Mi-Young. "South Korean Attitudes towards Foreign Subsidiaries of Multinational Corporations (MNCs): The Influence of Corporate Image and Country of Origin Image, and the Presence of Halo Effect." PhD diss., Southern Illinois University at Carbondale, 2001. ProQuest (251327561).

Oh examines how Koreans perceive and evaluate multinational corporations (MNCs), their countries of origin, and their foreign subsidiaries. The results indicate a positive relationship between MNCs' corporate image and country of origin image; this positive relationship is a predictor of attitudes toward foreign subsidiaries of MNCs.

Oh, Mi-Young, and Jyotika Ramaprasad. "Halo Effect: Conceptual Definition and Empirical Exploration with regard to South Korean Subsidiaries of US and Japanese Multinational Corporations." *Journal of Communication Management* 7, no. 4 (2003): 317–332. doi: 10.1108/13632540310807458.

Oh and Ramaprasad seek to understand if traits and impressions ascribed to multinational companies also translate to their Korean subsidiaries. Surveys among Koreans reveal that individuals' evaluations of subsidiaries were generally in line with their evaluations of parent companies.

Park, Se Jung, and Yon Soo Lim. "Information Networks and Social Media Use in Public Diplomacy: A Comparative Analysis of South Korea and Japan." *Asian Journal of Communication* 24, no. 1 (2014): 79–98. doi:10.1080/01292986.2013.851724.

The authors compare Korean and Japanese governments' use of information networks and social media to enact public diplomacy. Analyses of the countries' respective interorganizational information networks show that the organizations in both countries are well-connected online. Korea embraces two-way communication in its communication via Facebook, while Japan is less interactional.

Seo, Hyunjin, and Dennis F. Kinsey. "Three Korean Perspectives on U.S. Internet Public Diplomacy." *Public Relations Review* 39, no. 5 (2013): 594–596. doi: 10.1016/j.pubrev.2013.06.006.

Seo and Kinsey highlight the differences in Korean Internet users' assessment of relations with the United States. Using the responses of 60 Korean Internet users, the authors compare outcome-based, sincerity-based, and access-based perspectives and indicate that users of Café USA place a greater emphasis on sincerity-based communications than do other participants.

Yun, Seong-Hun, and Kelly Vibber. "The Strategic Values and Communicative Actions of Chinese Students for Sociological Korean Public Diplomacy." *International Journal of Strategic Communication* 6, no. 1 (2012): 77–92. doi: 10.1080/155311 8X.2011.634864.

Yun and Vibber investigate the positions of Chinese students in Korea who are attracted by the Korean Wave but have begun to dislike their host country as they interact with Koreans and daily culture. These negative experiences pose a risk to Korea's soft power.

Zhang, Juyan. "Beyond Anti-Terrorism: Metaphors as Message Strategy of Post-September-11 U.S. Public Diplomacy." *Public Relations Review* 33, no. 1 (2007): 31–39. doi: 10.1016/j.pubrev.2006.11.006.

This study examines the use of metaphor as a rhetorical strategy employed by the U.S. government in the wake of 9/11 attacks. Negative metaphors, such as "Axis of Evil" have been applied to several countries accused of criminal activities or engaging in violence against citizens or supporting terrorism, including North Korea.

Chapter 8

Intercultural Communication

Min-Sun Kim and Akira Miyahara

Intercultural communication scholarship is increasingly becoming one of the most powerful forces in social science due to the effects of globalization and increased cultural contacts in the twenty-first century. Development of the original paradigm of intercultural communication was established by an anthropologist Edward T. Hall and others at the Foreign Service Institute in Washington, DC, during 1950–1955.[1] The study of intercultural communication first appeared in the United States as part of communication study in the late 1960s. American and Korean intercultural communication scholars began studying U.S. and Korean communication behavior in the 1970s, stressing the differences in individualism and collectivism, low-context and high-context cultures.

Intercultural communication scholars T. Youn-ja Shim, Min-Sun Kim, and Judith Martin, in their book *Changing Korea,* stated that, in the last 70 years, South Korea has undergone unprecedented cultural transformations from an agrarian, Confucian-based society into a global, technological powerhouse.[2] Living in a global world with a rapidly changing sociocultural landscape, Korean people are confronting many challenges to their traditional values, attitudes, and worldviews.

Since the 1990s, an increasingly greater attention has been paid to the crucial role of intercultural communication scholarship in addressing the inevitable challenges posed by cultural changes in Korea. Intercultural communication publication on Koreans, conducted primarily by both U.S. and Korean intercultural communication scholars, expanded tremendously in the

---

1. Everett M. Rogers and Thomas M. Steinfatt, *Intercultural Communication* (Prospect Heights, IL: Waveland Press, 1999).

2. T. Youn-ja Shim, Min-Sun Kim, and Judith N. Martin, *Changing Korea: Understanding Culture and Communication* (New York: Peter Lang, 2008).

following decades. Today there are more English-language studies of Korean and American communication than of intercultural communication between any two other cultures, with the possible exception of Japanese and American communication.

An early and influential Korean scholar of intercultural communication was Professor Young Yun Kim at Oklahoma University. In 1976, her dissertation, titled "Communication Patterns of Foreign Immigrants in the Process of Acculturation: A Survey among the Korean Population in Chicago,"[3] led the way toward theoretical approaches to intercultural communication that are compatible with the Korean cultural realities.

Several distinctive approaches to intercultural communication research involving Koreans can be identified in English-language publications. Most notably, Korea has tended to be treated as part of its neighboring countries, either China or Japan, due to the close geographical proximity of these nations and certain shared cultural traditions. Professor Min-Sun Kim at the University of Hawaii at Manoa has suggested that Korea and other East Asian societies, including Japan and China, tend to exhibit similar cultural characteristics and social values, thus frequently lumped together as "East Asians."[4]

Another problematic trend in Korean intercultural communication is that often the stereotypical images of cultural groups portrayed in cross-cultural communication research have created a polarity that tends to exaggerate cultural contrasts. In 2002, Professor Kim noted that the Western model of intercultural communication has often created stereotypical images of "Asian" culture, including Korea. The idea of Euro-American paradigms has clearly become the dominant way of understanding Korean culture and communication.[5]

Korean intercultural communication research was primarily conducted to compare and contrast cultural communication behaviors of Koreans and English-speaking people, particularly with Americans, in English. This limited conception of intercultural communication scholarship involving Koreans and Americans has produced more English-language publications than any other languages. With the above mentioned challenges, highlighting the available English-language publications in Korea-related intercultural communication

3. Young Yun Kim, *Communication Patterns of Foreign Immigrants in the Process of Acculturation: A Survey among the Korean Population in Chicago* (PhD diss., Northwestern University, 1976).

4. Min-Sun Kim, "Intercultural Communication: Challenges of Studying 'Korean' Culture and Communication in a Globalizing World," in *Communication, Digital Media and Popular Culture: Contemporary Research and Future Prospects,* ed. Dal Yong Jin and Nojin Kwak (Lanham, MD: Lexington Books, 2018), 363–380.

5. Min-Sun Kim, *Non-Western Perspectives on Human Communication: Implications for Theory and Practice* (Thousand Oaks, CA: Sage, 2002).

will indicate a need for further examination of the divergent perspectives in understanding contemporary Korean society in a globalizing world.

INTERCULTURAL COMMUNICATION
RESEARCH ON KOREANS

In taking inventory of recent developments in the English-language intercultural communication field involving Koreans, it is useful to adopt two basic approaches to studying communication and culture in general. In understanding intercultural processes, the most frequently described distinction is the contrast between *culture-general* (etic) and *culture-specific* (emic) approaches. The terms "emic" and "etic" were first coined by the linguistic theoretician Kenneth Pike in 1954.[6] The *Culture-specific (emic)* approach is defined as being focused upon one particular culture, providing detailed cultural knowledge and interpretations that are indigenous to the culture. On the other hand, the etic approach involves the comparison of two or more cultures as a means of identifying specific characteristics that occur across cultures. Major trends in English scholarship in intercultural communication involving Koreans tended to be based on the distinction between the culture-general and culture-specific approaches.

Korean Cultural Values and Communication: Emic Approach

The undergirding of much of Korean intercultural communication studies stemming from the *emic* approach can be traced to the traditional Korean values found in the social relational guidelines. Past literature focuses on the impact of those values upon the intercultural communication patterns involving Korean society. While contemporary Koreans find themselves negotiating between "new" values and traditional values, past literature seems to suggest the Koreans are still firmly holding to the Confucian traditional values.

The main values and rules of social interaction that have been studied include the traditional Korean concepts *cheong*, *chemyeon*, and *nunchi*. *Cheong*, a culture-specific emotion, is described as the affective bond that unites groups of people together, or an attachment to objects, places, or things that the person has come in contact with. *Chemyeon* or "social face" has also been considered to reflect Korean culture and social behavior. *Nunchi* is the sensitivity to be aware of the other person's thoughts or emotion and having

---

6. Kenneth L. Pike, *Language in Relation to a Unified Theory of the Structures of Human Behavior* (The Hague: Mouton, 1954).

an understanding of the situation by observing the circumstances. *Cheong, chemyeon,* and *nunchi* are Korean cultural concepts that have been studied extensively to help explain the cultural characteristics of Korean society and interaction patterns. These "indigenous" Korean concepts have spurred many English-language publications, which frequently provide communicative implications in general.

Intercultural Communication Styles: Etic Perspectives

There is extensive cross-cultural research explaining how communication varies as a function of certain cultural values. Focusing on broader cross cultural comparisons, the majority of intercultural communication studies involving Koreans are conducted from etic (culture-general) perspectives within the last three decades. Intercultural communication studies on Koreans typically focus on the comparison with the Westerners, especially Americans, with some notable exceptions in studies led by Professor Akira Miyahara of Seinan Gakuin University in Japan,[7] which compared "collectivistic" cultures (e.g., Korea and Japan).

Central to the comparative approach in intercultural communication research has been cultural dimensions proposed by Geert Hofstede, a well-known Dutch social psychologist. According to Hofstede's 2010 study, Korea, with a score of 18, is considered a collectivistic society.[8] Typical English intercultural communication studies of Koreans have compared the communication traits between Koreans and Americans based on certain assumptions of underlying cultural values. In these studies, cultural variables were often used to explain the difference between the communication styles of Koreans and Americans. Korea is defined as collectivistic, high-context culture with heavy influence from Confucianism. In the Confucian culture, explicit communication is avoided and people tend to avoid direct communication. Back in 1988, Professor June Ock Yum at the State University of New York at Albany provided systematic cultural distinctions between East Asians (including Koreans) and Americans on social relationship versus task-orientation abound in the literature.[9]

An important factor that determines the differences between Koreans and Americans in their communication behavior is the in-group versus out-group

---

7. Akira Miyahara, Min-Sun Kim, Ho-Chang Shin, and Kak Yoon, "Conflict Resolution Styles among 'Collectivistic' Cultures: A Comparison between Japanese and Koreans," *International Journal of Intercultural Relations* 22, no. 4 (1998): 505–525.

8. Geert Hofstede, *Culture and Organization: Software of Mind* (New York: McGraw Hill, 2010).

9. June Ock Yum, "The Impact of Confucianism on Interpersonal Relationships and Communication Patterns in East Asia," *Communication Monographs* 55, no. 4 (2015): 378–388.

distinction, proposed by cross-cultural psychologist Harris C. Triandis.[10] Korea has traditionally been a group-oriented society where there is a strong distinction between in-groups and out-groups in everyday interactions. In fact, Koreans are known to have deeply rooted Confucian values that include the use of high-context communication that allows for all interaction partners to save face if possible. For instance, a systematic line of research focusing on cross-cultural communication styles by UH-Manoa Professor Min-Sun Kim and her colleagues find Koreans to be more concerned for face-related conversational goals (e.g., avoiding hurting the other's feelings, minimizing imposition, and avoiding negative evaluation from the other) than Americans.[11]

Publications focusing on nonverbal communication styles seem to parallel the results of verbal communication styles noted above. Regarding cross-cultural differences in American and Korean non-linguistic communication, Americans and Koreans seem to follow different public display rules that govern conduct. Specifically, the degree of touch avoidance seems to vary by culture. In fact, in 1966, anthropologist Edward T. Hall,[12] who is generally acknowledged to be the founder of the intercultural communication field, designated societies on the basis of how much they avoid touching. At least in terms of public touch, Hall designated both Korea and the United States as being touch-avoidant cultures. Studies have found results that supported Hall's characterization of Korea as a culture possessing a disinclination toward touch.

In sum, English-language publications on Koreans' communication traits in both face-to-face as well as on-line communication contexts seem to support that Koreans are usually more communicatively avoidant, more indirect in communication, and less argumentative than Americans. The common tendency that emerges from the communication patterns among Koreans is that the styles of Korean communication strategies also vary in relation to the status of interlocutors.

All in all, there are systematic cultural variations in preferences for communication styles and the perceptions of intercultural communicative competence. The general research findings regarding relationship orientation (Korean) versus task orientation (American) in verbal styles are grounded in shared cognitive knowledge about communication behavior, and that this culturally shared value can explicitly be shown to distinguish Koreans from other cultural groups.

---

10. Harry C. Triandis, "The Self and Social Behavior in Differing Cultural Contexts," *Psychological Review* 96, no. 3 (1989): 506–520.

11. Min-Sun Kim and Steven R. Wilson, "A Cross-Cultural Comparison of Implicit Theories of Requesting," *Communication Monographs* 61, no. 3 (1994): 210–235.

12. Edward T. Hall, *The Hidden Dimension* (New York: Doubleday, 1973).

CROSS-CULTURAL ADAPTATION

Going beyond comparative examination of communicative similarities and differences involving Koreans, there is another broad domain of interests that generated English-language publications: the communicative adaptations made by Koreans when they move between cultures. Cultural adaptation by Koreans is a relatively new area, which seeks to understand changes in communication behavior that are related to the process of acculturation and communicative implications.

Significant research attention has been given to adaptation-related communication phenomena in many countries (including Korean immigrants) due to a dramatic increase in migration population. A number of studies have focused on adaptive changes taking place over time within individuals and in their relationship to the new cultural environment. In *Becoming Intercultural: Integrative Theory of Communication and Cross-Cultural Adaptation* (1977), the leading intercultural communication scholar Young Yun Kim at the University of Oklahoma has provided insights into what happens over time when someone crosses cultural boundaries and what factors facilitate or impede his or her adaptation to the host culture.[13] Underscored in this communication perspective on cross-cultural adaptation is that communication is the necessary vehicle without which adaptation cannot take place. Since OU Professor Kim's early work, cultural adaption and communicative changes involving Korean immigrants has been amply demonstrated in many studies for the last three decades.

CULTURAL BIAS

There have been some major developments of the landscape in English-language intercultural communication research on Koreans since the mid-2000s. However, our in-depth review of English intercultural communication scholarship relating to Koreans reveals several challenges. While Korean culture has played a significant role in the past decade in studying communication and culture, there is a growing awareness of the limitations of Korean communication theories so steeped in Eurocentrism.

There is a widespread feeling among communication scholars in Asia (including Korea) that Asian cultures and traditions demand a pressing need to re-examine Western communication theories. According to Professor Min-Sun Kim's 2002 book, the dominant ideal of personhood in the United States

---

13. Young Yun Kim, "Communication Patterns of Foreign Immigrants in the Process of Acculturation," *Human Communication Research* 4 no. 1 (1977): 66–77.

is achieved through self assertion, by displaying "yang" communication behavior: confronting, demanding, talking, being assertive, being aggressive, being competitive, bragging, and expanding in human (communication) behavior.[14] Integration is furthered by "eum" communication behavior: being responsive, indirect, cooperative, intuitive, yielding, and aware of and considerate of the other's feelings. In Korea, lack of verbal communication or argument also does not mean failing to meet social norms or personal expectations. Rather, it can be viewed as sensitivity to social contexts.

MULTICULTURALISM AND HYBRID IDENTITY

As pointed out earlier, the cultural level analyses (e.g., accounts of Korean communication styles) tend to categorize all "Koreans" as collectivistic. For instance, a bulk of intercultural communication research has centered on the preferred communication styles of "culture-typed" ("Korean") individuals. Rapid changes in the modern world compel communication scholars to delve into the dynamic nature of individuals' cultural identity, including hybrid identities formed through on-line communication. More recent publications point out that individuals' identities are much more complex than previously thought, and certainly more complex than a generalized view of static national (e.g., "Korean") values.

Independent and interdependent construals of self, as individual-level cultural orientations, have been considered one of the most prominent self-schemata for distinguishing culture, which have been shown to affect communication styles in various communication settings. Self-construals are conducive in formulating views of the self-concept that include the newer ideas of multiple or hybrid identities among Koreans. Researchers have made several inroads into investigating theoretical consequences of self-construal for Koreans' communication styles.

Korea's fast-growing economy has created cultural changes resulting in a transformation from a face-saving culture to a modern culture. The increased exposure of Korea to the world has led some intercultural communication scholars to believe that Koreans may have become more individualistic. If this is the case, then past English-language research findings on Korean and U.S. communication may not adequately reflect present Korean communication.

There is an urgent need for more fine-grained analyses in English and other languages that capture the subtlety of particular outlooks and both the

---

14. Min-Sun Kim, *Non-Western Perspectives on Human Communication: Implications for Theory and Practice* (Thousand Oaks, CA: Sage, 2002).

heterogeneity and overlap that exists between and within different cultural communities represented in Korea. Communication scholars will continue to take up the challenges to investigate the heterogeneity found beyond traditional Korean ethnic boundaries across diverse interaction contexts, including on-line communication. The opportunities posed by multiculturalism in Korea will allow intercultural communication scholarship to play a more central role in contemporary Korean society of the global twenty-first century.

ANNOTATED BIBLIOGRAPHY

General

De Mente, Boye Lafayette. *The Korean Mind: Understanding Contemporary Korean Culture.* North Clarendon, VT: Tuttle Publishing, 2012.

Although Korean attitudes and behavior may be influenced by the modern world, the Korean mindset is still very much shaped by ancient culture and traditions. One of the keys to understanding traditional Korean attitudes and behavior is the language of the people—or more precisely, key words in the language. These key terms reveal both the heart and soul of Koreans and provide bridges for communicating and interacting with Koreans on the most fundamental level.

Kim, Donghoon, Yigang Pan, and Heung Soo Park. "High-versus-Low Context Culture: A Comparison of Chinese, Korean, and American Cultures." *Psychology and Marketing* 15, no. 6 (1998): 507–521.

The Korean and Chinese participants are shown to exhibit tendencies that are consistent with Edward T. Hall's description of high-context cultures, and the American subjects consistent with low-context cultures. Furthermore, the participants from Korea and China are found to be more socially oriented, to be more confrontation-avoiding, and to have more trouble dealing with new situations.

Kim, Min-Sun. *Non-Western Perspectives on Human Communication: Implications for Theory and Practice.* Thousand Oaks, CA: Sage, 2002.

Kim challenges the very core assumptions underlying the study of human communication and points out the limitations of longstanding individualistic, Western models on which much intercultural research is based. Frequently drawing on examples from Korean cultural contexts, she proposes a non-Western way of conceptualizing identity, or the "self"—the cornerstone of cultural research—illuminating how traditional Western and non-Western views can be blended into a broader, more realistic understanding of cultures and communication.

Kim, Suk-hyon. "Korean Cultural Codes and Communication." *International Area Review* 6, no.1 (2003): 93–114. doi: 10.1177/223386590300600107.

This study explores the relationship between Korean culture and communication by examining the Korean cultural codes unfamiliar to foreigners: *chemyon, nunchi, kongson*, harmony of *eum* and *yang, chong* and *euiri.* Specific examples from everyday Korean life today are used to illustrate the relationship among the cultural codes and to Korean communication styles and patterns. The author argues that there may have been a broad generalization and oversimplification.

Kincaid, D. Lawrence, ed. *Communication Theory: Eastern and Western Perspectives.* San Diego: Academic Press, 1987.

The first chapters of this edited book elaborate on Asian (including Korean) perspectives on communication theory; Korean philosophy and contemporary human communication theory; communication in Korean values. Discussions focus on the philosophical principles of communication systems among Korean and other East Asian countries.

Park, Myung-seok, and Moon-soo Kim. "Communication Practices in Korea." *Communication Quarterly* 40, no. 4 (1992): 398–404. doi: 10.1080/01463379209369857.

The communication practices of Koreans examined are divergent from those employed elsewhere in the world. Distinction in social behavior impinging on communication includes Confucian ethics, filial piety, age, gender, and hierarchical structure. Verbal and nonverbal differences relate to maintaining harmony in inter-personal relationships. The essay concludes with analyses from six research reports comparing Korean communication styles to those in other cultures.

Shim, T. Youn-ja, Min-Sun Kim, and Judith N. Martin. *Changing Korea: Understanding Culture and Communication*. New York: Peter Lang, 2008.

Korea is no longer an agrarian, Confucian-based culture but a global and techno-logical powerhouse that is one of the world's most important political and eco-nomic forces. Based on previous research and in-person interviews, the book shows how contemporary Koreans negotiate traditional Confucian values and Western capitalistic values in their everyday encounters—particularly in business and professional contexts.

Culture-Specific Values: Emic Approach

Alford, C. Fred. *Think No Evil: Korean Values in the Age of Globalization.* New York: Cornell University Press, 1999.

The author asks what we can learn about the contemporary notion of evil and about ourselves by examining a society where language contains no word for the English term "evil." In conversations with hundreds of Koreans, Alford found that Koreans regard evil not as a moral category but as an intellectual one, the result of erroneous Western thinking. Alford notes imported ways of thinking and how Koreans' responses to globalization matched Westerners' views about evil.

Byon, Andrew Sangpil. "Sociopragmatic Analysis of Korean Requests: Pedagogical Settings." *Journal of Pragmatics* 36, no. 9 (2004): 1673–1704. doi:10.1016/j. pragma.2004.05.003.

This article identifies and describes the sociopragmatic features of American learners of Korean as a foreign language in the Korean communicative act of request. Overall, the request-supportive move formulae of the respective Korean as a foreign language (KFL) groups support a stereotypical description of Koreans as being more hierarchical, collectivistic, roundabout, and formalistic in comparison to Americans.

Choi, Sang Chin, and Soo Hyang Choi. "*Cheong*: The Socio-Emotional Grammar of Koreans." *International Journal of Group Tensions* 30, no. 1 (2001): 69–80.

Based on the replies of 36 Korean university students, the authors analyze the structural properties that underpin the culture-bound concept of *cheong*. *Cheong* embodies the emotional links among Koreans connected to each other by feelings of we-ness and exhibiting the humanistic side of their selves. Their study concludes that Western models of the nature of persons and of social relationships are insufficient to account for the socio-emotional characteristics of Koreans.

Choi, Sang-Chin, Uichol Kim, and Soo-Hyang Choi. "Indigenous Analysis of Collective Representations: A Korean Perspective." In *Cross-Cultural Research and Methodology Series, Vol. 17. Indigenous Psychologies: Research and Experience in Cultural Context,* edited by Uichol Kim and John W. Berry, 193–210. Thousand Oaks, CA: Sage, 1993.

This book chapter examines the nature of Korean collective representations that are indigenous to Korean people and outline an alternative conceptual framework delineating the indigenous Korean perspective, specifically focusing on the nature of collective representations in Korean culture. They present two empirical studies investigating the Korean concepts of *woori* (we, us) and *cheong* (human affection).

Choi, Sang Chin, and Suk-Jae Lee. "Two-Component Model of *Chemyon*-Oriented Behaviors in Korea: Constructive and Defensive *Chemyon*." *Journal of Cross-Cultural Psychology* 33, no. 3 (2002): 332–345. doi: 10.1177/0022022102033003 3008.

The present study develops a *Chemyon*-Oriented Behaviors Scale, measuring individual differences in proclivity for doing *chemyon*-oriented behaviors and examines the dimensions of *chemyon*. Data collected from Korean undergraduate students indicate that the *chemyon*-oriented behaviors consist of two distinct components: constructive and defensive, and that the two components are significantly correlated.

Hatfield, Hunter, and Jee-Won Hahn. "What Korean Apologies Require of Politeness Theory." *Journal of Pragmatics* 43, no. 5 (2011): 1303–1317. doi: 0.1016/j. pragma.2010.10.028.

This study examines a corpus of Korean apologies to discover why people apologize and why they choose the form of apology that they do instead of choosing a strategy based upon the weight of a face-threatening act. Koreans actively manage and create expectations for behavior in their relationship.

Kim, Yungwook, and Jungeun Yang. "The Influence of *Chemyon* on Facework and Conflict Styles: Searching for the Korean Face and its Impact." *Public Relations Review* 37, no. 1 (2011): 60–67. doi: 10.1016/j.pubrev.2010.09.007.

The purpose of the study is to explore the elements of *chemyon*, the Korean face, and to investigate their influence on facework and conflict styles. Social *chemyons*, including social performance *chemyon*, social personality *chemyon* and social pride *chemyon*, are related to the others' recognition of one's performance, personality, and status while personal *chemyons* share commonality with the Western face.

Lee, Choong Y. "Korean Culture and Its Influence on Business Practice in South Korea." *Journal of International Management Studies* 7, no. 2 (2012): 184–191.

Korea has its unique cultures and these cultures influence people's daily life as well as its business practices, especially in international business. This article mainly focuses on six parts of the Korean culture, which are *kibun, inhwa*, the power distance and hierarchy, Confucianism, the personal relationships in doing business, and business etiquette in Korea. All of these critical aspects of the Korean culture have strong influences on how to do business in Korea.

Lim, Tae-Seop, and Soo Hyang Choi. "Interpersonal Relationships in Korea." In *Communication in Personal Relationships across Cultures,* edited by William B. Gudykunst, Stella Ting-Toomey, and Tsukasa Nishida, 122–136. Thousand Oaks, CA: Sage, 1996.

This chapter accounts for the value that Korean people attach to their interpersonal relationships by demonstrating the culturally unique facets of human relationships and the "strategies" employed to establish, maintain, and develop their interpersonal relationships. The three fundamental concepts underlying the Koreans' social behavior are: *chemyon* or face, *jung* or love or a psychological bond that connects two people, and *nunchi*, mind- as well as situational-reading that gives rise to tacit communication.

Yum, June Ock. "Communication Competence: A Korean Perspective." *China Media Research* 8, no. 2 (2012): 11–17. *Academic OneFile*, Accessed 12 Mar. 2018.

In Korea, appropriate communication is important especially with its elaborate honorific language system that accommodates an intricately interconnected hierarchical social structure. From a Korean perspective, harmony is a crucial dimension of communication competence. Five major such constructs are discussed in this article: empathy, sensitivity, indirectness, being reserved, and transcendality.

Verbal Communication Behavior: Etic Approach

Ambady, Nalini, Jasook Koo, Fiona Lee, and Robert Rosenthal. "More Than Words: Linguistic and Nonlinguistic Politeness in Two Cultures." *Journal of Personality and Social Psychology* 70, no. 5 (1996): 996–1011.

This article extends the validity of politeness theory by investigating the nonlinguistic aspects of politeness in two cultures. The results reveal that Koreans' politeness strategies are influenced more by relational cues, whereas Americans' strategies are influenced more by the content of the message.

Choi, Jinny K. "Identity and Language: Korean Speaking Korean, Korean-American Speaking Korean and English?" *Language and Intercultural Communication* 15, no. 2 (2015): 240– 266. doi: 10.1080/14708477.2014.993648.

Choi studies native language maintenance and ethnic identity of first-, 1.5-, and second-generation Korean Americans in the United States, through the lenses of various identity construction and sociolinguistic theories. The study identifies social factors that affect linguistic behaviors and identity formation. It further provides detailed analysis of the issues relevant to the conflict of identity where a pluralist ideology is strongly discouraged, as in the case of the United States.

Edwards, Peter. A. "Willingness to Communicate among Korean Learners of English." PhD diss., University of Nottingham, 2006. ProQuest (301677713).

This research investigates underlying factors that influence Korean learners' decision over whether to use English in a particular situation. Findings suggest that the quality and quantity of previous contact with the non-Korean world, for example, through travel and friendship, along with the presence and relative status of other Koreans at the communication event, significantly influence language use.

Gudykunst, William B., Seung-Mock Yang, and Tsukasa Nishida. "A Cross-Cultural Test of Uncertainty Reduction Theory: Comparisons of Acquaintances, Friends, and Dating Relationships in Japan, Korea, and the United States." *Human Communication Research* 11, no. 3 (1985): 407–454.

The authors test a model of uncertainty reduction theory derived from Charles R. Berger and Richard J. Calabrese's (1975) theory of initial interactions and recent extensions of the theory across three relationships (acquaintances, friends, and dates) in Korea, Japan, and the United States. For the United States, more variance is explained in attributional confidence in acquaintances than dates; however, the findings are reversed for the Korean and Japanese data.

Gudykunst, William B., Young-Chul Yoon, and Tsukasa Nishida. "The Influence of Individualism-Collectivism on Perceptions of Communication in Ingroup and Outgroup Relationships." *Communication Monographs* 54, no. 3(2009): 295–306. doi: 10.1080/03637758709390234.

The authors test the perceptions of communication in relationships with strangers (outgroup) and classmates (ingroup) in Korea, Japan, and the United States. The results indicate that individualism-collectivism is related systematically to perceptions of communication in ingroup relationships, but its perceptions of communication in outgroup relationships are more complicated.

Han, Saem. "The Refusal Speech Acts of Two Generations of Korean Women: Mother-in-Law and Daughter-in-Law in Interaction." PhD diss., Louisiana State University, 2001; https://digitalcommons.lsu.edu/gradschool_dissertations/1787.

The aim of this study is to analyze and interpret the refusal speech acts of two generations of Korean women: mothers-in-law and daughters-in-law. The data are collected from three soap operas. The results indicate that age is a critical factor in choosing polite refusals in the Korean language, but social distances far outweigh age differences among family members. Korean daughters-in-law usually follow indirect or implicit strategies to turn down their mothers-in-law's request or suggestion.

Holtgraves, Thomas, and Joong-nam Yang. "Politeness as Universal: Cross-Cultural Perceptions of Request Strategies and Inferences Based on Their Use." *Journal of Personality and Social Psychology* 59, no.4 (1990): 719–729. doi: 10.1037/0022-3514.59.4.719.

This study attempts to explain how face management processes (and the variables that affect face management) motivate the manner in which speakers in any culture will phrase their remarks. Several hypotheses derived from this theory are tested with subjects from Korea and the United States. The results indicate that inferences of speaker power and relationship closeness can be made on the basis of request forms, and this effect is similar for both Koreans and Americans.

Jwa, Soomin. "Facework among L2 Speakers: A Close Look at Intercultural Communication." *Journal of Multilingual and Multicultural Development* 38, no. 6 (2017): 517–529. doi: 10.1080/01434632.2016.1212864.

Jwa's study explores situations of intercultural communication in which facework is used to remedy moments of potential face loss. The data are drawn from communication among Korean, Malaysian, and Japanese students. Tensions among the intercultural group, which could lead to a potential break in face maintenance, emerge. These tensions result from discrepancies within the cultural groups concerning recognition of face, cultural assumptions, and language use.

Jin, Borae, and Sohyun Oh. "Cultural Differences of Social Network Influence on Romantic Relationships: A Comparison of the United States and South Korea." *Communication Studies* 61, no. 2 (2010):156–171. doi: 10.1080/10510971003604042.

This study examines the association between social network support and relationship quality of romantic partners among American and Korean college students. Findings indicate that Americans involve their family and friends more in their romantic relationships and get more support from them for their relationships than Koreans do. The results do not support the hypothesis that Koreans would perceive social network support as more important for their romantic relationships.

Kim, Donghoon, Yigan Pan Kim, and Heung Soo Park. "High versus Low-Context Culture: A Comparison of Chinese, Korean, and American Cultures." *Psychology and Marketing* 15, no. 6 (1998): 507–521.

Subjects from Korea, China, and the United States, representing both high- and low-context cultures, are studied. The Chinese and Korean subjects are shown to exhibit tendencies that are consistent with Edward T. Hall's description of high-context cultures, and the American subjects consistent with low-context cultures. For example, the subjects from China and Korea are found to be more socially oriented, to be more confrontation-avoiding, and to have more trouble dealing with new situations.

Kim, Eun Joo, Joohan Kim, Charles Berger and Min-Sun Kim. "Which Self-Presentation Style Is More Effective?: A Comparison of Instructors' Self-Enhancing and Self-Effacing Styles across the Culture." *Teaching in Higher Education* 19, no. 5 (2014): 510–524. doi: 10.1080/13562517.2014.880686.

This study examines how college students from Korea, the mainland United States, and Hawaii perceive professors' self-presentation styles in terms of competence and likability. Professors with self-enhancement are perceived as more competent but less favorable in the mainland United States and Hawaii, but not in Korea. Structural equation models indicate that self-construals are significant variables in the mainland United States and Hawaii, but not in Korea. Academic motivations, on the contrary, appeared as significant variables in Korea only.

Kim, Heeman, and Zizi Papacharissi. "Cross-Cultural Differences in Online Self-Presentation: A Content Analysis of Personal Korean and US Home Pages." *Asian Journal of Communication* 13, no. 1(2003): 100–119. doi: 10.1080/01292980309364833.

Korean and U.S. individual home pages are analyzed to examine how cultural differences are displayed online. While the U.S. virtual actors present themselves in a direct and personal manner, the Korean virtual actors structure the online self by providing interlinks to special interests. Virtual actors in the United States are more likely to present themselves with still pictures, while those in Korea are more likely to use manipulated graphics.

Kim, Jung Sik, Min-Sun Kim, Karadeen Kam, and Ho-Chang Shin. "Influence of Self-Construals on the Perception of Different Self-Presentation Styles in Korea." *Asian Journal of Social Psychology* 6, no. 2 (2003): 89–101. doi: 10.1111/1467-839X.t01-1-00013.

The present study investigates how self-construals influence the perception of others who use self-enhancement or self-effacement in communication. Results show that people with independent self in Korea evaluated the positive presentation more favorably, whereas people with interdependent self in Korea evaluated the negative presentation more favorably.

Kim, Min-Sun. "Cross-Cultural Comparisons of the Perceived Importance of Conversational Constraints." *Human Communication Research* 21, no. 1 (1994): 128–151.

Kim investigates how cultural groups may differ in their perceptions about preferred communication behavior. It focuses on the importance attached to "conversational constraints" in conversation. Data are collected from undergraduates studying in Korea, Hawaii, and the mainland United States. The results indicate that the perceived importance of clarity is higher in the more individualistic cultures. But the perceived importance of avoiding hurting the hearer's feelings and of minimizing imposition is higher in the more collectivistic cultures.

Kim, Min-Sun, Krystyna Aune, John E. Hunter, Hyun-Joo Kim, and Jung Sik Kim. "The Effect of Culture and Self-Construals on Predispositions toward Verbal Communication." *Human Communication Research* 27, no. 3 (2001):382–408. doi: 10.1111/j.1468-2958.2001.tb00786.x.

Effects of culture and self-construals on predispositions toward verbal communication are studied, focusing on communication apprehension and argumentativeness are the main focus. The theoretical model predicts that individualism increases one's construal of self as independent, which leads to a higher degree of argumentativeness and a lower level of communication apprehension. Data from Korea, Hawaii, and the mainland United States are partially consistent with the theoretical predictions.

Kim, Min-Sun, Ho-Chang Shin, and Deborah Cai. "The Influence of Cultural Orientations on the Preferred Forms of Requesting and Re-Requesting." *Communication Monographs* 65, no. 1 (1998): 47–66.

The study aims to compare the preferred linguistic forms for the first- and second-attempt requests by people of different cultural orientations. Data drawn from undergraduate participants from Korea, Hawaii, and the mainland United States reveal that the higher one's interdependence, the higher the effectiveness and likelihood of using hint strategies in the first- as well as for the second-attempt request. Independence, however, is positively associated with the likelihood of use ratings of direct statement strategies for both first- and second-attempt requests.

Kim, Min-Sun, and Steven R. Wilson. "A Cross-Cultural Comparison of Implicit Theories of Requesting." *Communication Monographs* 61, no. 3 (1994): 210–235.

The primary objective is to identify cross-cultural similarities and differences in people's implicit theories of requesting. Native speakers of Korean and native American English speakers studying in their respective countries read a hypothetical request situation, and evaluated request strategies. U.S. participants consider the direct statement strategy as the most effective, while Korean participants rated it as the least effective.

Kim, Tae-Yeol, Chongwei Wang, Mari Kondo, and Tae-Hyun Kim. "Conflict Management Styles: The Differences among the Chinese, Japanese, and Koreans." *International Journal of Conflict Management* 18, no. 1 (2007): 23–41. doi: 10.1108/10444060710759309.

This article examines how the Koreans, Chinese, and Japanese resolve an interpersonal conflict with their supervisors and how cultural factors explain the differences. Koreans, compared with the Chinese and Japanese, are more likely to use a compromise style. In addition, the Japanese, compared with the Chinese and Koreans, are less likely to dominate and are more likely to oblige their supervisors.

Kim, Yunguk and Jungeun Yang. "Impact of *Chemyeon* on Koreans' Verbal Aggressiveness and Argumentativeness." *Korea Journal* 53, no. 3 (2013): 48–77.

How is the level of verbal aggressiveness and argumentativeness of Korean people affected by *chemyeon* (roughly translated as "face")? In particular, the relationship between *chemyeon* and Korean verbal aggressiveness is examined with regard to the type of argument taking place and the social status of one's counterpart in the argument. All of these factors (i.e. *chemyeon*, type of argument, counterpart's status) are found to have a decisive impact on the level of one's verbal aggressiveness.

Klopf, Donald W. and Ronald E. Cambra. "Communication Apprehension among College Students in America, Australia, Japan, and Korea." *Journal of Psychology* 102, no. 1 (1979): 27–31. doi: 10.1080/00223980.1979.9915091.

Little is known about the effects of apprehension about oral communication in countries other than the United States. This study investigates the prevalence of communication apprehension in Korea, the United States, Australia, and Japan. The results indicate that the Americans have a significantly lower incidence of apprehension than the Japanese but a significantly higher incidence than the Australians and Koreans.

Kwon, Jihyun. "Expressing Refusals in Korean and in American English." *Multilingual Journal of Cross-Cultural and Interlanguage Communication* 23, no. 4 (2004): 339–364. doi: 10.1515/mult.2004.23.4.339.

Kwon analyzes refusals of Korean speakers in Korea and American English speakers in the United States. Although a similar range of refusal strategies are available to the two language groups, cross-cultural variation is evident in the frequency and content of semantic formulas used by each language group in relation to the contextual variables, which include the status of interlocutors and eliciting acts (i.e., requests, invitations, offers, suggestions).

Lee, Chang-Won. "Relative Statues of Employees and Styles of Handling Interpersonal Conflict: An Experimental Study with Korean Managers." *International Journal of Conflict Management* 1, no. 4 (1990): 327–340. doi: 10.1108/eb022687.

An on-site experimental study is conducted in order to observe conflict management styles of 90 middle-level managers from a large Korean furniture manufacturing company. Conflict management styles differ significantly when the managers interact with superiors, peers, or subordinates: The managers are mainly avoiding with superiors, compromising with peers, and competing with subordinates.

Lee, Hye Eun, and Hee Sun Park. "Why Koreans Are More Likely to Favor 'Apology,' While Americans Are More Likely to Favor 'Thank You.'" *Human Communication Research* 37, no. 1 (2011): 125–146. doi: 10.1111/j.1468–2958.2010.01396.x.

How do apologies and thanks relate to perceptions of reduction in positive and negative face threats in the United States and Korea? The findings of two studies show that (a) Koreans more frequently include apologies in favor-asking messages, while Americans more frequently include thanks; and (b) Americans consider repeated thanks to reduce the threat to hearers' negative and positive face, but Koreans consider repeated apologies to reduce the threat to speakers' positive face.

Lewis, Carmen C., and F. George Joey. "Cross-Cultural Deception in Social Networking Sites and Face-to-Face Communication." *Computers in Human Behavior* 24, no. 6 (2008): 2946–2964. doi: 10.1016/j.chb.2008.05.002.

This study proposes a framework for understanding the role Korean and American culture plays in deceptive behavior for both face-to-face (FTF) and computer-mediated communication (CMC). Results from online questionnaires show that Korean respondents exhibit greater collectivist values, lower levels of power distance, and higher levels of masculine values than Americans.

Lyuh, Inook. "The Art of Refusal: Comparison of Korean and American Cultures." PhD diss., Indiana University, 1992. ProQuest (304006583).

Lyuh's doctoral dissertation examines refusals in English and Korean. By using discourse completion task (DCT), its results establish that Koreans and Americans differ in the use of refusal strategies and in the content of their refusals. Unlike Americans whose refusals reflect the features of individualistic society, Koreans' refusal semantic formulas show the characteristic of a collectivistic culture.

Merkin, Rebecca S. "Cross-Cultural Communication Patterns: Korean and American Communication." *Journal of Intercultural Communication* 20 (May 2009): 5–15.

The purpose of this study is to test and thereby update communication research of the 1990s on Korean in contrast to American communication practices. Students in Korea and the United States fill out questionnaires testing their direct, indirect, immediate, verbally aggressive and communicatively apprehensive communication. Results show that Koreans use less direct and more indirect communication than Americans and that Koreans are also more communicatively apprehensive and less nonverbally immediate than Americans.

Miyahara, Akira, and Min-Sun Kim. "Requesting Styles among 'Collectivist' Cultures: A Comparison between Japanese and Koreans." *Intercultural Communication Studies* 6 (1993): 104–128.

How many Koreans and Japanese differ in the structure and content of their perceptions about preferred communication behavior, focusing on the importance attached to conversational concerns in requesting situations? The five conversational constraints used for the study are: (1) concern for clarity; (2) concern for minimizing imposition; (3) concern for avoiding hurting the hearer's feelings; (4) concern for avoiding negative evaluation by the hearer; and (5) effectiveness. The study finds that Koreans are more collectivistic in cultural orientation than Japanese.

Miyahara, Akira, Min-Sun Kim, Ho-Chang Shin, and Kak Yoon. "Conflict Resolution Styles among 'Collectivistic' Cultures: A Comparison between Japanese and Koreans." *International Journal of Intercultural Relations* 22, no. 4 (1998): 505–525. doi: 10.1016/S0147–1767(98)00021–2.

The important cultural differences (possibly subtle) in conflict management styles among the two collectivist Korean and Japanese cultures have been overlooked by intercultural communication scholars. Undergraduate students studying in Japan and Korea participate in the study. The study finds that Japanese are focusing more on clarity constraint than Koreans, and Koreans are more concerned about social-relation constraints more than Japanese.

Oak, Susan, and Virginia Martin. *American/Korean Contrasts: Patterns and Expectations in the U.S. and Korea.* Elizabeth, NJ: Hollym, 2000.

Authors highlight how average Americans and Koreans behave and what they expect in similar circumstances—American ways and Korean ways. This book is designed for anyone who interacts with Americans or Koreans and wishes to know more about the differences and similarities between American and Korean culture and society. It has been written in a simple and direct style, with emphasis on the more practical aspects of human social interactions and customs.

Park, Hee Sun, and Hye Eun Lee. "Cultural Differences in 'Thank You.'" *Human Communication Research* 31, no. 2 (2012): 138–156. doi: 10.1177/0261927X12438536.

This research investigates cultural differences in the use of, and responses to, gratitude statements in unsolicited email advertising messages. They find that Americans, compared with Koreans, are more positive about a message that included a gratitude statement (i.e., "thank you"). Furthermore, Americans, compared with Koreans, view the gratitude statement more positively and considered the advertiser of the gratitude statement–included message as more credible.

Park, Hee Sun, Hye Eun Lee, and Jeong An Song. "'I Am Sorry to Send You SPAM': Cross-Cultural Differences in Use of Apologies in Email Advertising in Korea and the US." *Human Communication Research* 31, no. 3 (2005): 365–398. doi: 10.1111/j.1468–2958.2005.tb00876.x.

A series of studies investigating cultural differences in apology usage in unsolicited email advertising messages (i.e., SPAM) is reported. In comparison to American SPAM, a greater percentage of Korean SPAM include apologies. Koreans consider advertising messages with apologies as more credible and normal and exhibit a greater tendency to model other people's apology use than do Americans.

Park, Mi Young, W. Tracy Dillon, and Kenneth L. Mitchell. "Korean Business Letters: Strategies for Effective Complaints in Cross-Cultural Communication." *International Journal of Business Communication* 35, no. 3 (1998): 328–345. doi: 10.1177/002194369803500302.

This case study examines international business letters of complaint written in English by U.S. managers whose first language is English and by Korean managers for whom English is a second language. Important differences exist in rhetorical choices between the two groups. The U.S. writers use a direct organizational pattern and tend to state the main idea or problem first before sharing explanatory details that clearly relate to the stated problem. By contrast, the standard Korean pattern is indirect and tends to delay the reader's discovery of the main point.

Stowell, Jessica A. "The Influence of Confucian Values on Interpersonal Communication in South Korea, as Compared to China and Japan." *Intercultural Communication Studies* 12, no. 4 (2003): 105–116.

This article asks: In what ways have the different paths pursued by Korea, China, and Japan on their way to modernization, impacted the Confucian cultural values of their people? While each of the three cultures has Confucian influence, they are dealing with Confucianism somewhat differently. Comparison of Godwin C. Chu's two studies demonstrates that Korean traditional values are more firmly entrenched than Japanese or Chinese.

Tamaoka, Katsuo, Hyunjung Lim, Yayoi Miyaoka, and Sachiko Kiyama. "Effects of Gender-Identity and Gender-Congruence on Levels of Politeness among Young Japanese and Koreans." *Journal of Asian Pacific Communication* 20, no. 1 (2010): 23–45. doi:10.1075/japc.20.1.02tam.

Tamaoka and others analyze university student politeness levels in Korea and Japan when they ask various people to purchase a concert ticket. A decision tree analysis reveals the hierarchies of factors predictive of politeness levels specific to young Japanese and Koreans. Among Koreans, power appears to override distance, resulting in the descending order of power and gender-identity and gender-congruence.

Ting-Toomey, Stella, Ge Gao, Paula Trubisky, Zhizhong Yang, HakSoo Kim, Sung-Ling Lin, and Tsukasa Nishida. "Culture, Face Maintenance, and Styles of Handling Interpersonal Conflict: A Study in Five Cultures." *International Journal of Conflict Management* 2, no. 4 (1991): 275–296. doi: 10.1108/eb022702.

This study tests Ting-Toomey's theory on conflict face-negotiation. More specifically, the study examines the relationship between face maintenance dimensions and conflict styles in Korea, Japan, China, Taiwan, and the United States. The results are: Cultural variability influences conflict styles, with Americans using a higher degree of dominating conflict style than their Japanese and Korean cohorts, and the Chinese and Taiwanese members using a higher degree of obliging and avoiding conflict management styles than Americans.

Yu, Kyong-Ae. "Culture-Specific Concepts of Politeness: Indirectness and Politeness in English, Hebrew, and Korean Requests." *Intercultural Pragmatics* 8, no. 3 (2011): 385–409. doi:10.1515/iprg.2011.018.

This study compares indirectness and politeness scales in Korean, Hebrew, and English, and it re-examines the link between indirectness and politeness cross-culturally. Its results show that neither non-conventional indirectness nor some strategies of conventional indirectness imply politeness in Korean and imply that politeness is differently perceived cross-culturally.

Yum, Young-ok. "Culture and Self-Construal as Predictors of Responses to Accommodative Dilemmas in Dating Relationships." *Journal of Personality and Social Relationships* 21, no. 6 (2004): 817–835. doi: 10.1177/0265407504047839.

Yum's study tests and expands the existing research on the effects of culture and self- construal on reports of accommodative dilemmas in dating relationships. Data are collected from members of three different regional cultures: Korea, the mainland United States, and Hawaii. Collectivism–individualism is related consistently with the type of accommodation, and the four self-construal types also display a reliable pattern of associations with accommodation and non-accommodation.

Nonverbal Communication Behavior: Etic Approach

Jung, Hyo Sun, and Hye Hyun Yoon. "The Effects of Nonverbal Communication of Employees in the Family Restaurant upon Customers' Emotional Responses and Customer Satisfaction." *International Journal of Hospitality Management* 30, no. 3 (2011): 542–550. doi: 10.1016/j.ijhm.2010.09.00.5.

The purpose of this study is to understand interrelationships among customers' perception of nonverbal communication, customers' emotional responses and customer satisfaction in the family restaurant. A total of 333 customers in Korea participated. The results show that employees' kinesics and proxemics among non-verbal communications have a significant effect on customers' positive emotions, while employees' kinesics and paralanguage affect customers' negative emotions.

Kim, Min-Sun. "A Comparative Analysis of Nonverbal Expressions as Portrayed by Korean and American Print-Media Advertising." *Howard Journal of Communication* 3, no. 3–4 (1992): 317–339. doi: 10.1080/10646179209359758.

Relating to various nonverbal behaviors of advertising models, Kim finds that Korean couples avoid any outward displays of affection in comparison with American advertising models. Korean magazine advertising models seem to engage in less explicit nonverbal display rules than U.S. magazine advertising models.

Lee, Ye Jin, and Yoshiyuki Matsumoto. "Emotional Display Rules of Japanese and Korean." *Shinrigaku Kenkyu* 82, no. 5 (December 2011): 415–423. doi: 10.4992/jjpsy.82.415.

Hypothetical stories designed to arouse feelings of happiness, sadness, or anger are presented to Koreans and Japanese university students. They rate the intensity of the emotion experienced, and to select the corresponding facial expression to display in an individual situation and in a social situation. The study shows that Japanese and Koreans share the emotional display rules about the expressions of emotions in individual situations more than in social situations.

Matsumoto, David, Sachiko Takeuchi, Sari Andayani, Natalia Kouznetsova, and Deborah Krupp. "The Contribution of Individualism vs. Collectivism to Cross-National Differences in Display Rules." *Asian Journal of Social Psychology* 1, no. 2 (1998): 147–165. doi: 10.1111/1467–839X.00010.

Display rules of emotion and the degree to which those differences could be attributed to individualism and collectivism are measured. Participants in Korea, Japan, the United States, and Russia complete a measure of display rules. The authors find that Koreans exert the highest control over their expressions, which is likely to be a reflection of the Confucian value of restraint. Meanwhile, Americans have the least controlled emotions in their sample.

Cultural Adaptation, Hybrid Identity, and Multicultural Communication Competence

Brannen, Francis, and Debra MacLellan. "A Perspective of Cultural Change in Korea and Its Effect on Multicultural Children." *Journal of Humanities and Social Science* 19, no. 6 (2014): 19–30. doi: http://dx.doi.org/10.9790/0837-19631930.

Multicultural schools in Korea enroll Amerasian children; one Korean parent and one American parent, *Damunhwa*; one parent of Korean ethnicity and one parent of another country, and children of migrant workers. This research is conducted in an Amerasian school. Multicultural children who attend Korean public schools often have trouble adapting to the Korean educational culture. The paper delves into the deeper effects on multicultural children and offers their perspectives of living in Korean society.

Choi, Jeonghwa, and Ronald Tamborini. "Communication-Acculturation and the Cultivation Hypothesis: A Comparative Study between Two Korean Communities in the U.S." *Howard Journal of Communications* 1, no. 1 (1988), 57–74. doi: 10.1080/10646178809359669.

Based on the communication-acculturation perspective, this study assumes active roles of mass media during the acculturation process among foreign immigrants. There is little substantial support among two Korean-American communities for the cultivation hypothesis in general, nor for the "resonance effect." While the intercultural testing of the hypothesis fails to find evidence for television's perceptual influence, the study generally supports previous findings of positive associations of various media orientations with antecedent factors including perceived language proficiency, and educational background.

Choi, Yeju. "Conflict-Handling Behaviors of Korean Immigrants in the United States." *Conflict Resolution Quarterly* 34, no. 4 (2017): 375–407.

Although there is a great deal of literature that has focused on conflicts faced by monocultural people, cross-cultural conflict scholars have not yet focused on the conflicts faced by bicultural people. Among many immigrants, Choi's study focuses on Korean immigrants in the United States through the Conflict Communication Scale (CCS) and compares the results with nationality, the amount of time that the immigrants have lived in the United States, the level of acculturation, and gender.

Froese, Fabian Jintae. "Acculturation Experiences in Korea and Japan." *Culture and Psychology* 16, no. 3 (2010): 333–348. doi: http://dx.doi.org/10.1177/13540 67X10371138.

This article adds new insights to the study of acculturation based on a phenomenological research design. The in-depth descriptions illustrate the plurality and complexities inherent in the social networks and languages of highly skilled migrants in Korea and Japan. Westerners may enjoy a moot advantage of being foreigners to whom superior knowledge and skills are ascribed, while simultaneously facing subtle forms of discrimination.

Froese, Fabian Jintae, Vesa Peltokorpi, and Kkug A. Ko. "The Influence of Intercultural Communication on Cross-Cultural Adjustment and Work Attitudes: Foreign Workers in South Korea." *International Journal of Intercultural Relations* 36, no. 3 (2012): 331–342. doi:10.1016/j.ijintrel.2011.09.005.

The authors examine how foreign workers in Korea are affected by their host country language proficiency, English in the workplace, communication styles, and social interaction frequency with host country nationals. While host country language proficiency and social interaction frequency with host country nationals (i.e., Koreans) has a more positive influence on general and interaction adjustment facets, English use in the workplace, congruent communication and conflict styles are more relevant to work adjustment and work attitudes.

Han, Eun-Jeong, and Paula G. Price. "Communicating across Difference: Co-cultural Theory, Capital, and Multicultural Families in Korea" *Journal of International and Intercultural Communication* 11, no. 1 (2018): 21–41. doi: 10.1080/17513057.2017.1367026.

This study examines the lived experiences and the communicative interactions employed by members of seven multicultural families in Korea. For Korean husbands, economic and social capital are the most critical influential factors in their choices of communication orientations, while for immigrant wives, cultural and symbolic capital are most significant. Additionally, contrary to previous research, Confucianism and patriarchy play key roles in the marginalization of Korean men in multicultural families and influence their co-cultural communication orientations.

Huh, Nam Soon, and William J. Reid. "Intercountry, Transracial Adoption and Ethnic Identity: A Korean Example." *International Social Work* 43, no. 1 (2000): 75–87. doi: 10.1177/a010522.

Adoptions of Korean and Chinese children by American families raise questions about the formation of ethnic identities of the adoptees. This study of 40 Korean adopted children and their American parents addresses such questions. A high degree of involvement by children in Korean cultural activities is positively associated with the strength of the children's Korean identity and ease of communication with their parents about their adoptions.

Inglis, Margaret, and William B. Gudykunst. "Institutional Completeness and Communication Acculturation." *International Journal of Intercultural Relations* 6, no. 3 (1982): 251–272. doi: 10.1016/0147–1767(82)90032–3.

The study examines the effects of institutional completeness upon the ethnic interpersonal and mass communication patterns. The research question is tested by applying some methods used in a study of an institutionally complete ethnic group, the Chicago Korean community to a less institutionally complete ethnic group, the Greater Hartford Korean community. According to the study results, the institutional completeness of an ethnic community influences certain aspects of the communication acculturation patterns of the immigrants within that community.

Kim, A. Eungi. "Global Migration and South Korea: Foreign Workers, Foreign Brides, and the Making of a Multicultural Society." *Ethnic and Racial Studies* 32, no. 1 (2008): 70–92. doi: 10.1080/01419870802044197.

Korean society is rapidly becoming a multicultural society and this process is inevitable and irreversible. The article examines various social factors that are contributing to the making of a multi-ethnic Korea, including the continuing influx of foreign workers, rapid ageing of the population, low fertility rate, and shortage of brides. The Korean case affirms the globalization and acceleration of international migration, as practically every society is affected by it and as the number of migrants continues to increase.

Kim, Eunjung, and Seth Wolpin. "The Korean American Family: Adolescents versus Parents Acculturation to American Culture." *Journal of Cultural Diversity* 15, no. 3 (2008): 108–116.

Acculturation and characteristics of Korean-American families are discussed in this cross-sectional study. Self-reports are gathered from families in the Midwest of the United States. Mothers, fathers, and adolescents maintain Korean cultural and linguistic characteristics while adopting some American cultural and linguistic features. The adoption of American culture and English is more evident among adolescents than their parents. The association between Korean-American parents' acculturation attitudes and their characteristics are consistent with the acculturation framework.

Kim, Irene J., Luke I. C. Kim, and James. G. Kelly. "Developing Cultural Competence in Working with Korean Immigrant Families." *Journal of Community Psychology* 34, no. 2 (2006): 149–165. doi: 10.1002/jcop.20093.

The authors provide an in-depth examination of the historical background, cultural values, family roles, and community contexts of Korean Americans as an aid to both researchers and clinicians in developing cultural competence with this particular group. Three indigenous concepts that may be useful in developing cultural competence include *haan* (suppressed anger), *jeong* (strong feeling of kinship), and *noon-chi* (ability to evaluate social situations through implicit cues). Clinical case examples and accounts from a community-based research perspective illustrate these cultural values.

Kim, Kyung-Hee, and Haejin Yun. *"Cying* for Me, *Cying* for Us: Relational Dialectics in a Korean Social Network Site." *Journal of Computer-Mediated Communication* 13, no. 1 (2007): 298–318. doi: 10.1111/j.1083–6101.2007.00397.x.

This study employs a relational dialectics approach to the nature of relational communication via Cyworld, a Korean social network site. The results suggest that Cyworld users routinely negotiate multiple dialectical tensions, transferred from face-to-face contexts, or imposed by interpersonal principles that relate to Korea's collectivistic culture. Cy-Ilchons (online buddies) extend the Korean cultural concept of blood ties, intensifying the openness-closedness contradiction at early stages of relationship formation.

Kim, Nam-Kook. "Multicultural Challenges in Korea: The Current Stage and a Prospect." *International Migration* 52, no. 2 (2014): 100–121. doi: 10.1111/j.1468–2435.2009.00582.x.

Kim explains the current stage of societal development in Korea toward multiculturalism through a three-stage framework: tolerance, legalization of non-discrimination, and multiculturalism. Democratization in Korea has confirmed the relevance of liberal democracy thesis, which presupposes two conditions: the increasing demand for cultural rights by minorities and liberal constitutional government's inevitable acceptance of such demands. Unlike the claim of state-initiated instrumental multiculturalism, strong voices of NGOs in civil society since the mid-1990s have influenced the development of a multiculturalism friendly atmosphere.

Kim, Yang-Soo. "Communication Experiences of American Expatriates in South Korea: A Study of Cross-Cultural Adaptation." *Human Communication* 11, no. 4 (2008): 505–522.

The communication experiences of American expatriates in Korea are examined by Professor Yang-Soo Kim at Middle Tennessee State University. Kim's analysis uses verbal transcripts obtained through 20 in-depth personal interviews in 2002. It shows that cultural differences reflected in verbal/nonverbal behaviors and work styles are important sources of psychological challenge for the American expatriates. The majority of American respondents report that positive and genuine relationships/friendships with host nationals (i.e., Koreans) contribute to their positive and rewarding life experience overseas.

Kim, Yeon Kyeong. "Becoming 'American' and Maintaining 'Korean' Identity through Media: A Case Study of Korean Married Immigrant Women in Mizville. org." PhD diss., University of Iowa, 2012. ProQuest (1293058280).

This dissertation takes a critical look at the everyday use of different media (U.S. and Korean traditional media, U.S. and Korean online media, and mizville. org) in building and maintaining the identity of Korean married immigrant women. Also, it examines the applicability of the segmented assimilation theory and the new assimilation theory in discussing the assimilation process to the mainstream U.S. culture and the maintenance of Korean identity.

Kim, Young Yun. "Communication Patterns of Foreign Immigrants in the Process of Acculturation." *Human Communication Research* 4, no. 1 (1977): 66–77. doi: 10.1111/j.1468–2958.1977.tb00598.x.

Professor Young Yun Kim of the University of Oklahoma reports the theoretical development and testing of a causal model of communication patterns of foreign immigrants in the process of acculturation. She conceptualizes communication patterns on two levels: cognitive and behavioral. Kim identifies three causal factors as major determinants of the immigrant's communication patterns: language competence, acculturation motivation, and accessibility to host communication channels. The acculturation theory is tested and supported by a survey of randomly selected Korean immigrants in Chicago.

Kim-Jo, Tina, Verónica Benet-Martínez, and Daniel J. Ozer. "Culture and Interpersonal Conflict Resolution Styles: Role of Acculturation" *Journal of Cross-Cultural Psychology* 41, no. 2 (2010): 264–269. doi: 10.1177/0022022109354643.

This study explores the role of acculturation and bicultural identity processes in the interpersonal conflict resolution preferences of monoculturals (Koreans and European Americans) and biculturals (Korean Americans). Korean Americans display a complex bicultural pattern of conflict resolution: They endorse "competing" (a traditionally individualistic style) more than Koreans while also endorsing "avoidance" (a traditionally collectivistic style) more than both European Americans and Koreans.

Lee, Eun Kyung. "Formation of a Talking Space and Gender Discourses in Digital Diaspora Space: Case of a Female Korean Immigrants Online Community in the USA." *Asian Journal of communication 23* no. 5 (2013): 472–488. doi: 10.1080/0 1292986.2013.772216.

Lee investigates the formation of a digital diaspora of female Korean immigrants in the United States. The findings show that these women's shared identity is an important element in the formation and development of the online community, especially in the creation of a candid talking space—*sokpuri*—where they vent their innermost feelings. The Missy image (of a young, independent, and modern woman) and ajuma image (of a less individualistic woman, who is active in sharing information and helping others) are the two salient identity discourses.

Lewis, Carmen C., and Joey F. George. "Cross-Cultural Deception in Social Networking Sites and Face-to-Face Communication." *Computers in Human Behavior* 24, no. 6 (2008): 2945–2964. doi: 10.1016/j.chb.2008.05.002.

This study proposes a framework for understanding the role Korean and American culture plays in deceptive behavior for both face-to-face (FTF) and computer-mediated communication (CMC). Results from online questionnaires indicate Korean respondents exhibit greater collectivist values, lower levels of power distance, and higher levels of masculine values than Americans. Furthermore, deceptive behavior is greater for FTF communication than for CMC for both Korean and American respondents.

Matsunaga, Masaki, and Chie Torigoe. "Looking at the Japan-Residing Korean Identities through the Eyes of the 'Outsiders within': Application and Extension of Co-Cultural Theory." *Western Journal of Communication* 72, no. 4 (2008): 349–373. doi: 10.1080/10570310802446007.

The co-cultural theory serves as a framework of this study in analyzing the publicly available narratives of Japan-residing Koreans and in exploring how these marginalized people in Japan manage their ethnic identity. The study states that Japan-residing Koreans' identity management is complex and challenging due to the ambivalence of their positionality. The "neither/nor" nature of their identity makes the pursuit of assimilation and separation difficult.

Moon, Seung-jun, and Cheong Yi Park. "Media Effects on Acculturation and Biculturalism: A Case Study of Korean Immigrants in Los Angeles' Korea Town." *Mass Communication and Society* 10, no. 3 (2007): 319–343. doi: 10.1080/15205430701407330.

The central focus of this study is on the effects of American and Korean mass media on Korean immigrants' acculturation process. The survey results show that exposure to American mass media is a significant positive predictor for the acceptance of American cultural values and a significant negative predictor of the affinity for Korean cultural identity. However, exposure to Korean mass media is related to neither immigrant's affinity for Korean cultural identity nor acceptance of American cultural values.

Cultural Bias: Non-Western Perspectives

Kang, Myungkoo. "There Is No South Korea in South Korean Cultural Studies: Beyond the Colonial Condition of Knowledge Production." *Journal of Communication Inquiry* 28, no. 3 (2004): 253–268. doi: 10.1177/0196859904264688.

This study examines the colonial condition of cultural studies in Korea that have brought this new stream of thought to both the social sciences and the humanities. Its author's review provides a critique of Korean cultural studies and reflects on why cultural studies are needed in the twenty-first century. He also offers the ways in which Korean cultural studies has adopted, appropriated, and utilized Western theories of cultural studies since the late 1980s.

Chapter 9

Korean Wave (*Hallyu*) Studies

Dal Yong Jin and Ju Oak Kim

The Korean Wave, *Hallyu* in Korean, refers to the rapid growth of Korean cultural industries and the exports of their cultural products to Asia and beyond. *Hallyu* began in 1997 with a few Korean TV dramas, including *What Is Love All About?*, *Winter Sonata*, and *Dae Jang Geum*. In the early 2000s, *Hallyu* was led by the success of Korean films like *Joint Security Area* (*JSA*) alongside H.O.T. and other K-pop musicians.

The Korean Wave's milieu has changed since the late 2000s, when fans in North America and Western Europe began to enjoy Korean popular culture. A few notable changes characterize *Hallyu* as a true transnational cultural phenomenon in recent years. To begin with, the global fans' acceptance of Korean local culture has shifted from television programs and films to K-pop, digital games, and animation. K-pop has emerged as a driving force for *Hallyu*'s remarkable growth on the global stage since Psy's *Gangnam Style* became a huge hit.

Equally significant is the global fans' growing use of social media to enjoy Korean popular culture. Korean-made smartphones and digital technologies have spurred the Korean Digital Wave as the major part of *Hallyu*. At the center of *Hallyu* 2.0, which started in the late 2000s, is the advancement of new digital technology and social media.[1]

Korean and non-Korean communication scholars did not publish about *Hallyu* in English until the early twenty-first century, when they started to write English-language journal articles, book chapters, and books. The huge success of the Korean Wave, which celebrated its twentieth anniversary in

---

1. Dal Yong Jin, *New Korean Wave: Transnational Cultural Power in the Age of Social Media* (Urbana: University of Illinois Press, 2016), 5–6.

2017, has led a number of scholars in the United States and abroad to publish about *Hallyu* in English.

EMERGENCE OF *HALLYU* STUDIES IN THE WEST

Hallyu studies has expanded in its regional coverage, subjects, and methodological directions. The early stage of *Hallyu* studies was limited to *Hallyu* in East Asia. But recent *Hallyu* studies covers the global reception of Korean popular culture in Europe, North America, and Latin America. The English-language research papers in the 2010s have concentrated on K-pop, animation, webtoons, and television programs. Some of them identify the social media's increasing role in the growth of the Korean Wave phenomenon in the global cultural markets.

Over the years, the number of English research publications on *Hallyu* has substantially increased. *Hallyu* papers in English numbered 76 as of 2016, and the number jumped from 1 in 2004 to 7 in 2011, 16 in 2013, although it dropped to 9 in 2015.[2] In 2017, 24 new publications—2 books, 8 journal articles, and 14 book chapters—were added to the growing body of the Korean Wave scholarship in English. In early 2018, the total number of academic English publications on *Hallyu* studies we used for this chapter stood at 107.

HALLYU STUDIES BY RESEARCH SUBJECTS

Major research topics have evolved from *Hallyu* studies. Our chapter aims at research topics broadly covering media, communication, and culture. We emphasize the focal areas of *Hallyu* studies so that our readers can get core information on *Hallyu*. The themes of scholarly Korean Wave publications in English help identify several research topics, such as concept and theory, policy and diplomacy, popular culture, social media, and representation.

Concept and Theory

The majority of English research publications on *Hallyu* during its first few years tended toward the regional spread of Korean popular culture in East and South East Asia. These early publications attempted to dissect the reason

---

2. The number until 2016 is mostly based on Tae-Jin Yoon and Bora Kang's chapter. See Tae-Jin Yoon and Bora Kang, "Emergence, Evolution, and Extension of Hallyu Studies: What Have Scholars Found from Korean Pop Culture in the Last Twenty Years," in *The Korean Wave: Evolution, Fandom, and Transnationality*, ed. Tae Jin Yoon and Dal Yong Jin, 3–21 (Lanham, MA: Lexington Books, 2017).

Korea's cultural industries grew and Asian audiences who had previously enjoyed Japanese and American popular cultures turned to Korean culture. Some of the articles also sought to confirm the possibility of regional cultural identity as Korean popular culture rapidly established itself as one of the most enjoyable and dependable local cultures in Asia.

As the Korean Wave spreads to many parts of the world, academic discourses on *Hallyu* have fundamentally shifted. Unlike the early phase of the Korean Wave, communication scholars were attracted to the popularity of *Hallyu* in the West, and their recent works try to explain why *Hallyu* becomes globally popular and at the same time theorize or conceptualize a new *Hallyu* trend. The leading *Hallyu* scholar Dal Yong Jin at Simon Fraser University compares the more recent phase of the Korean Wave with its early stage. He pays critical attention to *Hallyu*'s sociocultural conditions that develop local popular culture and media technology, which shapes the new Korean Wave. Jin advances non-Western theoretical discussions of transnational cultural flows and consumptions.[3] French *Hallyu* specialist Youna Kim, drawing attention to the Korean Wave's sociocultural implications as a global cultural force,[4] invokes "soft power" in discussing the use of cultural power to enhance national images[5] and cultural diplomacy[6] to dissect the politics of the Korean Wave.

Policy and Diplomacy

The Korean Wave came suddenly during the 1997 economic crisis. When their country endeavored to survive the worst economic recession, Korean broadcasters had to cut their budgets to import foreign TV programs while struggling to develop their own programs. And several East Asian countries that used to import Japanese popular culture needed to secure cheaper programs. Korean broadcasters and film corporations were able to quickly, yet with few specific plans, to penetrate the East Asian region.

But several key state-sponsored policy measures were instrumental in initiating and supporting the Korean Wave. The Korean government has used financial and legal mechanisms to promote *Hallyu*. The conservative Lee Myung-bak and Park Geun-hye administrations (2008–2017) sought to develop the Korean Wave as soft power. In his 2015 study, researcher Hyungseok Kang at King's College London argues that the government-led

---

3. Jin, *New Korean Wave*.
4. Youna Kim, ed., *The Korean Wave: Korean Media Go Global* (London: Routledge, 2013).
5. Joseph Nye, "Soft Power and American Foreign Policy," *Political Science Quarterly* 119, no. 2 (2004): 255–270.
6. Irena Kozymka, *The Diplomacy of Culture: The Role of UNESCO in Sustaining Cultural Diversity* (New York: Palgrave, 2014).

construction of national cultural identity is driven by the national agenda of globalization, which has enabled the Korean culture industries to boost cultural exchanges as part of Koreans' cultural diplomacy.[7]

In his 2014 journal article, Professor Jin at Simon Fraser University analyzes the Korean government's active engagement in the transnational consumption of Korean popular content. He takes a special note of the growing concerns among *Hallyu* experts and industry practitioners about government interventions in shaping popular culture as a commodity and the government's undervaluing of cultural diversity in the policy-making process.[8] Two University of South Wales researchers investigate the empowerment of the Korean cultural industries in connection with the Korean government's cultural policies. The Korean government has supported the cultural industries by helping develop technological infrastructures and distribution systems.[9]

Popular Culture

As the Korean Wave phenomenon started with a few television programs, films, and music in the late 1990s and early 2000s, many *Hallyu* works revolved around local popular culture. Several journal articles in English raised a significant question about the Korean Wave's cultural dimension in the global markets,[10] while asking whether Korean popular culture has propelled the East Asian cultural industry.

Several Korean musicians, whether idol groups or solo artists, have penetrated the global music markets, including Japan, China, the United States, Canada, France, and Chile. Professor Ju Oak Kim of Texas A&M International University has researched the Korean music industry's production system in discussing the global popularity of K-pop. Based on her interpretive analysis of SM Entertainment, one of Korea's largest music companies, Kim argues that the hybrid forms of K-pop, localizing policies, and social media marketing are the major factors of the *Hallyu* phenomenon.[11] Meanwhile, the transnational popularity of Korean pop music was examined

7. Hyungseok Kang, "Contemporary Cultural Diplomacy in South Korea: Explicit and Implicit Approaches," *International Journal of Cultural Policy* 21, no. 4 (2015): 433–447.

8. Dal Yong Jin, "The Power of the Nation-State amid Neoliberal Reform: Shifting Cultural Politics in the New Korean Wave," *Pacific Affairs* 87, no. 1 (2014): 71–92.

9. Seung-Ho Kwon and Joseph Kim, "The Cultural Industry Policies of the Korean Government and the Korean Wave," *International Journal of Cultural Policy* 20, no. 4 (2014): 422–439.

10. Jeongsuk Joo, "Transnationalization of Korean Popular Culture and the Rise of Pop Nationalism in Korea," *Journal of Popular Culture* 44, no. 3 (2011): 489–504; Eun-Young Jung, "Transnational Korea: A Critical Assessment of the Korean Wave in Asia and the United States," *Southeast Review of Asian Studies* 31 (2009): 69–80.

11. Ju Oak Kim, "Establishing an Imagined SM Town: How Korea's Leading Music Company Has Produced a Global Cultural Phenomenon," *Journal of Popular Culture* 49, no. 5 (2016): 1042–1058.

by *Hallyu* experts in Hong Kong and Australia, who asked what has led Korea, a peripheral nation, to produce a global phenomenon and what has influenced Asian culture to emerge as a center of the global pop industry.[12]

Audience Reception and Fandom

One of the most notable areas of research for *Hallyu* scholars has been audience reception and fandom as fans are the primary consumers of Korean popular culture. In-depth interviews or ethnographic field studies have enabled several scholars to analyze the major characteristics of fandom in many different regions. Professor Michelle Cho at McGill University posits television as a central space for constructing the Korean public's perception of the Korean Wave and for fictionalizing the Korean creative industries. Understanding the intertextuality of Korean pop music and Korean television dramas, she asserts that K-dramas commodify sentiment about K-pop and that the meta-textual presentation of K-pop on K-dramas has influenced the national public's understanding of the success of the Korean Wave.[13] Similarly, Ben Han, a communication professor at Tulane University, contends that K-pop has created transcultural fandom via digital platforms, making it an important subculture in Latin America. Relying on in-depth interviews with K-pop fans in Latin America, he observes that K-pop has become a huge sensation in Latin America because of its cultural affinity, not its exoticism and cultural novelty.[14]

Digital *Hallyu* Studies

Some scholarly works have addressed digital *Hallyu*. The digital technologies and cultures of Korea have become some of the largest *Hallyu* components in Korea's foreign exports. Besides, Korea has developed Webtoons (web comics) with the surge of smartphone use. The exports of these digital technologies and cultures have continued to soar, and they have played key roles in diversifying the Korean Wave.

In his 2010 book on Korean online gaming, the first of its kind in English, Simon Fraser's Jin explores how the Korean online game industry became one of the important players in the global game market in the 2000s. He analyzes the context in which the Korean game industry has been transformed

12. Jung Bong Choi and Roald Maliangkay, *K-Pop–The International Rise of the Korean Music Industry* (London: Routledge, 2015).

13. Michelle Cho, "Domestic Hallyu: K-Pop Metatexts and the Media's Self-reflexive Gesture," *International Journal of Communication* 11 (2017): 2308–2231.

14. Ben Han, "K-Pop in Latin America: Transcultural Fandom and Digital Mediation," *International Journal of Communication* 11 (2017): 2250–2269.

into a major sector of the national economic system in the process of global-ization.[15] Jin further examines the transitional expansion of Korean online gaming culture, while identifying the potential of local online games that generate contra-flow of digital culture.[16]

Korea's digital mediascapes have been analyzed as an important topic for discussion of the Korean digital wave. Professor Ben Goldsmith at the University of the Sunshine Coast in Australia and his co-authors have connected the advancement of digital technologies with the proliferation of the Korean culture and creative industries. They offer a critical perspective on the Korean government as a key player in developing digital culture in Korean society.[17]

Social Media

Social media has risen as a hot topic for *Hallyu* scholars as the global fans of Korean popular culture heavily use YouTube, Facebook, Instagram, and other social media Many of the latest books and other scholarly publications in English on *Hallyu* have concerned the global fans' use of social media and the social media's implications for the growth of local culture. Most important, Professor Jin at Simon Fraser and Professor Kyong Yoon of the University of British Columbia in Canada develop a theory on the spreadability of digital technologies in explaining North American fans' consumption of Korean popular culture. They claim that social media have fundamentally changed the level and range of media consumption. Jin and Yoon continue that this new media environment facilitates the geographically separated audiences in creating a participatory culture in their social contexts.[18] Cinema studies scholars Sangjoon Lee at Nanyang Technological University in Singapore and Abé Mark Nornes at the University of Michigan place the Korean Wave's new global stage in a theoretical, political, and cultural context. Considering Korean pop and television dramas as the important tools for reproducing *Hallyu,* Lee and Nornes study how social media have dramatically advanced the Korean Wave.[19]

15. Dal Yong Jin, *Korea's Online Gaming* EMPIRE (Cambridge, MA: MIT Press, 2010).

16. Dal Yong Jin, "The Digital Korean Wave: Local Online Gaming Goes Global," *Media International Australia* 14 (2011): 128–136.

17. Ben Goldsmith, Kwang-Suk Lee, and Brian Yecies, "In Search of the Korean Digital Wave," *Media International Australia* 141 (2011): 70–77.

18. Dal Yong Jin and Kyong Yoon, "The Social Mediascape of Transnational Korean Pop Culture: Hallyu 2.0 as Spreadable Media Practice," *New Media & Society* 18, no. 7 (2014): 1277–1292.

19. Sangjoon Lee and Abé Mark Nornes, *Hallyu 2.0: The Korean Wave in the Age of Social Media* (Ann Arbor: University of Michigan Press, 2015).

FUTURE ENGLISH RESEARCH PUBLICATIONS

Our chapter provides a concise overview of the 20 years of *Hallyu* scholarship in English through the books, book chapters, journal articles, theses, and dissertations. Since the Korean Wave's inception in the late 1990s, a number of scholarly works have been published first in Korean and then in English.

A 2017 study of the history of *Hallyu* studies selected a total of 666 research papers written in Korean between 2001 and 2016,[20] and compared them with 107 English publications annotated for our chapter. The study indicates that many scholars in Korea analyze *Hallyu* for their major research area. Given that the majority of *Hallyu* articles in English have been published in the 2010s, academic books, book chapters, and journal articles are more likely to appear in English in the future.

A growing body of *Hallyu* research in English in recent years has helped media scholars, students, journalists, and others learn how *Hallyu* has spread globally and why it's now one of the most important non-Western cultures. As the growth of K-pop and digital technologies in the global markets continues, more research on *Hallyu* is expected to be published in English for the international audience of the twenty-first century.

ANNOTATED BIBLIOGRAPHY

General

Huat, Chua Beng, and Koichi Iwabuchi, ed. *East Asian Pop Culture: Analysing the Korean Wave*. Hong Kong: Hong Kong University Press, 2008.

> Based upon a comparative analysis of the cultural phenomenon of Korea in Japan, China, and other countries, Huat and Iwabuchi examine how the Korean Wave has provided the space for proliferating cross-border connections and for producing the impression of Asianness in Asia.

Jin, Dal Yong, and Tae-Jin Yoon. "The Korean Wave: Retrospect and Prospect." *International Journal of Communication* 11 (2017): 2241–2249.

> In commemoration of its twentieth anniversary, this study looks into a historical trajectory of the Korean Wave. Jin and Yoon demonstrate that the phenomenon began with the inter-regional consumption of Korean television dramas and advanced to several other cultural forms, including Korean pop and online games.

---

20. Suk Kyong Hong, Dae Min Park, and So Jung Park, "Knowledge Network Analysis on *Hallyu* Research.," *Korean Journal of Journalism & Communication Studies* 61 no. 3 (2017):318–353.

Ju, Hyejung. "Glocalization of the Korean Popular Culture in East Asia: Theorizing the Korean Wave." PhD diss., University of Oklahoma, 2010. ProQuest (858609071).

Using in-depth interviews of Japanese consumers of Korean television dramas, Ju claims that the glocalization strategy helps East Asian audiences develop their emotional affinity with Korean media content.

Kim, Do Kyun, and Min-Sun Kim, ed. *Hallyu: Influence of Korean Popular Culture in Asia and Beyond.* Seoul: Seoul National University Press, 2011.

Kim and Kim offer a comprehensive articulation of the Korean Wave from its unprecedented emergence to its future directions. Multidisciplinary debates about the Korean phenomenon among Korean scholars of sociology, communication, history, and international relations help international audiences identify Korean perspectives on the Korean Wave.

Kim, Jeongmee. "Why Does Hallyu Matter? The Significance of the Korean Wave in South Korea." *Critical Studies in Television* 2, no. 2 (2007): 47–59. doi: 10.7227/CST.2.2.6

The meaning of the term, the Korean Wave, has enormously expanded to explain the transnational visibility of Korean popular culture and lifestyles. However, Kim identifies the paucity of research on the origin of the term's usage and points out that numerous researchers have used the term in a nationalistic perspective.

Kim, Ju Oak. "The Korean Wave as a Localizing Process: Nation as a Global Actor in Cultural Production." PhD diss., Temple University, 2016. Proquest (1794195875).

Focusing on the power dynamics of three major players—the government, television networks, and music agencies—in expanding the Korean Wave, Kim proposes that the phenomenon rekindles national forces in spreading local culture globally.

Kim, Kyung Hyun, and Youngmin Choe, ed. *The Korean Popular Culture Reader*. Durham, NC: Duke University Press, 2014.

By analyzing how its transnational popularity is associated with Korean society's modernization, neoliberal globalization, and post-industrialization, the authors emphasize the importance of local knowledge production in the Korean Wave phenomenon.

Kuwahara, Yasue, ed. *The Korean Wave: Korean Popular Culture in Global Context*. New York: Palgrave Macmillan, 2014.

The contributing authors discuss the implications of the transnational expansion of Korean popular culture. In their view, Korean popular culture has transformed hegemonic relationships between Western and non-Western countries in cultural production and consumption.

Marinescu, Valentina, ed. *The Global Impact of South Korean Popular Culture:* Hallyu *Unbound.* Lanham, MD: Lexington Books, 2014.

By analyzing the global expansion of Korean popular culture, this volume maps the export of Korean cultural products throughout Asia, Europe, Latin America, and the United States. The book not only offers transnational comparisons of those countries but also proposes a critical perspective on the future of *Hallyu*.

Yoon, Kyong, and Dal Yong Jin. "The Korean Wave Phenomenon in Asian Diasporas in Canada." *Journal of Intercultural Studies* 37, no. 1 (2016): 69–83. doi: 10.1080 /07256868.2015.1119810

Drawing on in-depth interviews in Toronto and Vancouver, the study examines how transnational cultural flow is articulated with social media and ethnic sociality. While the transnational flow of Korean media content largely relied on social media, the authors state, it was renegotiated by the users' positions as ethnic minorities.

Yoon, Tae-Jin, and Dal Yong Jin, ed. *The Korean Wave: Evolution, Fandom, and Transnationality.* Lanham, MD: Lexington Books, 2017.

Yoon and Jin pinpoint changes in the nature and appearance of the Korean Wave, mentioning conceptual and theoretical shifts in the studies of the Korean Wave and the influences of the development of media technologies on the Korean Wave. This edited volume provides an in-depth understanding of the various components of the Korean Wave and its global fandom that has led to the expansion of the phenomenon.

Concept and Theorization

Choi, JungBong. "Of the East Asian Cultural Sphere: Theorizing Cultural Regionalization." *China Review* 10, no. 2 (2010): 109–136.

In this study, the concept of cultural regionalization is employed as a theoretical framework to grasp cultural exchanges between East and Southeast Asian countries. The term, "the East Asian cultural sphere," is introduced to explicate how the Korean Wave has emerged from the encounter of two different waves, interregional political tensions and economic integrations that East Asia has made.

Jin, Dal Yong. "Reinterpretation of Cultural Imperialism: Emerging Domestic Market vs. Continuing US Dominance." *Media, Culture & Society* 29, no. 5 (2007): 753–771. doi. 10.1177/0163443707080535.

The cultural imperialism thesis is applied to discuss the role of Korean popular culture in the East Asian media market. Jin indicates that the rise of the Korean Wave does not change the global domination of U.S. media culture and practice and, therefore, cultural imperialism remains valid to explain the transnational dynamics of cultural products, capital, and industries.

———. "*Hallyu* 2.0: The New Korean Wave in the Creative Industry." *Journal of International Institute* 2, no. 1 (2012): 3–7.

Since the late 2000s, online users have easily accessed Korean pop music, animation, and video games. So the Korean Wave has opened up a new stage. In this new era of the Korean Wave, Jin adds, the intellectual property (IP) rights have become crucial for boosting the national economy and protecting creative products.

———. *New Korean Wave: Transnational Cultural Power in the Age of Social Media*. Urbana: University of Illinois Press, 2016.

In analyzing the new phase of the Korean Wave in comparison with the initial stage of the Korean phenomenon, Jin pays attention to the sociocultural conditions of Korea that develop local popular culture and media technology, which shape the characteristics of the new Korean Wave and advance non-Western theoretical discussions of transnational cultural flows and consumptions.

Kim, Youna, ed. *The Korean Wave: Korean Media Go Global*. London: Routledge, 2013.

This edited volume examines the sociocultural implications of the Korean Wave as a global cultural force, uncovering the continued inequalities of power relationships in global cultural flows. The contributing authors utilize the notion of soft power to discuss the politics of the Korean Wave and highlight the de-Westernized production of global culture.

Ravina, Mark. "Introduction: Conceptualizing the Korean Wave." *Southeast Review of Asian Studies* 31 (2009): 3–9.

Ravina analyzes the Korean Wave in the context of Korean studies, East Asian studies, and cultural studies. The author illuminates the national and transnational aspects of the Korean Wave and calls on others to explore further the logic of the cross-cultural expansion of the Korean phenomenon

Ryoo, Woongjae. "Globalization, or the Logic of Cultural Hybridization: The Case of the Korean Wave." *Asian Journal of Communication* 19, no. 2 (2009): 137–151. doi: 10.1080/01292980902826427.

Ryoo centers on cultural regionalization as a logic of transnational cultural flows. He states that the Korean Wave has confirmed that peripheral countries can find niche markets and become major actors in the process of global cultural transformations.

Shim, Doobo. "Hybridity and the Rise of Korean Popular Culture in Asia." *Media, Culture & Society* 2, no. 1 (2006): 25–44. doi: 10.1177/0163443706059278

Shim explores how the Korean culture industry has utilized cultural hybridization to produce global cultural forms. He points out that the creative hybridization of

Western and Asian values is critical to expanding the popularity of Korean popular culture to East Asian communities.

Policy and Diplomacy

Chen, Steven. "Cultural Technology: A Framework for Marketing Cultural Exports: Analysis of (the Korean Wave)." *International Marketing Review* 33, no. 1 (2016): 25–50. doi: 10.1108/IMR-07–2014–0219.

This study centers on the removal of cultural odor to facilitate Korea's popular products in neighboring markets, and the fusion of two cultural elements generates a third space for constructing new identities and cultural meanings of Korean popular content in the global market.

Huang, Shuling. "Nation-Branding and Transnational Consumption: Japan-Mania and the Korean Wave in Taiwan." *Media, Culture & Society* 33, no. 1 (2011): 3–18. doi: 10.1177/0163443710379670.

Korean popular products have swept over East Asian societies with a mixture of Western cultures and Asian sentiments. This study concludes that national cultures can be transnationally consumed with hybrid forms of cultural products, cultivating national images in the transnational markets.

Jin, Dal Yong. "The Power of the Nation-State amid Neo-Liberal Reform: Shifting Cultural Politics in the New Korean Wave." *Pacific Affairs* 87, no. 1 (2014): 71–92. doi: 10.5509/201487171.

Jin calls attention to the Korean government's involvement in the transnational consumption of Korean popular content. He indicates the intervention of the government as the turning point of the phenomenon in which the government has caused the shaping of popular culture as a commodity and the underestimation of cultural diversity in the policy-making process.

Kang, Hyungseok. "Contemporary Cultural Diplomacy in South Korea: Explicit and Implicit Approaches." *International Journal of Cultural Policy* 21, no. 4 (2015): 433–447. doi: 10.1080/10286632.2015.1042473.

Kang discusses that the Korean government considers cultural products as symbolic capital, providing "a 'developmental state' model of governance" in global trade. He concludes that the Korean culture industries have promoted cultural exchanges as part of cultural diplomacy.

Kim, Hwa Kyung, Andrew Eungi Kim, and Daniel Connolly. "Catching up on *Hallyu*? The Japanese and Chinese Response to South Korean Soft Power." *Korea Observer* 47, no. 3 (2016): 527–558.

The authors critically point out that the Korean government has strategized the Korean Wave to seek economic benefits, and that China and Japan have employed new forms of cultural protectionism.

Kim, Ju Young. "Rethinking Media Flow under Globalization: Rising Korean Wave and Korean TV and Film Policy Since 1980s." PhD diss., ProQuest (301682670).

Understanding that the paradigm of globalization has changed the landscape of the Korean culture industry, the author discusses that the Korean culture industry has experienced the qualitative growth of cultural content as well as the quantitative expansion of cultural exports, based on an exploration of the changing relationship between the Korean government and cultural industries since the late 1990s.

Kim, Regina. "South Korean Cultural Diplomacy and Efforts to Promote the ROK's Brand Image in the United States and around the World." *Stanford Journal of East Asian Affairs* 11, no. 1(2011): 124–134.

The Korean government has promoted its national image (particularly within the United States), and this article analyzes some of the obstacles and potential challenges the government has faced. Its author seeks to assess the effectiveness of the government's nation-branding projects and present the general prospects of the campaign.

Kim, Tae Young, and Dal Yong Jin. "Cultural Policy in the Korean Wave: An Analysis of Cultural Diplomacy Embedded in Presidential Speeches." *International Journal of Communication* 10 (2017): 5514–5534.

The Korean government has developed its strategies for enhancing the Korean Wave since the late 1990s. Through a textual analysis of presidential speeches and announcements, the authors propose that the Korean government has actively employed the phenomenon as a major tool for promoting national images.

Kwon, Seung-Ho, and Joseph Kim. "The Cultural Industry Policies of the Korean Government and the Korean Wave." *International Journal of Cultural Policy* 20, no. 4 (2014): 422–439. doi: 10.1080/10286632.2013.829052.

Over the last two decades, the Korean government has provided support to the cultural industries, including the development of technological infrastructures and distribution systems. The authors address that the Ministry of Culture has taken initiatives in implementing governmental support, by using a comparative approach to analyze the former regimes' cultural policies.

——— "From Censorship to Active Support: The Korean State and Korea's Cultural Industries." *Economic and Labour Relations Review* 24, no. 4 (2013): 517–532. doi: 10.1177/1035304613508873.

This article provides a historical trajectory of the Korean cultural industries, focusing on how the Korean government has shifted its understanding of the cultural industries from labor-centered manufacturing industries to knowledge-based creative industries.

Sohn, Dehyun, and Seung Ho Youn. "Fundamental Sources and Sustainable Development of the Korean Cultural Entertainment Industry with the Korean Wave." *International Journal of Tourism Sciences* 16, no. 1–2 (2016): 83–92. doi: 10.1080/15980634.2016.1212600.

A particular focus is given to the cultural entertainment industry (CEI), which expands the Korean Wave to other industries, including tourism, electronics, food, and fashion industries. For the authors, the key to sustaining the Korean Wave is to produce new and unique cultural content through finding and training new faces.

Yim, Haksoon. "Cultural Identity and Cultural Policy in South Korea." *International Journal of Cultural Policy* 8, no. 1 (2002): 37–48. doi: 10.1080/10286630290032422.

Yim comprehends the evolution of Korean cultural policy as the process of constructing cultural identity, developing arts and cultures, improving the quality of cultural life, and boosting cultural industries. A particular focus is given to the relationship between cultural identity and cultural policy.

Popular Culture

Cho, Younghan. "Desperately Seeking East Asia amidst the Popularity of South Korean Pop Culture in Asia." *Cultural Studies* 25, no 3 (2011): 383–404. doi: 10. 1080/09502386.2010.545424.

The usage of the term, "East Asia," in Korean society reflects how East Asia has reshaped the geographic imaginary of the region. The author proposes that the transnational expansion of Korean popular culture, shared memories of the pasts and desires for modernization, and the increasing connectivity of economic structures have produced a new sense of inter-regional identity in Asia.

Joo, Jeongsuk. "Transnationalization of Korean Popular Culture and the Rise of Pop Nationalism in Korea." *Journal of Popular Culture* 44, no. 3 (2011): 489–504. doi: 10.1111/j.1540–5931.2011.00845.x.

Considering that the transnational popularity of Korean popular culture has fueled popular nationalism in Korea, the author discusses that Korean popular culture has become a new engine for the East Asian entertainment industry and this new phenomenon has constructed the nationalistic discourse in Korean society.

Jung, Eun-Young. "Transnational Korea: A Critical Assessment of the Korean Wave in Asia and the United States." *Southeast Review of Asian Studies* 31 (2009): 69–80.

Through interpretive analyses of the Korean television drama *Winter Sonata* and Korean pop celebrities like BoA and Rain, this study raises a significant question regarding the cultural dimension of the Korean Wave. The author contends that the popularity of Korean pop is a result of its hybridity rather than its indigenousness.

Lie, John. "South Korean Literature in the Age of the Korean Wave: Soft Power, Literary Value, and Cultural Policy in South Korea." *Korea Observer* 44, no. 4 (2013): 647–668.

Few have given attention to Korean literature outside of the country. The author points out that the Korean government has relatively neglected to support writing and art, including novels, plays, and poems, defining culture as a commodity.

Films

Choi, Youngmin. *Tourist Distractions: Traveling and Feeling in Transnational Hallyu Cinema.* Durham, NC: Duke University Press, 2016.

After textually and historically examining domestic films, Choi delves into how the Korean cinema inspired both domestic and global tourists to visit movie sets and filming sites. Choi clarifies the crucial relationships between Korean cinema—with a focus on the impact of the Korean Wave's emerging core characteristics, such as its attempt to convert economic interests into affective feeling—and tourism.

Jin, Dal Yong. "Cultural Politics in Korea's Contemporary Films under Neoliberal Globalization." *Media, Culture & Society* 28, no. 1 (2006): 5–23. doi: 10.1177/0163443706059274

Market deregulation and state decentralization fundamentally transformed the Korean film industry in the late 1980s. The Motion Picture Promotion Law of Korea allowed the government to support local film companies, which led to the revitalization of Korean film production and the enrichment of cultural diversity in the 1990s.

Kim, Kyung Hyun. *Virtual* Hallyu: *Korean Cinema of the Global Era.* Durham, NC: Duke University Press, 2011.

Drawing on Gilles Deleuze's concept of the virtual, Kim analyzes social anxieties and controversies embedded in recent Korean films. He argues that going beyond the state-driven political and socio-economic approaches, the Korean Wave should be discussed in the context of post-nationalism, capitalism, and neoliberalism.

Kuotsu, Neikolie. "Architectures of Pirate Film Cultures: Encounters with Korean Wave in 'Northeast' India." *Inter-Asia Cultural Studies* 14, no. 4 (2013): 1–21. doi : 10.1080/14649373.2013.831196.

This study explores the consumption of Korean films in Northeastern India, focusing on the contribution of socio-political agents, digital technologies, and distribution systems to the localization of Korean film culture. The author identifies the Korean Wave as a form of Asian modernity that reflects specific aesthetics of Asian media culture.

Yecies, Brian. "The Chinese–Korean Co-Production Pact: Collaborative Encounters and the Accelerating Expansion of Chinese Cinema." *International Journal of Cultural Policy* 22, no. 5 (2016): 770–786. doi:10.1080/10286632.2016.1223643.

Yecies analyzes Korea-China coproduction, which has been popular since 2004. He emphasizes that with the rise of Korean-Chinese connections, Korean creators have expanded their activities at the regional level and, in turn, have changed the production culture in China.

Yecies, Brian, and Ae-Gyung Shim. "Contemporary Korean Cinema: Challenges and the Transformation of Planet Hallyuwood." *Acta Koreana* 14, no. 1 (2011): 1–15. doi: 10.18399/acta.2011.14.1.001.

The authors employ the term "Planet Hallyuwood" to explain that the Korean film industry has made a name in the global market while maintaining the locality of its culture, language, and market.

Television Dramas

Cho, Younghan, and Hongrui Zhu. "Korean Wave Studies as Method: Reconsidering the Television Format Phenomenon between South Korea and China through Inter-Asian Frameworks." *International Journal of Communication* 11 (2017): 2332–2349.

Centering on the Chinese remakes of Korean television formats, the authors propose inter-regional frameworks for analyzing the flows of television programs. They view television formats as cultural assemblages that highlight the inter-Asian characteristics of media culture.

Chuang, Lisa M., and Hye Eun Lee. "Korean Wave: Enjoyment Factors of Korean Dramas in the U.S." *International Journal of Intercultural Relations* 37, no. 5 (2013): 594–604. doi:10.1016/j.ijintrel.2013.07.003.

The notion of disposition is employed to analyze the U.S. audience's enjoyment of Korean television dramas. The authors assert that the U.S. audience's emotional connections with characters in Korean television dramas yield the cross-cultural enjoyment of Korean television dramas.

Han, Ben. "Reliving *Winter Sonata*: Memory, Nostalgia, and Identity." *Post Script* 27, no. 3 (2008): 25–36.

Han brings the notion of memory and nostalgia to explain why a Korean television drama, *Winter Sonata*, attracted older audiences in Japanese society. In his view, the nostalgic theme of first love in the series helped the Japanese audience revisit the traditional values that Japanese dramas no longer contain.

Hanaki, Toru, Arvind Singhal, Min Wha Han, Do Kyun Kim, and Ketan Chitnis. "Hanryu Sweeps East Asia: How *Winter Sonata* Is Gripping Japan." *International Communication Gazette,* 69, no. 3 (2007): 281–294. doi: 10.1177/1748048507076581.

This article examines the Japanese audience's fascination with the Korean television drama, *Winter Sonata*, based on the authors' in-depth interviews with middle-aged Japanese female viewers and archival data analysis. The authors note four reasons: the description of pure love, cinematic scenery, the inclusion of traditional Japanese values, and nostalgic sentiment.

Jeon, Won Kyung. "The 'Korean Wave' and Television Drama Exports, 1995–2005." PhD diss., University of Glasgow (United Kingdom), 2013. ProQuest (1535017722).

Jeon focuses on how the Korean government's nationalistic viewpoint has often failed to improve the cultural industry's actual circumstances although the importance of governmental policy has been identified in the inter-regional consumption of Korean television dramas.

Kim, Do Kyun, Arvind Singhai, Toru Hanaki, Jennifer Dunn, Ketan Chitnis, and Min Wha Han. "Television Drama, Narrative Engagement and Audience Buying Behavior: The Effects of *Winter Sonata* in Japan." *International Communication Gazette* 71, no. 7 (2009): 595–611. doi: 10.1177/1748048509341894.

The popularity of the Korean television drama, *Winter Sonata*, has increased the exports of the drama-related products, such as DVDs and CDs of the program, clothing, and cosmetics in Japanese society. The authors explain that the Japanese audience has valued the high quality of the program narrative and has attempted to purchase *Winter Sonata* products.

Kim, Jeongmee, Michael A. Unger, and Keith B. Wagner. "Beyond *Hallyu*: Innovation, Social Critique, and Experimentation in South Korean Cinema and Television." *Quarterly Review of Film and Video* 34, no. 4 (2017): 321–332. doi: 10.1080/105 09208.2016.1241623.

The authors discuss that the global fans of Korean popular culture have actively participated in the spread of the Korean Wave by using digital platforms. More importantly, the authors call attention to "Beyond *Hallyu*" products, referring to unconventional and independent works that have been relatively underestimated in the discussion of Korean popular culture.

Lee, Minu, and Chong Heup Cho. "Women Watching Together: An Ethnographic Study of Korean Soap Opera Fans in the U.S." *Cultural Studies* 4, no. 1 (1990): 33–46. doi:10.1080/09502389000490031.

An ethnographic study of Korean immigrants who prefer Korean soap operas to American series uncovers that the collective experience of viewing television dramas maintains their preference of Korean dramas to American ones.

Miller, Laura. "Korean Dramas and Japan-style Korean Wave." *Post Script* 27, no. 3 (2008): 17–24.

Laura analyzes the economic and sociocultural impact that the Korean television drama *Winter Sonata* has made in Japanese society. Middle-aged Japanese fans of the television drama have made donations for victims of the tsunami disaster in Korea; have purchased all of the media content in which Bae Yong Jon, the main actor of the drama, has appeared; and have toured the drama's filming locations.

Popular Music

Choi, JungBong, and Roald Maliangkay. *K-Pop—The International Rise of the Korean Music Industry*. London: Routledge, 2015.

Choi and Maliangkay question how the Korean pop industry has become a central sector of the global music market. The authors employ a variety of theoretical frameworks, including modernization, digitalization, and regionalization, to analyze the transnational expansion of Korean pop music.

Fuhr, Michael. *Globalization and Popular Music in South Korea: Sounding Out K-Pop*. New York: Routledge, 2016.

Fuhr calls attention to the Korean pop industry that has strategically developed its production system to adopt global trends. He first looks at the history of Korean music production since the late nineteenth century and then explains the unequal relationship between music producers, celebrities, and audiences.

Howard, Keith, ed. *Korean Pop Music: Riding the Wave.* Kent, UK: Global Oriental, 2006.

Taking an interdisciplinary approach to the construction and development of Korean pop music culture from the aspects of musicology, Korean studies, and cultural studies, this edited volume traces back to the early 1930s to discuss the influence of Japanese pop music and uncover the political deployment of popular music in the 1970s.

Jin, Dal Yong, and Woongjae Ryoo. "Critical Interpretation of Hybrid K-Pop: The Global-Local Paradigm of English Mixing in Lyrics." *Popular Music and Society* 37, no. 2 (2014): 113–131. doi: 10.1080/03007766.2012.731721.

Cultural hybridization has produced new types of global popular culture and generated transformations in local pop music production. The utilization of English lyrics is thus the key to spreading Korean pop globally but brings about debates regarding the balance between Western and local pop culture.

Kim, Gooyong. "Between Hybridity and Hegemony in K-Pop's Global Popularity: A Case of Girls' Generation's American Debut." *International Journal of Communication* 11 (2017): 2367–2387.

Kim examines a Korean girl group Girls' Generations' visibility in the U.S. media while applying a political economy approach to the analysis of a hybrid form of Korean pop music. He proposes that the Korean pop boom be understood as the continuation of American popular culture's global dominance and neoliberalism.

Kim, Ju Oak. "Establishing an Imagined SM Town: How Korea's Leading Music Company Has Produced a Global Cultural Phenomenon." *Journal of Popular Culture* 49, no. 5 (2016): 1042–1058. doi:10.1111/jpcu.12463.

Kim centers on the Korean music industry's production system to discuss the global popularity of Korean pop music. Based on an interpretive analysis of SME Entertainment, one of the leading music companies in Korea, she argues that the hybrid forms of Korean pop music, localizing policies, and social media marketing are major factors of the phenomenon.

Lee, Gyu Tag. "De-Nationalization and Re-Nationalization of Culture: The Globalization of K-pop." PhD diss., George Mason University, 2013. Proquest (1428746844).

Lee focuses on the development of Korean popular music in the historical context, embracing the intersection of culture, media, and communication technology. Defining Korean pop music as the localization of global pop music, he contends that Korean pop has significantly influenced East Asian audiences by providing pan-East Asian culture and practice.

Lee, Jamie Shinhee. "Linguistic Hybridization in K-Pop: Discourse of Self-assertion and Resistance." *World Englishes* 23, no. 3 (2004): 429–450. doi: 10.1111/j.0883–2919.2004.00367.x.

Lee explores how young Korean listeners consider Korean pop as a discursive space for asserting self-subjectivity and challenging traditional ideas and values. In this sense, she analyzes English lyrics in Korean pop music as a cultural form of resistance and negotiation. She concludes that its hybridity enhances the transnational expansion of Korean pop music.

———. "Crossing and Crossers in East Asian Pop Music: Korea and Japan." *World Englishes* 25, no. 2 (2006): 235–250. doi: 10.1111/j.0083–2919.2006.00462.x.

Employing the notion of crossing to discuss the transnational activity of Korean pop artists in the Japanese entertainment industry, Lee asserts that the transnational popularity of Korean pop renegotiates the long-standing power relationship between Korea and Japan, helping Korean pop artists overcome the sense of inferiority to Japanese popular culture.

Lie, John. *K-Pop: Popular Music, Cultural Amnesia, and Economic Innovation in South Korea.* Berekley: University of California Press, 2015.

Lie analyzes the three dimensions of Korean pop music: the impact of Japanese and U.S. music upon Korean pop music in the twentieth century, the portrayal of Korean society in Korean pop music, and the rise of Korean pop in connection with social transformations, economic development, and the specificity of production culture.

Lee, Jung-Yup. "Contesting Digital Economy and Culture: Digital Technologies and the Transformation of Popular Music in South Korea." *Inter-Asia Cultural Studies* 10, no. 4 (2009): 489–506. doi: 10.1080/14649370903166143.

Lee studies how digital technologies have transformed the Korean music industry. He emphasizes that the individualization of music consumption, promoted by digital technologies, has diversified popular music culture and has led to the reorganization of industrial structures.

Oh, Ingyu. "The Globalization of K-Pop: Korea's Place in the Global Music Industry." *Korea Observer* 44, no. 3 (2013): 389–409.

Oh proposes the development of Korean pop as a complicated process of globalization and localization in music production. He points out that Korean pop is deeply associated with European pop mixture in which Korean music producers have considerably used European sounds and beats.

Otmazgin, Nissim, and Irina Lyan. "*Hallyu* across the Desert: K-Pop Fandom in Israel and Palestine." *Cross-Currents: East Asian History and Culture Review* 3, no. 1 (2014): 32–55.

Israeli and Palestinian fans of Korean pop have significantly contributed to expanding Korean popular music to the Middle East, in which these fans have become mediators between the Korean pop industry and local fans.

Russell, Mark James. *Pop Goes Korea: Behind the Revolution in Movies, Music and Internet Culture.* Berkeley, CA: Stone Bridge Press, 2008.

Russell explains seven key factors that have driven the development of the Korean entertainment industry over the past decade: the establishment of media conglomerates, the production of blockbuster films, the introduction of film festivals, the growth of television culture, the development of the idol music system, the internet revolution, and the popularity of comic books and animation.

Shin, Hyunjoon. "Have You Ever Seen the *Rain*? And Who'll Stop the *Rain*?: The Globalizing Project of Korean Pop (K-Pop)," *Inter-Asia Cultural Studies* 10, no. 4 (2009): 507–523. doi: 10.1080/14649370903166150.

Through a case study of a male Korean artist, Rain, who has attempted to enter the U.S. music industry, Shin argues that whether or not Korean artists are successfully making their entry into the U.S. music market, their attempts reflect the desire for globalization within the Korean pop industry.

Siriyuvasak, Ubonrat, and Hyunjoon Shin. "Asianizing K-Pop: Production, Consumption and Identification Patterns among Thai Youth." *Inter-Asia Cultural Studies* 8, no. 1 (2007): 109–204. doi: 10.1080/14649370601119113.

Ubonrat and Shin propose that the domination of Korean pop could cause the standardization of cultural production in the Southeast Asia region, by analyzing Thai fans of Korean popular culture who tend to follow the trends of neighboring counties.

Sung, Sang-Yeon. "Globalization and the Regional Flow of Popular Music: The Role of the Korean Wave (Hanliu) in the Construction of Taiwanese Identities and Asian Values." PhD diss., Indiana University, 2008. ProQuest (287993719).

This dissertation on the inter-regional consumption of Korean pop music focuses on how Taiwanese audiences construct their national identity through the consumption of Korean pop music. Sung claims that Taiwanese audiences actively construct the notion of Asian values and learn about Korean nationalism while listening to Korean pop.

Audience and Fandom

Ahn, Jungah. "The New Korean Wave in China: Chinese Users' Use of Korean Popular Culture via the Internet." *International Journal of Contents* 10, no. 3 (2014), 47–54. doi:10.5392/IJoC.2014.10.3.047.

Ahn discusses that the growth of online streaming services is a significant factor for Chinese audiences to enjoy Korean television dramas and pop music, and their mundane consumption of Korean popular content has positively changed Korean image in Chinese society.

Anderson, Crystal, and Doobo Shim. "Filling the Void: Researching the Korean Wave (*Hallyu*) Fandom." *Journal of Fandom Studies,* 3, no 1 (2015): 3–6. doi: 10.1386/jfs.3.1.3_1.

The transnational popularity of Korean television dramas and pop music open up the audience's participation in the production process. Their feedback influences television writers and directors to change their storylines. Understanding the interaction between K-pop celebrities and their fans, Anderson and Shim contend that the participatory culture that K-pop fans have developed challenges the long-standing structure of global cultural production and consumption.

Chen, Brenda and Xueli Wang. "Of Prince Charming and Male Chauvinist Pigs: Singaporean Female Viewers and the Dream-World of Korean Television Dramas." *International Journal of Cultural Studies* 14, no. 3 (2011): 291–305. doi: 10.1177/1367877910391868.

Chen and Wang discuss that Singaporean viewers have identified the characteristics of Korean television dramas as "fairytale fantasies, traditional morality, and gender and equality," and have developed their self-identities through the consumption of Korean television dramas.

Cho, Michelle. "Domestic *Hallyu*: K-Pop Metatexts and the Media's Self-Reflexive Gesture." *International Journal of Communication* 11 (2017): 2308–2231.

Cho defines television as a central space for constructing the Korean public's perception of the Korean Wave. Understanding the intertextuality of Korean pop music and Korean television dramas, she indicates that K-dramas commodify sentiment about K-pop and that the meta-textual presentation of K-pop on K-dramas has influenced the national public's understanding of the success of the Korean Wave.

Ha, Jarryn. "Uncles Generation: Adult Male Fans and Alternative Masculinities in South Korean Popular Music." *Journal of Fandom Studies* 3, no. 1 (2015): 43–58. doi: 10.1386/jfs.3.1.43_1.

The emergence of the so-called *samchon* (uncle) fans reflects the new patterns of consuming popular culture in Korea. Ha states that, considering that patriarchal male figures are devoted to work and family care, male fans of K-pop have brought alternative masculinity to the fore of discussions on the Korean socio-political landscape.

Han, Ben. "K-Pop in Latin America: Transcultural Fandom and Digital Mediation." *International Journal of Communication* 11 (2017): 2250–2269.

Han illuminates that Korean pop has made a huge sensation in Latin America due to its cultural affinity rather than its exoticism and cultural novelty. More importantly, the author identifies Korean pop as getting accommodated into the mainstream culture of the region through local fans' various activities, deconstructing the long-standing East-West paradigm in the discussion of globalization.

Igno, Jay-Ar M., and Marie Cielo E. Cenidoza. "Beyond the 'Fad': Understanding *Hallyu* in the Philippines." *International Journal of Social Science and Humanity* 6, no. 9 (2016): 723–727. doi: 10.18178/ijssh.2016.6.9.740.

Korean popular culture has dominated the landscape of the Southeast Asian media industry over the last two decades. The authors note that Filipinos tend to find a sense of hope from Korean culture that their culture does not contain. Additionally, they connect the aggressive Korean Christian missionaries with a negative image of the Korean Wave among Southeast Asians.

Jeong, Jae-Seon, Seul-Hi Lee, and Sang-Gil Lee. "When Indonesians Routinely Consume Korean Pop Culture: Revisiting Jakartan Fans of Korean Drama." *International Journal of Communication* 11 (2017): 2288–2307.

Following up an earlier study in 2006, the authors explore the influence of digital technologies in the consumption of Korean popular content in Indonesia and identify the local specificity in the appropriation of hybrid cultural experiences. Indonesian consumers have constructed their image of "Koreanness," which reflects the transnational impact of Korean popular culture.

Ju, Hyejung, and Soobum Lee. "The Korean Wave and Asian Americans: The Ethnic Meanings of Transnational Korean Pop Culture in the USA." *Continuum: Journal of Media & Cultural Studies* 29, no. 3 (2015): 323–338. doi:10.1080/10304312.2014.986059.

The authors use the notion of ethnic media in pointing out that Korean media content contributes to constructing a pan-ethnic identity among East Asian communities. They emphasize that Korean popular content allows them to feel connected to East Asian culture and move beyond their perception of being marginalized from American society.

Jung, Sun, and Doobo Shim. "Social Distribution: K-Pop Fan Practices in Indonesia and the 'Gangnam Style' Phenomenon." *International Journal of Cultural Studies* 17, no. 5 (2014): 485–501. doi: 10.1177/1367877913505173.

Jung and Shim focus on how Korean pop reveals bottom-up cultural flows in the age of social media. The authors analyze the complexity and diversification of Korean pop circulation through an empirical study of Indonesian fandom and the "Gangnam Style" phenomenon.

Ko, Nusta Carranza, Song No, Jeong-Nam Kim, and Ronald Gobbi Simões. "Landing of the Wave: *Hallyu* in Peru and Brazil." *Development and Society* 43, no. 2 (2014): 297–350.

The past years have illuminated the arrival of the Korean Wave in Latin America. The authors challenge the notion of cultural proximity that is often used to explain the popularity of Korean popular culture in East Asia and suggest that individuals' cultural subjectivity is deeply involved in the global expansion of the phenomenon.

Kwon, Jung Min. "Queering Stars: Fan Play and Capital Appropriation in the Age of Digital Media." *Journal of Fandom Studies* 3, no. 1 (2015): 95–108. doi: 10.1386/jfs.3.1.95_1.

Kwon draws attention to fan writings on homoerotic relationships between two members of Korean pop groups. The author concludes that the strategic partnership between the Korean pop industry and fans has considerably appropriated media products and cultures.

Lyan, Irina, and Alon Levkowitz. "From Holy Land to '*Hallyu* Land': The Symbolic Journey Following the Korean Wave in Israel." *Journal of Fandom Studies* 3, no. 1 (2015): 7–21. doi: 10.1386/jfs.3.1.7_1.

This Israeli case study examines how Korean popular culture has expanded to the marginalized regions, such as Africa and the Middle East. The authors argue that online fan communities help geographically and culturally separated fans enjoy authentic experiences and domesticate Korean culture.

Madrid-Morales, Dani, and Bruno Lovric. "'Transatlantic connection': K-pop and K-Drama Fandom in Spain and Latin America." *Journal of Fandom Studies* 3, no. 1 (2015): 23–41. doi: 10.1386/jfs.3.1.23_1.

Madrid-Morales and Lovric explain the characteristics of Korean pop and drama fans in Latin America and Spain, identifying their demographic difference from Asian fans of Korean popular culture. They employ the theory of use and gratification to discuss their self-appropriation of Korean cultural content. They point out collaborative connections between Latin American and Spanish fans in the consumption of Korean pop culture.

Oh, Chuyun. "Queering Spectatorship in K-Pop: The Androgynous Male Dancing Body and Western Female Fandom." *Journal of Fandom Studies* 3, no. 1 (2015): 59–78. doi:10.1386/fs.3.1.59_1.

Analyzing K-pop cross-dressing from a genealogical context, Oh compares it with a traditional art form, *talnori*, in which male artists have traditionally performed cross-gender roles. She views K-pop cross-dressing as a hybrid performance that challenges the articulation of masculinity and heteronormativity in Korean society and deconstructs a boundary between queering dominance and resistance.

Oh, David. "K-pop Fans React: Hybridity and the White Celebrity-Fan on YouTube." *International Journal of Communication* 11 (2017): 2270–2287.

Bringing the reaction video of Korean pop to the discussion of the Korean Wave, Oh asserts that white celebrity-fans of Korean pop perform hybridity by producing reaction videos and by displaying their fascination with non-white music and celebrities. The author claims that white racial logic is still influential in their activities.

Shim, Doobo. "Korean Wave and Korean Women Television Viewers in Singapore." *Asian Journal of Women's Studies* 13, no. 2 (2007): 63–82. doi: 10.1080/1225927 6.2007.11666025.

Shim examines how Korean female immigrants in Singapore have consumed homeland media content and how their media consumption has helped to construct ethnic pride in their daily lives. He underlines that Korean television dramas play an important role in the centralization of Korean women in the expansion of the Korean Wave to the Southeast Asian region.

Sung, Sang-Yeon. "Constructing a New Image. *Hallyu* in Taiwan." *European Journal of East Asian Studies* 9, no. 1 (2010): 25–45. doi: 10.1163/156805810X517652.

Sung questions how the Korean Wave has reshaped Korea's image among Taiwanese audiences. Noting that Taiwanese people had a collective memory of Korea's rupture of diplomatic relations with their country, the author claims that the consumption of Korean television dramas and pop music has improved their perception of Korea's image.

———. "The Role of *Hallyu* in the Construction of East Asian Regional Identity in Vienna." *European Journal of East Asian Studies* 11, no. 1 (2012): 155–171. doi: 10.1163/15700615–20120010.

This ethnographic research investigates how Korean popular culture has helped East Asian immigrants in Europe construct their regional identity. This study shows that immigrants have maintained their own identities through the consumption of Korean popular content via digital platforms.

———. "K-Pop Reception and Participatory Fan Culture in Austria." *Cross-currents* 3, no. 3 (2013): 56–71.

Sung explores how Korean pop has been expanded to Austria after the global sensation of Korean pop singer Psy's music video "Gangnam Style." Analyzing the role of local private and public sponsors and fans in receiving Korean pop music, the author challenges the argument that Korean sponsors have initiated the expansion of Korean pop music beyond the Asian region.

Williams, J. Patrick, and Samantha Xiang Xin Ho. "'*Sasaengpaen*' or K-Pop Fan? Singapore Youths, Authentic Identities, and Asian Media Fandom." *Deviant Behavior* 37, no. 1 (2016): 81–94. doi:10.1080/01639625.2014.983011.

Patrick and Ho look into the emergence of the *sasaeng* fan in Singapore, who are interested in the personal lives of Korean pop stars. The authors focus on how they construct their mediated identities as a *sasaeng* fan and how fan identities are influenced by the politics of knowledge production. They conclude that social media has complicated the relationship between local fans and Korean pop idols and have generated more deviant and extreme types of fans.

Yin, Fu Su, and Khiun Liew. "*Hallyu* in Singapore: Korean Cosmopolitanism or the Consumption of Chineseness?" *Korea Journal* 45, no. 4 (2005): 206–232.

Yin and Liew indicate that the rise of Korean popular culture in Singapore is closely associated with Chinese communities. The authors conclude that the Korean Wave confirms the locality of cultural tastes in the region, and Southeast Asian societies have become part of globalizing Koreaness. Singapore fans consume Korean media content, study the Korean language, and travel to Korea.

Yoon, Kyong. "Cultural Translation of K-Pop among Asian Canadian Fans." *International Journal of Communication* 11 (2017): 2350–2366.

Yoon investigates the ways in which young Asian Canadian fans have consumed Korean pop. The author, based on in-depth interviews with Korean pop fans, identify that these relatively marginalized groups in Canada have positively rearticulated the meaning of race through the consumption of Korean pop. He states that they communicate with Korean pop stars via social media and attempt to construct self-driven cultural identities.

———. "Global Imagination of K-Pop Pop Music Fans' Lived Experiences of Cultural Hybridity." *Popular Music and Society* (2017): 1–17. doi: 10.1080/0300 7766.2017.1292819.

Based on qualitative interviews with Canada-based audiences, Yoon identifies the pattern of Korean pop consumption. In Yoon's view, they negotiate and interpret cultural hybridity, and their experience of globalization is limited to their temporary escape from their daily lives.

Yoon, Sunny. "East to East: Cultural Politics and Fandom of Korean Popular Culture in Eastern Europe." *International Journal of Media & Cultural Politics* 12, no. 2 (2016): 213–227. doi: 10.1386/macp.12.2.213_1.

Yoon pays attention to the increasing consumption of Korean popular culture in Eastern Europe. The author employs soft power as a theoretical framework to argue that the reception of Korean media in Eastern Europe is an attempt to diversify their cultural experiences.

Online Games

Jin, Dal Yong. "The Digital Korean Wave: Local Online Gaming Goes Global." *Media International Australia* 14, no. 1 (2011): 128–136. doi: 10.1177/1329878X 1114100115.

Centering on the potential of local online games that generate the contra-flow of digital culture, Jin notes that the local game industry produces globally appealing content through the development of hybrid narratives and characters and the deployment of local marketing in the Western markets.

————. *Korea's Online Gaming Empire*, Cambridge, MA: MIT Press, 2010.

Jin turns to how the Korean online game industry has recently become one of the major players in the global game market. He indicates that online games have significantly occupied the daily lives of young Koreans in the digital era. He further discusses the context in which the game industry has become a major sector of the national economic system in the process of globalization.

————. *Smartland Korea: Mobile Communication, Culture, and Society.* Ann Arbor: University of Michigan Press, 2017.

Jin highlights the advancement of smartphones and their applications, which have created new capital for information and communication technology corporations and have changed the way people communicate. It looks into a largely neglected focus of scholarly inquiry, a localized mobile landscape, with particular reference to young Koreans' engagement with their devices and applications.

Social Media

Chung, Peichi. "Co-Creating Korean Wave in Southeast Asia: Digital Convergence and Asia's Media Regionalization." *Journal of Creative Communication* 8, no. 2–3 (2013): 193–208. doi: 10.1177/0973258613512912.

Chung calls attention to the digitalization and regionalization of Asian media culture in the expansion of Korean popular culture. She identifies the interdependence between East Asian media professionals and Southeast Asian consumers and highlights the role of Southeast Asian media producers and institutions in the reproduction of the Korean Wave in Southeast Asia.

Goldsmith, Ben, Kwang-Suk Lee, and Brian Yecies. "In Search of the Korean Digital Wave." *Media International Australia* 141 (2011): 70–77. doi: 10.1177/1329878X 1114100109.

Korea's digital mediascapes have become an important topic of analysis in the discussion of the Korean digital wave. The authors demonstrate that the advancement of digital technologies is closely associated with the proliferation of the Korean culture and creative industries. The authors provide a critical perspective on the involvement of the government in the development of digital culture in Korea.

Jin, Dal Yong. "Digital Platform as a Double-Edged Sword: How to Interpret Cultural Flows in the Platform Era." *International Journal of Communication* 11 (2017): 3880–3898.

Jin considers digital platforms as a central engine for renegotiating the notion of cultural flows and for resolving the unequal relationship between Western and non-Western countries in cultural exchanges. But the author offers a critical perspective on the deepened power hierarchy between them, pointing out the domination of U.S.-centered digital platforms such as Google, YouTube, and Facebook.

———. "An Analysis of the Korean Wave as Transnational Popular Culture: North American Youth Engage through Social Media as TV Becomes Obsolete." *International Journal of Communication* 12 (2018):404–422.

Jin explores the ways in which the new Korean Wave is integrated into a social media–embedded cultural landscape in North America. It discusses the increasing role of social media and changing media consumption habits among youth. It maps out why social media has contributed to the enhanced popularity of the transnational media culture produced in a non-Western region.

Jin, Dal Yong, and Kyong Yoon. "The Social Mediascape of Transnational Korean Pop Culture: *Hallyu* 2.0 as Spreadable Media Practice." *New Media & Society* 18, no. 7 (2014): 1277–1292. doi: 10.1177/1461444814554895.

Social media have fundamentally changed the level and range of media consumption, and this new media environment allows geographically separated audiences to develop a participatory culture in their social contexts. Jin emphasizes the spreadability of digital technologies in which North American fans have consumed Korean popular culture.

Jung, Sookeung, and Hongmei Li. "Global Production, Circulation, and Consumption of Gangnam Style." *International Journal of Communication* 8 (2014): 2790–2810.

Jung and Lee analyze the global circulation and consumption of Psy's music video, "Gangnam Style." The authors emphasize the global audience's active participation in the expansion of the Korean music video via digital media platforms. They further mention Psy's marketing strategies and the universal attraction of the video as a major reason for creating the global fad.

Lee, Sangjoon, and Abé Mark Nornes, ed. *Hallyu 2.0: The Korean Wave in the Age of Social Media*. Ann Arbor: University of Michigan Press, 2015.

Lee and Nornes analyze the new stage of the Korean Wave in the theoretical, political, and cultural contexts. They attempt to discuss how social media have dramatically advanced the nature and range of the phenomenon. The book also sets agendas, theorizes the phenomenon, criticizes the role of government, and explains the various aspects of the consumption of Korean pop culture.

Xu, Weiai, Ji Young Park, and Han Woo Park. "The Networked Cultural Diffusion of Korean Wave." *Online Information Review* 39, no. 1 (2015): 43–60. doi: 10.1108/OIR-07-2014-0160.

Taking a combined approach to profile analysis, social network analysis, and semantic analysis, the authors conclude that American male users took initiatives in the diffusion of Korean music videos in the early stage and that users in culturally approximate societies tend to have affinities for Korean music videos.

Representation

Lee, Claire Shinhea, and Ji Hoon Park. "'We Need a Committee for Men's Rights': Reactions of Male and Female Viewers to Reverse Gender Discrimination in Korean Comedy." *Asian Journal of Communication* 22, no. 4 (2012): 353–371. doi:10.1080/01292986.2012.681664.

Lee and Park posit Korean reality television as a cultural portrayal of women's empowerment, examining the different reactions of male and female audiences to the show's way of depicting gender differences. They discuss that male viewers have increased their concerns about their social positions through the consumption of reality shows like *Nambowon*, which provide relatively progressive gender discourse.

Jung, Sun. *Korean Masculinities and Transcultural Consumption: Yonsama, Rain, Oldboy, K-Pop Idols*. Hong Kong: Hong Kong University Press, 2011.

Jung underscores the hybridity of Korean popular culture, looking at how international audiences have consumed Korean masculinity. The author points out that the hybridity of Korean masculinity enables local audiences to negotiate, to reconstruct, and to redefine their ambivalent desires in the consumption of Korean male celebrity.

Kim, Kyung Hyun. *The Remasculinization of Korean Cinema*. Durham, NC: Duke University Press, 2004.

Kim looks into how Korean cinemas have employed masculinity as a vehicle for displaying sociopolitical transformations over the past three decades. Understanding that the development of democratic and cosmopolitan culture has weakened male identity in Korean society, he considers the increasing visibility of violence in Korean films as the symptom of the society's ongoing attempt for remasculinization.

McHugh, Kathleen, and Nancy Abelmann, ed. *South Korean Golden Age Melodrama: Gender, Genre, and National Cinema*. Detroit, MI: Wayne State University Press, 2005.

Kathleen and Abelmann explore the national specificity of Korean cinemas and television dramas during the mid-1990s, giving a particular focus on the melodramatic narrative of Korean films and dramas. The editors deepen the discussion of a national film movement, providing a historical context of the nation's remarkable cultural and political movements.

Chapter 10

Cinema Studies

Dong Hoon Kim, Hye Seung Chung, Ji-yoon An, and N. Trace Cabot

"South Korean cinema is finding its place in the sun. At the dawn of the new millennium, the growing enthusiasm for Korean movies around the world is evidenced by intense activity on multiple fronts," wrote the editors of *New Korean Cinema* in 2005. "Film Studies, too, has responded to the interest and importance of contemporary Korean Cinema."[1] While conveying the excitement toward the emergence of Korean films on the global stage at the time, this opening passage from the edited book that probes the new developments in Korean film industry succinctly illuminates how and when Korean cinema began to garner scholarly attention beyond Korea.

Our chapter aims to annotate major English research publications on Korean cinema studies. It includes an introductory essay and an annotated bibliography, which constitutes the main portion of the chapter. The bibliography covers materials on Korean cinema, including books, book series, journal articles, book chapters, and dissertations. The selection of bibliographic entries was determined by multiple factors. We have carefully considered each English publication's contribution to the field, but at the same time tried to be as comprehensive as possible in historical periods and film-theoretical questions addressed (i.e., film authorship, genre studies, industrial studies, studies of regulations and policies, identity politics, and so on). Given the limited number of single-authored books on Korean cinema, our chapter prioritizes them. As for edited books, we have annotated three edited volumes because they simply cannot go unacknowledged owing to their significant contributions to the Korean cinema studies. Almost all the publications are geared toward academic readership with a few exceptions.

---

1. Chi-Yun Shin and Julian Stringer, eds., *New Korean Cinema* (Edinburgh, UK: Edinburgh University Press, 2005), 1.

German writer Johannes Schönherr's *North Korean Cinema: A History*[2] and Korean Film Council's *Korean Film Directors* book series[3] that are intended for a general, non-scholarly readership are noted in the bibliography, for these books would allow readers to explore more diverse aspects of Korean cinema.

THE ORIGIN OF CINEMA STUDIES

Korean film was rarely known to viewers outside the Korean peninsula until about a decade before the English-language publication of *New Korean Cinema*. As a result, even long after the global rise of Cinema Studies as an academic discipline since the 1950s, the study of Korean cinema was largely contained within the two Koreas. It was not until the 1990s that the continued success of films from South Korea at prestigious international film festivals, as well as the country's rapidly developing film and media industries, brought about a germinal academic interest in Korean cinema around the world. The subsequent global dissemination and popularity of Korean popular culture known as the Korean Wave (*Hallyu*) since the late 1990s further facilitated critical explorations of Korean film history, industry, and culture. While its history is short, the contributions that Korean cinema studies has made to such disciplines as cinema studies, media studies, Asian studies, and Korean studies are as conspicuous as the impressive accomplishment of Korean film, media, and cultural productions in the past two decades.

Though its entry into the discipline of cinema studies was considerably late, Korean cinema has quickly emerged as one of the most rigorously studied national film traditions globally since the late 1990s. As is typical with other national cinemas, the study of Korean cinema started with introducing canonical filmmakers who received global recognition through their success at film festivals, tracking their careers, and unpacking their films. *Im Kwon-Taek: The Making of a Korean National Cinema*,[4] the first English-language scholarly book on Korean cinema (2001), for instance, explores the career and opus of the famed Korean filmmaker Im Kwon-Taek. *The Remasculinization of Korean Cinema*[5] by Kyung Hyun Kim, the director of the University of California–Irvine Center for Critical Korean Studies,

---

2. Johannes Schönherr, *North Korean Cinema: A History* (Jefferson, NC: McFarland, 2012).

3. Korean Film Council, *Korean Film Directors*, 22 vols. (Seoul: Seoul Selection, 2007–2009).

4. David James and Kyung Hyun Kim, eds., *Im Kwon-Taek: The Making of a Korean National Cinema* (Detroit, MI: Wayne State University Press, 2001). This edited book includes contributions from the scholars from South Korea, Europe, and North America, and it was translated into Korean in 2005. See David James and Kyung Hyun Kim, eds., *Im Kwon-Taek: Minjok yeonghwa mandeulgi* [The Making of a Korean National Cinema], trans. Kim Hee-Jin (Paju, South Korea: Hanwool, 2005).

5. Kyung Hyun Kim, *The Remasculinization of Korean Cinema* (Durham, NC: Duke University Press, 2004).

a groundbreaking study of Korean cinema since the 1980s, examines how Korean film has used the trope of masculinity to address the nation's socio-political issues by analyzing canonical filmmakers' works.

Such auteur studies soon became coupled with studies on Korean film-industrial practices. In their edited volume *New Korean Cinema*, Chi-Yun Shin and Julian Stringer, the film scholars based in the United Kingdom, note that their book followed *Im Kwon-Taek: The Making of a Korean National Cinema* as the second English-language collection of academic essays to be dedicated to the Korean film industry outside Korea.[6] Taking cues from this important book, film scholars Jinhee Choi[7] and Darcy Paquet[8] offered excellent introductions to contemporary Korean film industry with their respective studies on its key players, newly emerging genres, domestic and international success, and ambivalent relation to Hollywood.

Importantly, reflecting the growing scholarly interest in transnationalism and globalization in the field of Cinema Studies in the late 1990s and early 2000s, a considerable number of studies began to examine Korean cinema with these new critical frameworks. While endeavoring to expound the global circulations and transnational appeals of Korean film, film and media scholars often present contemporary Korean cinema's global success as an iconic event that corroborates media globalization's varied impacts on film cultures. Korean cinema, therefore, has become an important part of theories developed about border-crossing film production and consumption practices, which leads more film historians and theorists to turn their attention to Korean cinema.

KOREAN STUDIES AND KOREAN CINEMA

It should be also noted that studies of Korean film and media in English have considerably expanded (and continue to expand) the boundary of Korean studies and spurred the growth of the field. Indeed, Korea's growing soft power has fundamentally transformed the nature of Korean studies, a regional studies developed in close association with security issues and international relations during the Cold War period. With increasing academic and public interest in the Korean Wave, the disciplinary focus of Korean studies has shifted from social sciences to humanities, including studies of film, media,

---

6. Shin and Stringer, 1–2.

7. Jinhee Choi, *The South Korean Film Renaissance: Local Hitmakers, Global Provocaeurs* (Middletown, CT: Wesleyan University Press, 2010).

8. Darcy Paquet, *New Korean Cinema: Breaking the Waves* (London: Wallflower Press, 2009).

culture, and literature. With this major transformation, the field has seen an unprecedented growth in recent years.

According to the statistics compiled by the Modern Language Association (MLA) in 2015, for instance, enrollments for the Korean language at every institutional level in the United States increased by 44.7 percent between 2009 and 2013, which made Korean one of only four languages—the other three being American sign language (19%), Portuguese (10%), and Chinese (2%)—that saw the increase in enrollment, while the total foreign language enrollment fell by 6.7 percent.[9] In response to the mounting interest in the Korean language and demand for Korean content courses, more and more colleges and universities across the globe have introduced new Korean programs and courses on Korea. Consequently, Korean cinema has become a staple in Asian and Korean studies curriculums.

DISCIPLINARY TENDENCIES

Despite its substantial contributions to multiple academic fields and continuing growth, certain tendencies in Korean cinema studies in English expose its relatively short history. Readers will easily notice from our chapter bibliography that a majority of the English-language publications on Korean cinema focus on South Korean films produced since the 1980s. There are few book-length studies that explore film cultures before the 1980s.

Another lacuna that deserves a mention here is North Korean cinema. There are several books authored by non-film experts and a handful of article-length studies.[10] Yet there is no single book dedicated entirely to film traditions of North Korea. Film historian Hyangjin Lee's *Contemporary Korean Cinema: Culture, Identity and Politics*,[11] theater and performance studies scholar Suk-Young Kim's *Illusive Utopia: Theater, Film, and*

---

9. A full report of 2015 on "Enrollments in Languages Other Than English in United States Institutions of Higher Education" is available at www.mla.org/Resources/Research/Surveys-Reports-and-Other-Documents/Teaching-Enrollments-and-Programs/Enrollments-in-Languages-Other-Than-English-in-United-States-Institutions-of-Higher-Education.

10. See Charles Armstrong, "The Origins of North Korean Cinema: Art and Propaganda in the Democratic People's Republic," *Acta Koreana* 5, no. 1 (2002), 1–19; Dong Hoon Kim, "The Politics and Poetics of North Korean *Juche* Cinema," *Asian Cinema* 25, no. 2 (2014), 205–22; Immanuel Kim, "*Snow Melts in Spring*: Another Look at the North Korean Film Industry," *Journal of Japanese and Korean Cinema* 7, no. 1 (2015), 41–56; Kyung Hyun Kim, "The Fractured Cinema of North Korea: The Discourse of the Nation in *Sea of Blood*," in *In Pursuit of Contemporary East Asian Culture*, edited by Xiaobing Tang and Stephen Snyder, 85–106 (Boulder, CO: Westview Press, 1996); Dima Mironenko, "North Koreans at the Movies: Cinema of Fits and Starts and the Rise of Chameleon Spectatorship," *Journal of Japanese and Korean Cinema* 8, no.1 (2016), 25–44.

11. Hyangjin Lee, *Contemporary Korean Cinema: Culture, Identity and Politics* (Manchester, UK: Manchester University Press, 2001).

Everyday Performance in North Korea[12] and Korean film scholar at Princeton University Steven Chung's *Split Screen Korea: Shin Sang-Ok and Postwar Cinema*[13] offer a rare glimpse into some aspects of North Korean film, but a more in-depth account of North Korean cinema has yet to arrive.

NEW DEVELOPMENTS

Recently published books have shown a clear sign of a long-awaited expansion of South Korean cinema studies into different chapters of Korean film history. Film historians Brian Yecies, Ae-Gyung Shim,[14] and Dong Hoon Kim[15] have significantly expanded the topography of Korean cinema studies with their research on the understudied film culture of colonial Korea. University of California-Berkeley Professor Jinsoo An's forthcoming *Parameters of Disavowal* excavates and analyzes seldom-examined Korean classic films from the 1960s and 1970s in its attempt to probe the lasting effects of colonialism on Korean cultural productions and sentiments.[16]

Noted film scholars Hye Seung Chung and David Scott Diffrient's *Movie Migrations: Transnational Genre Flows and South Korean Cinema*[17] is another noteworthy example that shows new developments in the field. This insightful study of Korean film genres not only demonstrates Korean cinema studies' continuing contributions to transnational film theories, but also greatly broadens our understanding of cinematic transnationalism by historicizing the influence of transnational film practices on Korean film genres.

It is also worth mentioning that a transnational group of film scholars such as Han Sang Kim, Soon-jin Lee, and Gyeong-hye Wi in South Korea, Christina Klein in the United States, and Sangjoon Lee in Singapore has begun to explore film cultures developed in Korea from the late 1940s to the 1950s. There are also a few junior scholars working on their dissertations in English about war-time and post-war film cultures. In this regard, a compound development of film culture marked by historical "disruptions" in the Korean peninsula from the end of colonization through the immediate

---

12. Suk-Young Kim, *Illusive Utopia: Theater, Film, and Everyday Performance in North Korea* (Ann Arbor: University of Michigan Press, 2011).

13. Steven Chung, *Split Screen Korea: Shin Sang-ok and Postwar Cinema* (Minneapolis: University of Minnesota Press, 2014).

14. Brian Yecies and Ae-Gyung Shim, *Korea's Occupied Cinemas 1893–1948* (New York: Routledge, 2011).

15. Dong Hoon Kim, *The Eclipsed Cinema: the Film Culture of Colonial Korea* (Edinburgh, UK: Edinburgh University Press, 2017).

16. Jinsoo An, *Parameters of Disavowal: Colonial Representation in South Korean Cinema* (Berkeley: University of California Press, 2018).

17. Hye Seung Chung and Scott Diffrient, *Move Migrations: Transnational Genre Flows and South Korean Cinema* (New Brunswick, NJ: Rutgers University Press, 2015).

post-war period will likely emerge as a major subject of critical inquiries. These new studies in English will continue to grow and diversify the field of Korean cinema studies.

ANNOTATED BIBLIOGRAPHY

Pre-Colonial and Colonial Korean Cinema

Chung, Chonghwa. "Negotiating Colonial Korean Cinema in the Japanese Empire: From the Silent Era to the Talkies, 1923–1939." *Cross-Currents: East Asian History and Culture Review* 2, no. 1 (2013): 139–169. doi:10.1353/ach.2013.0006.

Explores the interlocking histories of imperial Japanese cinema and colonial Korean cinema with a focus on various forms of collaborations between Korean and Japanese filmmakers, ranging from co-productions to Korean filmmakers' training in Japanese studios and individual partnership. By shedding light on rarely explored aspects of colonial film history, the author critically examines the prevailing nationalist film historiography.

Kim, Dong Hoon. "Segregated Cinemas, Intertwined Histories: The Ethnically Segregated Film Cultures in 1920s Korea under Japanese Colonial Rule." *Journal of Japanese and Korean Cinema* 1, no. 1 (2009): 7–25. doi:10.1386/jjkc.1.1.7_1.

Examines ethnically segregated film cultures in Korea under Japanese colonial rule, focusing on film exhibition and film-viewing practices in segregated urban areas in Seoul of the 1920s. Through the examination of separated but at times intertwined film cultures of Japanese migrants and local Koreans, this study ultimately attempts to examine issues in film historiography and explore a shared film history between the two national cinemas.

———. *The Eclipsed Cinema: The Film Culture of Colonial Korea.* Edinburgh, UK: Edinburgh University Press, 2017.

Investigates the film culture of colonial Korea (1910–1945). Through extensive archival research, Kim's book explores the under-investigated aspects of Korea's colonial film culture, such as the representational politics of colonial cinema, the film unit of the colonial government, the social reception of Hollywood cinema, and Japanese settlers' film culture. *Eclipsed Cinema* substantially expands the critical and historical scopes of early cinema and Korean and Japanese film histories.

Kim, Jina E. "Intermedial Aesthetics: Still Images, Moving Words, and Written Sounds in Early Twentieth-Century Korean Cinematic Novels (Yeonghwa Soseol)." *Review of Korean Studies* 16, no. 2 (2013): 45–79. doi: 10.25024/review.2013.16.2.003.

Focusing on *yeonghwa soseol* (cinematic novels) of colonial Korea, the article examine the ways in which the newly forged relationship between literature and new media (such as cinema) affected the practices of creating literature itself. In tracing the emergence of this hybrid genre and offering analysis of cinematic novels, the author shows how the emergence of new print media, film, photography, and radio influenced traditional literary forms.

Workman, Travis. "Stepping into the Newsreel: Melodrama and Mobilization in Colonial Korean Film." *Cross-Currents: East Asian History and Culture Review* 3, no. 1 (2014): 153–184.

Examines the ways in which films from the late colonial period blurred the boundaries between colonial Korean newsreel documentary and fiction films in an attempt to draw the viewer into spectacles of war mobilization. Drawing on theories of melodrama, the article compares the earlier fiction film *Sweet Dream* (1936) with the wartime film *Straits of Joseon* (1943) in order to trace how the genre conventions of melodrama were transformed through its incorporation of the aesthetics and politics of political propaganda.

Rhee, Jooyeon. "*Arirang*, and the Making of a National Narrative in South and North Korea," *Journal of Japanese and Korean Cinema*, 1, no. 1 (2009): 27–43. doi: 10.1386/jjkc.1.1.27_1.

Examines the nationalist elevation of *Arirang* (1926), a landmark film from the colonial period. By detailing the varied efforts of postcolonial film scholars, the article interrogates in what ways the nationalist historiography has affected the writing of colonial film history and the conceptual formation of *minjok yeonghwa* (Korean national cinema) in both North and South Korea.

Yecies, Brian and Ae-Gyung Shim. *Korea's Occupied Cinemas 1893–1948*. London: Routledge, 2011.

Charts the development of film industry in Korea chronologically from the pre-colonial period and the colonial occupation (1910–1945) to U.S. Army Military period (1945–1948). Moving beyond the text-oriented approach of previous studies, the authors engage in extensive archival research in their attempts to follow the development of exhibition, film policy, and filmmaking from 1893 to 1948 and draw links between the arrival of cinema and the cultural, political and social environment.

Zur, Dafna. "Landscape of the Heart in *Homeless Angels* and *Hometown of the Heart*," *Journal of Japanese and Korean Cinema* 7, no. 1 (2015): 10–27. doi: 10.1 080/17564905.2015.1035001.

Examines the colonial film *Homeless Angels* (1941) and the post-liberation *Hometown of the Heart* (1949) in terms of their shared *Bildung* narrative. Zur's analysis emphasizes their staging of childhood and pro-social self-awakening as variations of a push toward modernization following Imperial Japanese and American models for Korea.

North Korean Cinema

Armstrong, Charles. "The Origins of North Korean Cinema: Art and Propaganda in the Democratic People's Republic." *Acta Koreana* 5, no. 1 (2002): 1–19.

Tracks the early formation of film industry in North Korea, focusing on the political and cultural functions cinema played in North Korea's endeavors to create a national identity. The article highlights Soviet cinema's influence on early North Korean cinema and thus explores technical, aesthetical, and ideological contributions Soviet cinema made to North Korean film production in its formative years.

Kim, Dong Hoon. "The Politics and Poetics of North Korean *Juche* Cinema." *Asian Cinema* 25, no.2 (2014): 205–222. doi: https://doi.org/10.1386/ac.25.2.205_1.

Sheds light on the seldom-studied aesthetics of North Korean *Juche* (self-reliance) cinema. Instead of putting too much emphasis on cinema's political functions, the article places the cinematization process of North Korean *Juche* ideology in conversation with political questions through the analysis of film theories developed in North Korea and filmic conventions of North Korean *Juche* films.

Kim, Immanuel. "*Snow Melts in Spring*: Another Look at the North Korean Film Industry." *Journal of Japanese and Korean Cinema* 7, no. 1 (2015): 41–56. doi: 1 0.1080/17564905.2015.1035005.

Examines the transformation of North Korean film industry in the 1980s with a focus on political, social, and historical factors that contributed to the rapid of growth of North Korean cinema in this decade. The author employs *Snow Melts in Spring*, a co-production between North Korean filmmakers and *zainichi* Korean filmmakers, as a case study in exploring North Korean filmmakers' efforts to demonstrate their creative visions while limiting political expressions.

Kim, Kyung Hyun. "The Fractured Cinema of North Korea: The Discourse of the Nation in *Sea of Blood*." In *In Pursuit of Contemporary East Asian Culture*, edited by Xiaobing Tang and Stephen Snyder, 85–106. Boulder, CO: Westview Press, 1996.

Interrogates in what ways North Korean cinema intervenes in the discourse of the nation and formation of North Korea's national identity. In unpacking the representation of North Korea as a unified nation in cinema, the author pays a particular attention to how North Korean film tackles the contradictions generated by the nation's division. Kim's analysis focuses on *Sea of Blood* (1969), a classical film whose purpose is, according to the author, to retrieve and project an imaginary of the unified nation-state.

Mironenko, Dima. "North Koreans at the Movies: Cinema of Fits and Starts and the Rise of Chameleon Spectatorship." *Journal of Japanese and Korean Cinema* 8, no.1 (May 2016): 25–44. doi:10.1080/17564905.2016.1171563.

Introduces models of film spectatorship developed in North Korea in the wake of the Korean War (1950–1953) by historicizing North Korean audiences and their experiences at the cinemas during the 1950s and early 1960s. With its analysis of film spectatorship in North Korea, this intriguing research challenges an assumption that North Koreans are passive recipients of official propaganda produced by the state and ultimately exposes the limits of effectiveness we often attribute to propaganda.

Schönherr, Johannes. *North Korean Cinema: A History*. Jefferson, NC: McFarland, 2012.

Analyzes North Korean film history from its beginnings to today, introducing film industry, key players, canonical works, film festivals, and film distribution and exhibition practices. Intended for a non-academic readership, the book serves as an important primer to North Korean cinema with its dozens of images, stills, and interviews.

South Korean Cinema

Film History

Choe, Steve. *Sovereign Violence: Ethics and South Korean Cinema in the New Millennium.* Amsterdam: Amsterdam University Press, 2016.

Examines "images of violent brutality and narratives of bleak nihilism" in Korean films of the new millennium. The book focuses on key films that induce a spectatorial discomfort in viewers through either harrowing images or psychologically disturbing narratives. Choe sees this chosen body of works as allegorically critiquing the formation of power in the post-IMF era. The violence in these films is interpreted as posing an urgent ethical dilemma that is reflective of life in an age of neoliberal globalization.

Chung, Hye Seung. "From National to Transnational: A Historiography of Korean Cinema." In *Communication, Digital Media, and Popular Culture in Korea*, edited by Dal Yong Jin and Nojin Kwak, 443–468. Lanham, MD: Lexington Books, 2018.

Offers an overview of Korean film history. Chung's historical examination is broken down into five distinct stages: the colonial period, the Golden Age, the Dark Age, the New Wave, and the contemporary era of global media and transnational flows. The author notes an exclusion of a discussion of North Korean cinema in the chapter, a decision resulting from the author's limited access to the films made in North Korea.

Kim, Kyung Hyun. *The Remasculinization of Korean Cinema*. Durham, NC: Duke University Press, 2004.

Analyzes South Korean film since the 1980s in relation to representations of masculinity, with particular emphasis on the traumatic, auteur studies of directors associated with New Korean Cinema, and anxieties born from both the end of authoritarian rule and the crises of the late 1990s.

———. *Virtual* Hallyu: *Korean Cinema of the Global Era*. Durham, NC: Duke University Press, 2011.

Taking up Gilles Deleuze's concept of the virtual, Kim analyzes South Korean film, primarily *Hallyu* cinema but also colonial film, in relation to topics including nationalist and capitalist ideology, the anxieties and ambivalent desires surrounding temporality and modernity, and space. Colonial film and contemporary representations of the period, relations with the North, and several works by many of the most prominent *Hallyu* auteurs are additionally explored in detail.

Klein, Christina. "Cold War Cosmopolitanism: The Asia Foundation and 1950s Korean Cinema." *Journal of Korean Studies* 22, no. 2 (2017): 281–316. doi: 10.1353/jks.2017.0014.

Focuses on two of the earliest South Korean films to be introduced to the world stage in the 1950s. In order to depict the complex workings at play behind this phenomenon, the paper traces the history of the Asia Foundation, which was not only instrumental to the global debut of Korean films, but also to the American cultural Cold War in Asia. Klein labels the post-colonial post-war discourse exemplified in the two films' "Cold War cosmopolitanism."

Lee, Hyanjin. *Contemporary Korean Cinema: Identity, Culture and Politics*. Manchester, UK: Manchester University Press, 2000.

As one of the first books on Korean cinema in the English language, the book offers a general review of both North and South Korean cinema's developments, as well as thematic analyses of specific films. Namely, these are gender, nationhood, and class conflicts and identities. Each chapter explores the theme in a selection of North Korean films, before offering a comparison in South Korean works. In particular, a chapter is dedicated to the various cinematic adaptions of *Chunhyangjeon* across the histories of both North and South Korean cinemas.

Lee, Sangjoon, "On John Miller's 'The Korean Film Industry': The Asia Foundation, KMPCA, and Korean Cinema, 1956." *Journal of Japanese and Korean Cinema* 7, no. 2 (2015): 95–112. doi: 10.1080/17564905.2015.1087143.

Introduction to and reproduction of former Hollywood producer and the Asian Foundation's special motion picture officer in Tokyo, John Miller's 1956 report on the South Korean film industry. The report was the first comprehensive overview (in any language) of the Korean film industry, compiled at the behest of the Asia Foundation. Miller's overview is accompanied by recommendations for further developing the industry.

Min, Eungjun, Jinsook Joo, and Han-ju Kwak. *Korean Film: History, Resistance, and Democratic Imagination.* Westport, CT: Praeger Publishers, 2003.

Analyzes Korean cinema in relation to questions of national cinema, the major historical and political events informing Korean film and its development from its introduction to the peninsula into the 1990s, questions of modernity and postmodernity in post-dictatorship South Korean film, and the convergences and distinctions between North and South Korean cinema and their respective engagements with history and nation.

Moon, Jae-cheol. "The Meaning of Newness in Korean Cinema: Korean New Wave and After." *Korea Journal* (2006): 36–59.

Consideration of "post-Korean Wave" cinema in relation to the notions of newness, accompanied by an expanding interest in irony, mass culture, and genre material. Competing notions of innovation, the emergence of new filmmakers, and a renewed interest in a universal cinematic language drive these developments.

Park, Seung Hyun. "Korean Cinema after Liberation: Production, Industry, and Regulatory Trends." In *Seoul Searching: Culture and Identity in Contemporary Korean Cinema*, edited by Frances K. Gateward, 16–35. Albany, NY: SUNY Press, 2007.

Chronological history of the Korean film industry and regulatory interventions in 1973–1997, particularly focused on the interplay between protectionism and censorship during the authoritarian period and the formation of the New Wave through the relaxation of state restrictions on content, the emergence of independent producers, and the entrance of new directors.

———. "Film Censorship and Political Legitimation in South Korea, 1987–1992." *Cinema Journal* 42, no. 1 (2002): 120–138. doi:10.1353/cj.2002.0024.

Documents the greater leniency in South Korean censorship laws following the June 1987 antigovernment protests, the use of censorship in this period, and the legitimacy-producing narrative that freedom of expression was offered by the authorities. Park also provides a background context for this development with an examination of censorship in 1973–1986, the introduction of the Public Performance Ethics Committee in 1975, and "invisible" economic censorship by producers avoiding state scrutiny.

———. "Structural Transformation of the Korean Film Industry, 1988–1993." *Asian Cinema* 11, no. 1 (2000): 51–68. doi:10.1386/ac.11.1.51_1.

Explores the changes in the South Korean film industry caused by the direct distribution of Hollywood cinema to Korean theaters and the removal of the domestic film production quota. The article is divided into sections accounting for production, distribution, and exhibition. The author notes that this deregulation led to investment in larger-budget domestic productions capable of attracting audiences independently of the quota system.

Shin, Chi-Yun, and Julian Stringer, eds. *New Korean Cinema*. Edinburgh, UK: Edinburgh University Press, 2005.

This edited book followed David E. James and Kyung Hyun Kim's *Im Kwon-Taek* as the second edited collection dedicated to the South Korean film industry. Taking into account the new revival of the Korean film industry at the turn of the new millennium, this book looks at film from the early 1990s to the mid-2000s—a period labelled by the editors as "the post-*Sopyeonje* era"—to seek reasons for this commercial breakthrough and to assess its defining characteristics.

Shin, Jeeyoung. "Globalisation and New Korean Cinema." In *New Korean Cinema*, edited by Chi-Yun Shin and Julian Stringer, 51–62. Edinburgh, UK: Edinburgh University Press, 2005.

Outlines South Korea's globalization policy as it promoted domestic growth and international popularization of the film industry. The Busan International Film Festival and efforts at promoting Korean cinema, including the 1995 Film Promotion Law, the involvement of *Chaebol* in modernizing the film industry prior to the 1997 IMF crisis, and media regionalization are all examined accordingly.

Yecies, Brian, and Ae-Gyung Shim. *The Changing Face of Korean Cinema: 1960–2015*. London: Routledge, 2016.

Traces South Korean state policies and censorship from the 1960s to 2015, examining government cultural policy and industrial practices. Topics include the establishment of international co-productions and other transnational engagements, attempts to both circumvent and adhere to state guidelines, efforts in the Golden Age to establish creative credibility and cleave to governmental policy, women in the industry, and erotic film of the 1970s and 1980s.

Film Industry

Ahn, Soo Jeong. *The Pusan International Film Festival, South Korean Cinema, and Globalization*. Hong Kong: Hong Kong University Press, 2012.

Examines the history and development of the Busan (Pusan) International Film Festival (BIFF) between 1996 and 2005. The book elucidates the strategies taken by the BIFF to position itself as a key platform for Asian cinema, while revealing the institutional dynamics of the film festival, by focusing on key programs of the past, such as retrospectives and the Pusan Promotion Plan.

Choe, Youngmin. *Tourist Distractions: Travelling and Feeling in Transnational Hallyu Cinema.* Durham, NC: Duke University Press, 2016.

Identifies travel, both as in filmic representations and "screen tourism," as a central critical characteristic of *hallyu* cinema. Choe's book is organized through the association of three affective categories with spatial and temporal relations. Intimacy, associated with Japan and Korea, and amity, identified between China and Korea, are explored through joint productions. Remembrance, relating North and South Korea, is examined through representations of the DMZ (demilitarized zone).

Choi, Jinhee. *The South Korean Film Renaissance: Local Hitmakers, Global Provocateurs.* Middletown, CT: Wesleyan University Press, 2010.

Examines the developments of the South Korean film industry and the corresponding formal changes between 1986 and 2006—what Choi coins as the second South Korean film renaissance. Choi first gives an overview of the industry and the transformations it undertook in order to adapt to regional and global demands. In the following five chapters, Choi then examines the major production trends and cycles of the renaissance—namely, blockbusters, gangster cinema, romance films, teen pics, and lastly, "high-quality" films.

Jin, Dal Yong. "Cultural Politics in Korea's Contemporary Films under Neoliberal Globalization." *Media, Culture & Society* 28, no. 1 (2006): 5–23. doi:10.1177/0163443706059274.

Offers a political economic analysis of the growth in domestic film production and audiences in relation to the neoliberal globalization thesis and state cultural policy. The author further examines the transnationalization of the film industry, and the role of these developments in preserving or constructing notions of Korean identity and nationalism.

Kim, Darae, Dina Iordanova, and Chris Berry. "The Busan International Film Festival in Crisis Or, What Should a Film Festival Be?" *Film Quarterly* 69, no. 1 (2015): 80–89. doi:10.1525/fq.2015.69.1.80.

Though the turbulence faced by the Busan International Film Festival (BIFF) and the Korean film industry in 2014–2015 was often discussed in the Korean media, little scholarship has fully addressed this topic. The journal article by three scholars gives attention to this crisis, offering a solid summary in English of both the BIFF's challenge of 2014–2015 and the Korean film industry's current climate and raising larger questions about the role of a film festival at a time of neoliberalism.

Kim, Eun-Mee. "Market Competition and Cultural Tensions between Hollywood and the Korean Film Industry." *International Journal on Media Management* 6, no. 3–4 (2004): 207–216. doi:10.1080/14241277.2004.9669403.

Examines the performance of domestic and Hollywood productions in the South Korean theatrical and home video markets, providing an empirical analysis of film performance demonstrating increased emphasis on larger-budget domestic productions, domestic audience preference for Korean productions, and the interrelation of markets and cultural production.

Lee, Nikki J. Y. "Localized Globalization and a Monster National: 'The Host' and the South Korean Film Industry." *Cinema Journal* 50, no. 3 (2011): 45–61. doi: 10.1353/cj.2011.0031.

Focuses on the industrial practices and the national and transnational ambivalences in Korean film production and their global popularity, in addition to the monopolization of domestic theatrical distribution by major entertainment companies. An engagement with historic traumas in blockbusters identifies them with a national register thrilling to domestic audiences, while Hollywood conventions and style lend global appeal.

Park, Young-a. *Unexpected Alliances: Independent Filmmakers, the State, and the Film Industry in Postauthoritarian South Korea.* Stanford, CA: Stanford University Press, 2015.

Asserts the importance of independent filmmakers, and the organizations they fostered, in the explosion of Korean film's popularity. Park employs ethnography, her personal connection to the discussed personalities, and Bourdieuan theory in her analysis of how film-activists were redeployed as "independent filmmakers" to elite Busan International Film Festival-goers, while noting that their activist legacy remains.

Paquet, Darcy. *New Korean Cinema: Breaking the Waves.* London: Wallflower Press, 2009.

Examines South Korean cinema's diversifying film output of the 1990s and 2000s. Though the endpoint of this phenomenon remains yet to be clarified in the continuing scholarship on Korean cinema, Paquet—the founder of the website koreanfilm.org who has become a leading expert on Korean films and the film industry—demarcates the movement to be between the 1980s and the mid-2000s. This book is dedicated to the creative and commercial rebirth of Korean cinema in this period.

———. "An Insider's View of a Film Industry in Tradition: Darcy Paquet's Meditations on the Contemporary Korean Cinema." *Acta Koreana* 14, no. 1 (2011): 17–32.

In this article, Paquet introduces what he believes to be the particular character and identity of Korean cinema in the "post-boom" years of 2007 to the present. From his insider position as a film columnist and journalist, Paquet recognises the evolving film landscape and the new challenges that are faced by the Korean film industry as it recovers from its industrial crisis in 2007.

Ryoo, Woongjae. "The Political Economy of the Global Mediascape: The Case of the South Korean Film Industry." *Media, Culture & Society* 30, no. 6 (2008): 873–889. doi:10.1177/0163443708096098.

Assuming the position that globalization will not necessarily lead to the disappearance of the state, Ryoo uses the South Korean film industry as a case study in the state's active cultural policy to promote the development of high value-added media as an industry congruent with globalization.

Shin, Chi-Yun. "Art of Branding: Tartan 'Asia Extreme' Films." *Jump Cut, Past and Present* no. 50 (Spring 2008).

Charts the rise of Tartan Films' "Asia Extreme" distribution label, which introduced many of the internationally best-known South Korean films to Western audiences. The author provides both commercial contexts and analysis of the "genre-fication" of East Asian cinema through its marketing in terms of "extreme" affects, with the consequence of collapsing national and genre categories in its branding effort.

Wilson, Rob. "Korean Cinema on the Road to Globalization: Tracking Global/Local Dynamics, or Why Im Kwon-Taek Is Not Ang Lee." *Inter-Asia Cultural Studies* 2, no. 2 (2001): 307–318. doi:10.1080/14649370120068603.

Tracks the tensions between the local and globalization, primarily through its extended consideration of Jang Sun Woo's *Cinema on the Road*, emphasizing the "inward turn" toward a Korean national-imaginary, represented by Im Kwon-Taek, which stands in contrast to a Chinese and Taiwanese "outward turn" represented primarily through Ang Lee.

Authorship

Berry, Chris. "The Documentary Production Process as a Counter-Public: Notes on an Inter-Asian Mode and the Example of Kim Dong-Won." *Inter-Asia Cultural Studies* 4, no. 1 (2003): 139–144. doi: 10.1080/1464937032000060276.

Drawing on what the author calls the "socially engaged" mode of independent documentary filmmaking in East Asia, this article analyzes the works of Kim Dong-Won, one of South Korea's leading independent documentary activists. The author's comparative framework compares Kim's documentaries with the works of other East Asian documentary filmmakers such as Ogawa Shinsuke, a renowned Japanese documentary filmmaker, to probe in what ways documentary productions are employed by East Asian filmmakers to address social issues.

Chung, Hye Seung. *Kim Ki-duk.* Champaign: University of Illinois Press, 2012.

Investigates the controversial motion pictures written and directed by Korean independent filmmaker Kim Ki-duk. Challenging misunderstandings of Kim's cinema among both Korean and Western critics, Chung questions the validity of reducing the iconoclastic director's socially conscious work to the categorical ghetto of "extreme cinema." Instead, the author reads his films as a necessarily brutal cinema of *ressentiment* (resentment) that accurately depicts the cruelty of a classist society and revolves around the psychological and physical pain endured by outlaw heroes.

Chung, Steven. *Split Screen Korea: Shin Sang-ok and Postwar Cinema.* Minneapolis: University of Minnesota Press, 2014.

Follows the career trajectory of the filmmaker Shin Sang-ok, a central figure who has stood as a representative filmmaker for the military dictatorships of both South and North Korea. Though Shin has been overdetermined by rumors surrounding his period in North Korea, the author returns to the core ideas behind Shin's identity, such as authorship, national cinema, and Cold War ideological polarity. Shin becomes a means through which the author examines the multi-layered cultural and visual politics of both divided Korea and the global Cold War.

Demir, Anaïd. "Kim Ki-duk, Serial Painter." In *Kim Ki Duk*, edited by Adrien Gombeaud, 37–54. Paris: Dis Voir, 2006.

Analyzes the influence of other mediums, particularly painting and photography, on Korean filmmaker Kim Ki-duk's films. Demir's auteur analysis notes the importance of Kim's fine arts training in Paris in his aesthetic sensibilities. The author utilizes the extended "serial painter" metaphor to analyze the content of Kim's work as well, emphasizing the intertextual dimensions of his filmography.

James, David, and Kyung Hyun Kim, eds. *Im Kwon-Taek: The Making of a Korean National Cinema.* Detroit, MI: Wayne State University Press, 2001.

The first English-language academic book on South Korean cinema published outside of Korea presents Im Kwon-Taek biographically and as a filmmaker, the history and development of a Korean national cinema, and analyses of a number of Im's films from a variety of theoretical perspectives. Nationalism, Buddhism, tradition, and gender are considered at length in relation to Im's films.

Kim, Han Sang. "Cold War and the Contested Identity Formation of Korean Filmmakers: On Boxes of Death and Kim Ki-yŏng's USIS Films." *Inter-Asia Cultural Studies* 14, no. 4 (2013): 551–563. doi: 10.1080/14649373.2013.831194.

Examines the seldom-explored film culture of the 1950s. By unpacking Kim Ki-Young's films produced in the 1950s, the article explores in what ways the Korean War, cold war politics, Korea-U.S. relations, and newly introduced ideals of democracy influenced the formation of national, social and cultural identities in post-colonial, post-war South Korean society.

Korean Film Council. *Korean Film Directors*. 22 vols. Seoul: Seoul Selection, 2007–2009.

This book series is a collection of auteur studies on individual directors, some-times collected as groups based on their status in the industry as newcomers in three "Rookie Directors" books, from various authors. All provide biographical details and complete filmographies, with variations in content from book-to-book including interviews, film analysis, and reprinted articles. The series also includes substantial amounts of translated content originally published in Korean.

Lee, Nikki J. Y. "Salute to Mr. Vengeance!: The Making of a Transnational Auteur Park Chan-wook." In *East Asian Cinemas: Exploring Transnational Connections on Film*, edited by Leon Hunt and Leung Wing-Fai, 203–219. London: I.B. Tauris, 2008.

Analyzes the rise of the renowned Korean filmmaker Park Chan-wook as an inter-national auteur director to determine the significance of "commerce of the auterist" in relation to transnationality. The author argues that if its original configuration is tied to the industrial and marketing concerns of Hollywood, transnational auterism ties into international circulation.

Shin, Chi-Yun. "Locating Cosmopolitanism in the Films of E J-Yong." In *Korean Screen Culture: Interrogating Cinema, TV, Music and Online Games*, edited by Andrew David Jackson and Colette Balmain, 35–54. Bern, Switzerland: Peter Lang, 2016.

E J-Yong (aka Lee Je-yong) is a well-known auteur filmmaker in the Korean film industry, known for his diverse array of works that freely cross over boundaries of genres and controlled visuals. Shin's book chapter examines E's eclectic filmog-raphy of feature films to argue that what binds this body of works together is the common cosmopolitan aspiration toward multiplicity, acceptance of difference, and transcendence from localized loyalties.

Film Genre

An, Jinsoo. "Popular Reasoning of South Korean Melodrama Films (1953–1972)." PhD diss., University of California at Los Angeles, 2005. ProQuest (305000964).

Analyzes the relationship between the melodramatic mode of representation and nationhood in Korean popular film from 1953 to 1972. An defines melodrama as "popular reasoning" of postwar Korea at the time of political repression, social dislocation, and national reconstruction. Her dissertation explores ways in which the dominant mode of melodrama manifests itself across different genres (such as

Manchurian action, historical drama, and courtroom drama) in Golden Age Korean cinema.

Cho, Michelle. "Genre, Translation, and Transnational Cinema: Kim Jee-woon's *The Good, the Bad, the Weird*." *Cinema Journal* 54, no. 3 (2015): 44–68. doi:10.1353/cj.2015.0022.

Analyzes *The Good, the Bad, and the Weird*, a Korean western movie, in relation to genre translation in transnational cinema. The article focuses particularly on its relation to revisionist and Manchurian westerns, distinctions between genre translation in film versus conceptions of literary translation, and the bypassing genre normativity through the identification of the transnational and translational dimensions of genre cinemas.

Chung, Hye Seung. "From *Acacia* to *The Uninvited*: The Adoption Anxiety in Korean Horror Cinema." In *Korean Horror Cinema*, edited by Daniel Martin and Alison Peirse, 87–100 Edinburgh, UK: Edinburgh University Press, 2013.

Explores the theme of adoption in *Acacia* (2003) and other horror films. The essay contextualizes the social stigma of adoption in South Korea which has long been known as a "baby exporter" in the West. Then it offers an in-depth textual analysis of *Acacia* in which a six-year-old adopted son for an upper-middle class family functions both as a victim and a threat. Unlike its Hollywood counterparts, *Acacia* eschews the clear-cut dichotomy between good and evil and reveals the collective social guilt about abandoned children.

———, and David Scott Diffrient. *Movie Migrations: Transnational Genre Flows and South Korean Cinema*. New Brunswick, NJ: Rutgers University Press, 2015.

Examines global genre transformations and the concept of cross-cultural inter-textuality through analyses of South Korean melodramas, literary adaptations, comedies, Westerns, historical dramas, monster movies, psychological thrillers, and multicultural films. It reconceives cross-cultural adaptations and remakes as examples of transnational *détournement* (a technique of cultural recycling and political resistance adopted by French Situationists), providing historical context-ualization that helps explain how such appropriations constitute a form of creative transformation reflecting South Korea's postcolonial state.

Diffrient, David Scott. "'Military Enlightenment' for the Masses: Genre and Cultural Intermixing in South Korea's Golden Age War Films." *Cinema Journal* 45, no. 1 (2005): 22–49. doi: 10.1353/cj.2006.0005.

Examines two war films from the 1960s by Lee Man-hee, one of Korea's most renowned directors of the Golden Age. Textual Analyses of each film offer detailed examination of the generic hybridity and its significance. Particularly insightful are the cross-cultural references and comparisons to Hollywood's musicals of the time and the analysis of Western diegetic music. Equally useful are the introductions to both the filmmaker and the industrial background of the time.

————. "The Face(s) of Korean Horror Film: Toward a Cinematic Physiognomy of Affective Extremes." In *Korean Horror Cinema*, edited by Alison Peirse and Daniel Martin, 114–130. Edinburgh, UK: Edinburgh University Press, 2013.

Examines the role of physiognomy in Korean horror films. Using Gilles Deleuze's concept of *visagéité*, Diffrient explores the effects of showcasing close-ups of "faces of affective extremes" in the horror genre. Arguing that horror is most horrific when its constituent polarities are fully operative—in effect, when amusement and pleasure coexist alongside terror and pain—the chapter analyses several examples of such scenes in Korean horror films of the 2000s.

————. "The Unbearable Lightness of Hong Sang-soo's *HaHaHa*: Awkward Humor, Nervous Laughter, and Self-Critique in Contemporary Korean Comedy." *New Review of Film and Television Studies* 12, No. 1 (January 2014): 1–23. doi: 10.10 80/17400309.2013.857487.

Analyzes the humorous elements and comic sensibilities in Hong Sang-soo's films, focusing on his 2010 film *HaHaHa*. Drawing from and expanding on theories of laughter in comedy studies, the author closely examines Hong's use of textual and extratextual frames in service of a critical self-reflexivity.

Kim, Kyu Hyun. "Horror as Critique in *Tell Me Something* and *Sympathy for Mr. Vengeance*." In *New Korean Cinema*, edited by Chi-Yun Shin and Julian Stringer, 106–116. Edinburgh, UK: Edinburgh University Press, 2005.

Examines two well-known Korean horror films: *Tell Me Something* and *Sympathy for Mr. Vengeance*. Narrative and formal analyses of each film are provided, through which the author aims to reveal the potential of horror films to challenge and critique cultural conventions. Kim sees each film as an insightful critique of the ideological strictures imposed by mainstream Korean society, namely, the patriarchal ideology in *Tell Me* and the problems of modern subjectivity in *Sympathy*.

Kim, Molly Hyo J. "Whoring the Mermaid: The Study of South Korean Hostess Film (1974–1982)." PhD diss., University of Illinois at Urbana-Champaign, 2014. ProQuest (1706284343).

Focuses on cinematic representations of prostitute women in Korean hostess films in the Korean context of the 1970s and 1980s. The exploitive employment of female sexuality and the repeated theme of women's extreme and perpetual sacrifice are explored beyond the usual narrative of Park Chung-hee's state censorship operation. Kim reads hostess films as culturally complex texts, not just as by-products of the state power, linked to the film movement "The Era of Image" (1975).

Kim, Sung Kyung. "'Renaissance of Korean National Cinema' as a Terrain of Negotiation and Contention between the Global and the Local: Analysing two Korean blockbusters, *Shiri* (1999) and *JSA* (2000)." *Essex Graduate Journal of Sociology, Past and Present* no. 6 (2006): 75–88.

Traces the role of nationalism in the Korean film renaissance, the textual elements leading to the success of major blockbusters, and sources of domestic audience's enjoyment. The author identifies the joining of global conventions with nationally specific sentiments at the core of these phenomenon.

Klein, Christina. "Why American Studies Needs to Think about Korean Cinema, Or, Transnational Genres in the Films of Bong Joon-ho." *American Quarterly* 60, no. 4 (2008): 871–898. doi: 10.1353/aq.0.0041.

Focuses on Bong Joon-ho's redeployment of Hollywood monster and crime film genre conventions in *The Host* and *Memories of Murder* as they attest to the ambivalent relationship between the United States and South Korea. Klein further notes Korean film's utility in examining the global circulation of American cultural products and their relation to transnationality.

Lee, Sangjoon. "Destination Hong Kong: The Geopolitics of South Korean Espionage Films in the 1960s." *Journal of Korean Studies* 22, no. 2 (2017): 343–364. doi: 10.1353/jks.2017.0016.

Against the unprecedented global popularity of espionage films in the 1960s, Lee's article looks to Korea's very own Bond-mimetic espionage films of the late 1960s. While noting the Cold War politics that drove American and Europe espionage narratives, Lee observes that Korea too vigorously adopted anti-communist doctrines in this genre in order to uphold their militant dictatorships. The article focuses particularly on the South Korea-initiated inter-Asian coproduction of espionage films that were produced during this period.

Lee, Eunha. "Monster Mothers and the Confucian Ideal: Korean Horror Cinema in the Park Chung-hee Era." PhD diss., Southern Illinois University at Carbondale, 2012. ProQuest (1027588741).

Psychoanalytic feminist analysis of Korean horror films during the Park Chung-hee era, Lee examines the reconfiguration of patriarchal Confucian virtues along the regime's developmentalist line within the genre. It focuses specifically on the monstrous feminine and pleasurably aberrant viewing by female spectators capable of navigating this configuration and female agency within it.

McHugh, Katherine, and Nancy Abelmann, eds. *South Korean Golden Age Melodrama: Gender, Genre, and National Cinema*. Detroit, MI: Wayne State University Press, 2005.

South Korean Golden Age Melodrama is another landmark edited collection. Focusing on a period of Korean cinema that had been buried by the then contemporary revival of the Korean film industry, this is one of the first works in the English language to examine the "Golden Age" of the 1960s and its influences on the contemporary scene. The collection of nine essays examines this period of Korean cinema that produced a body of works on a par with Italian Neorealism, French New Wave, and New German Cinema.

Martin, Daniel. "South Korean Cinema's Postwar Pain: Gender and National Division in Korean War Films from the 1950s to the 2000s." *Journal of Korean Studies* 19, no. 1 (2014): 93–114. doi: 10.1353/jks.2014.0005.

Surveys two genres over the past sixty years: the Korean War film and the postwar thriller. The article observes the ways that certain themes and subtexts are transformed in these genres over the years, seeing these changes as reflections of shifting ideologies and attitudes in the postwar period. Also drawn to attention are repeated tropes and themes, such as the figure of the North Korean female spy, to explore the potent role of gender as a national metaphor.

———. "Between the Local and the Global: 'Asian Horror' in Ahn Byung-ki's *Phone* and *Bunshinsaba*." In *Korean Horror Cinema*, edited by Alison Peirse and Daniel Martin, 145–157. Edinburgh, UK: Edinburgh University Press, 2013.

Auteur study of Ahn Byung-ki, emphasizing both his influential role in the development of Korean and pan-Asian horror. Combines individual close-readings of many of Ahn's films, a consideration of his international rise to prominence through the rise of Tartan Extreme, and global and regional interest in Asian horror.

Morris, Mark. "War Horror and Anti-Communism: From *Piagol* to *Rainy Days*." In *Korean Horror Cinema*, edited by Alison Peirse and Daniel Martin, 48–59. Edinburgh, UK: Edinburgh University Press, 2013.

Provides a fresh reading of combat war films as generically hybrid works that are as horrific as, if not more than, actual horror films of their period. While focusing specifically on scenes of transgressive violence (in particular with the usage of bamboo spears), Morris deconstructs the complex nature of these narratives that are interwoven with political, historical, and psychological components.

Film Analysis

An, Ji-yoon. "Blood Is Thicker than Water, or Is It? Depictions of 'Alternative Families' in Contemporary Korean Cinema." In *Korean Screen Culture: Interrogating Cinema, TV, Music and Online Games*, edited by Andrew David Jackson and Colette Balmain, 35–54. Bern, Switzerland: Peter Lang, 2016.

Examines the recurring representations of "alternative families" in Korean films of the mid-2000s. An argues that new kinds of family forms emerge on screen in the films *Family Ties* and *Five Is Too Many*, where families are arguably matriarchal (as opposed to patriarchal), inclusive (as opposed to exclusive) and based on choice (as opposed to blood relations). Such depictions, according to the author, are linked to the social backdrop of family law reforms, feminist movements, and changing family discourses.

Beven, Jake. "Welcome to Panmunjeom: Encounters with the North in Contemporary South Korean Cinema." *New Cinemas: Journal of Contemporary Film* 8, no. 1 (2010): 45–57. doi: 10.1386/ncin.8.1.45_1.

Examines how the tensions between the two Koreas are represented in contemporary South Korean film productions. The author closely analyzes a few film texts that capture the changing political climate in the Korean peninsula to track the evolution of cultural representational politics in North Korea as demonstrated in recent South Korean films.

Chung, Hye Jin. "'The Host' and 'D-War': Complex Intersections of National Imaginings and Transnational Aspirations." *Spectator-The University of Southern California Journal of Film and Television* 29, no. 2 (2009): 48–56.

Analyzes the titular films as they reflect the relationship between the national and transnational, reimagining Korean identity in their movement toward globalized conventions associated with Hollywood film. This quality is associated with CGI effects and the imaginary liminal spaces they produce, reflecting transnational flows.

Chung, Hye Seung. "From Saviors to Rapists: G.I.s, Women, and Children in Korean War Films." *Asian Cinema* 12, no. 1 (2001): 103–116. doi: https://doi.org/10.1386/ac.12.1.103_1. Reprinted in Heroism and Gender in War Films, edited by Jakub Kazecki and Karen Ritzenhoff, 115–130. New York: Palgrave McMillan, 2014.

Examines the images of American G.I.s in relation to Korean women and children in three films: the Hollywood production *Battle Hymn* (1957) and two Korean films, *Silver Stallion* (1990) and *Spring in My Hometown* (1998). Drawing upon "gaze theories" of Laura Mulvey, E. Ann Kaplan, and Michel Foucault, the essay charts out the relationship between vision and power, specularity and subjectivity, identity and otherness reflected in the war-time encounters of white American male colonizers and Korean colonial subjects.

——— and David Scott Diffrient. "Forgetting to Remember, Remembering to Forget: The Politics of Memory and Modernity in the Fractured Films of Lee Chang-dong and Hong Sang-soo." In *Seoul Searching: Culture and Identity in Contemporary Korean Cinema*, edited by Frances Gateward, 115–139. Albany, NY: SUNY Press, 2007.

Explore fractured narration in Lee Chang-dong's *Peppermint Candy* (2000) and Hong Sang-soo's *The Virgin Stripped Bare by Her Bachelors* (2000). The former film interweaves personal time with national time through chronologically reversed narration that identifies the 1980 Kwangju massacre as the inciting event for the tragic hero and nation's moral, spiritual downfall. While the latter film is not explicitly political, its repetitive, overlapping, and contradictory narration similarly allegorizes modern Korea's social upheavals and fragmentary national identity with deep internal divisions.

James, David E. "Art/Film/Art Film: *Chihwaseon* and Its Cinematic Contexts." *Film Quarterly* 59, no. 2 (2005): 4–17. doi:10.1525/fq.2005.59.2.4.

Contextual introduction and analysis of Im Kwon-Taek's *Chihwaseon*. The film's painter protagonist reflects artistic frustrations, the process of filmmaking through painting, and the revival of a lost past allegorically tied to Im's own background. James further elaborates on the reflexivity of films about art in Korean, Western, and Chinese contexts, noting their specific critical functions, particularly as they relate to disillusionment.

Jeon, Joseph Jonghyun. "Memories of Memories: Historicity, Nostalgia, and Archive in Bong Joon-ho's 'Memories of Murder.'" *Cinema Journal* 51, no. 1 (2011): 75–95. doi: 10.1353/cj.2011.0065.

Offers an in-depth examination of the famed Korean filmmaker Bong Joon-ho's hit feature, *Memories of Murder*. The article reads this film as a commentary on the possibilities of historicity in the medium of film, particularly within the framing of a detective story. Jeon argues that the film instantiates a kind of spectral historiography, which is in turn seen as a comment on not only the archive's possibility but also its limits.

Lee, Nam. "*Repatriation* and the History of Korean Documentary Filmmaking." *Asian Cinema* 16, no. 1 (2012): 16–27. doi: 10.1386/ac.16.1.16_1.

One of the few studies on Korean documentary, this article examines how social and political changes have presented new opportunities and challenges for contemporary documentary filmmakers in South Korea. It focuses on *Repatriation* (2004) by the renowned documentary filmmaker Kim Dong-Won, the winner of the Freedom of Expression Award at the Sundance Film Festival in 2004.

Magnan-Park, Aaron Han Joon. "Peppermint Candy: The Will *Not* to Forget." In *New Korean Cinema*, edited by Chi-Yun Shin and Julian Stringer, 159–169. Edinburgh, UK: Edinburgh University Press, 2005.

Examines one of Lee Chang-dong's most famous works, *Peppermint Candy*. Magnan-Park explores the reverse narrative structure alongside theories of psychoanalysis and historiography to assess the film's ability to engage with issues of national trauma and recovery. The author reads the film as the director's provocation to the national audience to collectively redress the repressed aspects of South Korea's military-dominated past—a *rapprochement* that the author sees as coinciding with the government's relaxation of its hold over official history in the mid-2000s.

Martin-Jones, David. "Decompressing Modernity: South Korean Time Travel Narratives and the IMF Crisis." *Cinema Journal* 46, no. 4 (2007): 45–67. doi: 10.1353/cj.2007.0044.

Scholars have duly noted and discussed how South Korean films of the IMF crisis years explored issues pertaining to national history and identity. Martin-Jones adds to the debate by looking specifically at time travel narratives in three commercially successful works of the time. Martin-Jones postulates that the time travel narratives enabled a decompression, an exploration, and ultimately a sense of mourning for the recent past, while romance stories demonstrated the desire for conservative gender politics.

Ogawa, Shota Tsai. "Revisiting *Through the Night* (2002): A Paradigm or Anomaly in Japanese–Korean Co-production and Cross-Media Adaptation." *Journal of Japanese and Korean Cinema* 6, no. 2 (October 2014): 152–166. doi: 10.1080/17 564905.2014.961712.

Focuses on the Japanese-Korean co-production *Through the Night*, spearheaded by *Zainichi* Koreans without previous experience in the film industry, in an expansion of scholarly considerations of East Asian co-production, emphasizing the role of South Korean media's rising popularity and utilization by the Korean diaspora.

Ok, Hye Ryoung. "The Politics of the Korean Blockbuster: Narrating the Nation and the Spectacle of 'Glocalisation' in *2009 Lost Memories*," *Spectator* 29, no. 2 (Fall 2009): 37–47.

Analyzes "globalization through localization" as a phenomenon linked with resurgent nationalist sentiments and the need to confront globalization following the IMF crisis, culminating in the compromise between Korean specific stories and the practices and Hollywood sensibilities. Ok proposes that the active appropriation of Hollywood resists its hegemonic imposition, while still allowing for wider circulation abroad.

Shin, Chi-Yun. "Two of a Kind: Gender and Friendship in *Friend* and *Take Care of My Cat*." In *New Korean Cinema*, edited by Chi-Yun Shin and Julian Stringer, 117–131. Edinburgh, UK: Edinburgh University Press, 2005.

Examines two Korean films *Friend* and *Take Care of My Cat* to compare the different ways in which gender affects not only the stylistic characteristics but also the publicity and reception of these works. *Friend* is read as a commercial film that was tailored to the mass appeal of hyper-masculine ethics at the time, while *Take Care of My Cat* is interpreted as resisting the male dominant ideology of the time by revising and updating the conventionally male buddy film genre with a feminist consciousness.

Shin, Chi-Yun, and Julian Stringer. "Storming the Big Screen: The *Shiri* Syndrome."
In *Seoul Searching: Culture and Identity in Contemporary Korean Cinema*, edited
by Frances Gateward, 115–139. Albany, NY: SUNY Press, 2007.

Offers an in-depth study of *Shiri* (1999), one of the first South Korean movie
blockbusters that facilitated the rapid commercialization of Korean film industry.
In addition to the analysis of the film, the authors examine how the blockbuster
prompted social debates about the increasing importance of film, media and culture
industry in Korea's pursuit of globalization that commenced in the 1990s.

Identity Politics

An, Ji-yoon. "Family Pictures: Representations of the Family in Contemporary
Korean Cinema." PhD diss., University of Cambridge, 2017. DOI: https://doi.
org/10.17863/CAM.13956.

Examines the central narrative theme of family in contemporary Korean cinema.
It brings together films on the family and writings on them in Korean and Western
scholarships to identify trends and patterns that have gone undetected. An's dissertation is thematically structured to explore: the breakdown of the patriarchal
nuclear family, the depiction of mothers as dark and dangerous beings in recent
thrillers, the emergence of new family forms, and the experiences of the "Korean
family" by those living outside of Korea.

Bae, Juyeon. "Searching for Traces of Absence: Korean Diaspora in Contemporary
Korean Cinema." In *Korean Screen Culture: Interrogating Cinema, TV, Music and
Online Games*, edited by Andrew David Jackson and Colette Balmain, 239–256.
Bern, Switzerland: Peter Lang Publishing, 2016.

Noting that non-native ethnic Koreans have become increasingly represented in
South Korean films, the author examines the complexities of their filmic representation with a focus on portrayals of *joseonjok* (Chinese-Korean) and *goryeoin*
(ethnic Koreans from Russia or Central Asia). Bae illustrates the different ways
that ethnic Koreans are "otherized" in contemporary films in light of the absence
of their history in mainstream Korean history.

Chung, Hye Seung, and David Scott Diffrient. "Interethnic Romance and Political
Reconciliation in *Asako in Ruby Shoes*." In *New Korean Cinema*, edited by Chi-
Yun Shin and Julian Stringer, 193–209. Edinburgh, UK: Edinburgh University
Press, 2005.

Analyzes the politics of interethnic romance in E.J. Yong's *Asako in Ruby Shoes*
(2000), the first Korean-Japanese coproduction which is set in both Seoul and
Tokyo. While rejecting the nationalist and masculinist narrative and accommo-
dating diverse images of "otherness" (queer, ethnic Chinese, Japanese, etc.),
the film is symptomatic of an emergent trend in post-IMF crisis South Korean

cinema in which aggressive Korean women are replaced by more docile, feminine counterparts of other ethnic origins.

Hübinette, Tobias. "Comforting an Orphaned Nation: Representations of International Adoption and Adopted Koreans in Korean Popular Culture." PhD diss., Stockholm University, 2005. https://perma.cc/7N6H-PXPZ.

Focuses on the numerous popular cultural representations of international adoption and adopted Koreans in Western countries. Hübinette provides a history of international adoption from Korea and an account of its development in the political sphere. Cinematic and lyrical representations are framed by theories of nationalism, globalization, and postcolonialism to argue that the Korean adoption issue can be conceptualized as an attempt to overcome a difficult past and to imagine a common future for all ethnic Koreans at a transnational level.

Jeong, Kelly Y. *Crisis of Gender and the Nation in Korean Literature and Cinema: Modernity Arrives Again.* Plymouth, UK: Lexington Books, 2011.

Examines the changing constructs of modernity, masculinity, and gender relations in Korean literature and cinema from the 1920s to the 1960s. Each chapter explores a decade and are organized around questions about gender, modernity, class, and the nation that are crucial to understanding the selected texts and their contexts. This is a useful text that offers critical readings based on both Western and Korean-language sources, using methods and texts from Korean studies, comparative literature, postcolonial studies, and film studies.

Kim, Phil Ho, and C. Colin Singer. "Three Periods of Korean Queer Cinema: Invisible, Camouflage, and Blockbuster." *Acta Koreana* 14, no.1 (2011): 117–136.

While the history of queer cinema may not be as rich in the Korean context as in other cinemas, it is unique, as noted by the authors, in breaking ground in the LGBT (lesbian, gay, bisexual, and transgendered) realm before the onset of social activism. Kim and Singer make a most welcome attempt at periodizing the history of Korean queer cinema. According to both the queer content and the reception of films, three periods are proposed: the Invisible Age (1976–1998), the Camouflage Age (1998–2005), and the Blockbuster Age (2005–present).

Lee, Helen. "A Peculiar Sensation: A Personal Genealogy of Korean American Women's Cinema." In *Dangerous Women: Gender and Korean Nationalism*, edited by Elaine H. Kim and Chungmoo Choi, 291–323. London: Routledge, 1998.

Somewhat of an anomaly to the canon of scholarly works on Korean cinema, this book chapter traces Korean-American women's cinema and examines the independent artistic works of various female Korean-American artist-filmmakers, from well-known figures such as Theresa Hak Kyung Cha to lesser-known figures like the author herself. It explores the relationship between diasporic identity and artistic representation, investigating issues that are often deconstructed in these personal and autobiographical works, such as cultural and geographical displacement, gender and race (dis)identification, and dispersal and difference.

Shin, Jeeyoung. "Male Homosexuality in *The King and the Clown*: Hybrid Construction and Contested Meanings." *Journal of Korean Studies* 18, no. 1 (2013): 89–114. doi: 10.1353/jks.2013.0006.

Offers an in-depth examination of the 2005 Korean box-office hit, *The King and the Clown*. Focusing on the representation of male homosexuality, the article illuminates the multilayers at work when contested issues are camouflaged in commercial works. Shin reads the historical and traditional settings, along with gendered characterizations, as means to avoid controversy around the gay identity, while the *kkotminam* phenomenon and the tailored-appeal to the *yaoi* subculture are seen as tactics to capitalize on such cultural trends.

Mobile Video Content

Ok, Hye Ryoung. "Cinema in Your Hand, Cinema on the Street: The Aesthetics of Korean Mobile Cinema." *Public*, no. 40 (2012): 110–117.

Focusing on the *Yigong: Twenty Identities* series (2002), a larger scale mobile content project commissioned by South Korea's leading wireless service provider SK Telecom, the author analyzes the formal characteristics of early original mobile video content that explored mobile screen-specific aesthetic forms and thus represented a concrete aesthetic and cultural imagination of ideal moving images for the mobile screen.

Screen Personae

Yecies, Brian. "Somewhere between Anti-Heroism and Pantomime: Song Kang-ho and the Uncanny Face of the Korean Cinema." *Acta Koreana* 14, no. 1 (2011): 33–71.

Explores the trajectory of popular Korean actor Song Kang-ho's screen performances, from his fourth film *Number 3* (1997) to *Thirst* (2009). By examining Song's various screen personae and in particular the numerous close-ups of his facial expressions, the author argues Song's screen characters to have enabled audiences "to peer into a cinematic surface that reflects back a mixture of anti-heroism and pantomime."

Afterword

Eyun-Jung Ki and Seungahn Nah

About two years ago a small band of Korean American Communication Association (KACA) members began to talk casually about how to celebrate the organization's upcoming fortieth anniversary. The first thought was to quickly put together a book just for the sake of publishing something to celebrate the anniversary, but, wisely, self-restraint prevailed. Instead, the vision came to be two important companion volumes—*Communication, Digital Media, and Popular Culture in Korea: Contemporary Research and Future Prospects,* edited by Dal Yong Jin (Simon Fraser University) and Nojin Kwak (University of Michigan), and *Korean Communication, Media, and Culture: An Annotated Bibliography,* which you now hold in your hands.

In the course of compiling this bibliography, the seemingly unending revisions of chapter drafts challenged some, if not all, of the project's participants, perhaps more than they were prepared for. In the end, however, this is a beautiful story of our history-making bibliography coming to fruition. Not surprisingly, we are full of good feelings about this project, and we would like to share them with you.

The editors, Professor Kyu Ho Youm (University of Oregon) and Professor Nojin Kwak (University of Michigan), became the driving force behind this monumental project, which offers an informative overview of Korean communication publications in English. This ten-chapter annotated bibliography contains one thousand entries encompassing nearly all the major English-language books, book chapters, journal articles, theses, and dissertations on the subject. For them as published communication scholars, this Korean bibliography project was challenging but invaluable for several reasons.

The editors were meticulous in their approach to editing each chapter, striving to bring everything together in a timely fashion. And, although they stopped counting how many rounds of revisions were required before chapters were "approved," they can tell you it was certainly more than five. Each revision improved the chapters and reflected the editors' exceptional dedication and commitment to the project, which was done for readers more than anyone else. The editors communicated regularly with project participants, keeping them updated about the ongoing project and the ever-changing number of entries, helping all contributors check their progress in real time. In addition, the editors facilitated the exchange of ideas, questions, and answers among the project contributors. While primarily working with co-authors on their own chapters, editors and chapter authors eagerly collaborated in pursuing the highest standard of excellence. Kudos to all the authors and special thanks to Kyu Ho Youm and Nojin Kwak.

This extensive bibliography covers ten topical areas of Korea-related communication. Its completion was made possible only by the enthusiastic participation of Korean and non-Korean scholars around the world. What is especially notable about the project is its authorial variety. The participation of seven non-Korean scholars demonstrates a refreshingly inclusive perspective on communication studies related to Korea. It also showcases the scholarly interest in Korean communication that goes far beyond native Korean researchers. Equally important, the authors are nearly all front runners in their specialties and among the most productive and influential scholars in Korean communication. Their readable styles and chapter organization help not only each chapter but the book as a whole to epitomize first-rate bibliographical scholarship in Korean media, communication, and culture.

This book should serve as an essential English-language reference resource for scholars and students in Korean communication and for librarians who work with Korean culture, politics, sociology, the Internet, international studies, law, and other subjects. Anyone interested in learning about and researching Korea should consider this book a go-to resource. Each chapter provides a historical evolution of works on its primary topic, providing readers with a revealing snapshot of the key information they need about each source. Although it will be published initially in hardcopy, our goal is for an online version to be available in due course.

We live in an age when books and other hardcopy publications are often outdated even before they are accessible in print. Offering the most up-to-date information online will define this kind of ever-expanding bibliography of Korean communication studies in English. Hence, this current bibliography project, the first of its kind, is not the end but the beginning of a comprehensive resource on Korean communication as a global topic.

Dr. Eyun-Jung Ki, KACA President (2017–2019)
Professor
Department of Advertising and Public Relations
University of Alabama

Dr. Seungahn Nah, KACA President (2015–2017)
Professor and Associate Dean for Graduate Affairs and Research
School of Journalism and Communication
University of Oregon

Names Index

Subject Index

About the Contributors

Ji-yoon An is a visiting assistant professor in Korean studies at Eberhard Karls Universität Tübingen in Germany. Coming from a background in music and film studies, An's scholarly interests are cultural trends and flows. She received full funding from the Arts and Humanities Research Council in the United Kingdom for her doctoral study at the University of Cambridge. An was also awarded the Fellowship for Field Research from the Korea Foundation. She has contributed to Andrew D. Jackson and Colette Balmain's *Korean Screen Cultures: Interrogating Cinema, TV, Music and Online Games* (2016) and has presented at numerous international conferences. Her dissertation, titled "Family Pictures: Representations of the Family in Contemporary Korean Society," is forthcoming as a book.

Charles R. Berger is professor emeritus in the Department of Communication, University of California at Davis. He is a former editor of *Human Communication Research* and co-editor of *Communication Research.* Berger is a fellow and past president of the International Communication Association and a National Communication Association distinguished scholar. He has advanced theories that explain communication under uncertainty (uncertainty reduction theory), message production processes (planning theory), and, most recently, narrative impact (story appraisal theory). Berger edited *Interpersonal Communication,* volume 6, published in 2014 and co-edited *The International Encyclopedia of Interpersonal Communication* in 2016.

N. Trace Cabot is a PhD student and Annenberg Fellow in the Department of Cinema and Media Studies at the University of Southern California's School of Cinematic Arts. He was a research associate at the Institute for Communication Arts and Technology and a film lecturer at Hallym University in Korea. His research focuses on early film theory and contemporary

Lacanian-Marxist thought guided by case studies drawn from Korean and Japanese film and animation. He has presented research on Korean film at conferences hosted by the Korean Association of Broadcasting and Telecommunications Studies and the Society for Cinema and Media Studies.

John C. Carpenter is a PhD candidate at the University of Iowa School of Journalism and Mass Communication. His dissertation examines how language of publication informs journalistic practice and conceptualization among English-language news organizations in Korea, including the *Korea Times, Korea JoongAng Daily*, and *Korea Herald*. Among Carpenter's journal articles are "The Face of Multiculturalism in Korea: Media Ritual as Framing in News Coverage of Jasmine Lee" (*Journalism,* 2014), "Service at the Intersection of Journalism, Language, and the Global Imaginary: Indonesia's English Language Press" (*Journalism Studies*, 2017), and "Creating English as a Language of Global News Contraflow: Al Jazeera at the Intersection of Language, Globalization, and Journalism" (*Journal of Arab & Muslim Media Research,* 2017).

Hye Seung Chung is an associate professor of film and media studies at Colorado State University. She is the author of *Hollywood Asian: Philip Ahn and the Politics of Cross-Ethnic Performance* (Temple University Press, 2006) and *Kim Ki-duk* (University of Illinois Press, 2012). Her latest co-authored book, *Movie Migrations: Transnational Genre Flows and South Korean Cinema* (with David Scott Diffrient), was published by Rutgers University Press in 2015.

Jae Eun Chung is an associate professor in the Cathy Hughes School of Communications at Howard University. Her research interests include new media technologies, their psychosocial impacts, and health communication. Her work has been published in the *Journal of Communication, Communication Research, Journal of Computer-Mediated Communication, Journal of Health Communication,* and *Computers in Human Behavior*.

Chang-Dae Ham is an associate professor at the Charles H. Sandage Department of Advertising at the University of Illinois at Urbana-Champaign (UIUC). He has researched how consumers proactively cope with, and still themselves against, various persuasion attempts. Ham has published 25 peer-reviewed journal articles and book chapters in advertising, psychology, marketing, and mass communication in the United States and Korea. Ham has developed and managed an advertising professional training program for LG at UIUC.

Jacqueline Hitchon is the head of the Charles H. Sandage Department of Advertising at the University of Illinois at Urbana-Champaign (UIUC).

Her research interests in health communication include the relationship between exposure to marketing messages and eating disorders, and the impact on audiences of embedding health messages directly into the plots of entertainment programming. Hitchon's broader scholarship on advertising has included work on cause-related marketing and political advertising. She has published in major journals, including *Communication Research, Human Communication Research, Journal of Broadcasting and Electronic Media, Journalism and Mass Communication Quarterly* and *Political Communication*.

Yongick Jeong is an associate professor in the Manship School of Mass Communication at Louisiana State University. His primary research interests involve advertising in digital, social and entertainment media, privacy concerns on social media, visual attention to digital advertising, effectiveness of Super Bowl advertising, and health/environmental communication. In addition, Jeong is also interested in various international communication topics, including cultural differences between Korea and the United States in perceiving advertising creativity.

Dal Yong Jin is a professor in the School of Communication at Simon Fraser University. His major research and teaching interests are on platform technologies, mobile technologies and game studies, media (de-)convergence, globalization and media, transnational cultural studies, and the political economy of media. Jin is the author of several books, such as *Smartland Korea: Mobile Communication, Culture and Society* (University of Michigan Press, 2017), *New Korean Wave: Transnational Cultural Power in the Age of Social Media* (University of Illinois Press, 2016), *Digital Platforms, Imperialism and Political Culture* (Routledge, 2015), and *Korea's Online Gaming Empire* (MIT Press, 2010). He has also edited several volumes, including *The Korean Wave: Evolution, Fandom, and Transnationality* (Lexington, 2017).

Seok Kang is a professor in digital communication with an emphasis on mobile media effects, digital journalism, and media production at the University of Texas-San Antonio. His teaching and research centers on new communication technologies, mobile communication, marketing, social media, and digital message design. Kang has published 10 books on digital communication, 37 refereed journal articles, and five book chapters. His research has appeared in the *Journal of Broadcasting and Electronic Media, Mass Communication and Society, International Journal of Communication,* and *Health Communication,* among others.

Eyun-Jung Ki is a professor in the Department of Advertising and Public Relations at the University of Alabama. She has published 50-plus peer-reviewed articles in leading journals, including the *Journal of*

Communication, *Journalism & Mass Communication Quarterly*, and *Journal of Public Relations Research*. Ki was the lead editor of *Public Relations as Relationship Management: A Relational Approach to the Study and Practice of Public Relations* (Routledge, 2015). Her primary research revolves around organization-public relationships, emerging media, and global public relations. Public relations practice and scholarship in Korea have been an element of her academic work.

Dong Hoon Kim is an associate professor in the Department of Cinema Studies at the University of Oregon. His research interests include visual culture, early cinema, and East Asian film, media and popular culture. His book, *Eclipsed Cinema: The Film Culture of Colonial Korea* (Edinburgh University Press, 2017), explores the seldom-studied film culture in colonial Korea, analyzing the major development of colonial cinema from the 1910s through the 1930s. Kim has been engaged with a variety of activities in the field besides his academic research, directing short films, working for film festivals, and serving as consultant to film companies.

Hun Shik Kim is an associate professor in the Department of Journalism at the University of Colorado in Boulder. His teaching and research interests include broadcast journalism, telecommunication systems and policies, international communication, and Asian media cultures in global environments. His research has been published in a number of scholarly journals, and he is the author of two books on international journalism and global television industry. Kim is co-director of the CU International Media Certificate program. Before joining CU, he was a network television reporter and news producer for the Korean Broadcasting System (KBS) in Seoul for 13 years.

Ju Oak Kim is an assistant professor in the Department of Psychology and Communication at Texas A&M International University. Her research examines the changing nature of cultural production and content flows in the digitally restructured media world, with a particular focus on East Asia. Kim's work has been published in academic journals, such as the *Journal of Popular Culture*, *China Media Research*, and *Journal of Fandom Studies*. Kim is currently working on a monograph on the Korean Wave with the working title, *Korean Negotiators: Media Production as a Translocalizing Process*.

Min-Sun Kim is a professor of communicology at the University of Hawaii at Manoa. She is the author of *Non-Western Perspectives on Human Communication* (Sage, 2002), co-author of Hallyu: *Influence in Asia and Beyond* (Seoul National University Press, 2011) as well as *Changing Korea: Understanding Culture and Communication* (Peter Lang, 2008). Kim has published more than 120 articles, primarily on intercultural communication. She has served as the editor of *Korean Studies* published by Center for Korean Studies at the University of Hawaii.

Arunima Krishna is an assistant professor of public relations at Boston University's College of Communication. Her primary research interests lie in understanding how publics and corporations perceive and respond to controversial social issues. Her work has examined issues such as vaccine negativity and workplace gender discrimination to unpack how publics understand and respond to these issues. Her work has appeared in journals, including the *Journal of Public Relations Research, Health Communication, Management Communication Quarterly*, and *Public Relations Review*.

Nojin Kwak is a professor and chair of the Department of Communication Studies and director of the Nam Center for Korean Studies at the University of Michigan. He also serves as director of the BTAA Korean Studies e-School, the Big Ten Academic Alliance-wise course share consortium. Kwak's research examines the role of communication media in civic and political engagement and has published in major peer-reviewed journals, including *Communication Research, Journal of Communication, Human Communication Research, Political Communication, Journal of Computer-Mediated Communication, New Media and Society,* and *Political Research Quarterly*. His recent studies analyze the patterns of social media use and their influence on community involvement, deliberative openness, and political participation. He is a co-editor of a book series, *Perspectives on Contemporary Korea* (University of Michigan Press, 2017).

Hye-ryeon Lee is a professor of communicology at the University of Hawaii at Manoa, and is also on the faculty of the UH Cancer Center, the Center for Korean Studies, and the Public Health Program. As a scholar of health communication, she conducts research to examine the mechanism through which culture and communication influence health behaviors among socially and culturally diverse populations such as Koreans and Pacific Islanders in America. Lee's work has appeared in major journals, including the *Journal of Health Communication, American Journal of Public Health, Health Psychology, Journal of Community Health, Social Science and Medicine,* and *Cancer Epidemiology*.

Seungyoon Lee is an associate professor in the Brian Lamb School of Communication at Purdue University. Her research interest concentrates on the evolution of communication, knowledge, and collaboration networks and its implications for individual well-being and community resilience. Her recent work examined creative interaction and social ties of organizational members as well as information and communication behaviors of publics in Korea. Lee's work has been published in leading journals including the *Journal of Communication, Communication Research, Management Communication Quarterly,* and *Journal of Health Communication.*

Akira Miyahara is a professor of communication studies at Seinan Gakuin University and is a member-at-large for East Asia of the International Communication Association. He has published book chapters and journal articles involving cross-cultural studies of interpersonal communication among Koreans and Japanese. Miyahara's published work includes "Requesting Styles among 'Collectivist' Cultures: A Comparison Between Japanese and Koreans" (co-authored with Min-Sun Kim) in *Intercultural Communication Studies* and "Conflict resolution styles among 'collectivist' Cultures: A Comparison between Japanese and Koreans" in *International Journal of Intercultural Relations.* Miyahara has taught at Asia Pacific College to students from Seoul National University and Yonsei University in Seoul.

Seungahn Nah is a professor and associate dean for graduate affairs and research at the University of Oregon School of Journalism and Communication. He specializes in the interrelationships among communication, community, and democracy with special emphasis on the roles of digital communication technologies in community and democratic processes and outcomes. Nah has published numerous journal articles and book chapters regarding political and civic communication in the United States and Korea. His work has appeared in such leading journals as the *Journal of Communication, Communication Theory, Journalism and Mass Communication Quarterly, Journal of Computer-Mediated Communication, New Media & Society,* and *International Journal of Communication.*

Hye-Jin Paek is a professor in the Department of Advertising and Public Relations at Hanyang University in Korea. Prior to her current position, Paek was an assistant professor at the University of Georgia and then an associate professor at Michigan State University. Her major research areas include health and risk communication and social marketing. Paek has published more than 100 journal articles, 20 books and book chapters, and 150 conference presentations. Formerly a president of the Korea Health Communication Association, Paek frequently serves on advisory boards for the Korea Center for Disease Control and Prevention, the Korean Food and Drug Administration, the Korea Health Promotion Foundation, and the Korean Ministry of Health and Welfare.

Ahran Park is a senior researcher at the Media Research Center of the Korea Press Foundation in Seoul. Her research interests include comparative media law, Internet law, and media policy. A former news reporter of *Chosun Daily News,* Park has published media law books in Korean and media law articles in various Korean and international journals. Park has contributed to comparative books, including *Justices and Journalists: The Global Perspective* (Cambridge University Press, 2017), *International Libel and Privacy Handbook* (LexisNexis, 2016), and *Carter-Ruck on Libel and Privacy* (6th ed. 2010). She is the editorial director of the *Korean Journal of Journalism* and *Communication Studies* in Seoul.

Namkee Park is an associate professor in the Department of Communication at Yonsei University in Seoul. His research interests include social psychological implications of communication technologies as well as computer-mediated communication (CMC) and human-computer interaction (HCI). His work has been published in leading journals such as the *Journal of Communication, Communication Research, New Media & Society, Journal of Broadcasting & Electronic Media,* and *Computers in Human Behaviors,* among others.

Yoonmo Sang is an assistant professor in the Department of Strategic, Legal and Management Communication at Howard University. Before joining the Howard faculty, he worked for the American Library Association's Office for Information Technology Policy as a research associate. Currently, Sang is a member of the Howard Media Group. He has published a number of book chapters and journal articles, including those on U.S. and Korean communication laws. Sang is on the editorial boards of *Social Media + Society* and the *Journal of Media Law, Ethics, and Policy Research*, a journal of the Korean Society for Media Law, Ethics, and Policy Research.

Matthew A. Shapiro is an associate professor of political science at the Illinois Institute of Technology and an East Asia Institute Fellow. He is also a research affiliate at Argonne National Laboratory's Joint Center for Energy Storage Research. He was trained in political science, economics, and public policy at the University of Southern California, and his published and ongoing research focuses on how national innovation systems are formed and contribute to sustainable development, how climate change is addressed and impacted by relevant policies and political forces, and how communications from politicians, scientists, and the media impact both of these areas. Shapiro's work has been published in *Pacific Review, Environmental Communication, American Politics Research, Environment & Planning A, International Journal of Public Policy,* and *Scientometrics,* among others.

Minsun Shim is an associate professor in the Department of Communication and Information at Inha University in Korea. Her research centers on understanding the processes and effects of communication in promoting advances in public health. Specifically, Shim is interested in how communication processes, primarily in online and social media settings, influence health experiences and quality of life, and how such communication processes are influenced by individual characteristics and social interactions. Her work has appeared in major communication journals, including the *Journal of Communication, Journalism and Mass Communication Quarterly, Health Communication, Journal of Health Communication, and Journal of Applied Communication Research*.

Jae-Hwa Shin is a professor in the School of Mass Communications at the University of Southern Mississippi. Shin has published journal articles and book chapters and co-authored *Public Relations Today* (2007, Pearson), *Think: Public Relations* (2011, Pearson), and *Think: Public Relations* (2nd ed. 2013, Pearson). Her PR research focuses on strategic conflict management. Shin is on the editorial board of the *Journal of Public Relations Research*. Prior to her graduate study in the United States, she worked as public relations director at the Korea Economic Research Institute and the Center for Free Enterprise, affiliated with the Federation of Korean Industries in Seoul.

Peter J. Schulz is a professor of communication theory and director of the Institute of Communication and Health at the University of Lugano (Università della Svizzera italiana) in Switzerland. His recent work in health communication research examines health literacy and empowerment, doctor-patient communication, and on parental communication and media effect in the health domain. Schulz published more than 145 articles on health communication in a multitude of peer-reviewed publications. In 2017, he received the Ewha-KACA Research Award for a comparative project on "Recommendations and Warnings Against Vaccination: Media Texts and Other Communications" in Korea and Switzerland.

Kyu Ho Youm is the Jonathan Marshall First Amendment chair professor at the University of Oregon School of Journalism and Communication. He has published a number of books, journal articles, and monographs on U.S., Korean and other foreign communication laws. *Press Law in South Korea* (Iowa State University Press, 1996) was his first book. Youm has co-authored the Korea chapters for *Media, Advertising, and Entertainment Law Throughout the World* (Thomson Reuters, 2018) and *International Libel and Privacy Handbook* (LexisNexis, 2016–2017 ed.). His scholarly articles have been cited by U.S. and foreign courts, including the Supreme Court of Great Britain, the High Court of Australia, and the Supreme Court of Canada.

CPSIA information can be obtained
at www.ICGtesting.com
Printed in the USA
LVHW111454190320
650578LV00001B/58